BARBARIC CIVILIZATION

D1566602

Barbaric Civilization
A Critical Sociology of Genocide

CHRISTOPHER POWELL

McGill-Queen's University Press
Montreal & Kingston • London • Ithaca

© McGill-Queen's University Press 2011

ISBN 978-0-7735-3855-9 (cloth)
ISBN 978-0-7735-3856-6 (paper)

Legal deposit third quarter 2011
Bibliothèque nationale du Québec

Printed in Canada on acid-free paper that is 100% ancient forest
free (100% post-consumer recycled), processed chlorine free

This book has been published with the help of a grant from
the Canadian Federation for the Humanities and Social Sciences,
through the Aid to Scholarly Publications Program, using funds
provided by the Social Sciences and Humanities Research Council
of Canada.

McGill-Queen's University Press acknowledges the support of the
Canada Council for the Arts for our publishing program. We also
acknowledge the financial support of the Government of Canada
through the Canada Book Fund for our publishing activities.

Library and Archives Canada Cataloguing in Publication

Powell, Christopher John, 1971–
    Barbaric civilization: a critical sociology of genocide / Christopher Powell.

    Includes bibliographical references and index.
    ISBN 978-0-7735-3855-9 (bound). – ISBN 978-0-7735-3856-6 (pbk.)

    1. Genocide. 2. Civilization, Western. 3. Critical theory. I. Title.

HV6322.7.P69 2011   304.6'63   C2011-900675-8

This book was typeset by Interscript in 10.5/13 Sabon.

Contents

Acknowledgments

Groundwork for this book was laid in my doctoral dissertation, "Civilization and Genocide," which received financial support through the Social Sciences and Humanities Research Council of Canada's Doctoral Fellowship, the Ontario Graduate Scholarship, the Carleton University Graduate Scholarship, and the Zbigniew A. Jordan Scholarship. I would like to thank each of these funders for their support of independent academic scholarship in Canada.

Funding provided by the University of Manitoba's University Research Grants Program and through a Faculty of Graduate Studies research assistant grant paid for research that informed the early chapters of the book. I'd to thank Farzana Quddus and Mahmudur Bhuiyan for their diligent work on these grants.

Crucial reworking of the core theoretical model of the book took place on a research/study leave in winter 2006, and substantial rewriting of the historical chapters took place on a research/study leave in winter 2010, granted by the University of Manitoba Faculty of Arts. I would also like to thank the University of Manitoba Faculty Association for having negotiated the provisions for these leaves into our collective agreement, work for which I was not present but from which I benefited.

I would like to thank all of my colleagues in the Department of Sociology at the University of Manitoba for their unflagging practical and moral support of my research, for providing a welcoming and friendly environment as I carried out this idiosyncratic project, and for continuing to express confidence in my work even as I blew past one self-declared completion date after another.

Similarly, I wish to thank Philip Cercone of McGill-Queen's University Press for having remained interested in this project for over six years. I am grateful to Brenda Prince, Jessica Howarth, Joan McGilvray, Filomena Falocco, Jacqueline Davis, Katie Heffring, and Robert Lewis for patiently shepherding me through the various aspects of the publication process. I'd also like to thank the two anonymous peer reviewers for their indispensable contribution to this process and for their invaluable critical feedback.

Many friends and family members have contributed to the realization of this project through their encouragement and their intellectual engagement. Any list of those whom I especially wish to thank would necessarily be incomplete, so I will refrain from thanking people individually – with one necessary exception. I owe a debt of gratitude that no words can repay to Sheryl Peters for her inexhaustible conviction in the value of this work, for insightful criticism that pushed me to take my ideas further and closer to home than I had dared on my own, and for holding me accountable in practice to the relational egalitarianism that I have tried to articulate in theory. Her involvement in this process has made the document a better book, and me a better person.

BARBARIC CIVILIZATION

Introduction

The way out of a trap is to study the trap itself, learn how it is built.

Gunaratana 2002, 98

THE PROBLEM

This book investigates how civilization produces genocides. More specifically, it explains how genocides can result from the normal functioning of Western civilization. Not every genocide has resulted from Western civilization, nor is this civilization unique in producing genocides. But when a genocide happens within the ambit of Western civilization, a close inspection of the institutions of our civilization that regulate the use of violence in social life often shows that these institutions did not fail but functioned normally and that in functioning normally they engendered the very thing we might want and expect them to prevent.

I would like to be careful on this point. When we say an institution or a machine or a strategy "fails," this could mean a couple of different things. It could mean the institution has stopped doing what we wanted it to do – for example, protecting human life. Or it could mean the institution has stopped doing what it normally does, what its elementary components and the manner of their combination regularly impel it to do. Usually, we want these two meanings to refer to the same circumstances so that the normal functioning of our institutions produces a better, more humane world for all. But whether they do this or not depends all too little on our wishes. Just like a machine or a strategy, a social institution can fail our hopes without failing to operate normally. When this happens, we can learn something we did not know up until then about how that institution works. We are confronted with an occasion – which we can seize or ignore – to fundamentally revise some taken-for-granted assumptions about the world. If civilization can produce genocides, then civilization is not the unmitigated good that we often take it for.

Common sense and predominant scholarly opinion make genocide the very antithesis of civilization. The "advance of civilization" means the advance of humane values – of nonviolence, of consideration for others, of common decency. These same sources all tell us that by whatever measure, and despite its occasional lapses, our modern Western civilization is the most advanced of all civilizations that have existed in human history. If we accept this account of things, however, then we have a problem.

Why has the past century witnessed the largest extermination campaigns in human history? And not only the largest but also the most organized, the most efficient, and the most rapid? These include the mass murder and expulsion of the Armenians in the Ottoman Empire; the extermination programs under the Third Reich against Jews, Gypsies, Poles, homosexuals, communists, and disabled people; the cultivation of lethal famine on a mass scale in Joseph Stalin's Ukraine; the slaughter of half a million suspected communists, and the imprisonment of another half million, in Indonesia in 1965–66; and the murder of 800,000 Tutsis and political moderates in just one hundred days in Rwanda – a rate of killing that, according to Philip Gourevitch, exceeded the Nazi holocaust at its peak (Gourevitch 1998, 3).

More than this, why do some of the most advanced liberal democracies in the world have genocide, or multiple genocides, lurking in their pasts as guilty secrets? As David Stannard's *American Holocaust* (1992) shows vividly, the expansion into the Americas of Europe's civilization – its manners, its social and political institutions – has involved the systematic destruction of the many Indigenous societies encountered by the colonizers, over and above the devastation effected by introduced diseases. The means of genocide have varied by circumstance and have included not only outright mass slaughter – even biological warfare (Churchill 1998, 151–6) – but also dispossession, enslavement, forced migration, the prohibition of traditional religious and cultural practices, the destruction of cultural monuments, the suppression of Indigenous languages, confinement to marginal living conditions, and the large-scale abduction of children. The partial or near-total destruction of each of the many Indigenous cultures of the Americas has facilitated the expansion of European sovereignty and European manners into the so-called New World. Every nation-state in the western hemisphere has grown in part through a genocide or genocides against the Indigenous inhabitants of its present territories. In many cases, such genocide still continues; in others, overtly genocidal practices have only recently been ended and only in response to the unrelenting resistance of the victims. Without these genocides, the states of the New World would not have developed their present form.

Genocide in Canada

Most non-Indigenous Canadians tend to assume that Canada is an exception to this pattern, but a thorough examination of history indicates otherwise. The systematic study of genocide in Canada would make up a book in itself and would necessarily address the varying historical experiences of many different cultures. Methods of colonization and the relation between settlers and Natives have varied historically and geographically. Massacres perpetrated by settlers or by the settler state feature in these histories only in restricted contexts. But there are more ways to destroy a people than simply massacre. The simplest argument for understanding Indigenous experiences as genocide concerns the Indian residential school (IRS) system, operated by several Christian churches and funded by the British and then the Canadian state from the mid-eighteenth century until 1996. Through the operation of this system, "Indian" children were taken forcibly from their parents and raised in an environment that stigmatized every trace of Indigenous culture, working to produce children entirely assimilated to white-settler society. As Duncan Campbell-Scott, the principal architect of the IRS policy, put it, "Our objective is to continue until there is not a single Indian in Canada that has not been absorbed into the body politic, and there is no Indian question and no Indian Department ... I want to get rid of the Indian problem" (quoted in Titley 1986, 50; see also Dussault et al. 1996). This process clearly satisfies the definition of "genocide" established in the 1948 United Nations Convention on the Prevention and Punishment of the Crime of Genocide (UNCG), which includes among the means sufficient to effect genocide, "forcibly transferring children of the group to another group." It is no coincidence that physical, sexual, and psychological abuse of Indigenous children was endemic throughout the IRS system and that many thousands of Indigenous children died while in residential schools from preventable diseases and injuries (Grant 1996; for more personal accounts, see Knockwood 2001 and Fontaine 2010).

Indigenous authors have also argued that other practices, not intrinsically genocidal, have operated genocidally in the context of a Canadian colonialism. Such practices include the appropriation and commodification of Indigenous land (Davis and Zannis 1973; Weyler 1992), the manipulation of legal definitions of "Indian" status using blood quantum rules and sexist discrimination (Lawrence 2004), legislated exclusion from jobs in the settler economy (Lutz 2008), and welfare and development policies that impose absolute poverty on reserve populations (Roseau River Anishnabe First Nation Government 1997; Shewell 2004). Taken together, these practices have worked genocidally to impede Aboriginal cultural survival and to construct a Europeanized Canada with no space for Indigenous societies (Boyko 1995; Neu and Therrien 2003; Paul 2006; Robinson and Quinney 1985).[1]

Colonialism and Genocide Worldwide

The spread of civilization also brought genocide to those parts of the eastern hemisphere that Europe colonized. In Australia, for instance, settler colonialism took destructive forms resembling those in North America (e.g., Barta 1987; Moses 2000 and 2002; Ryan 1996). Throughout Africa and Asia, the project of colonialism frequently involved the "destruction, in whole or in part, of a national, ethnic, racial, or religious group," to cite the UNCG. The wrenching reconfiguration of local social systems, done to impose mechanisms of economic exploitation that profited the colonizers, frequently destabilized entire societies and claimed millions of lives. Some anthropologists have estimated that "from the time of their first contacts with the Europeans to the nadir of their population in the late nineteenth and early twentieth centuries, indigenous populations at the margins worldwide were reduced by some thirty million (a conservative figure) or, more likely, by about fifty million. In other words, indigenous populations were reduced to about one-fifth of their precontact numbers" (Maybury-Lewis 2002, 44). This estimate does not include the lethal consequences of the transatlantic slave trade, which killed or displaced up to 40 million Africans (Maybury-Lewis 2002, 47) and did untold damage to tribes and kingdoms throughout the continent. The instigators and ultimate beneficiaries of these

---

1 In chapter 2, I propose a definition of "genocide" designed to accommodate these arguments.

atrocities include those nation-states that are counted among the foremost exponents of the Enlightenment, of democracy, of civilization.

How Does Civilization Produce Genocides?

This is our puzzle: how is it that as civilization advances, bringing with it the values cherished by humanists, genocide seems to travel in its wake or in its bow wave? If the relationship between civilization and genocide were truly an inverse one, we would expect to find the largest, most efficient, and most highly organized genocides far in the past, not uncomfortably close to our present. We would expect that the spread of civilization through colonization brought with it a spread of peaceability, tolerance, inclusiveness. But even posing the issue in these terms shows up part of the answer to the puzzle. Colonization necessarily expands by force, by violence. And the modern Western civilization that colonialism has spread across the globe enjoys technological and logistical resources that enable the organized, efficient deployment of force on a historically unprecedented scale. Every human society has its own cruelties and its own atrocities, according to its means. As these means have grown, so too have their products, for good and for ill.

I will try show how civilization produces genocides, although certainly not all genocides everywhere in history and possibly not all genocides in the modern era. But many genocides, including all of those I discuss in this book, make sense as "civilizing genocides," genocides that either expanded the geographical scope of Western civilization, or deepened the extent to which it permeates society, or both.

To say that civilization produces genocides, I shall have to attach some specificity to the term "civilization," which can mean so many things to so many different people as to mean almost nothing at all. I will treat Western civilization as a definite thing. Just what kind of thing it is will take some explaining. But the point of treating it as a thing is that we are used to the idea that a thing can be produced or constructed or *made*, and we are used to the idea that a thing made by human effort can have many different uses or many different consequences, above and beyond those intended by those who made it. A hammer can be used to pound nails into lumber or to break a bank window; a scalpel can enable life-saving surgery, or a horrible mutilation, or an elective cosmetic alteration, or a fine brunoise of garlic. The products of our labour serve ends beyond those that we plan for them. If we treat civilization as a thing, the question of whether it produces genocide is distinct from the question of whether its makers intend it to do so.

The argument of this book unfolds in two main parts. The chapters in the first part deal with theoretical arguments, culminating in chapter 4, which proposes a theoretical framework for comparatively studying genocides. The chapters in the second part apply this framework to six historical examples of genocide. The book therefore proceeds deductively, dealing with the abstract conceptual and analytical framework before getting to the concrete particulars, which is how my own mind tends to work. Readers who tend to think inductively, who would rather get acquainted with the details of a topic before considering its overall form, may prefer to start reading the chapters in the second part before then turning back to the chapters in the first.

Analyzing Genocide Sociologically

This book analyzes genocide sociologically, which is to say, scientifically. My conception of science is not positivistic: I do not search for invariant general laws, or insist on quantitative data, or claim an objectivity understood as value-neutrality. At the same time, I aim to understand genocide as a structured social relation generated by other structured social relations. This approach is far from unique, but for anyone not immersed in critical sociology, it is unfamiliar enough to deserve some explaining. Chapter 1, "A Critical Sociology of Genocide," begins from a general account of some basics of sociological theorizing and proceeds to explain what is distinctive to my own approach. Sociologists generally agree that the social life of human beings generates a distinct type of phenomenon that cannot be properly explained by reduction to psychological or biological factors, but they disagree widely on how to characterize this phenomenon. One possibility is that social life generates distinct and self-reproducing patterns of action that exist independently of individual consciousness and that constrain individuals from outside themselves; another is that human interaction produces and is produced by subjective meanings that, although present in human consciousness, depend on interaction for their existence and are shared among the members of social groups. In contrast to these two general strategies for defining the social, which I call the *objectivist* and *subjectivist* strategies, I prefer to take a relational approach: the social is neither mind-independent nor mind-based but operates as the dynamic network of relationships into which people enter, partly willingly and partly unwillingly, and through which individuals make up their very selves. Social relations engender not only conflicts but also *contradictions*, dynamics through which the pursuit of some good generates its opposite and through which fundamental oppositions of interest are generated within and by our very means of coming together. If genocide results from a contradiction of this type, it can be eliminated altogether – but only through a transformation that goes to the very roots of social life.

What Counts as Genocide?

Chapter 2, "Identifying Genocide," explores the meaning of the term "genocide" and provides a new answer to the question of what should and should not count as genocide. Central to the debate has been the issue of whether genocide primarily means the physical or the cultural extermination of a people. Authors who take the former position tend to equate genocide with the mass murder of ethnic minorities by nationalist or totalitarian governments; authors who take the latter position consider liberal-democratic settler states like Canada and the United States to be culpable of genocide against Indigenous peoples within their borders. Defenders of the narrow view make the plausible argument that physical and cultural extermination are different kinds of events. However, a close reading of Raphaël Lemkin, the jurist who first coined the term "genocide," reveals that he conceived of genocide as a complex process involving attacks on the physical *and* the cultural life of nations. Lemkin's conception has problems of its own, which result from his primordialist understanding of nations: for Lemkin, the cultural life and the biological life of nations are organically interconnected, and nations are the natural bases of human culture. This limited conception, a symptom of the age of nationalism, prevents us from considering that genocide may be perpetrated against groups that are not nations. Using a relational conception of social structure, I argue that the object of genocide is the dynamic social network that sustains a collective social identity. Chapter 2 closes by proposing that we conceive of genocide as an identity-difference relation of violent obliteration.

Moving beyond Uniqueness

In 1990 Helen Fein claimed that there was a "sociological theory gap" separating the study of genocide from other concerns of the discipline. Chapter 3, "Closing the Theory Gap in the Sociology of Genocide," considers what is involved in bridging this gap. Doing so requires overcoming the tendency to think of genocide as a unique phenomenon, one that is categorically separate from the phenomena produced by normal social institutions. To understand how genocides are produced by the normal operation of normal institutions, I draw on Zygmunt Bauman's discussion of how specifically modern forms of rationality, in science and in the organization of state bureaucracies, made the Nazi holocaust possible by negating whatever spontaneous human compassion the thousands of ordinary soldiers and civil servants involved in its implementation might otherwise have felt for the victims. Michel Foucault's analysis of disciplinary power and biopower, as extensions of the power of sovereigns over the life and death of their subjects, also connects forms of rationality common to modern states with the specifically genocidal inflection that they sometimes take. Marxian analysis of state power and of imperialism helps to establish the systematic connection between class and sovereignty, revealing how genocide may be one of the many tactics a dominant class can use to establish or maintain relations of exploitation and thereby extend or preserve its privilege. Genocide scholars who draw on a more liberal tradition of conflict theory help to bring into focus those dynamics of state power that do not reduce to class in the Marxian sense, dynamics generated by states' monopolization of the means of military force. Finally, the work of feminist scholars traces the irreducibly gendered quality of genocide, establishing the continuity between genocidal violence and the more quotidian violences that maintain gendered heteronormativity in everyday/everynight life.[2]

---

2 Throughout this book, I follow Dorothy Smith's preference for the term "everyday/everynight" over the more familiar "everyday" (see Smith 2006). To the extent that the divide between day and night tends also to mark a divide between public life and private life, mention of "everynight" life draws attention to those activities that go on off of the public stage of daytime life, ranging from the intimacies of the bedroom to political acts committed under literal and figurative cover of darkness.

The Social Production of Genocides

Chapter 4, "Civilizing Genocides and Barbaric Civilization," presents the core argument of the book, a theory of how genocide can be produced through the expansion of Western civilization. I build upon Norbert Elias's analysis of the "civilizing process." Elias conceives of all social structures as *figurations* – that is, as dynamic networks of social relations unfolding as historical processes. So he examines the (Western) civilizing *process* historically, casting back over a thousand years to chart the rise of the institutions and the modes of conduct that today are called "civilized." In Elias's analysis, the civilizing process has two distinguishable but indivisible aspects: at the "macro" scale, it entails the progressive regional monopolization of the means of military violence leading to the emergence of the system of sovereign states; at the "micro" scale, it engenders the transformation of the habits and emotions of individuals toward increasing self-control and self-restraint in the performance of all things to do with the body – from sneezing, belching, and eliminating to laughing, weeping, and expressions of passion – a change that also involves increasing sensitivity to the perceptions and feelings of others. In Elias's account, these two developments enable and reinforce each other, and their progression brings with it an overall decrease in the use of violence in social life, especially a removal of violence from the conduct of everyday/everynight life, its concealment "behind the scenes" of the social order, and the growth of interdependencies between people that mitigate against violence. An important consequence of this theory is that when violence erupts into the world of the everyday, as it does in genocide, this eruption necessarily represents a reversal or a breakdown of the civilizing process.

To radically reformulate Elias's theory while preserving its useful core, I read him deconstructively. Although the overt meaning of Elias's texts asserts a hierarchical binary relationship between civilization and barbarism, in which the former progressively overtakes and suppresses the latter through the (reversible) advance of the civilizing process, a closer reading brings out an opposite picture, in which every advance of the civilizing process reproduces barbarism (or the objective and subjective conditions for violence) on an increased scale. The monopolization of military force by sovereign states enables the formation of ever-greater reserves of destructive

potential, up to and including the capacity for global nuclear omnicide. More subtly, the resolution of interpersonal conflicts through
increasingly refined codes of civility reinforces the dangerousness of
radical social difference, increasing the social distance between the
privileged subjects of civilization and its barbarous Others. Advances
in the civilizing process do not dissolve violence but *defer* it, and
through this deferral they produce networks of relations of *difference* that both connect and separate human beings.[3]

Like a plant producing a toxin and the antidote for the toxin at
almost equal rates, this barbarizing-civilizing process generates the
impunity to commit violence and the *interdependence* that prevents
violence at almost equal but uneven rates and on an ever-increasing
scale. The possibility of genocide results from social relations operating along three dimensions: identity-difference, which defines who is
included in and who is excluded from the universe of moral obligation; impunity-interdependence, which defines the relative balance of
power across the identity-difference relation, allowing or inhibiting
the use of force; and interest-indifference, the relative stakes of social
relationships (how much can be gained or lost through relations). In
sum: *a network of actors joined together by common identity will
pursue genocide across the boundary of difference if a sufficient interest exists to mobilize such a large-scale action and if the actors have
the impunity to do so.* In such a process, the sovereignty of the state
may be extended, along with the social dominance of the habitus of
its privileged members. Alarmingly, the civilizing process can produce, and be produced through, these *civilizing genocides*.

Six Historical Examples

The three chapters that make up the second part of the book each
analyze a pair of historical events that exemplify particular qualities of the process that produces civilizing genocides. Chapter 5,
"Genocides of Ideological Others in Languedoc and Guatemala,"

---

3 "Différance," Jacques Derrida's neologism for the semiotic process through
which meaning emerges from the endless process of making-difference between
signs, appears in my analysis as a material process in which the identities of
subjects are defined by the production of a hierarchical difference between them
that is based on class, on sex/gender, and on the relation of subjects to the means
of violence.

Mission and *The Killing Fields*, and I read historical novels about French and British colonialism in Canada and its effects on Indigenous peoples like the Haida and the Mi'kmaq. But although, as I have written elsewhere (Powell 2009), these encounters sank into me like a stone into a river, changing the course of my relation to the world, at a conscious level my awareness of them remained abstract. I didn't yet have any way to make use of this knowledge, so it lay dormant. And like most settler Canadians, I was entirely oblivious to the on-going effects of the genocide closest to home. Even after the stories of sexual abuse in Indian residential schools became public knowledge in the early 1990s, they long remained for me, as for many other settler Canadians, stories about exceptional abuses committed by bad individuals, not stories about the most visible symptoms of an institution designed to destroy cultures. Since childhood, I have found it distressingly easy to identify with victims of violence, whomever they are, and to be horrified by oppression and cruelty; it has taken longer for me to perceive how my own life is implicated in genocidal events and how I am personally connected to them.

But civilization is a contradictory process, and the same social context that implicated me in collective denial also set me on a path that would lead me to question this denial. For, like many Canadians with a certain amount of privilege, I grew up believing that the world was just. I held, naively, the belief that morally good actions brought practically good outcomes to those who performed them and that bad actions caused bad outcomes, with the effect that on the whole people got what they deserved and deserved what they got. This involved a certain amount of selective perception, of course. The effort of ignoring the evidence that didn't fit this image of a just world became a habit that I forgot I'd ever acquired. But I was motivated to perform this effort because I wanted to be a good person. In effect, and in the terms of relational theory, this desire to be a good person amounted to a desire to become part of a system of circulating actions whose macro and micro forms, as I experienced them, aligned harmoniously: a society without contradictions. In such a society, the conditions for social acceptance, for self-acceptance, and for material success would all match up perfectly, allowing the knowing, questing individual subject a kind of spiritual closure. I sought the ultimate bliss of knowing that I had, through my actions, made myself into everything that others expected of me while, by the same actions, obtaining everything that I needed for my own self.

But this closure proved elusive, and the search for it led me to some uncomfortable realizations.

Blame Carl Sagan and Farley Mowat. Sagan's *Cosmos* offers its readers a grand vision of systemic order in which the entire earth is just a speck of dust and all human history a half-heartbeat in the long slow life of the universe. Mowat's *Never Cry Wolf* dares its readers to deeply identify with the radical Other, to extend moral community even to nonhumans. Books like these lay ready at hand thanks to my parents' diligent efforts to impart to me significant cultural capital. And together, with others like them, they raised the bar for spiritual closure very high. Sagan's concern with the possibility of human extinction through global nuclear war and Mowat's concern with the extinction of natural difference through human overdevelopment of fragile ecosystems are just two of the ways that the scientific aspiration to totalize the natural universe *epistemologically* has shown up the negative *practical* consequences of modern attempts to totalize the social universe, either politically (through total monopolization of military force) or economically (through totally efficient exploitation of natural resources). Rigorously pursued, a universalizing, non-anthropocentric scientific attitude can, under the right conditions, turn back on itself, become reflexive. With this turning, contradictions become apparent; the universe cracks, becomes multiple, and the prospect of totality recedes like a mirage.

Relative privilege cultivating a selfish desire to be just, scientific cultural capital, and suburban leisure and isolation were the distinctive social conditions that, in hindsight, seem to have led me to this book. Between there and here stand a string of fairly predictable biographical details. But one of these might be worth mentioning. In the autumn of 1989 I made the acquaintance of the East Timor Action Network (ETAN), a student organization at the University of Toronto working to draw attention to the plight of East Timorese under Indonesian occupation. This plight included genocide: when East Timor declared independence after the withdrawal of Portuguese colonial power in 1975, Indonesian soldiers invaded, occupied the country, and murdered an estimated 60,000 of its 600,000 inhabitants; Amnesty International has estimated that from 1975 to 1999, one-third of the population, or 200,000 persons, died from military action, starvation, and disease. When the United Nations General Assembly voted eight times to condemn Indonesia for these actions, Canada abstained five times and voted "no" three times.

The members of ETAN proposed that this happened because of the Canadian government's preference for protecting the profits of Canadian businesses operating in Indonesia over securing the lives and the human rights of East Timorese subjects. As luck would have it, I was able to ask someone on the inside of Canadian diplomacy to explain Canada's position. My professor for an introductory course in political science in 1989–90, Jack T. McLeod, was unusually well connected, and one of the guest speakers for our course was Stephen Lewis, celebrated social-democratic political leader and, from 1984 to 1988, Canadian ambassador to the United Nations. Lewis spoke about his experiences with the United Nations and international diplomacy but didn't mention East Timor. In the hallway after his lecture, I caught up with Lewis and asked why Canada had abstained from the votes to condemn Indonesia for its actions in East Timor. Lewis's hurried reply was in effect that Canada considered the Indonesian annexation of East Timor to be a fait accompli, a done deal, so there was no point in opposing it.

Try as I might, I could not make out how this position was just. Such incomprehension has led me here.

Theoretical Goals

When I began the research that led to this book, I wanted a project that would do two things. First, it would tie theory to a politically and morally urgent issue. I wanted to ground the most abstract theoretical questions in the most concrete possible of problems, out of a conviction that only such a grounding would give theory any way of being validated. I take the nominalist view that the possibilities of theoretical innovation are endless, such that theoretical problems cannot be solved by exhausting all of the alternatives at an abstract level; theoretical positions can achieve only a relative adequacy, and for this to happen they need a purpose beyond themselves.

Second, I wanted my project to address some kind of limit phenomenon. I am generally interested in the limits of what is possible in social life. There is a theoretical and a practical reason for this. Theoretically, the problem of explaining social events, of saying why one thing happens and not something else, translates into a question about constraint: what constrained things to happen this particular way and impeded other, imaginable possibilities from becoming actual? And this type of question connects to a more general question:

what are the ultimate constraints on social life – the limits beyond which it cannot go, the conditions that have to obtain for it to exist at all? For the victims, at least, genocide is one limit beyond which social life is not possible. So if I take the ubiquitous question of why genocide happens where and when it does and turn this question on its head to ask, when genocide does not happen, why *not* and what prevents it, I have a question that gets at the conditions of possibility for any social life.

This way of approaching things makes my work consistent with *radical* projects in social theory. The word "radical" derives from the late Latin word "radix," which means "root," and the first definition of "radical" listed in the Oxford English Dictionary is "of or pertaining to a root or roots"; radically critical thought looks for the roots of social life and argues that the range of forms any given society can take is ultimately constrained by the nature of its roots. Karl Marx (1971; Marx and Engels 1976), for example, identifies the social organization of material production as a necessary condition for social life and argues that conflicts or contradictions built into the social relations of production fundamentally shape everything else that happens in society. Radical feminists like Shulamith Firestone (1970) make comparable claims about social relations of sex and reproduction. I have tried to use genocide as a way into a radical critique of the social relations of physical force.

My sense of "radical," or "radically critical," social thought is best understood in relation to the question of how the various events of social life are or are not systemically connected. In the view associated with uncritical versions of functionalism, societies form organically integrated wholes, like living organisms, such that genocide cannot possibly result from the inner logic of the system but must represent a pathology or breakdown of society. In the view distinctive to analytic conflict theory, conflict is inherent to social life, but there is no systemic relationship among all the various conflicts of any particular society; there are no deep roots to go to when explaining genocide. In a radical view, all social life is systematically interconnected, but this does not add up to a coherent whole: society is torn – and fuelled – by a limited number of fundamental contradictions, each rooted in the social relationships that organize a particular limit or condition of possibility for collective social life. In this view, all victimizations, and all struggles for human freedom and dignity, are connected: struggles for women's emancipation, working people's empowerment, military disarmament, sexual freedom, ecological sustainability, the abolition of racism, decolonization, and the search for an end to genocide are all inescapably intertwined. However, none of these struggles is the foundation of all the others. This makes my position postmodernist, in contrast with modernist radicalisms that assert one or another hierarchy of oppressions.

Two Qualifications

Now that I have introduced myself, I would like to offer two caveats before I get fully underway. The first concerns the scope of what this book accomplishes. It works well as a critique of the uncritical functionalism that is common sense for many of the more privileged members of Canadian society, the view that society is a relatively unified moral community and that something as evil as genocide must result from individual madness or collective social breakdown. It also does something to shake up another common-sense view of the privileged: the assumption that society is composed of individuals making choices and nothing more. I show the plausibility of thinking through genocide in terms of emergent and contradictory relational structures. But I have not given a proof of my position, in the strong sense of making the alternatives appear irrational. Functionalist and conflict theories can take sophisticated, nuanced, and critical forms. I provide a different framework, coherent and plausible on its own terms, that stands or falls by the insights that it offers, by the opportunities for empirical research that it opens up, and by the new thoughts and the new actions that it helps to make possible.

Second, my approach to this project owes a great debt to a range of critical projects – most especially feminism but also postcolonialism, critical race theory, and queer theory – that do not take explicit prominence in the text to come. In particular, the feminist questions of how the personal is political, how social relations are embodied, and how masculinity is bound up with violence were always on my mind as I researched and wrote this book. Only after I had written this book did I fully perceive how much of the social history of state formation is quite literally and directly a social history of patriarchy. If I could conduct this project over again from the beginning, analyses of gender relations would feature much more explicitly in my narrative than they currently do. I hope that you, the reader, will grant me the goodwill of seeing them as implicit.

In *Violence*, Slavoj Žižek approaches his topic "awry," through "sidelong glances," because, he writes, to confront violence too directly leads to mystification: on the one hand, "the overpowering horror of violent acts and empathy with the victims inexorably function as a lure which prevents us from thinking," but on the other hand, "a cold analysis of violence somehow reproduces and participates in its horror" (Žižek 2008, 4). If I agreed entirely, I would not have written this book in the way that I have. But I do agree that writing about violence calls for special care. In her remarkable book *Trauma and Recovery*, Judith Lewis Herman has described what I would most like to be true of my own work on this difficult topic:

> I expect this book to be controversial – first, because it is written from a feminist perspective; second, because it challenges established diagnostic concepts; but third and perhaps most importantly, because it speaks about horrible things, things that no one really wants to hear about. I have tried to communicate my ideas in a language that preserves connections, a language that is faithful both to the dispassionate, reasoned traditions of my profession and to the passionate claims of people who have been violated and outraged. I have tried to find a language that can withstand the imperatives of doublethink and allows all of us to come a little closer to facing the unspeakable. (Herman 2001, 4)

PART ONE

1

A Critical Sociology of Genocide

At the entrance to science, as at the entrance to hell, the demand must be posted: "Here all mistrust must be abandoned, and here perish every craven thought."

Marx 1971, 331

INTRODUCTION: EVERYBODY IN DENIAL

In 1999 the clothing retail chain The Gap ran a series of television advertisements for its new line of khaki pants. The ads showed a multiracial ensemble of mostly young women and men joyously dancing to swing jazz against a white background while wearing Gap khakis. At the end of each spot, the caption would appear: "Everybody in Khakis." At that time, The Gap was a focus of concern for activists as one of several popular clothing retailers that sold clothes made in sweatshops by workers, mostly women, who were required to labour long hours under dangerous and unhealthy conditions, had no legal or union protections and no job security, endured arbitrary harassment and termination, and subsisted on the barest possible wages so that the labour-cost of each garment was a tiny fraction of its retail value. In this context, the video for Rage against the Machine's 1999 single "Guerrilla Radio" opened with a shot of an ensemble of women of colour working steadily in neat rows of sewing machines to the sound of swing jazz and against the same white background, followed by the caption: "Everybody in Denial."

There's an activist slogan that says, "If you're not outraged, you're not paying attention." The sensibility this expresses goes beyond observing that outrageous injustice exists in the world to confronting how this injustice is all too frequently involved in maintaining what relatively privileged people take for granted as an ordinary, everyday/everynight life. It is a sensibility that believes it is not possible to be aware of the world and to be comfortable in it. It's also a sensibility that comes from a place of relative privilege: the privilege of having a choice between being outraged by injustice or living in denial about it. It's a sensibility demanding that those with the luxury of this choice use their privilege to oppose injustice, even if success brings with it a diminution of privilege.

There's some echo, at least, of this sensibility in the work of most scholars who study genocide, especially in the claim of Frank Chalk and Kurt Jonassohn that our culture, both lay and academic, suffers from *collective denial* regarding the importance of genocide in human history and as a contemporary phenomenon. Chalk and Jonassohn explain this denial as the residue of conventional historical practice, of histories written by the winners and news made by rulers. In their brief account, this hegemony of collective denial has been broken by "the shocks of the twentieth century," in which "the gap between practice and ideals simply became too great to support the intellectual foundations of such denial," and by the growth of democratic environments, in which "for the first time, it is the ruled who make the news" (Chalk and Jonassohn 1990, 8). Collective denial about genocide means that we try to think about it as little as possible. In particular, we try to think as little as possible about what the fact of genocide, or of particular genocides, might mean for our own everyday/everynight lives. We treat it as an aberration, a catastrophe, a monstrosity, or a horrible social dysfunction but in any case as something quite out of the ordinary and so as something that we can safely ignore most of the time. We push it to the margins of our consciousness. There are several ways we do this. One is by *wilful ignorance*: we simply abstain from learning more than we have to about genocides that we are connected to in any way, such as genocides that are happening now or have happened recently or genocides that are part of the history of our own societies. Another is by *theodicy*, a term Dirk Moses (2002) has used to describe how settler societies maintain denial about genocides committed against Indigenous peoples. A third method of denial, I think, is *sacralization*. Particular ethnic groups who have been victims of genocide sometimes treat their experiences or memories thereof as something holy, something set apart from the mundane world and not to be profaned by too close association with it. This makes sense as a method for reclaiming the dignity of one's identity after it has been abominably violated. But something that is sacred is, by definition, not part of this world. For those who have the luxury of a choice between outrage and denial, making genocide sacred can work as another way of ignoring it most of the time.

I think that for many well-meaning people, one force that perpetuates denial is the sense of being overwhelmed by something enormous, something too strange and complex to understand immediately, and something that one must act on somehow even though it isn't clear how. I think that we can defuse this feeling: we can make genocide smaller, simpler, and more comprehensible in ways that help us to think effectively about what to do about it. The general approach that I propose for doing this is something I call a *critical sociology of genocide*. A critical sociology of genocide does two things. First, it treats events like genocide, which involve the interconnected actions of many individual people, as definite things – in the same sense that tables and chairs are things, rocks and trees are things, neurons and DNA are things, electromagnetic fields and gravity wells are things. That's the sociology part. Second, it maintains that there is no neutral point of view on any social event. When we talk about the social world, we are embedded in the very processes we are talking about, in the conflicts and struggles that ripple through them, and whether we mean to or not we are always *taking sides*. That's the critical part. So in the next section of this chapter, I explain in more detail what I mean by these two words, "sociology" and "critical."

WHAT DIFFERENCE DOES SOCIOLOGY MAKE?

Subjectivity

I've been saying that social events are things, but what kind of things are they? This is an old question for sociologists and is a good way of introducing the discipline. For me, classical sociology has three general answers to this question: the subjectivist, the objectivist, and the relational. (These are contemporary terms, not the terms that classical sociologists themselves would have used.) The first is the *subjectivist* answer: social things are characterized by the subjective meanings that they have for human beings. This is the answer given by Max Weber, for whom the basic unit of sociological analysis was intentional *social action* (Weber 1978, 4–5, 15–16, 18, 22–4). Social events are to be explained first and foremost by *understanding* the subjective meanings and intentions that individuals attach to their actions (Weber 1978, 8–12). Understanding does not mean condoning. For Weber, it means being able to reconstruct the meaning that was actually attached to an action by the person who performed it. Actions such as writing a mathematical formula, chopping wood, and aiming a gun are more than just programmed behavioural mechanisms; they have meanings for the people who perform them and are caused by motives. I might chop wood to work out some stress, or because I am cold and my stove needs fuel, or to prepare for a romantic evening by the fireplace; I might aim a gun in target practice, or in self-defence, or in anger, or to perform a professional duty. Understanding these meanings is necessary to be able to say descriptively *what* a person is doing. "Getting married," "going to war," and "solving a puzzle" are events that depend on their meanings to be what they are. Understanding is also necessary to be able to say *why* people do what they do because our motivations and intentions are meaningful and because of the causal relation (however fraught) between our motives and our behaviours. However, Weber does acknowledge that intentional action can, and often does, have unintended consequences. One of the goals of sociology is to help diminish those unintended consequences by giving social actors improved knowledge of the likely consequences of their actions.

One important implication of a subjectivist social science concerns the nature of morality. Science can deal with morality only as an empirically observable phenomenon. That is, it cannot treat morality as a *metaphysical essence*. An essence could be understood as a definite and finite list of attributes that define a thing, which are permanent, inalterable, and eternal; these attributes are metaphysical because their connection to the object they define is held to obtain ahistorically – that is, outside of time and space, history and society. By definition, a metaphysical essence is not something that can be empirically observed, directly or indirectly. So empirical scientists of any stripe, social or natural, cannot have anything to say about essences; we can't explain them, and we can't use them to explain events in the physical universe, including social events. You might ask: why am I even talking about them? The answer is that in Western culture it is commonplace to speak of morality and also of ethics, criminality, and even law as metaphysical essences. For example, in a debate with Michel Foucault that addressed the nature of justice, Noam Chomsky took the essentialist position:

one does not necessarily allow the state to define what is legal. Now the state has the power to enforce a certain concept of what is legal, but power doesn't imply justice or even correctness; so that the state may define something as civil disobedience and may be wrong in doing so. (Chomsky and Foucault 1997, 133)

I think there is some sort of an absolute basis – if you press me too hard I'll be in trouble, because I can't sketch it out – ultimately residing in fundamental human qualities, in terms of which a "real" notion of justice is grounded. (Chomsky and Foucault 1997, 138)

This way of speaking accords with common sense, and Foucault's reply to Chomsky – that such a law does not exist, or more precisely that justice is a stake in power struggles and an instrument of power (Chomsky and Foucault 1997, 135–8) – seems radically alarming. However, an empirical science can examine concepts such as law, criminality, and justice only *as they manifest themselves in observable social life* – that is, in terms of how they are defined and used, or not used, by concrete human beings: "If it can be argued that the National Socialist state was by its very nature a criminal state because it violated God's laws or the laws of nature, one must ask what practical difference such violations made to the perpetrators. As long as the leaders of National Socialist Germany were free to exercise sovereignty, no superordinate system of norms constituted any kind of restraint on their behaviour" (Rubenstein 1987, 296–7). That which makes no difference explains nothing. Science cannot directly settle the question of whether metaphysical essences exist in any ultimate sense, any more than it can settle the question of whether God exists. Science is committed to a rule of *immanence* – to studying things or events in the physical universe and explaining them in terms of other things in the physical universe. So when social scientists examine morality, they can examine it only as something conceived of and practised by human beings.

Weber, then, treats morals as things, specifically social things, in the physical universe. Since he defines the "thing-ness" of social things in terms of their meaningful quality and their relation to intentional action, morals – or, more generally, values – are, for Weber, one type of subjective meaning that informs social action. This view has two important consequences. First, regardless of whether essential values exist or don't exist, subjective values clearly do exist – people have various ideas about what is right and wrong, good and evil, proper and improper – and we can *observe* people expressing these ideas and acting on the basis of them. Through observation, we can *understand* people's values if we work hard enough (Weber 1978, 4–13). We can also try to *explain* how these people have come to have these values and what the consequences will be of acting on these values in a given situation (Weber 1978, 85). Second, and even more important for understanding genocide, science cannot legitimately claim to say whose values are right and whose are wrong: "The one and only result which can ever be achieved by empirical psychological and historical investigation of a particular value-system, as influenced by individual, social and historical causes, is its *interpretive explanation*. That is no small achievement" (Weber 1978, 80, original emphasis). For Weber, one of the principal benefits of interpretive explanation is that it contributes to the "empirical causal study of human action" (Weber 1978, 80). To explain why people of a certain group act the way they actually do, it does not do us any good to ask whether their actions are morally right in some transcendental or metaphysical sense. We need to ask whether they themselves believe their actions to be morally right. We usually find that they do. For example,

> That Hitler and his helpers were masters of dissimulation and the spreading of deliberate lies, that their preachings contained a strong dose of hatred, humbug, and hypocrisy, was in no way incompatible with their fervent belief in the ultimate truth of their creed ... It is understandable that many representatives of the older educated elite experienced the extent of the regression under the Nazis as a shock out of the blue, because they could not discern beneath the lies, the propaganda tricks, and the deliberate use of falsehoods as a weapon against enemies, the sincerity with which the standard-bearers of the movement believed in ideas which appeared to them themselves as doubtful or patently absurd. (Elias 1996, 315–16)

As another example, let us consider Hannah Arendt's report of the trial of Adolf Eichmann. Arendt has described as immoral and criminal the actions of Eichmann and others responsible for the Final Solution. At first glance, this doesn't seem like a problem; she considers their acts immoral and criminal, and so do we. The problem is that Arendt tries to do more than pass judgment: she wants to understand the conditions of possibility for the Nazi genocides. Again and again, she asks how it was possible for human beings to engage in this sort of behaviour. Standing in the way of her answering this question is her assumption that morality and law exist outside of time and space. She calls the Final Solution criminal and its perpetrators criminals, even though what they did was in accordance with German law. The law itself was criminal: "it was not an order but a law which had turned them all into criminals" (Arendt 1994, 149). (The Final Solution arguably also did not contravene any international law to which Germany was a party, which created some difficulty when it came to trying the perpetrators after the fact.) Arendt's explanation for how an ordinary individual like Eichmann could participate in atrocity is that he acted "under circumstances that make it well-nigh impossible for him to know or to feel that he is doing wrong" (Arendt 1994, 276). But this is not accurate. Eichmann's own statements reveal that he felt strongly that what he was doing was *right* and that he acted, to the point of self-sacrifice, in accordance with the demands of moral duty. The Nazis explicitly exhorted people to be strong, overcome their animal pity, and resist being "tempted *not* to murder, *not* to rob, *not* to let their neighbours go off to their doom" (Arendt 1994, 150, original emphasis); that is, they exhorted people to suppress their personal impulses in the service of society. '

The sociologist Zygmunt Bauman makes the same mistake in *Modernity and the Holocaust*.[1] He claims that the mechanisms of scientific rationality and bureaucracy enabled the "social production of distance" (Bauman 1991b, 199), separating individuals who participated in the Holocaust from the consequences of their actions so that their moral sense would not be activated: "The Holocaust could be accomplished only on the condition of neutralizing the impact of primeval moral drives, of isolating the machinery of murder

---

1 As does Alex Alvarez in *Governments, Citizens and Genocide*. Alvarez's criminological approach treats genocide as deviance and so reifies its criminality and immorality. For example, he discusses the morality of genocide only in terms of the suppression of forms of morality that would inhibit participation in violence and treats the production of moralities that legitimate genocide under the heading of "ideology" (Alvarez 2001, 72–7, 95, 106–7, 112).

from the sphere where such drives arise and apply, of rendering such drives marginal or altogether irrelevant to the task" (Bauman 1991b, 188). As important as the social production of distance was, it is not he only factor that explains the participation of ordinary, nonpsychotic individuals in mass extermination. As Christopher Browning points out in his case study of Reserve Police Battalion 101, whose 500 members shot to death approximately 38,000 Jews, many killings were performed by reserve police forces "who were quite literally saturated in the blood of victims shot at point-blank range" (Browning 1992, 162), victims who included women, children, and elderly persons.[2] It is true that those who engaged in such killings felt a deep emotional repugnance about their actions, at least at first (Browning 1992, 184). But for the most part, they themselves did not understand this repugnance as a "primeval moral drive" but as a weakness that *stood in the way* of moral behaviour (Browning 1992, 185).

Claudia Koonz explains this puzzling phenomenon in *The Nazi Conscience*. Although a core of fanatics in the Nazi party were motivated by anti-Semitic hatred, persuading the majority of Germans to support the Nazi agenda meant appealing to their sense of virtue. To do this, the Nazis formulated a value-system with four principal features, three of which were common to other Western societies. First, the life of the people, or *Volk*, was understood to be like that of an organism, "marked by stages of birth, growth, expansion, decline, and death" (Koonz 2003, 6). The organic life required individuals to "put collective need ahead of individual greed" in order to ensure the health of the community. Second, values were conceived of as relative to the nature and environment of the community in which they evolved. But while anthropologists like Ruth Benedict (1934) and Frank Boas (1940) used cultural relativism to argue for humanistic tolerance, the Nazis asserted that the German *Volk*, not humanity as a whole, was the ultimate object of morality.[3] Third, aggression against undesirable populations in conquered lands was understood to be justified as a notion that had ample precedent – in

---

2 Nor can social distance and bureaucratic depersonalization explain killing of the sort that took place during the Rwandan genocide of 1994, where a great deal of killing was done face-to-face using not guns but machetes.

3 Cultural relativism and moral universalism are often assumed to be antithetical, but this is a mistake. For accounts of how moral universals can be socially constructed, see Alexander (2002) and Stammers (1999).

American attitudes toward Indigenous peoples, for example. Fourth, and distinct to Germany at the time, the government was accorded "the right to annul the legal protections of assimilated citizens on the basis of what the government defined as their ethnicity" (Koonz 2003, 8). Even this was not unprecedented, but the Nazis pushed the envelope of persecution by defining ethnicity and exclusion in terms that "bore no physical or cultural markers" (Koonz 2003, 8). Overall, the Nazis' successful effort to present themselves as bearers of an upright ethical standard must be appreciated to understand how the Final Solution became possible (Powell 2011).

Essentialist thinking about morality prevents us from inquiring deeply into the dynamics of genocide and from asking crucial questions. How do the perpetrators understand their own actions? Do they perceive their actions as immoral, or do they act in accordance with moral codes that make genocide a duty and a virtue? What are the contents of such codes? How do they come into being – what are their historical causes? What benefits do they provide that induce people to participate in them? We have to ask these questions not just so that we can understand genocide better but precisely because we condemn it – precisely because we want to find ways to prevent it from continuing to happen.

Weber's sociological conception of morality helps us to understand how ordinary, nonsociopathic people can participate in genocide and believe that they are acting morally.[4] However, an entirely subjectivist account of social action is not sufficient to the task of explaining genocide. Subjectivist sociology centres itself on the individual. Any aggregate or collective concepts that scientists might use to explain the actions of large numbers of people – concepts like bureaucracy or Protestant asceticism, for example – are just methodological tools and do not designate real things. One important problem with an individualistic sociology can be understood if we again consider an essentialist conception of morality. One reason why we are so willing to imagine that morality exits outside of time and space is that we often feel deeply that right and wrong exist

---

4 This is not to say that believing one's actions to be morally justified means that these acts have no effects whatsoever on one's state of mind. Frantz Fanon, for example, tells the story of a police officer who came to him seeking relief for psychiatric symptoms resulting from his work as a torturer for the colonial government – so that he could be a more effective and well-adjusted torturer (Fanon 1963, 264–7). Perpetrators of violence may suffer trauma from their acts without this leading them to classify their acts as morally wrong.

outside of our individual selves. We express this in the statement that some things "just are" wrong – as Chomsky did in his debate with Foucault. And although we feel this most strongly about very extreme moral issues like genocide, torture, or rape, the same feeling is at work in our experience of quotidian social rules: in why we cover our mouth when we cough, or stand facing the front of elevators, or refrain from bursting into song during ordinary conversations. We feel not just that morality is inside us but also that some aspect of it comes from outside ourselves.

A second problem with subjectivist sociology, related to the first, is that it does not allow for the existence of any social things on a larger scale than the individual. Although Weber acknowledges that intentional action can lead to unintended consequences, he does not account for how this is possible – for how people's intentional actions are shaped by forces that they do not intend or understand, forces that are not, in themselves, meaningful. We can understand this by analogy to natural forces. Rain, for example, is not in itself a meaningful phenomenon (Weber 1978, 7). Human beings can and do attach all sorts of meanings to it – personal, aesthetic, spiritual, and so on – and its occurrence or nonoccurrence certainly has important consequences for us, even life or death consequences. But the mechanisms that produce rain are not governed by the logic of our meanings. We may associate rain with sadness, but it doesn't rain because we're sad (except in the movies). Human intentional actions may affect whether it rains or not; for example, by cutting down or by planting large forests, human beings may decrease or increase rainfall in an area. This effect can be intended or not or can be intended by some participants and not by others. But to understand these dynamics, we need to distinguish between the meaningless natural forces that govern rainfall and the meaningful aspects of social interaction. In an analogous way, there are meaningless social forces generated by human action but not reducible to our intentions or our subjectivity, forces of which we can be quite unaware and that shape the circumstances of our lives in powerful ways. The forces that connect civilization with genocide fall into this category.

Objectivity

The objectivist answer is the second classic answer to the question of what kind of things social things are, and it is exemplified in the work of Emile Durkheim. It was Durkheim who insisted that the "first and most basic rule" of sociological method "is *to consider social facts as things*" (Durkheim 1982, 60, original emphasis). Social facts form the basic unit of analysis in Durkheimian sociology, and he defines them in this way: "A social fact is any way of acting, fixed or not, capable of exerting over the individual an external constraint" (Durkheim 1982, 59). Social facts exist "independent of their individual manifestations" and independent of individual human beings. Sociology is defined as the study of social facts, such that "Sociological method as we practice it rests wholly on the basic principle that social facts must be studied as things, that is, as realities external to the individual ... [I]f no reality exists outside of the individual consciousness, it [sociology] wholly lacks any material of its own" (Durkheim 1979, 37–8). Durkheim's prescription for studying social facts differs entirely from Weber's method for studying social action. Whereas Weber asserts that sociological research must begin with *verstehen*, the understanding of the subjective meanings individuals attach to their actions, Durkheim insists that social facts must be defined in terms of their objective and formal properties. For example, he defines crime as "any action that is punished" (Durkheim 1982, 75). At a price – namely the risk of neglecting important differences in how local cultures understand the practices they engage in – this approach allows sociologists to make comparisons among practices that might not be recognized as sharing similarities by those who engage in them.[5]

Objectivist sociology has the effect, intended by Durkheim, of taking features of social life that commonly are treated in a metaphysical manner and locating them within the natural universe.[6] Durkheim's method lets us explain historical events in terms of other historical events, human practices in terms of other practices. This leaves open

---

5 As Peter Winch has argued (Winch 1990, 45–51), it is not ultimately possible to define social actions in purely formal terms with no reference to how the participants themselves view their actions; the social meaning of an act makes it what it is. Neither is Durkheim's method as rigidly objectivist as I have made it out to be; the past generation of Durkheim scholarship has brought out the ways that he was sensitive to and engaged with the effects of meaning and subjectivity in constituting social phenomena (see Emirbayer 1996).

6 My use of the expression "natural universe" includes the social world of human relations as well as relations among nonhumans (see Callon 1988; Latour 1988 and 1993).

the possibility that knowing more about society enables us to change it in a deliberate, premeditated way – to subject the operation of meaningless mechanisms to our demand for meaningful lives. It also (more than Weber's approach) allows researchers to generate startlingly counterintuitive insights into familiar features of everyday/everynight life.

The most famous example of the counterintuitive potential of objectivist sociology is Durkheim's claim that crime is functional. As I've mentioned, Durkheim defines crime as "any action that is punished" (Durkheim 1982, 75) or, more narrowly, as actions that "have been repressed by regular punishment" (Durkheim 1982, 78). Durkheim proceeded to make the counterintuitive claim that crime is normal, not pathological, on three grounds (Durkheim 1982, 98–101). These were, first, that it is found in all societies and that "it is completely impossible for any society entirely free of it to exist" (Durkheim 1982, 99); second, that what is established as crime in any given society is relative to the moral sentiments of that society, such that as grosser violations become less common, finer offences come to be viewed with more seriousness; and third, that in all societies some random variation in individual temperament exists, which produces deviations from the norm that lead to the improvement of society, such that the suppression of all deviance, even if it were possible, would prevent gains as well as harms. "Thus, crime is necessary. It is linked to the basic conditions of social life, but on this very account is useful, for the conditions to which it is bound are themselves indispensable to the normal evolution of morality and law" (Durkheim 1982, 101).

In making this argument, Durkheim tends to conflate the *normal* with the *good* or at least the *necessary* by assuming that the normal must be the result of an inexorable and functionally optimal evolutionary process. In this book, I argue that by Durkheim's criteria *genocide itself appears both moral and functional*. Not surprisingly, I reject the assumption that the normal is either necessary or beneficial, and I also do not think the "moral" is something that should automatically command our approval or our obedience. On the contrary, the normalcy and the morality of genocide tell us something important and troubling about the limitations of ordinary social institutions.

Durkheim's definition of morality is complex and seems to have evolved over the course of his work. In *The Rules of Sociological*

Method, he defines as moral any precept whose violation is condemned by public opinion or by widespread, repressive sanction, saying, "Whenever we are confronted with a fact that presents this characteristic we have no right to deny its moral character, for this is proof that it is of the same nature as other moral facts" (Durkheim 1982, 80–1). In *Professional Ethics and Civic Morals* he echoes this, defining moral facts as "rules of conduct that have sanction" (Durkheim 1992, 2). In *Moral Education* he characterizes morality in terms of rules that are *customary*, and hence socially instituted, but that are also *authoritative*, that individuals do not feel free to alter according to their own interests or tastes (Durkheim 2002, 23–4, 29–31). The authority of morality comes from outside of individuals but not from outside of the physical universe; rather, it comes from society as a supra-individual entity existing within the physical universe (Durkheim 2002, 85–6). And in *The Division of Labour in Society*, Durkheim argues that the ultimate function of morality is social solidarity: "We must say that which is moral is everything that is a source of solidarity, everything that forces man [*sic*] to take account of other people, to regulate his actions by something other than the promptings of his own egoism, and the more numerous and strong these ties are, the more solid is the morality" (Durkheim 1984, 331).[7] Morality, for Durkheim, is not any specific set of values or rules but a *type* of rule; moral facts are recognizable by their form, not their content. This allows us to investigate actual moral practices in a non-ethnocentric way, to study the moral convictions of other people and other societies without our own values getting in the way.

The surprising consequence of this, quite unforeseen by Durkheim, is that when we study morality this way, we can see that genocide could be both moral and functional. If genocide is supported by widespread, repressive sanction, if the obligation to participate in genocide is experienced as a duty to something outside oneself, a rule that one does not feel free to alter, and if genocide really does

---

7 Or again: "Moral goals, then, are those the object of which is society. To act morally is to act in terms of the collective interest ... Above and beyond me as a conscious being, above and beyond those sentient beings who are other individual human beings, there is nothing else save that sentient being that is society. By this I mean anything that is a human group, the family as well as the nation, and humanity, at least to the extent that they constitute societies" (Durkheim 2002, 59–60).

contribute to the integration and solidarity of a society, then "we have no right to deny its moral character." These are all empirical conjectures, and they can be resolved in the affirmative.

It should already be clear that the Nazi holocaust meets these formal criteria of morality. However, as a project aimed at providing the basis for solidarity among the German *Volk*, the Nazi holocaust was ultimately unsuccessful: the Third Reich was defeated militarily, the perpetrators of the Holocaust were tried and convicted of crimes against humanity, and the Holocaust became a source of shame for the German people. To better show how genocide can be functional, I'd like to briefly consider a successful genocide: the destruction of the Armenian community in the Ottoman Empire by the Young Turk regime in 1915.

One of the ideological proponents of this genocide was a sociologist named Ziya Gökalp. Gökalp has been called "the father of Turkish nationalism" (Melson 1992, 164) and is regarded by many as "the pre-eminent Turkish thinker of the century" (Smith 1995, 46); he was also a dominant figure in Turkish sociology (Ertürk 1990, 39–40). He used the ideas of Auguste Comte, Herbert Spencer, and Durkheim about the organic unity of society to justify an "ultra-nationalist perspective which left no room for individual liberties and initiative" (Smith 1995, 48). In particular, he borrowed Durkheim's ideas about social solidarity, moral unity, the division of labour, and corporatist political structures (Smith 1995, 47–9; Kahveci 1995, 52–5; Melson 1992, 164) to argue that the removal of Armenians from the Ottoman Empire was necessary to create "a society consisting of people who speak the same language, have had the same education and are united in their religious and aesthetic ideals – in short those who have a common culture and religion" (Heyd 1950, 63).[8] These ideas resonated with the agenda of the Young Turk government, and they expressed what that government

---

8 This use of Durkheim's work was in direct opposition to Durkheim's own intentions. As Steven Lukes has noted in his "Introduction" to *The Rules of Sociological Method* (Lukes 1982, 19), Durkheim was both personally (he was from an Alsatian and Jewish family) and professionally opposed to ethnic fundamentalism. In works like *The Division of Labour in Society* and his lectures collected as *Professional Ethics and Civic Morals*, he was concerned to articulate a theory of social solidarity that privileged civic over ethnic nationalism. But the intentions of social scientists rarely constrain the uses to which their theories are put, as Western Marxists are painfully aware.

hoped to achieve by obliterating the Armenian community through massacre and forced expulsion. The Armenian genocide claimed over 800,000 lives (Dadrian 1997, 223), inspired the first attempts to criminalize genocide in international law (Lemkin 1947, 146), and may also have encouraged Adolf Hitler's genocidal ambitions (Dadrian 1997, 402–9).[9] Unlike Hitler's holocaust, however, the Turkish genocide succeeded in its larger aims. The multicultural and cosmopolitan Ottoman Empire, which had been dissolving over the previous several decades as ethnic minorities within its borders launched successful nationalist movements for secession, was reincarnated as the modern, ethnically based nation-state of Turkey. This state denies to this day that a genocide took place; discussion of any genocide against Armenians has been prohibited by law, and the state threatens repercussions against other states or even foreign individuals who recognize the genocide (e.g., CBC News Online Staff 2004). The Turkish solidarity that Gökalp dreamed of survives to this day.

However, there is one crucial problem with the objectivist account of morality as I have presented it. This is evident in Durkheim's statement that "whenever we are confronted with a fact that presents this characteristic *we have no right* to deny its moral character" (Durkheim 1982, 81, original emphasis). Durkheim seems to be saying that where a social rule meets the criteria of a moral fact, we have no right to object to it. Individuals must accept anything that society deems moral. This seems to smuggle a metaphysical and universal moral standard back into Durkheim's sociology, a totalitarian one at that! However, an endorsement of totalitarianism runs counter to the politics that Durkheim espoused in his own lifetime, which among other things was opposed to anti-Semitism and jingoistic nationalism in the France of his day. It seems more reasonable to conclude that Durkheim failed to predict that genocidal anti-Semitism would be instituted as a social norm a quarter-century after his death and that he was unaware of or in denial about genocides occurring in colonial contexts in his own lifetime. But how do

---

9 These events were followed by a second genocide against Armenians, this time committed by the Turkish army, which in September 1920 invaded the Republic of Armenia and in five months of conquest and occupation killed 200,000 Armenians in the region before being driven out by the Red Army (Dadrian 2001, 161; 1997, 361).

we keep the insight that genocide can be socially instituted as moral while also keeping our right to object to this moralization?

Part of the answer lies in language, in the distinction between what Jean-François Lyotard (1984, 9) calls denotative and performative utterances. A constative utterance is capable of being true or false; a performative utterance performs an action and hence makes something true. When I say, in the right setting and in my capacity as an instructor, "this class is now underway," I cause class to begin and am speaking performatively; if someone in the hallway overhears me and says to a friend on the phone, "I have to go, class is starting," he or she is speaking constatively. Durkheim's objectivist sociology fails to distinguish between the constative and performative ways of saying that whatever society values is moral. This is a symptom of a broader problem: objectivist sociology cannot deal well with performative statements because if social facts exist outside and independently of individual human beings, it's not at all clear how individual social action can be performative. That is, it's not clear how individuals can act to change social facts. To address this problem, I now turn to the third classic answer to the question "what kind of things are social things?" This is relational sociology.

Relationality

In the trio of figures most commonly recognized as the core of the classical tradition in sociology, it is Marx who presents a relational conception of the social.[10] But, for two reasons, I'd like to use the work of Norbert Elias to introduce this conception: first, because Elias makes the relational qualities of his sociology more explicit than Marx does; and, second, because I would like to use Marx to introduce ideas specific to critical sociology.

Elias insists on the *relational* quality of social action. To treat society as either an objective or a subjective phenomenon, he says, is to assume that individuals and society exist separately from one another: "The very concept of society has this character of an isolated object in a state of rest, and so has that of nature. The same goes for

---

10 For a detailed discussion of Marx as a relational thinker, see Ollman (1976), especially chapters 2, 3, 13, and 14 and all of part 3. For more information on relational thinking in contemporary sociology, see Emirbayer (1997), Breslau (2000), Bourdieu and Wacquant (1992), and Ball (1978).

the concept of the individual. Consequently we always feel impelled to make quite senseless conceptual distinctions, like 'the individual *and* society,' which makes it seem that 'the individual' and 'society' were two separate things, like tables and chairs, or pots and pans" (Elias 1978, 113, original emphasis). The dualism that treats subjectivity and objectivity as separate and opposed rests on a myth, which Elias calls the myth of *homo clausus*: that there is such a thing as "the individual" that exists prior to society, autonomous, monadic. Elias insists that this is a culturally specific and highly distorted image of human existence and that the ubiquitous human condition is not being but *being with others* (Elias 2000, 473–4; 1978, 13). By the same token, it is untenable or mystical to think that social facts could exist "externally" to individuals. Society exists as the network of relationships among individuals. In other words, the terms "society" and "individual" do not designate separate things, and still less do they connote two separate levels of reality. Individuals exist in and through their relations with others, and society exists as the network of these relations. And these relations are not fixed or static but are constantly and inexhaustibly dynamic.

It would not be inaccurate to say that the units of analysis in Elias's sociology are *social relations* (as opposed to social facts or social action), but Elias talks much more about *figurations*, the word he uses where other mid-twentieth-century sociologists would use "structure" to designate identifiable regularities or stable patterns in social interaction. Whereas sociologists inspired by Durkheim, especially Talcott Parsons, have tended to think of social structure in static (or *synchronic*) terms, a figuration is processual (or *diachronic*) by definition (Elias 2000, 456–7, 403). The difference is like the difference between chess and a dance (Elias 2000, 482). Chess can be plotted as the set of its board, pieces, and rules; glancing at the board at any moment between moves tells one everything one needs to know about the current state of the game. A dance, on the other hand, is constituted by movement. To understand a dance, it is necessary to add the dimension of time, observe it in motion. The same is true, says Elias, of social figurations. Whereas Auguste Comte, the inventor of the term "sociology," proposed that his new science should have two branches, social statics and social dynamics (Comte 1998), Elias abolishes statics entirely. Individuals and society exist as process, movement, change.

Elias's relational and dynamic conception of social things means that he rejects a whole series of dualisms that trouble sociologists of an objectivist or subjectivist inclination, dualisms in which the relation between the opposed terms forms an intractable problem. The first dualism is that between the self and society. In relational sociology, there is no question of the connection between self and society; social subjects relate directly to other social subjects. Social figurations exist neither within individuals nor outside of them but between them, among them, in their interactions and relations with each other (Elias 1987, 166). And more specifically, they exist in the power relationships that emerge through trials of strength among individuals and groups (Elias 1978, 78).

The second dualism abolished is that between the macro and the micro. The idea of "levels of analysis" is a vestige of what Elias calls *egocentric* thought, which places the individual, or *homo clausus*, at the centre of an expanding series of concentric circles that represent social environments of successively greater scales: the family, the school, the industry, the nation-state, and so on. Egocentric models are vestiges of the anthropomorphism that underlies all pre-scientific thought in the European tradition (Elias 1978, 16). For the concentric-circles model with its ascending "levels of analysis," Elias substitutes a network model with no centre and no definite periphery, where the network ties represent not static relationships but interactions, interdependencies, balances of power (Elias 1978, 15). There are no transcendent structures "outside" of anything. Order is immanent to this network as the pattern of motion and change within it; figurations exist as change.

This in turn abolishes a third dualism, that between social order and social change. Elias rejects the Hobbesian problem of order that preoccupied Parsons: how it is possible for order to exist despite social change. Instead, Elias says that social order exists "in the same sense that one talks of a natural order, in which decay and destruction as structured processes have their place alongside growth and synthesis, death and disintegration alongside birth and integration," and he maintains that "the distinction between 'order' and 'disorder,' so significant for the people involved, is sociologically speaking without significance. *Among men [sic], as in nature, no absolute chaos is possible*" (Elias 1978, 75–6, original emphasis).[11]

---

11 "The social life of people in societies always has, even in chaos or degeneration, in the greatest social disorder, a very particular form" (Elias, quoted in van Krieken 1998, 50).

Finally, since figurations exist as ensembles of dynamic relationships produced through social interaction, the opposition between structure and agency disappears. Structures do not exist apart from human agency, affected by or impervious to performative actions. Figurations that seem static are so only relative to an anthropocentric sense of time; viewed over a longer time scale, they always reveal their movement. What constrains individual actors is not the objectivity of social facts but the exigency of *power*.

In *What Is Sociology?* Elias proposes a hypothetical situation in which two groups of people compete, on a roughly equal basis, to forage food in a limited ecosystem whose resources are dwindling (Elias 1978, 76). Elias states that these two groups are dependent on one another and have a function for one another. He criticizes other sociologists for using the term "function" in ways that contain a concealed value-judgment. "Functional" ought not to imply amicable or harmonious: "fierce antagonists, in other words, perform a function for each other, because the interdependence of human beings due to their hostility is no less a functional relationship than that due to their position as friends, allies, and specialists bonded to each other through the division of labour. Their function for each other is in the last resort based on the compulsion they exert over each other by means of their interdependence" (Elias 1978, 77). He defines "function" in this way: "when one person (or a group of persons) lacks something which another person or group has the power to withhold, the latter has a function for the former" (Elias 1978, 78). Thus enemies have a function for one another through their power to withhold the necessities of social and physical integrity from each other. Power *always* informs social interdependencies – whether or not social actors themselves are conscious of this.

A figuration, then, is a dynamic network of functional relations, or in other words a dynamic network of power relations. We can see a genocide, in these terms, as a figuration: a definite and historically specific unfolding of power relations among social actors. By treating genocide as the same type of thing as the other things that make up social life, we remove its aura of sacredness and put it firmly back in the mundane, profane world, where we can get our hands on it and do something about it. We also allow ourselves to ask how it interacts with other figurations, like the nation-state system, capitalism, gender, racialization – and civilization.

WHAT DIFFERENCE DOES *CRITICAL* SOCIOLOGY MAKE?

If figurations are dynamic networks of power relations, if human beings and human action necessarily occur in the context of figurations, where does that leave sociology itself? In a figuration, presumably. If relational sociology seems to dispose of the possibility of objective knowledge, that's because it does: there is no way for a human mind to perceive society from the outside because there is no "outside" from which people can perceive society as an object separate from themselves. But neither is knowledge simply subjective, a matter of individual perspective. Our minds do not exist in isolation but are constrained by the relations with others that we necessarily enter into and through which we exist. If social relations are a condition of possibility for all human activity, then knowledge is irreducibly conditioned by social relations, and hence by power, and hence by struggles for power – and hence by *difference*.

Elias's work does not focus on the importance of difference as a constitutive feature of social relations. This lack of critical focus shows tellingly in his epistemology. Avoiding both objectivism and subjectivism, Elias characterizes the pursuit of scientific knowledge in terms of involvement and detachment. His paradigmatic example is that of two fishers caught in a whirlpool (Elias 1987, 45–6). The detached fisher observes that smaller objects sink more slowly than larger ones and determines that the smart thing to do is jump off the boat. The involved fisher is too caught up in the experience to grasp this information. Involvement and detachment are relative, and in Elias's example they are relative to what we might call a *problem-situation*. He compares the fishers in the whirlpool with citizens of the two nuclear superpowers during the height of the Cold War (Elias 1987, 92). Sociological detachment, he says, is required to perceive the spiral of mutual escalation that can lead only to human destruction and required to pursue the counterintuitive but more "reality-adequate" strategies that lead to disarmament. His diagnosis assumes that the problem-situation is the same for all parties: the avoidance of total human extinction through nuclear exchange. However, he does not consider how the problem-situation is different for different parties. Specifically, he does not consider that those who make nuclear weapons and those who control them benefit from a maintenance of mutual threat, so long as this threat does not actually materialize, whereas the rest of humanity gain no benefit whatsoever from the continuance of mutual threat or the very existence of nuclear weapons. Since the problem-situation is not the same for all parties, valid knowledge of the situation will not be the same for all parties. Considering this takes us beyond ordinary sociology and into critical sociology.

I propose that a critical sociology can be characterized in terms of three rules: the rule of immanence, the rule of reflexivity, and the rule of contradiction. The *rule of immanence* says that social phenomena result from other social phenomena. This rule is general to most sociologists, but critical sociologists place special emphasis on it. I have already given some indication of what this rule involves in my discussion of Weber, Durkheim, and Elias, so I won't go into more detail here, except to add one proviso. A *materialist* sociology includes, within the realm of what is considered "social," nonhuman factors like machines, natural resources, built environments, and even ecosystems, to the extent that these are produced by or are factors in human social relations. (Many sociologists are not materialist, and not all materialist sociologists are critical.) What material immanence still rules out are explanations of social phenomena in terms of purely nonsocial physical factors – that is, reduction to physiology or genetics, technological or ecological determinism, and the like. However consequential nonhuman physical factors are for social life, the way that they are consequential is conditioned by the structure (or figuration) of social relations in which they are involved. It also rules out explanations in terms of nonphysical phenomena – that is, metaphysical essences located outside of time and space.

The second feature of critical sociology is the *rule of reflexivity*, which states that any way of knowing, understanding, or explaining social phenomena is itself a social phenomenon. In other words, sociological knowledge is located inside, and is part of, the thing it knows. I take this idea from the work of sociologist Dorothy Smith and of philosopher-historian Michel Foucault. The third rule is the *rule of contradiction*. This rule states that social figurations can be contradictory, such that one and the same social figuration may generate opposing interests for subjects located differently within it. This rule is, of course, based on the work of Karl Marx.

Reflexivity

SMITH AND THE INESCAPABILITY OF STANDPOINT
Dorothy Smith begins her account of reflexivity from her own experience of a disjuncture. This disjuncture is between her life as a sociologist and her life as a woman. The former is a "conceptually ordered world" (Smith 1990, 16) in which the data and information they work with are stripped clean of any association with physical bodies and their sweat, their smells, their messiness. It is information that is organized in terms of the needs and interests of organizations, bureaucracies, and governmental agencies – that is, of the administration, or rule, of society. And the way sociologists work with this information is of the same order: they forget their physical body, become absorbed in the purely conceptual order, and see the social world as an object whose messiness is to be ordered by their conceptual activity. We might say that they become disembodied to deal with disembodied information, a brain on a stick dealing with pure data, an avatar in cyberspace. And male sociologists (we might also say, assuming they have the right class background) enter this world without a sense of transition; they feel right at home in it. But women, Smith says, notice the transition. They notice that "It has been a condition of a man's being able to enter and become absorbed in the conceptual mode, and to forget the dependence of his being in that mode upon his bodily existence, that he does not have to focus his activities and interests upon his bodily existence" (Smith 1990, 18). Men can do this because someone else is doing the work of looking after bodies, and women notice this because they are the ones doing the work: "Under the traditional gender regime, providing for a man's liberation from [Robert] Bierstedt's Aristotelian categories is a woman who keeps house for him, bears and cares for his children, washes his clothes, looks after him when he is sick, and generally provides for the logistics of his bodily existence" (Smith 1990, 18). The relationships that exempt men from, and oblige women to, the work of bodily reproduction are relations of domination and subordination. Smith calls them *relations of rule*. Male sociologists don't notice these relations because their position in them makes the relations invisible, a part of the natural order of things. Women sociologists notice them because as women and as sociologists they inhabit both sides of the relation, the subordinate

and the dominant. The point is that how you are located in social relations affects your ability to perceive them. Standpoint matters.

Standpoint is much more than a matter of individual perspective; it is socially structured, or figurational. There are two reasons for this. First, the categories and the assumptions through which we know the world – through which we explain our experiences – are acquired by us through social relationships. So are these experiences themselves. The categories and the assumptions are not given to us by society, as an objectivist would insist. Rather, we acquire them through the activity of relating to others. Dualist, or nonrelational, thinking accepts that knowledge must come either from the individual in isolation, or from society as a reality external to the individual, or from some combination of the two. Relational thinking abolishes the images of individuals in isolation and of society outside of individuals and claims that knowledge, like the rest of culture, comes through interactions and relations among actors. For example, consider an exchange of looks between a white woman on a moving train in Ontario and a family of Indigenous persons standing on a spur, watching the train (Smith 1990, 24). The way that each person in this situation knows what has happened is organized by culturally acquired assumptions about what things are – about prosaic things like train, spur, and watching and about more ideologically loaded things like race, gender, family, and class. It is also organized by the opportunities for interaction that the situation allows and does not allow.

Second, people's situations in social relationships are not just random but are also ordered by the inequalities in society and by projects of rule. For example, consider an actual case of two different accounts of a confrontation between police and street people in Berkeley, California, in 1968: one, a letter to an underground newspaper written by a bystander; the other, a response from the mayor based on the police report (Smith 1990, 63). Both are based on experience, but they are very different experiences. (Smith actually writes that the bystander's letter is based on "actual experience" and that the mayor's is not. This is an inconsistent use of the term "experience" and neglects the radical implications of contradiction, as I will further explain below.) The bystander's report is based on being physically present and having directly seen the events; he accuses the police of provoking and harassing the street people and using brutal and arbitrary force; his account is rooted in the particularities of who did what and how. The mayor's letter is based on police reports, which strip the event of its particularities, treating the individual officers as interchangeable and assimilating their actions to established categories of police procedure. It is also conditioned by the mayor's practical investment in maintaining the legitimacy (or the appearance of legitimacy) of the city's institutions. An account given by one of the harassed street people in question would be different again. But it is no accident that the voices of street people are rarely heard by the rest of society – or, to go back to my earlier example, that we are more likely to hear what a white sociologist thought about a family of Indigenous persons watching the train go by than we are to hear what the members of this family thought about the white sociologist. The point isn't that we should feel guilty for the privileges we enjoy (we might or might not do that also) but rather that our position in unequal social relations *systematically* affects our knowledge of the world and that we need to take this into account. This taking into account is what Smith means by a "reflexive critical inquiry" (Smith 1990, 205–6).

Along with other standpoint epistemologists, Smith is associated with the claim that women, racialized minorities, and other oppressed groups have a privileged standpoint in social science, and perhaps in science as a whole. This claim leads to some misperceptions that are worth addressing. It is not a moral claim, namely that oppressed groups deserve to be privileged simply because they have been oppressed. Smith, like other standpoint epistemologists such as Sandra Harding (1992), believes that objective knowledge is possible but that the effect of social inequality on knowledge has impeded this. Relations of rule are largely invisible to those who enjoy a privileged position in them, such that the knowledge produced by these persons is an ideological mystification of the real world. When women and other oppressed groups are admitted into the ranks of scientists, they bring with them their experience of large parts of social reality that have been previously ignored. This makes possible a more complete knowledge of reality and strengthens the objectivity of science.

Here we come to a problem, or rather two problems. The first problem is that Smith's use of the term "experience" is inconsistent. She claims that the bystander's knowledge is based on experience, whereas the mayor's is not because it is textually mediated. But the experience of reading a text is a kind of experience – different from being present at an event but possessing its own kind of concreteness and having definite effects on how readers know the world around them. (The occurrence of secondary trauma attests to just how forceful textually mediated accounts can be.) Nor is the bystander's experience unmediated by anything at all – nor, for that matter, are the experiences of the homeless people who were beaten. Smith wants to say that some experiences are real and others are illusory, but an *experience* is always real in itself, whether or not it tells us the truth about other real things. This leads to the second problem: Smith's account of how reflexivity affects knowledge is mostly negative. She considers how some people's standpoints blind them to realities that other people's standpoints give them access to: "The textual surfaces of discourse obliterate the structures of power sustaining their coherence and authority" (Smith 1990, 203). But if knowledge truly is embedded within its own object, it is itself a social thing, a figuration, and in addition to its ability to conceal or distort power relations, it ought also to be able to produce them, or at least to play a part in their production. This is precisely what the work of Michel Foucault addresses.

FOUCAULT AND THE PRODUCTIVITY OF DISCOURSE

Michel Foucault takes up the problem of how knowledge is embedded within its object in ways that bear more specifically on the problem of genocide. To understand this, we can begin with his analysis of power as he presents it in the first volume to *The History of Sexuality*.[12] Foucault's conception of power is entirely consistent with a relational sociology. First, power is not a substance that can be acquired, held, or lost but is the effect of a field of force relations. It is "exercised from innumerable points, in the interplay of nonegalitarian and mobile relations" (Foucault 1990, 94). Second, power is immanent to other types of social relationships (e.g., economic, knowledge-based, sexual) and yet produces distinct effects of

---

12 It would be a mistake to say that Foucault proposes a theory of power, as he himself states clearly: "In studying these power relations, I in no way construct a theory of power. But I wish to know how the reflexivity of the subject and the discourse of truth are linked – 'How can the subject tell the truth about itself?' – and I think that relations of power exerting themselves upon one another constitute one of the determining elements in this relation I am trying to analyze" (Foucault 1998, 451).

its own. Third, "power comes from below," from the "manifold relationships of force that take shape and come into play in the machinery of production, in families, limited groups, and institutions"
(Foucault 1990, 94). Large-scale structures of domination are the
effects of particular configurations of these innumerable local relations. Fourth, power relations are both intentional, strategic, and
calculated, on the one hand, and nonsubjective, socially objective,
and constraining, on the other. Finally, power is always accompanied by resistance; power and resistance are necessarily co-present
and embedded within each other. Just as twentieth-century physics
moved from thinking of energy as a substance to thinking of it as a
field and just as neoclassical economics reconceived value as a field
rather than a substance (Mirowski 1989), Foucault treats power as
a field, emerging from multiple force relations distributed over a
large, dispersed network, rather than as a substance that can be
hoarded or spent. And one important feature of this conception of
power is that it is a network of relations of force exerted on concrete
individual human bodies. This allows us to think of genocide – especially of genocide through physical extermination of groups of
people – as one form of power among others, different in its form of
expression but not in its basic makeup.

   For Foucault, thinking about power as force relations means that
the distinction between war and politics is blurred. Referring to the
famous statement of military strategist Carl von Clausewitz, that
"war is a continuation of politics by other means," Foucault writes:
"Should we turn the expression around, then, and say that politics is
war pursued by other means? ... [P]erhaps we should postulate rather that this multiplicity of force relations can be coded – in part but
never totally – either in the form of 'war,' or in the form of 'politics';
this would imply two different strategies (but the one always liable
to switch into the other) for integrating these unbalanced, hetero-
geneous, unstable, and tense force relations" (Foucault 1990, 93).
This way of thinking about politics has three important implications. First, the "disequilibrium of forces" that we see in war is also
at work in politics (Foucault 1980, 90). Social inequality is conditioned by unequal access to the means of force. Second, the effects of
war shape the form that peaceful politics will take; "even when one
writes the history of peace and its institutions, it is always the history
of war that one is writing" (Foucault 1980, 91). Third, the outcome

of political conflict depends on a "contest of strength,"[13] the ultimate form of which is war. This way of thinking about politics is very
troubling, for it suggests that war is implicit in politics or that politics necessarily depends on and invokes the possibility of war. This
is even more troubling if we add genocide to the picture and say that
politics, war, and genocide are all various strategies – always liable
to switch to each other – for "integrating these unbalanced, hetero-
geneous, unstable, and tense force relations." It is also useful, however, because it makes it easier to see how otherwise ordinary states
can commit genocide and why genocide can be such an endemic
feature of the contemporary nation-state system. If we consider the
close association of politics, war, and genocide to be the product of
historically specific social relations, rather than a timeless human
universal, Foucault's conception might help us to think of how to do
away with this association. Finally, the notion that the history of
peace is also always a history of war has important implications for
how we understand the growth of Western civilization and what
Norbert Elias calls "the civilizing process" – implications that I discuss in chapter 4.

The significance of Foucault's conception of power for the issue of
reflexivity is expressed in his notion of power-knowledge and his
analyses of specific forms of power-knowledge that produce particular modes of subjectivity, such as delinquency or sexuality. Normally,
we might think of power as something that distorts knowledge
and of knowledge as something that opposes the abuses of power.
Foucault observes that the two, however, often complement one another: power is based on knowledge and uses knowledge, and knowledge is obtained through the exercise of power over objects that are
shaped by power. For example, in *Discipline and Punish*, Foucault
traces the history of the prison in terms of the innovation and dissemination throughout society of techniques of disciplinary power.
Disciplinary power makes use of the ever-finer compartmentaliza-
tion of space and time, and the ever-more calculated and minimal
application of force to bodies, in order to get subjects to govern their
own behaviour in ways that suit the interests of dominant forces in
society. Its paradigmatic form is the panopticon, a situation in which

---

13 The parallels with Elias's account of how social relations emerge from
"trials of strength" (Elias 1978, 78) deserve special attention here.

the individuals of a group are made unable to observe or communicate with each other and may be observed at any time, but without their knowledge, by a central figure. The panopticon and other techniques of disciplinary power are evident not only in prisons but also in "factories, schools, barracks, hospitals" (Foucault 1995, 228) and other sites where precise control is exerted over masses of people. Disciplinary power both enables and depends on the collection of great quantities of information about many individual people; indeed, Foucault implies that the individualism that characterizes modern subjectivity is at least partly a consequence of disciplinary power.

The reflexive aspect of this is that the knowledge that is so generated – for example, criminological knowledge about delinquents – is part and parcel of a coercive apparatus. Such knowledge is not objectively true; that is, it does not simply reflect an object that exists independently of it. But it is not false either. It is knowledge about how people act when they are being disciplined, collected through the mechanisms of discipline and with an eye to intensifying these mechanisms. It is true because it affects power relations in ways that make it true. Disciplinary power produces certain types of people – the patient, the student, the delinquent – that do not exist apart from relations of discipline, even if some of the conditions or practices that distinguish them (e.g., hallucinating, studying, stealing) are fairly general throughout human societies. And a great part of the knowledge of the human sciences is knowledge about such types of people. In *The History of Sexuality*, Foucault extends this analysis to sexuality itself: although sex acts of all kinds can be found throughout human history, it is modern society that has produced "the homosexual" and "the heterosexual" as types of people. One of the deepest aspects of our selves, what we call our "sexuality," is a product of power-knowledge relations and hence of a calculated economy of force.

REFLEXIVITY: CONCLUSION

Both Smith and Foucault show how knowledge of the social world is reflexively embedded within its own object. Smith shows how our position in structured relations of social inequality makes other people's lived experience visible or invisible to us. Foucault shows how knowledge plays an active role in relations of power, not only disguising power but also enabling it to assume new forms and to achieve new objectives. He also proposes an explanation for how new types of people are produced through the combined operation of knowledge and power and for how this production of subjectivity is connected to broader transformations in the exercise of state sovereignty.

Taken together, these accounts of reflexivity have three implications for a sociology of genocide. The first is that researchers who study genocide need to be aware of their own location in relations of privilege and need to take care to correct for how this location may blind them to important aspects of genocide. The second is that researchers can and should pay attention to the ways that knowledge not only describes the world but also actively shapes it, even to the extent of producing types of people. This is especially important because genocide is all about *types of people*. For any given genocide, the process by which these types of people are made will tell us a great deal about why the genocide happened. Third, reflexivity suggests that there is no neutral point of view on genocide or any other social phenomenon. If knowing is something that necessarily happens through social relations, then a neutral point of view about any given thing could exist only if all human beings could share the same relation to that thing. The rule of contradiction states that this is impossible in any currently existing society.

Contradiction

The third rule of my critical sociology is the rule of contradiction, which says that social figurations can be contradictory, such that the same figuration generates opposed interests for subjects located within it. This rule is based on the work of Karl Marx.

Marx is often read as an objectivist, and at first glance he may seem like one. In *The German Ideology* he insists on the primacy of concrete, material factors in the shaping of human consciousness and social life. Throughout *Capital* he insists that social relations give rise to dynamics that operate independently of human consciousness and that inexorably constrain the conditions of life and the scope of action that human beings face, individually and collectively. His insistence, in *The Communist Manifesto*, that concrete human individuals make history under conditions they have not chosen is often read in terms of the dualist opposition between subjectivity and objectivity, agency and structure – with the emphasis placed on objectivity and structure. However, Marx can also be read relationally, and I think this is the more fruitful reading.

We can consider, for example, his claim in the *Manifesto* that "the history of all hitherto existing society is the history of class struggle" (Marx and Engels 1988a, 21). Many interpreters read this statement to mean that classes are first and foremost *groups of people* and that these groups of people enter into struggles that determine the development of society. This objectivist conception of social groups is at odds with Marx's tendency to use *social relations* as the elementary unit of analysis. Marx describes classes as being produced by a relational social process, the process of alienated labour. By producing goods for sale – that is, commodities[14] – workers turn their own labour into a commodity and, because labour is the expenditure of a person's time and energy, turn their own lives into a commodity (Marx 2000a, 86). In effect, they are separated from a part of their own lives, which then become the property of other human beings. Capitalists are nothing more nor less than people who own enough of other people's labour to live off of the surplus produced by that labour. Capital and labour are two ends of the same relationship; "capital presupposes wage labour; wage labour presupposes capital. They reciprocally condition the existence of each other; they reciprocally bring forth each other" (Marx 2000c, 283). Or, again, "wages and private property are identical" (Marx 2000a, 93). "The relationship of the worker to his labour creates the relationship to it of the capitalist, or whatever else one wishes to call the master of the labour. Private property is thus the product, result, and necessary consequence of externalized labour, of the exterior relationship of the worker to nature and to himself" (Marx 2000a, 93). Social classes are, first and foremost, positions defined by the relation between them. The tendency for the concrete actors who occupy these positions to identify as members of one or another social group is secondary. This is the sense in which Marx expects that the working class, in abolishing capital, will abolish class as such. There can be no workers without capital, or rather, without capital, those who labour are not "workers" because workers and capital exist in relation to each other. The revolution Marx imagines involves much more than doing away with a group of people; those concrete

---

14 A commodity is any item that has both a use-value and an exchange-value – that is, any item that serves some human purpose (whatever that might be, from basic needs to ephemeral desires) and that is exchanged either in barter or for money (Marx 1990, 125–6).

individuals who occupy the social position of capitalist are not the point. Revolution involves unmaking a social relation that lies coiled within every other social relation like a virus (Marx and Engels 1988b, 17; 1988a, 30; Marx 2000c, 281, 284).

One and the same social relation produces two classes, workers and capitalists, whose interests are systematically opposed to one another. For capital, labour is an object to be exploited for as much wealth as possible, whereas for labour, capital is parasitic. We can see this clearly in terms of an expanded concept of *praxis*. Marxists use the term "praxis" to mean several things: the free, creative labour of human beings that tends to escape the logic of capital; the unfree labour of workers exploited by capital; collective action in general; and the unity of theory and practice in the pursuit of revolutionary transformation. If we keep in mind Marx's insistence that the ability to transform the world through labour is the most important and defining human attribute, we can see all of these as aspects of the same thing: world-creating activity (Marx 2000a, 88–91; Marx and Engels 1988b, 4). In relations of alienated labour, the praxis of capitalists is directed (all other things being equal) to the transformation of workers into commodities from which the maximum possible wealth can be extracted – that is, to their objectification and dehumanization. Any effective attempt by workers to realize their own humanity must run contrary to the interest of capital. Although various compromises are possible, there is no logically possible way to satisfy both imperatives at the same time. This is the first sense of the term *contradiction* as I understand it: not just that groups engage in zero-sum-game struggles over finite goods but also that one and the same social relation generates systematically opposed interests. So just as "class" refers primarily to locations in a social relation, which produce more or less self-aware groups of people, "class struggle" refers primarily to the tensions and oppositions generated by this relation, which manifest in conflicts between groups. Or rather, since class implies class struggle, we could say that class struggle generates classes as more or less self-aware social groups. The movement of class difference produces class identity.

That workers are subordinated to capital means their praxis is captured by capital and used against them. This points to the second sense of the term "contradiction." The means by which workers seek to produce wealth – the exercise of their labour-power – produces their own poverty (often in absolute terms but always relative to the wealth enjoyed by capitalists and to the wealth that could be theirs). The means by which they seek to realize their humanity produce their own commodification and dehumanization. We are used to thinking of the term "contradication" in the context of logical abstractions, but for Marx, contradiction is practical and concrete. It can be resolved only by concrete, practical activity – by a change that goes to the very root of social relations, a radical change. This is the significance of his famous claim that "the philosophers have only interpreted the world, in various ways; the point is to change it" (Marx 2000b, 173).

What difference does contradiction make to the study of genocide? In the next chapter, I examine Marxian contributions to explaining genocides. But here I want to stress Marx's methodology of historical materialism rather than his specific observations about capitalism. In my reading, historical materialism emphasizes how social identities result from the production of social differences, which ensues from contradictions in material social relationships – those relationships that concern the material basis of human existence. Marx equates "material social relations" with relations of economic production. For this, he has been criticized by feminists (e.g., Barrett 1996), who see reproductive labour as a material social relation, one that does not reduce to relations of production, as Friedrich Engels claims it does (Engels 1972). Reproductive labour includes the bearing of children, which only women can do, as well as the noncommodified work of bodily care, which usually falls to women in patriarchal societies: childrearing, food preparation, household maintenance, and other so-called women's work. We could also criticize Marx for not considering that physical violence informs the material basis of human existence in ways that again do not reduce to economic production. Although Marx and Engels try to reduce the state's control of violence to the interests of the dominant production class (Marx and Engels 1988b, 18; Engels 1988a, 69), we could just as easily reverse the analytic priority and see relations of force as the basis of control over relations of property (e.g., Tilly 1985). We can observe how the state's control of force allowed a new dominant class to emerge in the Soviet Union even when private property had been formally abolished (Resnick and Wolff 1995). We can observe also that in contemporary societies the economic interests of the capitalist class may allow for two or more widely diverging rationalities of the application of force in society

(Foucault 1980, 88, 101). I think it is consistent with the spirit of historical materialism to say that just as contradictions in relations of production generate workers and capitalists, so too do contradictions in relations of reproduction generate women and men as women and men, and contradictions in relations of force generate states and subjects. The idea of contradiction allows us to systematically join together the organization of violence and the production of identity-difference. And genocide is all about these two things: identity-difference and the social organization of violence.

CONCLUSION

To sum up, what difference does critical sociology make to the study of genocide? I have three answers.

First, the rule of immanence means that there are no metaphysical guarantees in social life. Not only is genocide possible, but it can also be produced by otherwise ordinary social institutions. Even morality can be mobilized in the service of genocide. Once the potential victims of genocide have been excluded from the community of obligation, moral solidarity among those who remain inside this community can be increased by a successful genocide. It may well be the case, as Chalk and Jonassohn (1990, 416) argue, that genocide always inflicts certain harms on the society that perpetrates it. It is also the case, however, that it can confer certain benefits. There is no nonmetaphysical sense in which we can say, on a purely descriptive level, that genocide is wrong. And metaphysical realities, if they exist, seem not to make a difference where genocide is concerned. Affirming that genocide is evil is always a performative statement, an attempt to make something true by saying it – in this case, to institute a value. The good news is that, given a relational conception of society, the rule of immanence tells us that such performative acts are never pointless. Social institutions do not reduce to individual action, but they do not exist apart from the actions of concrete human beings either. They result from the stabilization of social relations and are always open to contestation. The very question of the morality or immorality of genocide is itself a power contest. The perpetrators of genocide quite often understand this. Those who oppose genocide should understand it also.

Second, the rule of reflexivity means that value-neutral knowledge is not possible. Knowledge of social relations is embedded within social relations: we know the social world from a definite standpoint within relations of privilege and dis-privilege, and our knowledge of it comes to us through these relations. Not only that, but knowledge is also part of what makes up the social world and can have performative effects of its own; knowledge can help to produce definite relations of power, with consequences that include the production of types of people or modes of subjectivity. If we are committed to the production of a more free and egalitarian world, our study of genocide needs to be informed by the voices of those who are normally denied a voice in official, institutionalized accounts of society; it needs to include as many standpoints as possible. As Sandra Harding (1992) points out, this may require a shift in the composition of the research community toward greater inclusiveness. Moreover, we also need to consider what sorts of power-knowledge relations are implied by the knowledge we produce and to consider the kinds of solutions this knowledge is oriented to. Solutions that rely on the power of nation-states, for example, have different ripple effects than do solutions that circumvent or even undermine the power of states.

This is all the more crucial if genocide is the product of a contradictory material social relation. If relations of force generate systematically opposed interests, as well as implicit class identities differentiated on the basis of those who control the means of force and those who do not, then a universally valid explanation of genocide will not be possible. Instead, explanations of genocide that are internally coherent and valid on their own terms will tend to bifurcate depending on whether those who produce them identify or dis-identify with sovereign authority. Within contradictory relations of force, alienation can be experienced from the sovereign's standpoint, as the persistent ungovernability of subjects, or from the standpoint of subjects of the sovereign, as the dangerous impunity of states. As you can guess, I will be writing from the latter perspective.

For the critical sociologist of genocide, the struggle to end genocide is a political and a social struggle. It is a *radical* struggle in that it goes to the roots of the institutions that make up our normal life. Strategies for ending genocide are bound up in larger projects of social change. We cannot end genocide and leave everything else just as it is. If we succeed, we will obtain for human beings an unprecedented security of person and of socio-cultural self-expression; we will guarantee the practical right to form collective identities at odds with the prevailing norms of society, to perpetuate minority traditions, and to innovate new ones. If we fail utterly, genocide will be institutionalized as moral in our emerging global culture, denial will prevail, and the very word "genocide" will fall into disuse. In this struggle, "even the dead will not be safe from the enemy if he wins" (Benjamin 1969, 255).

In societies that have successfully perpetrated genocide – in the colonial powers of Europe, in settler societies in the Americas and Australasia, even in contemporary Turkey – the habit of denial is being challenged and, to some extent, broken. In societies haunted by failed genocides, brave and precarious attempts are being made to come to terms with the past. It is even possible that some time in the near future, a genocide in the making will be prevented by the foresighted and compassionate intervention of bystanders who could just as easily have looked away. For those of us who are privileged enough to have the luxury to chose between denial and engagement, the latter option offers us the prospect of redemption on this earth: "The past carries with it a temporal index by which it is referred to redemption. There is a secret agreement between past generations and the present one. Our coming was expected on earth. Like every generation that preceded us, we have been endowed with a weak Messianic power, a power to which the past has a claim. That claim cannot be settled cheaply" (Benjamin 1969, 254).

2

Identifying Genocide[1]

Science is not politics. It is politics by other means.

Latour 1988, 229

INTRODUCTION

What is genocide? This is a surprisingly difficult question to answer. There is an official definition, set out in the 1948 United Nations Convention on the Prevention and Punishment of the Crime of Genocide (UNCG). But almost every author who writes about genocide also offers his or her own definition, and these differ substantially from the UNCG and from one another. These definitions place varying emphasis on the importance of single factors like mass killing, state complicity, the noncombatant status of victims, or the overt intentions of the perpetrator. On top of this, there are a number of variant, or specifying, terms in circulation – such as ethnocide, politicide, linguicide, gendercide, cultural genocide, ethnic cleansing, autogenocide, democide, mass murder, and others – which are understood by some authors as variants within the category of genocide and by others as distinct categories unto themselves. Most authors insist, implicitly or explicitly, that theirs is the true definition of genocide and that the others are in some way faulty or mistaken. Many authors regard the profusion of definitions as a problem, an impediment to coherent research and/or to effective action. Yet there seems to be no way forward out of the thickets of this "definitionalism."

In this chapter, I take the somewhat foolhardy approach of proposing not only a new definition but also a new *kind* of definition. Do we really need another definition of genocide? I think we do, for

---

1 A version of the argument in this chapter has been published in the *Journal of Genocide Research* (Powell 2007).

two reasons. First, the United Nations definition does not serve well the purposes of a sociological understanding of genocide. As a legal instrument, the UNCG is designed with the objective of charging specific individuals with a specific offence and finding them guilty or innocent of the charge. Sociology, like other scientific endeavours, is concerned not mainly with individual guilt or innocence but with understanding and explaining *what* happens in the world and *why* it happens. In the long run, rich and robust explanations might also clarify questions of guilt or innocence, but in the short term they often muddy those questions by showing them to be more complicated than most people had been prepared to believe. This might seem alarming, but I think we need to face these complexities and confusions if we hope to find ways to prevent genocide rather than to punish it after the fact. Second, I think social scientists' definitions of genocide are caught between the rock and the hard place of subjectivist and objectivist sociologies. Relational sociology opens up a new avenue of inquiry, one that turns irresolvable conceptual problems into solvable empirical questions.

In this chapter I do five things. First, I show how we can understand debates over the proper use of the word "genocide"[2] in terms of sociological subjectivism and objectivism, and I suggest what a relational conception might look like. Second, I show how genocide is what W.B. Gallie (1956) calls an *essentially contested concept*. When a concept is essentially contested, debates over its use cannot be resolved by a simple appeal to reason; Gallie suggests that a historical understanding is needed to clarify the stakes of the debate. Third, then, I look at the history of the concept of genocide and show how its emergence is part of broader developments in the nation-state system. The concept of genocide emerges as one symptom of a concern with the relation between state power and identity, and it represents an attempt to put limits on the means by which states seek to alter identity. Fourth, I look more closely at the UNCG definition and at how Raphaël Lemkin first defined the term "genocide"

---

2 In this chapter and throughout the book, quotation marks around a term (e.g., "genocide") indicate that I am *mentioning* rather than *using* the word – that is, talking about the concept of genocide and its various possible meanings rather than talking about those actual practices that the word "genocide" may designate. At no time do I use quotation marks to suggest disapproval of the term's use.

in *Axis Rule in Occupied Europe* to bring out the implicit sociological assumptions at work in these texts and to show how their
implications change when we bring these assumptions up to date.
Finally, I propose that we understand genocide sociologically as
directed not just at individuals or even groups but also at social
structures or figurations and, further, that we define it critically as *a
relation of violent obliteration*, a relation that involves the production of difference through the performance of violence.

DEFINITIONALISM

Questions about how to define the word "genocide" are of more
than merely semantic importance. Definitions tell us which events
should count as genocides and which should not. This affects how
we evaluate events morally or politically, our treatment of the survivors and the perpetrators, and also the theories we construct to
explain genocide and the strategies we formulate to attempt to prevent it. Almost every scholar who writes about genocide proposes
his or her own definition of "genocide." There are definitions that
more or less accept the UNCG formulation (e.g., Fein 1979 and
1984*; Porter 1982*); definitions that supplement the UNCG with
variants like "genocidal massacre" (Kuper 1981), "politicide" (Harff
and Gurr 1988*), or "democide" (Rummel 1994*); and definitions
that broaden the UNCG definition by adding to the list of groups
whose attempted extermination may properly constitute genocide
– whereas the UNCG lists "national, ethnical, racial, or religious
group[s]," Tal (1979) adds political and social groups generally,
Legters (1984, 65) adds classes, Hannum and Hawk (1986) allow
persons belonging to the same ethnicity as the perpetrators, and
Chalk and Jonassohn (1990, 23*) argue that the victim group need
exist only in the imagination of the perpetrators. Martin Shaw, focusing on genocide as a political strategy, defines genocidal action as
"action in which armed power organizations treat civilian social
groups as enemies and aim to destroy their real or putative social
power, by means of killing, violence, and coercion against individuals whom they regard as members of the groups" (Shaw 2007,
154*). Whereas all of these definitions assume the need for a specific

---

* Asterisked definitions are quoted more fully in the appendix.

intent to destroy a group or, more narrowly still, an intent to kill members of a group because they are members of that group – to kill Jews because they are Jews and so on – some definitions broaden the notion of "intent" by adding degrees of genocide comparable to degrees of murder in US criminal law (Charny 1994, 85*; Churchill 1998, 434*) or by requiring only an intent to commit actions that have the effect of destroying a group, either foreseeably (Reisman and Norchi 1988; El-Kaïm-Sartre and Sartre 1968; Huttenbach 1988)[3] or even regardless of foreseeability (Thompson and Quets 1987, 11; 1990, 246–8*; Barta 1987, 238–40). The definition espoused by John Thompson and Gail Quets, in which "genocide" is simply "the destruction of a group by purposive action" (Thompson and Quets 1990, 248), could include genocide as the outcome of "accidents, ecological and environmental damage" (Fein 1993, 17); this connotation foreshadows the claim of Mike Davis that El Niño famines in European colonial territories, brought on by the forcible commodification of agriculture, were "the exact moral equivalents" of the bombings of Hiroshima, Nagasaki, and Dresden (Davis 2001, 22). Tony Barta (1987, 239–40) goes furthest in eliminating intention from the definition of "genocide," proposing the notion of a "relationship of genocide," a relationship that perpetrators (e.g., white Australians) may enact for the most part unwittingly.[4]

Despite this bewildering profusion, we can organize most definitions of genocide into two general tendencies. On the one hand are definitions that, consistent with a subjectivist sociology, define

---

3 "The genocidal intent is implicit in the facts. It is necessarily premeditated. Perhaps in bygone times, in the midst of tribal wars, acts of genocide were perpetrated on the spur of the moment in fits of passion. But the anti-guerilla genocide which our times have produced requires organization, military bases, a structure of accomplices, budget appropriations. Therefore, its authors must meditate and plan out their act. *Does this mean that they are thoroughly conscious of their intentions? It is impossible to decide.* We would have to plumb the depths of their consciences – and the Puritan bad faith of Americans works wonders" (El-Kaïm-Sartre and Sartre 1968, 79, emphasis added). Interestingly enough, W. Michael Reisman and Charles Norchi discuss the Soviet war in Afghanistan, and Arlette El-Kaïm-Sartre and Jean-Paul Sartre discuss the American war in Vietnam – similar events that have prompted similar extensions of the notion of "genocide."

4 I provide a more detailed list of definitions of genocide in the appendix. Even this list is only a small sample since almost every author who writes about genocide defines it in his or her own way.

genocide in ways that emphasize the perpetrator's intentions – sometimes to the exclusion of all other factors. For example:

- Genocide is the intention to destroy physically a whole or substantial part of a group because the individuals are members of that group (Palmer 2000, 23).
- Genocide is a form of one-sided mass killing in which a state or another authority intends to destroy a group as that group and membership in it are defined by the perpetrator (Chalk and Jonassohn 1990, 23; Chalk 1994, 52; Jonassohn and Björnson 1998, 10).
- Genocide is the calculated murder of a segment or all of a group defined outside the universe of obligation of the perpetrator by a government, elite, staff, or crowd representing the perpetrator in response to a crisis or opportunity perceived to be caused by or impeded by the victim (Fein 1984, 4).

Definitions that emphasize the importance of intent take their inspiration from the UNCG definition itself:

In the present Convention, genocide means any of the following acts committed with intent to destroy, in whole or in part, a national, ethnical, racial, or religious group, as such:
(a) Killing members of the group;
(b) Causing serious bodily or mental harm to members of the group;
(c) Deliberately inflicting on the group conditions of life calculated to bring about its physical destruction in whole or in part;
(d) Imposing measures intended to prevent births within the group;
(e) Forcibly transferring children of the group to another group.

Thus the most important factor determining whether a particular act or course of action should be classified as genocide is the intentions of the person or people who have carried it out. From a sociological perspective, this approach has two principal advantages and two disadvantages.

The first advantage of this approach is the general one of incorporating a subjective understanding of actors' intentions into our examination of their actions. Subjective intentions are a part of social reality, and attending to them is an indispensable part of sociological research. The other, more specific, advantage of this approach is that it allows us to recognize as genocide violence against groups that existed partly or entirely in the imagination of the perpetrator. For example, it is generally recognized that the laws by which the Nazi government defined Jewishness only loosely resembled how Jews themselves defined Jewishness. The Nuremberg laws defined as Jewish anyone with three Jewish grandparents and as mixed-blood anyone with one Jewish grandparent, regardless of how they self-identified, their current religious or cultural practice, or how they were regarded in either Jewish or non-Jewish communities. The Nazi government wished to define Jews as a race, but *races do not exist among human beings* (American Association of Physical Anthropologists 1996). The human group that the Nazis attempted to exterminate was fictitious. But this fiction served as the basis for real atrocities. Similarly, many thousands of ordinary people in Guatemala and El Salvador – trade union leaders, parish priests, human rights advocates, Indigenous elders, and others – were disappeared, tortured, and murdered for being communists, when they were not communists. The most extreme example might be that of Cambodia under the Khmer Rouge, where an estimated 1.7 million people were murdered (Ebihara and Ledgerwood 2002, 275) for belonging to a rural bourgeoisie that in fact barely existed at all (Chalk and Jonassohn 1990, 399–402).

The first and general disadvantage of subjectivist, or *intentionalist*, definitions of "genocide" is that they tend to marginalize the subjective experiences of the victims of genocide, which are as much a part of social reality as are the experiences of the perpetrators. Aside from the general oddness of privileging the perpetrators' experiences over those of the victims, this approach rules out a priori the possibility of *unintended* genocide, which we could otherwise understand as intentional action that leads to the violent destruction of a group as that group identifies itself. The second and more specific disadvantage of intentionalism is that it ignores the *collective* dimensions of genocide that are otherwise visible. When Raphaël Lemkin first proposed the concept of genocide in *Axis Rule in Occupied Europe*, he stressed that genocide involves the "disintegration of the political and social institutions, of culture, language, national feelings, religion, and the economic existence of national groups, and the destruction of the personal security, liberty, health, dignity, and even the lives of the individuals belonging to such groups. Genocide is directed against the national group as an entity, and the actions involved are directed against individuals, not in their individual capacity, but as members of the national group" (Lemkin 1944, 79). In Lemkin's view, the object of genocide is not a collection of individuals but a "national group." But in the subjectivist sociology that intentionalist definitions of genocide presuppose, "national groups" do not exist, except either as ideas in individuals' minds or as a simple aggregate of individuals. This makes it difficult for those who rely on such definitions to understand what attacks on "political and social institutions" and on "culture, language, national feelings, religion," and economics have to do with genocide. If all of these things are mere abstractions, the only thing concrete about genocide is physical violence and, especially, murder. Genocide becomes a special form of murder, distinct for *why* it is committed. Taking this logic to its extreme, Ward Churchill (2002) argues that under the terms of the UNCG, if the phrase "in part" in reference to a "national, ethnical, racial, or religious group" has no lower limit and if the phrase "as such" means "because they belong to that group," then even the murder of a single person could be considered genocide if the murderer has been motivated by, for example, race hatred. Perhaps to avoid this interpretation, some scholars equate genocide with mass killing or distinguish it from other mass killings on the basis of the reasons for which it has been carried out. This leads to quite sterile debates over, for example, how many people must be killed for an event to qualify as genocide or over whether killing members of a group to obtain an economic or military objective, rather than as an end in itself, can qualify as genocide. Too great a focus on what was or what might have been going on in the minds of the perpetrators distracts us from the tangible consequences, and the preventable causes, of atrocity.

On the other hand are definitions that abstain from mentioning intent and define genocide, *à la* Emile Durkheim, in terms of purely formal, objective properties. For example:

> Genocide in the generic sense is the mass killing of substantial numbers of human beings, when not in the course of military action against the military forces of an avowed enemy, under conditions of the essential defenselessness and helplessness of the victims. (Charny 1994, 75)

or

> A formal distinction between genocide and assassination is also required. Genocide is herein defined as *a structural and*

systematic destruction of innocent people by a state bureaucratic apparatus. (Horowitz 2002, 23, original emphasis)

One conspicuous feature of these definitions is that in different ways they insist on the innocence of the victims of genocide in order to distinguish genocide from the large-scale killing of combatants in wartime. These restrictions feel arbitrary and create problems; for example, how do we understand genocides against people who resist their slaughter by force of arms or against people convicted of crimes or understand other situations where the victims are not obviously helpless and innocent? Again, the socio-cultural dimensions of genocide are neglected. More open-ended is this definition: "In short, given the problems which arise from restrictions, we define genocide as the destruction of a group by purposive action. This allows the role of intentional action to be explored, different subtypes of genocide to be compared, and the impact of different factors on genocide to be examined empirically" (Thompson and Quets 1990, 248). Key to this definition are the words "destruction" and "group"; what counts as each of these could be endlessly contested. Churchill proposes an entire revision of the UNCG to account for physical, biological, and cultural genocide in the first, second, third, and fourth degrees. The "degrees" of genocide he proposes are analogous to those of murder in American law and open the possibility of genocide that is not specifically intended but results from "reckless disregard" or "depraved indifference" to its likelihood (Churchill 1998, 432–5). However, the most objectivist of definitions is proposed by Tony Barta:

In Australia very few people are conscious of having any relationship at all with Aborigines. My thesis is that all white people in Australia do have such a relationship; that in the key relation, the appropriation of the land, it is fundamental to the history of the society in which they live; and that implicitly rather than explicitly, in ways which were inevitable rather than intentional, it is a relationship of genocide ... My conception of a genocidal *society* – as distinct from a genocidal state – is one in which the bureaucratic apparatus might officially be directed to protect innocent people but in which a whole race is nevertheless subject to remorseless pressures of destruction inherent in the very nature of the society. (Barta 1987, 239–40, original emphasis)

Here, genocide is an objective social structure, which is made visible by its consequences and which exists regardless of, or even when at odds with, the subjective intentions of those involved in its perpetration.

The advantages and disadvantages of these and other possible objectivist definitions partly mirror those of subjectivist definitions: they allow us to perceive the collective, nonindividual aspects of genocide, they avoid hair-splitting over what might or might not have been intended by the perpetrators, but they sideline the subjective, experiential dimensions of genocide – for the perpetrators, the victims, and bystanders. Dirk Moses has criticized objectivist, or structural, approaches for bypassing the issue of guilt and responsibility altogether and for being so rigidly determinist (note Barta's reference to inevitability) that no room is left for contingency, uncertainty, the possibility of alternative courses of action (Moses 2002, 27). These are common criticisms of objectivist sociology in general. More specifically, we can also ask what means and what types of victims make an event genocide. Thompson and Quets defer this question, whereas Barta seems to assume that the Aboriginal "race" exists as a natural human group.

There seems no easy way to resolve these debates. Each different definition captures something important about genocide, but these various definitions cannot all be made compatible with each other. Each new definition results from an author deciding what seems to him or her to be the most important thing about genocide and then constructing a definition that captures this *essence*. As you may recall from the start of chapter 1, I use the word "essence" to designate a definite and finite list of characteristics that define a thing, which are permanent, inalterable, and eternal and which exist ahistorically. All of the definitions I have quoted, and many others besides, attempt to specify the essence of genocide. We could say that this essence is being fought over, or contested, and that genocide is an *essentially contested concept*.

AN ESSENTIALLY CONTESTED CONCEPT

Disagreements over how the word "genocide" should be defined are functional disagreements – that is, disagreements over the work that the word is supposed to do or the function it should serve. These disagreements involve a strong element of political partisanship;

definitions affect, for example, whether the destruction of Indigenous peoples of the Americas or the firebombing of Japan during the Second World War counts as genocide and hence whether Western liberal democracies are guilty of genocide. The philosopher W.B. Gallie has observed that in many definitional debates, the contestants refuse to each go their own way; they will not just agree to disagree. Instead, "Each party continues to maintain that the special functions which the term ... fulfils on *its* behalf or on *its* interpretation, is the correct or proper or primary, or the only important, function which the term in question can plainly be said to fulfil. Moreover, each party continues to defend its case with what it claims to be convincing arguments, evidence, and other forms of justification" (Gallie 1956, 168). When we encounter this situation in ordinary life, Gallie says, we are tempted to view it as a simple conflict of interests and to regard the reasons offered by the differing parties as mere ideological justifications. In philosophy the same situation may hinge on metaphysical disagreement. In both situations argument is wasted because the crucial issues at stake are actually beyond argument. However, Gallie points to the existence of a third case: disputes "which, although not resolvable by argument of any kind, are nevertheless sustained by perfectly respectable arguments and evidence" (Gallie 1956, 169). These disputes are concerned with essentially contested concepts. "Genocide," it turns out, is an essentially contested concept *par excellence*.

Gallie specifies five primary and two supplementary conditions for the essentially contested quality of a concept. First, the concept must be appraisive. That is, it must imply a strong value-judgment.[5] Although not all authors conceptualize genocide specifically as an offence, all agree that it is an evil. The second and third criteria are closely connected: the object that the concept refers to must be of an internally complex character, and it must be possible to describe this object coherently in a variety of ways, such that its particular value can be accounted for by a plurality of different ways of arranging and prioritizing its component elements. Genocide involves a diverse array of elements: state power, mass murder, victims' defenselessness, collective identity, and so on. Its evil can be differently accounted for

---

5 Gallie speaks directly only of concepts that make positive value-judgments. However, nothing specifically prevents expanding the use of "essentially contested concepts" to include also negative appraisals.

through different arrangements of these elements, in which one element figures more prominently than the others or in which a particular arrangement of elements is specified. For example, debates about whether the destruction of Indigenous cultures in the Americas should be counted as genocide often hinge on the importance given, in the definition of "genocide," to destructive practices other than deliberate massacre: forced migration, confinement to inhospitable living conditions, removal of children from the group, and sporadic and disorganized violence by nonstate actors (settlers), as opposed to systematic state-run concentration and extermination of populations. Fourth, the concept must be open to being modified in the course of changing circumstances in ways that cannot be predicted in advance. For example, the massacres and mass starvation inflicted on Cambodians by the Khmer Rouge government did not involve a relationship of national, ethnic, racial, or religious difference between perpetrators and victims but resembled a genocide in many other ways. Despite the absence of this one crucial criterion, the event was labelled a genocide. The strangeness of the Cambodian genocide even prompted the invention of a new term, "autogenocide" (Lacouture 1978), to denote genocide against a group committed by members of that group.[6] Fifth, the different parties to the dispute must recognize that the concept is disputed and engage "aggressively and defensively" (Gallie 1956, 172) with other usages to maintain their own. In other words, they must be engaged in definitional debate.

To distinguish an essentially contested concept from a concept that is simply confused, Gallie introduces two supplementary conditions. First, the concept must be derived from an original exemplar, an event or example that all participants accept as an appropriate and unqualified application of the concept. In genocide studies this event is the Nazi genocide of European Jews, sometimes called the Shoah. Despite disagreement over whether the Holocaust includes only the Shoah or also includes Nazi mass murders of other groups – Gypsies, Poles, homosexuals, disabled persons, and so on – all genocide scholars are united in affirming that what happened to the Jews of Europe was genocide. To say otherwise is to be a Holocaust

---

6 It should be noted that this label is problematic, as Alexander Hinton points out: "it overlooks the fact that the Khmer Rouge also targeted ethnic minorities, including Muslim Chams, Vietnamese, and Chinese, and that ethnic Khmer were manufactured into different sorts of political beings" (Hinton 2005, 15).

denier and to lose all scholarly and moral credibility (except, of course, among other deniers). Finally, the way that the exemplar event is recognized must be somewhat open-ended; that is, it must be possible to plausibly claim that, by continuing to argue definitions, one is extending the salience of the term, furthering the point of having called the exemplar by that term in the first place. With respect to genocide, this means claiming that whatever point was served by inventing a term – "genocide" – to describe the Shoah, or the Nazi holocaust in general, this point is served and even advanced by extending the term to new events. Many scholars believe that the point of using the term "genocide" is to prevent a repetition of events like the Holocaust; for that to happen, it must be possible to speak of a general class of "events like the Holocaust." The more we investigate the matter, the more we learn that "events like the Holocaust," in ways that we deem relevant, don't just exist in some hypothetical future but are littered throughout our past and, appallingly, our present.

If a concept is essentially contested, logic will not avail to resolve definitional disputes because no general principle for deciding which usage is best can be found or specified (Gallie 1956, 189). Where does this leave us with respect to "genocide"? Gallie distinguishes between the "logical" and the "historical" senses of what it is to understand a concept. The distinction is that of synchronic (or static) and diachronic (or processual) conceptions of structure: the logical sense involves being able to state and conform to the rules governing a concept's use, whereas the historical sense involves knowing about "the whole gamut of conditions that have led to, and that now sustain, the way we use it" (Gallie 1956, 196–7). For certain types of concepts – for example, scientific concepts vindicated solely by their predictive accuracy – the logical sense is sufficient. However, for appraisative concepts, a purely logical understanding is insufficient, precisely because the rules of use may be essentially contested. In these cases a logical understanding must be supplemented by a historical understanding: "For, if we want to see *just what* we are doing, when we apply a given appraisative concept, then one way of learning this is by asking from what vaguer or more confused or more restricted version (or ancestor) our currently accepted version of the concept in question has been derived" (Gallie 1956, 198). This does not mean looking for an original historical definition of a term. There is no guarantee that earlier versions of a term are any less problematic than contemporary ones. The point of history is not to find an essence that has been accidentally lost but to retrace the events that produced and sustain a classifying *practice*.

THE HISTORICITY OF A CLASSIFYING PRACTICE

At the beginning of chapter 1, I defined a *metaphysical essence* as a definite and finite list of characteristics that define a thing, which are permanent, inalterable, and eternal because they exist outside of society and history. We can see that genocide scholars have attempted to define genocide as an essence by trying not only to specify a list of characteristics that define it but also to speak as though this list exists outside of history and is merely discovered or described rather than assembled or constructed. "The word is new, the crime ancient," says Leo Kuper (1981, 11), essentializing both the definition of genocide and, anachronistically, its status as a crime. In chapter 1, I argued that treating morality as an essence prevents us from coming to grips with the concrete dynamics of morality as a relational social practice. Here, I would like to make the same claim about *concepts*. Following the rule of immanence, we can say that concepts themselves exist as definite practices. We don't discover them; we make them. And by grouping phenomena together into a common category, treating various things as instances of the same thing, we do more than reflect or describe the world: we intervene in it; we alter it. A concept works as a tool that makes it easier for the people who use it to assemble their experiences in particular ways and to pursue particular courses of action – and, by extension, more difficult to pursue others. As a form of concrete action, then, every concept has a history. Knowing a bit of the history of the concept of genocide will help us to make more informed decisions about how to use it today.

The word "genocide" first appeared in print in 1944, as the title and the subject matter of chapter 9 of *Axis Rule in Occupied Europe*, by Polish jurist and legal activist Raphaël Lemkin. Briefly, it meant "the destruction of a nation or of an ethnic group" (Lemkin 1944, 79), although Lemkin's conception of genocide is much more complex than this. Lemkin formed the word by combining "the ancient Greek word *genos* (race, tribe) and the Latin *cide* (killing)," although he indicated in a note that the word "ethnocide" would be equivalent (Lemkin 1944, 79). He coined the term to refer not only to what the Nazi regime was doing to Jews but also to what it was doing and planned to do to certain other ethnic groups throughout the Reich, particularly in the territories it had conquered in eastern Europe. Lemkin stated that he wanted the concept of genocide to protect the right of national groups to exist, just as the concept of homicide protects the right to life of human individuals (Lemkin 1944, 79, 91).

"Genocide" was Lemkin's second attempt to create such a legal protection. In 1933 he had submitted a proposal to the International Conference for the Unification of Criminal Law in Madrid "to declare the destruction of racial, religious, or social collectivities a crime under the law of nations." This proposal included two crimes: "barbarity," defined as "action against the life, bodily integrity, liberty, dignity, or economic existence" of a person, if taken "out of hatred towards a racial, religious, or social collectivity, or with a view to the extermination thereof"; and "vandalism," defined as destruction of cultural or artistic works for the same reason (Lemkin 1947, 146). Just as the concept of genocide was invented in response to Nazi atrocities, Lemkin's concepts of barbarism and vandalism were invented in response to the atrocities committed against the Armenian national group by the Young Turk government of the Ottoman Empire and, subsequently, by the state of Turkey (see also Cooper 2008, 9–15).

Elements of both barbarism and vandalism, of physical and cultural destruction, are incorporated in Lemkin's 1944 concept of genocide. But the latter was de-emphasized during the drafting of the UNCG (in which Lemkin was a key participant). For example, an earlier draft of the resolution included political groups among the groups whose destruction could constitute genocide, but this was opposed by representatives of the Soviet Union and others (Kuper 1981, 23–30); an entire article delineating criteria of cultural genocide was removed at the urging of US representatives (Churchill 1998, 365). The present wording of the UNCG, therefore, reflects the desire of its framers not to criminalize their own behaviour. Even with these modifications, the United States did not ratify the convention until 1988, and then only with modifications that narrowed the definition of genocide still further and that stipulated the United States can be prosecuted only with its own consent.

So where does the concept of genocide originate, and which is the original definition – the 1948 UNCG, 1944's *Axis Rule in Occupied Europe*, or Lemkin's 1933 proposal regarding barbarism and vandalism? None of these. Both Michel Foucault (1984, 80) and Norbert Elias (2000, 52; 1987, 121) warn us against the conceit of thinking we can identify the precise origin of an idea or an institution. No early definition of genocide is original any more than the Nazi holocaust was an unprecedented event; both express the transient culmination of long-term historical developments. The Nazi holocaust had its precedents in the Armenian holocaust, in the German genocide of the Herero in South Africa in 1905 (Drechsler 1990), and in the normalcy with which genocide had been used as a tool of colonization and nation building throughout the modern period. Lemkin himself recognized the colonial aspects of the Nazi genocides (see Lemkin 1944, 80–1; McDonnell and Moses 2005; Moses 2002 and 2004; Schaller 2005). And the formulation of a law against genocide finds a home among the formulation of other laws regulating the state's use of force against noncombatants: the Hague Conferences of 1899 and 1907, the Kellogg-Briand Pact of 1928, and the Geneva Conventions of 1929 and 1949, to name a few. As Lemkin himself put it, an idea of war that automatically and unproblematically involves the massacre of enemy noncombatants gave way to a belief that war occurs only between states and that the massacre of civilians is an outrage (which he called the "Rousseau-Portalis Doctrine") (Lemkin 1944, 80). We should be struck by the fact that these two developments occurred more or less at the same time and that the era in which genocide was made criminal for the first time is also the era in which it achieved effects of scale, efficiency, and frequency that stun the imagination.

I think that this double process – the intensity of genocide and its criminalization – reflects the joint fruition of nationalism and of imperialism. By the time the European scramble for Africa was complete at the onset of the First World War, there was no longer any outside to the nation-state system: from then on, genocide could no longer take place at the frontiers or margins of the Eurocentric world-system but had to take place within one or another nation-state. Moreover, states with imperial ambitions, like Germany, had no unclaimed territory to venture into. We can understand the Nazi holocaust as an introversion of the same process that had led to colonial genocide in Spanish, Portuguese, British, French, Belgian, and other European colonies and settler states over the preceding five centuries. Also by the end of the nineteenth century, states had become *nation*-states. Those who controlled the sovereign monopoly of military force were concerned with cultivating language, religion, custom – and race – as bases of solidarity and allegiance. Lemkin was concerned with protecting the right to existence of national groups, as though nations were a natural and universal feature of human social life. They are not; they are historically specific social figurations. Among other things, nations are, in Benedict Anderson's memorable phrase, "imagined communities" (Anderson 1991). The Turkish and Nazi genocides, and Lemkin's activism in response to them, reflect the importance that these imagined communities had acquired by the first half of the twentieth century.

The history of "genocide" after 1948 shows two opposed but related tendencies. On the one hand, the UNCG itself did nothing at all for half a century after it was passed – or almost nothing: it inspired a certain tension in observers who noted the gap between the theory and practice of international law. But for half a century this law designed to compromise the sovereign authority of states could only strain against the leash of its dependence on these very sovereign states for its implementation. On the other hand, the term "genocide" did circulate widely outside of legal and diplomatic circles. Its meaning broadened as members of different minority groups used it to express their historical experiences. For example, black Americans in the civil rights movement in the 1950s expressed fears of a genocide by white supremacists (e.g., Griffin 1977). Both the transatlantic trade in African slaves, in particular, and the general condition of blacks in racist America have been called genocidal. During the Vietnam War, the International War Crimes Tribunal headed by Bertrand Russell accused the United States of having committed genocide in southeast Asia (El-Kaïm-Sartre and Sartre 1968). Of course, Aboriginal peoples throughout the Americas, whose historical experiences fit both the 1948 and 1944 formulations, have used "genocide" to describe both their past and present circumstances (Churchill 1998). The term has also been invoked to defend established forms of privilege; for example, antichoice activists have tried to label abortion a "genocide of the unborn."

We could say that the viability of the word "genocide" is today sustained through three sets of practices. First, it is used in *practices of state politics* to delegitimate certain uses of state power, namely the acts to which it is applied, and to legitimate other uses of state power, such as the International Criminal Tribunals for both Rwanda and the former Yugoslavia as well as the NATO invasion of Kosovo. It can be used in this way by nonstate actors as well as by states themselves (and perhaps more easily). Ward Churchill invokes a history of genocide as a basis for the aims and means of the American Indian Movement; the Russell Tribunal accused the United States of genocide in southeast Asia to oppose the invasion of Vietnam. Second, the concept of genocide is invoked in *practices of memorialization* through which past events are actively remembered as genocides. In the most conspicuous examples, different actors attempt to construct or assemble out of diverse traces – documents, survivors' narratives, physical sites – a unitary truth about a unified event; but it is also possible to recognize an irreducible multiplicity in memory. Third, "genocide" is mobilized in *practices of identification,* projects to form, maintain, or strengthen collective identities. For Jews, Armenians, Aboriginals, African Americans, and others, the existence of a genocidal past both modifies and reaffirms identity. We can see all three practices coming together in the ensemble of ways that historical memory of the Shoah has been important to national identity and practical politics in the State of Israel.

The fourth set of practices – scholarly or social-scientific examination of genocide – is inseparable from the other three. The rule of reflexivity reminds us that, whether we like it or not, any attempt to explain genocide sociologically is shaped by, and acts back on, this context of state politics, memorialization, and identification. When I speak, what you hear depends on how you are invested in these other fields of practice. For the same reason, however, these other practices necessarily invoke sociological assumptions – about what kind of things make up the social world and what their dynamics are. Because of this, I can reread the various competing definitions, including those put forward by jurists or diplomats or activists, for their hidden sociological assumptions and can revise them by modifying these assumptions.

REINSERTING SOCIOLOGY INTO THE DEFINITION

I would like to look briefly at the UNCG definition and in more detail at the conception of genocide put forward by Raphaël Lemkin in *Axis Rule in Occupied Europe*. Despite their differences, the two texts share three key points: first, they conceptualize genocide as a crime that, second, is committed against natural human groups that, third, form the basis of nation-states. If we reconsider all of these points, we can formulate a conception of genocide that is critical, relational, and sociological, one that directly extends and builds upon these earlier definitions.

The UNCG defines "genocide" in terms of three sets of criteria: the types of groups that can be victims, the types of means that can be used to perpetrate it, and the presence of intent to destroy all or part of a group as such.[7] Each criterion makes a definite sociological claim. The set of protected groups, for example, leaves out many other possibilities: groups defined by sexuality or by disability, both of which were subjected to extermination under the Third Reich, groups defined by social class, and so on. This selectivity invites the question: what is important about nationality, ethnicity, race, and religion? The answer is that they are all forms of identity that have been crucial to the cultivation of modern nationalism. The UNCG's first assumption is that genocide is always about *state formation*. Second, the means specified all involve the use of physical violence to inflict biological destruction on a social group as such. The "as such" suggests that the group is understood to have an existence of its own, above and beyond the existence of its members. Nonphysical ways of destroying a group are not considered: prohibition of language, dance, artwork, or religious practices, destruction of cultural monuments, dissolution of sustaining institutions, and forced deportation or dispersion. Social groups are imagined in their biological aspect; their life is imagined as a biological life. Implicitly, the UNCG recognizes the groups it protects as natural groups; it *naturalizes nationhood*. Third, the UNCG makes genocide a *crime*; it *moralizes* genocide from the outset. This is obvious, but it has important implications. Making it a crime means that specific agents must be criminals. The law must therefore emphasize intent. Genocide can never be accidental or inadvertent; it can never be the consequence of an impersonal structural process (the way global warming is understood to be). The outcome of a course of action matters less than the intent behind it; put another way, the experiences of the victims count for less than the moral quality of the accused perpetrator. This makes it

---

7 These are not metaphysical essences, although it is easy to mistake them for such. In its "Preamble," the UNCG situates itself in a definite historical context. Article 2 opens by announcing its own *performativity*: "In the present Convention, genocide means ..."

easier to assume that genocide is committed by bad people, and by bad governments, and more difficult to imagine that governments we consider to be good – our own, perhaps, or those found in liberal democracies, perhaps – might be guilty of it. This assumption has cast a long shadow over popular and scholarly thinking about genocide.

Genocide is a *crime* against the *natural groups* on which *nation-states* are based. For all that the UNCG omits of Lemkin's conception of genocide, these three points establish a continuity between the two. I would like to focus on the naturalness of national groups as this idea appears in *Axis Rule in Occupied Europe*. Lemkin's germinal book, nearly 700 pages in length, provides a detailed, country-by-country account of the practices by which Nazi Germany and its allies governed social life in the territories under their control and describes the violence and destruction inflicted on persons and on social, political, economic, and cultural institutions of various subject peoples, including Jews and other groups. Chapter 9 of *Axis Rule* proposes the new concept of "genocide" to refer to certain aspects of this occupation and, by implication, to any similar actions by other states. It is a vigorously contested text: authors who propose fundamentally differing definitions of and explanations for "genocide" all claim to be working out the proper implication of Lemkin's ideas. I think that the irresolvable quality of these debates results in part from a confused sociological assumption made by Lemkin about how social groups exist.

Is the crux of genocide the *physical extermination* of a group, or is it the destruction of a group as a *cultural entity*? Authors on both sides of this question claim support from Lemkin. His discussion of genocide specifies a range of "fields" in which the Nazi genocides were being carried out: political, social, economic, biological, physical, religious, and moral (Lemkin 1944, 82–90). However, as Dirk Moses (2004) has pointed out, the physical field (which includes mass killings, endangering of health, and restriction of food supply) is crucial to what makes genocide distinct from other crimes. Lemkin states that "denationalization," for example, is an inadequate term because, among other considerations, "it does not connote the destruction of the biological structure." The same is true for terms like "Germanization," "Magyarization," and so on. The Germanization of the Poles, for example, "means that the Poles, as human beings, are preserved and that only the national pattern of the Germans is imposed on them. Such a term is much too restricted to apply to a process in which the population is attacked, in a physical sense, and is removed and supplanted by populations of the oppressor nations" (Lemkin 1944, 80). Although Lemkin's conception of genocide includes the destruction of cultural institutions and of the "national pattern" of a group, physical destruction is also a necessary component of genocide, and so cultural genocide on its own is not genocide according to the 1944 formulation.

But there are more complications. Lemkin's conception is explicitly concerned with national or ethnic groups: "By 'genocide' we mean the destruction of a nation or of an ethnic group" (Lemkin 1944, 79). He is not concerned to protect social groups in general. Why not? It turns out that culture is the *point* at stake when genocide is committed:

> The world represents only so much culture and intellectual vigor as are created by its component national groups ... The destruction of a nation, therefore, results in the loss of its future contributions to the world. Moreover, such destruction offends our feelings of morality and justice in much the same way as does criminal killing of a human being: the crime in the one case as in the other is murder, though on a vastly greater scale. (Lemkin 1944, 91)

National or ethnic groups are more than just populations of people with common characteristics. They have an existence of their own, above and beyond the individuals who make them up. And they are what produces culture. Lemkin is specifically concerned to establish for national groups a collective right to existence, comparable to the individual's right to life, because of the unique value of national groups, vis-à-vis other types of social groups, as the engines of cultural production.

If we recognize that Lemkin defines "genocide" in terms of the violation of a nation's right to its collective existence, we can identify an important source of confusion over what he has said. This is that he combines performative statements about what the word "genocide" *means* ("by 'genocide' we mean the destruction of a nation or of an ethnic group") with descriptive statements about how he thinks genocide *works* and what it *does*. Many subsequent authors do this also; for example, Helen Fein defines genocide as "the calculated murder of a segment or all of a group defined outside the universe of obligation of the perpetrator" (Fein 1984, 4), conflating what genocide is with how it happens. We can separate out these two aspects of Lemkin's thinking. Genocide *is* the destruction of a nation. However, it may *happen* in two ways: immediately, through the "mass killings of all members of a nation" (but "generally speaking" it "does not necessarily" involve this); or it may involve "a coordinated plan of different actions aiming at the destruction of essential foundations of the life of national groups" (Lemkin 1944, 79). The different fields described on pages 82 to 90 of *Axis Rule* (political, social, economic, biological, physical, religious, and moral) are fields in which genocide "is being carried out" (Lemkin 1944, 82) by the German occupiers. These fields do not form part of the definition of "genocide," but they do form part of a theory about what comprises the "essential foundations of the life of national groups." In other words, chapter 9 of *Axis Rule* can be read as a theoretical exposition of how and why nations or ethnic groups are destroyed, and it makes sociological claims about the nature or structure of nations and their conditions for survival. As Moses observes (2004, n21), these claims are of a communitarian nature and thus "baffle" anyone who thinks in exclusively individualist terms. To sum up, Lemkin seems to assume three things about national groups: first, they exist objectively, like Durkheimian social facts; second, they have essential foundations of life; and third, they are the natural bases or units of human culture.

A CRITICAL RELATIONAL CONCEPTION OF GENOCIDE

To sociologists, these kinds of claims are familiar; they are associated with the functionalism of Durkheim and of American sociological theorist Talcott Parsons. In *The Rules of Sociological Method*, Durkheim claims that societies exist objectively and that societies have objective functional needs that vary according to which evolutionary stage they have reached (Durkheim 1982, 97). Parsons elaborates upon these claims to formulate a system theory which claims that societies are bounded, self-sufficient, and integrated systems that make up organic wholes, which evolve historically the way that individual organisms evolve (Parsons 1951 and 1966). Parsonian functionalism has been subjected to very strong criticisms and has lost its dominant position in sociological theory, but we can make two criticisms that apply as much to Lemkin as to Parsons. The first is that claims about the universality of any particular form of social organization are always anachronistic. As Elias (2000, 466–7) points out, Parsons took the American society that existed in his day for the universal template of all human communities, when in fact this society has a historically limited and – in the long view – very recent existence. The same can be said of "nations" in the sense that Lemkin understood them. Nationalism is a modern invention. It is younger even than the sovereign state, the origin of which is conventionally pinned on the 1648 Treaty of Westphalia.[8] Nationalism includes, among its inventions, the claim that nations are ancient and the construction of narratives that assemble history into the collective memories of imagined communities (Anderson 1991, 187–206). The second criticism is more abstract: to a relational sociologist, social systems are not as highly integrated as functionalists understand them to be; that is, they are less, not more, highly integrated than individual organisms. This means that they are more changeable than organisms. Nations are an important engine of cultural production, but they are far from the only possible such engine.

What is it, then, that genocide destroys and that the criminalization of genocide protects? What kinds of things are "national, ethnic, racial, and religious groups"? The subjectivist answer is that they are merely aggregates of individuals engaged in social action; the objectivist answer is that they are social facts that exist independently of individuals. A relational answer is that they are *figurations*. That is, they are processes made up of dynamic networks of social relationships and constituted through the material practices of concrete human individuals. They exist not inside people as ideas or

---

8 Although the Treaty of Westphalia incorporates the idea or recognition of sovereignty, the practice of sovereignty as a monopoly of military force has a more complicated history. Elias charts the growth of this monopoly, in France at least, in *The Civilizing Process*. Three historical moments stand out: the reversal of the centrifugal dispersion of military power in the twelfth century; the subjugation by the kings of Paris of all their territorial rivals in the sixteenth century; and the complete stripping of a military function from the aristocracy, and consolidation of military power in the hands of the sovereign, in the sixteenth and seventeenth centuries.

labels and not outside people as independent realities but between and among people. If we insert the concept of figurations into Lemkin's observations of Nazi practices, we can say that the point of genocide is to destroy certain kinds of social figurations and that the point of the concept of genocide and of its criminalization is to protect these figurations.

Thinking of nations as figurations makes it easier to decide when genocide has and has not taken place. Consider, for example, the American firebombing campaign in Japan during the Second World War. This strategic bombing deliberately targeted civilian population centres, killed hundreds of thousands of noncombatant men, women, and children, and rendered millions homeless. Was this genocide? Answering this question in subjectivist terms requires that we find evidence of a specifically genocidal intent. Answering it in objectivist terms is somewhat easier because if we conceive of the Japanese nation as a social fact, we can say that this nation was partly destroyed through intentional action. But an objectivist sociology, as I've already said, cannot easily deal with those cases in which people are subjected to violence in order to destroy a group that is partly or wholly imagined by the perpetrator, as with anticommunist violence in 1980s Central America or with antibourgeois violence in Cambodia under the Khmer Rouge. A relational conception of social groups can handle both kinds of situations: those in which an existing group is subjected to destruction but without clear evidence of intent; and those in which a perpetrator intends to destroy a group that had not previously existed. Each type of situation raises some interesting questions about the causes and consequences of genocidal violence.

In relational sociology, groups are neither objective nor subjective, being composed of relations among people. But they have what we could call quasi-objective qualities and quasi-subjective ones. Their quasi-objective qualities result from the fact that, although the existence of social groups depends on individuals, it does not reduce to individuals. A group, like any figuration, is composed of the relations of power and interdependency that both enable and constrain practical action. In general, individuals may or may not be conscious of the fields of practical possibilities open to them and of the practical consequences of their actions. This is possible because of the *complexity* of these fields. This complexity exists because figurations result from the practices of many individuals, each of whom relates to the others in a variety of ways.[9] As a result, individuals can experience the social world as an object, as something that exists outside of themselves, even though they are a part of it. This phenomenon accounts for the possibility that our actions may have unintended consequences and that patterned regularities or mechanisms can exist, generated by the matrix of social practice, of which individuals are quite unaware. One of my fundamental convictions in writing this book is that genocide is produced by just such mechanisms and that the job of sociology is to make them perceptible and hence susceptible to change. But another implication of the phenomenon I have described is that, because groups have a quasi-objective existence, it may be possible to destroy a group in whole or in part without intending to. There may be such things as accidental genocides.[10]

The quasi-subjective qualities of social groups, on the other hand, result from the fact that social practices are always meaningful and from the fact that meaning is an indispensable part of the reality of these practices. Social groups exist in part because people imagine that they do and invest this meaning in their practical relationships with each other. In any intentional genocide, the victim is an imagined group in the same sense that nations are imagined communities: "It is *imagined* because the members of even the smallest nation will never know most of their fellow-members, meet them, or even hear of them, yet in the minds of each lives the image of their communion" (Anderson 1991, 6, original emphasis). Thus whether the way that perpetrators of a genocide imagine the victim group agrees with the way that the victims imagine themselves and each other can vary enormously, from a relatively close fit (such as the genocide of Ottoman Armenians) to a partial mismatch (as in the genocide of European Jews) to wild cases of mistaken identity (e.g., Guatemalan communists and Cambodian bourgeoisie). But even in these latter cases, it would be a mistake to say that the victim group was wholly

---

9 A network of relations among individuals has, at a minimum, one fewer dimension than the number of individuals in it. A network between two people consists of one relation in one dimension; between three people, of three relations in two dimensions; between four people, of six relations in three dimensions; and so on. Even this is a simplified analogy that assumes, for example, only one type of relation. The complexity of a network composed of thousands or millions of people is formidable.

10 In chapter 6, I explore the question of whether the genocide of the Aboriginal Tasmanians was an accidental genocide.

fictive. The community imagined by the perpetrator becomes the basis for very tangible relationships of violence and annihilation. Once individuals are assigned to the victim group, they belong to it for all practical purposes – or at least, for the practical purposes that matter most in such a situation. Such groups are, in effect, *constituted through genocide*. Genocidal violence produces its victims *qua* victims in the course of its own actualization. Or, stated in another way, genocide produces difference even as it annihilates it.

This fact raises another implication that relational sociology has for our understanding of genocide. In a relational sociology, social difference and social identity entail each other. Identity for any subject, whether the subject is an individual or a group, does not reside in the subject itself but in the relations between the subject and its various Others. Differing identities exist in relation to each other; the relation between them is difference. Identity and difference are distinguishable but indivisible aspects of the same relational entity,[11] hence the term "identity-difference." The boundaries of the community of obligation are defined by who is not in the community. This is not just a cognitive fact but also a practical one; if people are members of the same group or belong to different groups, such is the case because they are *made* members or outsiders in practice. Identity and difference exist as processes, as the ongoing work of identification and differentiation. If genocide works to produce difference, it also and by the same gesture works to produce identity. We can thus see genocide as one among many other tools for achieving this effect. In this sense, genocide is not just destructive but also productive; it works to produce relations of identity-difference through a process of annihilation. Knowing this can help us to explain why genocide happens. By producing relations of identity-difference, it joins the perpetrators together into a community of obligation, building a social solidarity out of the stuff of life and death. We can ask what else it produces, what other benefits it provides, and to whom.

---

11 "[Auguste] Comte turned resolutely against this separation of form from content, of scientific method from scientific subject matter, and of thought from knowledge. A distinction can be made, he implied, but not a division" (Elias 1978, 41). This notion of being able to make a distinction but not a division between two phenomena or two aspects of a phenomenon applies so well to features of Elias's own theory that I have appropriated it broadly in my discussion.

One pair of questions remains: if genocide involves the destruction of social groups, understood as figurations, should we privilege a particular list of types of groups whose members can be victims of genocide, and should we privilege a particular list of means by which genocide can be accomplished? I do not see any reason to answer either of these questions in the affirmative. As Alexander Hinton points out,

> While the marking of difference occurs in every society, the social groupings that are constructed vary dramatically. Race, ethnicity, nation, and religion are favored categories in modern discourse. However, as anthropologists and other scholars have demonstrated, many other social classifications exist, including totemistic groups, clans, phratries, lineages, castes, classes, tribes, and categories based on sexual orientation, mental or physical disability, urban or rural origin, and, of course, economic and political groups ... The criterion that distinguishes genocide as a conceptual category is the intentional attempt to annihilate a social group *that has been marked as different*. (Hinton 2002, 4, emphasis added)

Lemkin's inclination to define "genocide" in terms of national groups resulted from mistaken sociological assumptions about the natural primacy of nations among other types of human groups. Some authors have argued that not restricting the types of possible victim groups will lead to an unmanageable profusion of spurious claims to victimhood that denude the word "genocide" of its effective meaning. But a relational conception of genocide defends against this outcome because groups do not only exist in the minds of individuals; they also exist in practical relations among people, relations that can be observed empirically. What it means for a group to be destroyed, either in whole or in part, and what kinds of methods produce this destruction are also empirical questions. We don't yet entirely know what determines the viability of social groups; this is a question that needs to be researched, and it is premature to restrict the list of genocidal methods to those we already know about. A relational conception thus connects the empirical study of genocide to the empirical study of social groups and social identity in general.

In conclusion, what does a critical relational conception of genocide look like? There are many possibilities, but I think the most succinct is this: *genocide is an identity-difference relation of violent obliteration*. That genocide is a relation should come as no surprise: genocide is itself a figuration, a relation-process that works to destroy certain other figurations called "social groups." It is an identity-difference relation because social groups do not exist in themselves but are constituted as social identities connected by relations of difference. That genocide is violent goes without saying. The ambiguity of the word "violent" is, I think, a necessary evil. Just as we cannot specify in advance what kinds of human social groups are possible, we cannot specify in advance what kinds of relations people experience as violent; sociologists have barely begun to investigate this question empirically.

Finally, I have chosen to characterize genocide in terms of "obliteration" because this term seems appropriate to thinking of genocide as a relation and a process. To obliterate is to "destroy completely; to devastate, demolish, or lay waste," but also to "blot out ... so as to leave no distinct traces; to erase, delete, efface" (Oxford English Dictionary 2010). Within a relation of genocide, the genocidaires perceives the victims as having some identity, but in the same gesture they use violence to efface, blot out, erase this identity. This erasure works not only objectively but also subjectively; genocide not only destroys the figurational network of the victim group but also removes the traces of this network from the perpetrators' experience of the world. Moreover, as a dynamic relation, genocide has no built-in stopping point short of total annihilation. Given enough energy and left sufficiently unopposed, genocide proceeds until nothing of the victim identity survives, not even ruins. Very few genocides reach this end; usually, some opposition or exhaustion halts the obliterating gesture before it achieves totality. However, as a reference point, total obliteration serves to distinguish partial obliteration from something that is merely damaging or harmful to one's interests.

Whether a given social process tends toward the obliteration of a group or identity figuration is, again, not something that can be determined in advance but something that must be understood in the relevant socio-historical context. At some point, consideration of *what something is* turns out to depend on questions of *how it works* and hence on questions of *why it happens* – to which I now turn.

3

Closing the Theory Gap
in the Sociology of Genocide

If indeed genocide expresses some, though obviously not all, of the dominant trends in contemporary civilization, it would hardly be surprising that
few researchers would want to spend much time on the dark side of the
world we have made for ourselves.

Rubenstein 1987, 284

WHAT IS THE THEORY GAP?

In 1990 the American sociologist Helen Fein claimed that a "sociological theory gap" separated the study of genocide from the interests of other sociologists: "No stream of sociology or major theorist
since 1945 has considered genocide focally, either to explain genocide or to consider its implications for theories of the state, of development, and of community and society" (Fein 1993, 32).[1] Writing
in 1989, Zygmunt Bauman, in *Modernity and the Holocaust*, had
made a similar assertion: "*the Holocaust has more to say about the
state of sociology than sociology in its present shape is able to add
to our knowledge of the Holocaust*. This alarming fact has not yet
been faced (much less responded to) by sociologists" (Bauman
1991b, 3, original emphasis). More than ten years later, Alex Alvarez
repeated the sentiment: "While there have been a few noteworthy
exceptions to this omission, genocide has remained largely outside
the mainstream of contemporary social science. This is surprising,
to say the least" (Alvarez 2001, 1). And in an overview of genocide

---

1 Fein's diagnosis of a theory gap first appeared in 1990, in a special issue of
the journal *Current Sociology*, which was republished by Sage in 1993 as the
book *Genocide: A Sociological Perspective* – and which, sadly, was out of print
by the late 1990s.

scholarship, Australian political scientist Colin Tatz examines history, philosophy, religion, and psychology but not sociology (Tatz 2003, 18–42). What is this sociological theory gap with respect to genocide?[2] And what can a critical sociology contribute to remedying it?

I think that the best way to understand the notion of a theory gap, one that is still relevant today, is as an inability to explain genocide in the same terms that are used to explain ordinary social phenomena. Part of this inability may come from a reluctance of sociologists to confront extreme violence at all: "There is a similar paucity of social scientists who consider state violence, terror and repression or the development of human rights: social science most often glosses over blood and victims in antiseptic abstraction, masking the nature of the state" (Fein 1993, 32). In other words, one culprit is *collective denial*, the problem that I introduced at the beginning of chapter 1. However, if collective denial were the only problem, then after ten years or more of vigorous scholarship on genocide, we would expect more progress than Alvarez reported in 2001. I think there is another cause of the theory gap, namely the tendency even of genocide scholars to put genocide in a category by itself, separate from other social events, and to explain it as an extraordinary event, an exception to social life. In other words, there has been a tendency by some sociologists to treat genocide as *categorically unique*. And this tendency derives in turn from the movement among some Holocaust scholars to treat the Jewish experience of genocide under the Third Reich as a unique and sacred event in human history.

---

2 Sociology is not alone in its reticence. Alexander Hinton, for example, has observed that "with few exceptions anthropologists have remained remarkably silent on the topic of genocide" and that "although anthropologists have long been at the forefront of advocating for the rights of indigenous peoples and have conducted rich analyses of violence, conflict, and warfare in substate and prestate societies, they have only recently (since the 1980s) begun to focus their attention intensively on political violence in complex state societies" (Hinton 2002, 1). Comparable silences can be observed in other disciplines. Since each discipline is organized around a different core network of theoretical assumptions and debates, the epistemological consequence of these silences, and the effects of treating genocide as central rather than marginal, are likely to be different for each discipline.

THE PARTICULAR UNIQUENESS OF THE SHOAH[3]

In 2001 Westview Press published a collection of essays titled *Is the Holocaust Unique? Perspectives on Comparative Genocide*. The appearance of this book signalled the importance of a debate that had been gathering steam for some time, particularly in American scholarly circles. There are several authors who claim, and claim vocally, that the Nazi genocide of European Jewry (the Shoah)[4] was a historically unique event, such that no other events belong in the same category with it or are even comparable to it. They insist that this uniqueness is not only empirical but also moral, such that ultimately any attempt to compare the Shoah with other events or to situate it in a broader category such as "genocide" is a moral offence or even a covert form of Holocaust denial – "the equivalent of David Duke without his robes," as Deborah Lipstadt (1993, 215) puts it. For Jewish Canadian philosopher and Holocaust survivor Emil Fackenheim, the uniqueness of the Shoah is explicitly sacred: "whoever dissolves the starkly unique tragedy of the Holocaust (whether in terms psychological, sociological, historical, moral, philosophical, or theological) sooner or later blasphemes against God, man, and in any case against the Truth" (Fackenheim 1978, ix). A more nuanced position is taken by Yehuda Bauer, who distinguishes between "genocide" as defined by the UNCG and "Holocaust" understood as a category to which the Shoah uniquely belongs (Bauer 1978, 35–38;

---

3 The Hebrew word "Shoah" (also spelled "Sho'ah," meaning literally "holocaust" in the sense of a consuming fire) refers specifically to the genocide of European Jews undertaken by the Nazis and their collaborators (it is also called the "Khurbn" or "Churban").

4 It is important to recognize that the Nazi holocaust involved not one but several genocides, of which the most systematic were those against Jews and against Gypsies (Romany and Sinti peoples); other victims included communists, homosexuals, and disabled persons. The expression "the Holocaust" is fraught with confusion, inasmuch as it is often used synonymously with Shoah in order to equate the two or even to deny that other groups suffered genocide (Finkelstein 2000, 3). To be precise, I use "Nazi holocaust" to refer to all Nazi-perpetrated genocides taken together, and I follow Ian Hancock's (2001, 88) practice of using ethnically specific terminology wherever such exists and is applicable: "Shoah" for the Nazi genocide of Jews, "Porrajmos" for the Nazi genocide of Gypsies, and so on.

2001, 10–12).[5] Far less moderate and more systematic than Bauer's position has been the particularism of Steven Katz, who asserts what he calls the "phenomenological" uniqueness of the Shoah: "the Holocaust is phenomenologically unique by virtue of the fact that never before has a state set out, as a matter of intentional principle and actualized policy, to annihilate physically every man, woman, and child belonging to a specific people. A close study of the relevant comparative historical data [shows] that only in the case of the Jews under the Third Reich was such all-inclusive, noncompromising, unmitigated murder intended" (Katz 2001, 49). Claims to uniqueness tend to reduce to this claim of the Nazis' singular, unprecedented, and unparalleled intentionality; Bauer refers to it, as do Lucy Dawidowicz (1981, 11, 14), Deborah Lipstadt (1993, 213), and Michael Marrus (1987, 24).[6] Katz acknowledges that the uniqueness of the Shoah cannot be maintained on grounds of quantitative scale; neither the absolute number of Jews killed nor the proportion of all European Jews killed are without equal among mass murders in history (Katz 1983, 296; 1994, 65, 580). Uniqueness has been affirmed on other grounds as well, such as the unique religious significance of Christian anti-Semitism (Rubenstein 2001), but as a claim about a concrete historical process, the significance of Christian anti-Semitism tends to depend on a claim about the unique intentions of those who put the Final Solution in motion.

There are several problems with affirming the particular uniqueness of the Shoah. The most obvious and important of these, for genocide scholars, is that it makes any comparative study of genocide impossible – and in turn, forestalls any contribution that scholarship can make to putting a stop to the ongoing practice of genocide. The second problem is that many of the arguments made in favour of uniqueness are not historically sound, even the narrow claim that the Shoah is unique for being the only case in which a state has "set out,

---

5 However, the sense of nuance occasionally disappears from Bauer's arguments, notably when he conflates Nazis' intentions with their acts, as in this example: "Total physical annihilation I prefer to call Holocaust, and that of course means that whereas that *is what happened* to Jews – and the fact that a percentage of Jews survived in Europe was due not to any lack of desire on the part of the Nazis to kill them, but their failure to catch all of them – it could, mutatis mutandis, happen to others as well" (Bauer 1991, 40, emphasis added).

6 For a more extensive listing of authors who have maintained the uniqueness of the Shoah, and of authors who deny such uniqueness, see Churchill (1998, 77n24).

as a matter of intentional principle and actualized policy, to annihilate physically every man, woman, and child belonging to a specific people"; for example, as Ian Hancock (2001) demonstrates, Nazi policies toward Gypsies were just as exterminatory as those toward Jews. Lipstadt dismisses the genocide of the Cambodians in Eurocentric, if not racist, terms: "The Khmer Rouge's massacre of a million of their fellow Cambodians ... was barbaric. But what they did was quite different from the Nazis' annihilation of the Jews, which was 'a gratuitous act carried out by a prosperous, advanced, industrial nation at the height of its power'" (Lipstadt 1993, 212, quoting Evans 1989, 87).[7] A third problem is that a preoccupation with the uniqueness of the Shoah tends to support collective denial about genocides other than the Shoah, especially about genocides that do not closely resemble it in the manner of their implementation. This applies especially to genocides against Indigenous peoples in settler societies like Canada, the United States, and Australia (Stannard 1992). American Indian scholar Ward Churchill has accused those who insist on the Shoah's uniqueness of being genocide deniers (Churchill 1998, 31ff). And indeed, Steven Katz has put considerable energy into arguing *against* claims that peoples other than Jews – including Gypsies and homosexuals under the Nazis, Turkish Armenians, American Indians in general, the Pequot in particular, and even Bosnian and Rwandan minorities – have ever suffered genocide (see Katz 1988, 216; 1991; 1994, 20, 514–24; 2001, 62–7; see also McMillen 1994, A13),[8] and he has done so on questionable evidentiary grounds.[9]

---

7 It can also call upon more specific patriotic loyalties, as when Dawidowicz rebuts claims that the atomic bombings of Hiroshima and Nagasaki constituted genocide by saying that such claims "bespeak a vicious anti-Americanism. Their purpose is to depict America as Amerika, a Nazified United States, heir as it were to the unredeemed evil which the Nazis represented" (Dawidowicz 1981, 17).

8 Worth mentioning is Katz's startling claim that "the depopulation of the New World, for all its death and terror, was largely an *unintended* tragedy, a tragedy that occurred despite the sincere and indisputable desire of the Europeans to keep the Indian population alive" (Katz 1994, 20, original emphasis). That *some* Europeans wished to prevent the extinction of First Nations peoples is true enough, but that this desire informed the dominant tendencies of European colonialism in the Americas is a complete fantasy, as David Stannard amply demonstrates in *American Holocaust* (see also Churchill 1998; Maybury-Lewis 2002).

9 Churchill claims that Katz "has been known to rely on the work of notorious Turkish deniers, even when they've been exposed as 'full-blown revisionists' and more accurate sources are readily available" (Churchill 1998, 33n).

Finally, at least part of the motive for the uniqueness thesis seems to be an uncritical support of the State of Israel and of Jewish-Israeli nationalism. So Bauer, for example, claims that "the denial of the Holocaust as a specifically Jewish tragedy is therefore connected with the dangers of anti-Semitism" (Bauer 1980, 43) and that "all these universalizing attempts [regarding the Holocaust] seem to me to be, on the Jewish side, efforts by their authors to escape their Jewishness" (Bauer 1998, 17). The uniqueness of the Shoah is a source of "moral capital" for "the Jewish people," capital that is threatened with "plunder" by those who wish to give it a more general significance (Alexander 1980 and 1994; see also Bauer 1980). And if this moral capital belongs to the Jewish people, its proper executor is the State of Israel: "the heart of every *authentic* response to the Holocaust – religious and secular, Jewish and non-Jewish – is a commitment to the autonomy and security of the State of Israel" (Fackenheim 1977, 212, original emphasis);[10] "those few who have continued to demur from the Zionist project even in the face of the crematoria ... have sinned against both God and man in what can only be construed as the arrogant blindness of their own confused self-righteousness" (Katz 1992, 290). The insistence on uniqueness, as Dirk Moses has pointed out, offers "identity politics in the name of disinterested scholarship" (Moses 2002, 15). Since Jewish-Israeli nationalism cannot protect non-Jews from genocide, it is an identity politics that impedes both a critical interrogation of genocide and an effective solution to it.

THE GENERAL UNIQUENESS OF GENOCIDE

I have suggested that we can understand the theory gap as an inability to explain genocide in the same terms that are used to explain ordinary social phenomena. From this perspective, insistence on the particular uniqueness of the Shoah is a major obstacle to closing this gap. However, it is possible to recognize the Shoah as one member

---

10 Or again: "Zionism is the momentous Jewish response to modernity ... Even for those whose ideological commitments run in other directions, who would prefer a Kantian teleology or a non-nationalist universalism predicated upon an aversion to ethnicity and religious particularism, the brute, barbarous realities of the murderous *Einsatzgruppen* and the genocidal imperatives of Himmler's SS silences [sic] their conceptual, principled, but abstract representations" (Katz 1992, 289).

among others of the general category of genocide, while insisting that this category as a whole is unique among *types* of social phenomena. This insistence on the *general uniqueness of genocide* would pose a second, more subtle and invisible, obstacle to closing the theory gap. I think that many genocide scholars who earnestly desire to close the theory gap have unwittingly fallen into this second trap. Despite the valuable contributions their work makes to our empirical knowledge of genocides and of some of the patterns it displays, this work cannot explore how genocide is deeply rooted in ordinary social practices – not because of any lapse in the diligence of their research but because of tacit assumptions that they make prior to the research process. Among these tacit assumptions, four stand out most prominently: an essentialist approach to the question of definitions, the use of typologies to explain genocide, the search for the unique predictors of genocide, and a focus on armed humanitarian intervention as the main solution to genocide.

To begin with, general uniqueness results from a preoccupation with the search for an essentialist definition of "genocide". Essentialism means that "genocide" is defined unto itself rather than being defined in terms of its relation to other phenomena. Three types of arguments are frequently advanced to defend what amounts to an essentialist approach, whether it is recognized as such or not. The first is scientific: that to have a coherent object of study one must be able to determine what is genocide and what is not. The second is political or juridical: that if genocide is to be punishable through international law, one must be able to specify objectively who has committed genocide and who has not. The third is moral: that "genocide" carries a unique stigma and that one must be careful not to mitigate the force of this stigma through indiscriminate application. But even though these arguments imply the need for a single generally agreed upon definition, the practical consequence of definitionalism has been the opposite, as we have seen at the outset of chapter 2. What is significant about essentialist definitions is that they try to delineate exactly the boundaries of "genocide," to foreclose the possibility of ambiguous or indeterminate cases, to construct a categorization scheme in which every historical event either is genocide or is not. The problem with this approach is that, for any definition of a complex social event, ambiguous borderline cases can always be found. This ambiguity is not necessarily a bad thing. It can provide avenues of scientific exploration: starting from genocide, we could trace the

networks of social relations that connect genocide to the wider figurations in which it is embedded, like state power, or capitalist exchange, or gender, and to familiar settings that we don't associate
with genocide, like elected assemblies, or stock markets, or family
living rooms. The fuzziness of definitional boundaries could help
genocide studies cast a fresh light on familiar phenomena, showing
new aspects of how power, violence, and subjectivity (for example)
are bundled together in practice. But many genocide scholars still
have unbounded enthusiasm for an unrealizable project: the "quest
for a fundamental formula ... as to what essentially lies at the heart
of genocide and the genocidal" (Huttenbach 2001, 8).

This preoccupation with essences leads many scholars to investigate genocide by producing typologies. If genocide has a single fixed
essence, then differences among actual genocides can be explained as
typological variations on this essence, and concentrating study on
specific types would then help to isolate causal factors more efficiently. And so, for example, Frank Chalk and Kurt Jonassohn propose four types of genocide "according to their motive":

(1) to eliminate a real or potential threat;
(2) to spread terror among real or potential enemies;
(3) to acquire economic wealth; or
(4) to implement a belief, theory, or an ideology.
    (Chalk and Jonassohn 1990, 29)

Typologies proposed by Helen Fein (1984, 8–22; reproduced in
Alvarez and Bachman 2008, 295–8) and by Roger Smith (1987,
24–9) resemble that of Chalk and Jonassohn, especially in the inclusion of "ideological" as a type, of which the Jewish and Armenian
holocausts are exemplars. Typing genocides according to the apparent intentions of the perpetrators involves a huge assumption,
namely that the rationalizations with which the perpetrators of violence seek to legitimate their actions reflect the real motives that actually cause them to engage in genocide.[11] But to understand why

---

11 Even in Weberian terms, although explicit statements form a real component of any actual genocide understood as a meaningful social event, willingness
to accept them at face value constitutes a failure of *verstehen*.

genocides happen, we need to inquire into the broader political projects within which genocide is situated.

For example, the Athenian genocide of Melos was implemented to terrorize potential enemies or neutrals in a war in which Athens had put its own sovereignty at risk, and in which the stakes included great economic wealth. Does this make it a genocide of type 1, 2, or 3 within Chalk and Jonassohn's typology? To classify it as type 2 would ignore its context in the Peloponnesian War and the fact that Athens sought through this war to achieve regional economic hegemony. Only psychotic individuals spread terror for the sake of spreading terror; political actors like states, or insurgents trying to overthrow states, spread terror as a means to achieve some larger strategic project. The same is true for "implementing a belief, theory, or an ideology." For example, along with the Nazi holocaust, the Turkish genocide of Armenians is often considered a paradigmatic instance of ideological genocide because of the importance of Turkish nationalist ideology in legitimating it. But as I have already argued, the Armenian holocaust produced very concrete benefits for its perpetrators – as much as we wish it had not. Ideologies of nationalism are only a part of the wider networks of practice that make up nationalist movements, just as beliefs, theories, and ideologies in general are only a part of what makes up material social relations. It may be convenient for us to claim that genocides are implemented because of beliefs or ideologies that we can comfortably demonstrate to be mistaken, and it may be convenient to separate concrete factors like "real threats" (type 1) or "economic wealth" (type 3) from mere "ideologies" (type 4). But these typologies enforce abstract separations between things that are intimately interconnected in practice.

A third aspect of general uniqueness is the search for the unique predictors of genocide. Any unique type of phenomenon, seen against the background of normal social institutions, must appear as a breakdown or aberration of these institutions: as a pathology. A unique pathology implies a unique pathogen, one whose presence can be detected amidst the system's natural elements. If this pathogen could be detected in the early stages of the disease, or even before its onset, palliative measures would be more efficacious. And being unique, the pathogen must be something we don't already know of, something we have to discover. Assuming the general uniqueness of genocide leads to a curious blindness about the

connection between genocide and other forms of violence. Amnesty
International's secretary general, Pierre Sané, writes, "None of the
human rights tragedies of recent years was unpredictable or un-
avoidable ... The problem is not a lack of early warning, but a lack
of early action" (Sané 2000, 8–9). In contrast, Chalk and Jonassohn
write: "A number of people have argued that the establishment of an
early warning system would be a better approach to prevention. But
surely the establishment of such a system presumes the availability
of a number of reasonably reliable indicators. In our opinion, there
has not been nearly enough research done on the preconditions of
genocide to specify such indicators with any degree of reliability"
(Chalk and Jonassohn 1990, 4).[12] There is a crucial difference of
orientation between these two statements. Sané says, "only by protecting all human rights everywhere, every day, will we render the
debate over humanitarian intervention obsolete" (Sané 2000, 9). For
him, the problem of genocide and the problem of human rights
abuse are generally continuous with one another; the former is made
possible by the latter, and their remedies overlap. Sané connects the
spectacle of genocide to isolated acts of torture and extrajudicial
execution, political disappearance, and acts of censorship and repression – and through more extended conceptions of human rights,
to clean water, housing, and education.[13] "Genocide" is tied to
problems of global governance and state violence, of freedom and
equality, of everyday/everynight life. Treating genocide as unique
prescribes a search for predictors of genocide performed in isolation from any examination of dictatorship, violence, or repression,
more generally. This implies a form of political practice that tries

---

12 Chalk reiterated the need to search for predictors in his panel-discussion
paper at the seminar "Genocide and Collective Memory" (Chalk 2000).
Jonassohn and Karin Björnson approach the problem slightly differently in
their 1998 text: "If we lack the means to make predictions credible and
the actors who will rely on them as guides to action, then we need preventative measures that do not require a prediction" (Jonassohn and Björnson
1998, 94).

13 The concept of "human rights" includes under its umbrella not only the
rights to political liberty and security of the person, on which Amnesty
International concentrates ("first-generation" human rights), but also second-
generation social rights, which include the right to housing, clean water, education, and so on, and third-generation rights, which relate to collective existence
and community identity (Weston 2006).

to solve the problem of genocide while leaving other forms of violence unaddressed.[14]

Finally, assuming the general uniqueness of genocide makes it reasonable to privilege armed humanitarian intervention as the main solution to genocide. If genocide is an exception to normal social life, if it exists separately from other types of social phenomena, it will be enough for us to treat it in isolation. In particular, we do not have to inquire into how the ordinary conduct of states makes genocide possible. On this point, general uniqueness shows an affinity, through a particular strategy for eliminating genocide, with the broader praxis of political liberalism.

General Uniqueness, Liberalism, and the Politics of Intervention

The scholars whose work assumes the general uniqueness of genocide tend to be those whom Dirk Moses (2002, 19) calls "liberal." Whereas "postliberal" scholars explain genocide in terms of the "structural determinants of policy development," liberal scholars stress "the agency of the state as the intending genocidal subject" (Moses 2002, 19). That is, they explain genocide in terms of choices made by collective subjects, understood as individual subjects writ large, choices made on the basis of intentions that are present in the consciousness of these subjects. They tend to conflate intentions (what a subject means to do) with motives (why they mean to do it). Consequently, liberals "are inclined to typologize genocides according to motive, distinguishing for example between 'developmental' or 'utilitarian' genocides of indigenous peoples and 'ideological' genocides of scapegoated or hostage groups" (Moses 2002, 20). Liberals also "insist on the primary role of the state as the genocidal perpetrator" (Moses 2002, 21) because the state is the largest and

---

14 The need to search for predictors of genocide is also discussed in Charny (1982) and Kuper (1985), in the various contributions to Charny (1984) and to Fein (1992), and elsewhere. Israel Charny's germinal approach to the search for predictors tends to move away from general uniqueness; his "Genocide Early Warning System" involves the monitoring of violations of basic human rights as a key component (Charny 1982, 289). The approach to prediction taken by Chalk and Jonassohn (1990) in effect represents a move *away* from Charny's more integrative approach and toward the ideal-typical form of general uniqueness.

most powerful example of a collective subject to which we could attribute a genocidal intent.

Assuming the general uniqueness of genocide serves the interests of political liberalism in the same gesture as it maintains the theory gap. By treating genocide as outside of and separate from the field of normal social relations, general uniqueness aims to solve the problem of genocide on terms that leave everything else about the social world as unchanged as possible – especially on terms that do not call into question those structures or figurations that are at the core of liberal-democratic society. This is consistent with a liberal emphasis on states as intending subjects: if genocide results from the intentions of states, then there are two kinds of states in the world – good states, those that do not practise genocide, and bad states, those that do. As Moses observes, "Because the state is conceived of in Rankean terms as an individual personality, genocide is held to issue from ideologies about it (like fascism) rather than a prior cause in civil society ... Liberal theories of genocide are really theories of totalitarianism" (Moses 2002, 21). Good states have a moral responsibility, not only to their own subjects but also to the subjects of bad states, to intervene diplomatically and militarily if necessary to protect them from great evils such as genocide and other gross human rights abuses. Social science does not need to search for a solution to genocide, only for the predictors of genocide so that the liberal solution can be implemented effectively. Ending genocide is mainly a question of doing something where nothing is being done.

One should take these generalizations with a grain of salt. Political liberalism is a broad, complex, and very diverse ensemble of outlooks and projects, one whose members, like those of any similarly broad political tendency, are connected more by family resemblance than by any one set of common principles. Nevertheless, Moses's characterization of liberal genocide scholarship resonates with the tendency of scholars to define genocide in terms that make it Other to the ideals of Western liberal democracy. As Mark Levene observes,

Looked at from the standpoint of 'the West' genocide is something which happens 'out there,' the product of societies that lack the civic institutions, the separation of executive and legislative branches, and above all the democratic, liberal traditions which act as a bulwark against the overwhelming and untrammeled power of the state and, hence, of its genocidal tendency ...

By implication, if Western states commit genocide it must be a regrettable oversight, whereas if carried out by 'totalitarian' ones it is par for the course. (Levene 2005a, 173)

As early as 1951, Hannah Arendt's *The Origins of Totalitarianism* established the association of genocide with totalitarianism and of totalitarianism with radical and utopian ideologies attributed to Joseph Stalin's Soviet Union and to Nazi Germany. This association persists in contemporary genocide scholarship: for instance, in Zygmunt Bauman's stress on the dangers of utopian thinking when joined with state power (Bauman 1991b); conspicuously in the very title of Eric Weitz's *A Century of Genocide: Utopias of Race and Nation*; in Benjamin Valentino's assertion that genocides result mainly from radical communism, ethnic nationalism, and regimes trying to defeat guerrilla insurgencies (Valentino 2004, 4–6); and in Stéphane Courtois's questionable attempt to represent communism as morally worse even than Nazism (Courtois 1999). At worst, the a priori association of genocide with the Others of liberalism produces "the stain of hypocrisy that attaches to regimes that are avowedly democratic in character, that allow comparative freedom and immunity from naked state violence domestically, but that initiate or participate in atrocious actions beyond their borders" (Jones 2004c, 9). But even in its mildest forms, this association puts ethnocentric brackets around any systematic inquiry into the roots of genocide. And in practical terms, it implicitly supports the privileging of armed humanitarian intervention by liberal states into genocidal states as the solution to genocide.

It's important not to homogenize the positions taken by liberal genocide scholars. Some liberal writers have focused on preventing genocide through diplomacy and socio-economic development (e.g., Hamburg 2008, 267–73). However, intervention has emerged as the *primary* strategy proposed for ending genocide. For example, the organization Genocide Watch makes this strategy its main focus:

The International Campaign to End Genocide has four goals:
1 The provision of public information on the nature of genocide and creation of the political will to prevent and end it.
2 The creation of an effective early-warning system to alert the world and especially the U.N. Security Council, NATO and other regional alliances to potential ethnic conflict and genocide.

3 The establishment of a powerful United Nations rapid
response force in accordance with Articles 43–47 of the U.N.
Charter, as well as regional rapid response forces, and international police ready to be sent to areas where genocide threatens or has begun.

4 Effective arrest, trial, and punishment of those who commit
genocide, including the early and effective functioning of the
International Criminal Court, the use of national courts with
universal jurisdiction, and the creation of special international
tribunals to prosecute perpetrators of genocide. (Genocide
Watch 2010b)

The Board of Advisors of Genocide Watch includes some of the most
prominent social scientists who write about genocide: Alexander
Alvarez, Yehuda Bauer, Frank Chalk, Steven Jacobs, Erich Leowy,
Eric Markusen, Robert Melson, Linda Melvern, Samantha Power,
Eric Reeves, Rudy Rummel, Ervin Staub, Colin Tatz, Eric Weitz, and
others (Genocide Watch 2010a). And the idea of armed humanitarian intervention is also prominent in public discussions of genocide.
After the Rwandan genocide of 1994, for example, public debate
about what ought to have been done focused almost entirely on the
question of an armed UN intervention during the weeks immediately
before or after 6 April. To pick a more everyday humble: at a panel
discussion on "Genocide and Collective Memory" at the National
Gallery of Canada in November 2000, the bulk of audience questions were directed to Frank Chalk, who argued for the need to have
a UN rapid-intervention force, and ignored the other three panelists
who spoke on other topics. Intervention was then and continues to
be the single most prominent solution to the problem of genocide in
the academic and the public imagination.

In the aftermath of the Rwandan genocide, Lieutenant General
Roméo Dallaire, commander of the United Nations Mission for
Rwanda, claimed that with a well-supported force of only 3,000
soldiers, he could have saved hundreds of thousands of lives (Dallaire
and Beardsley 2003). Events like the Rwandan genocide, where the
United Nations was already involved in the internal affairs of the
country, where a fairly small military effort might have been greatly
effective, where advance warning was given, and where genocide
was unambiguously what happened, suggest that intervention could
be appropriate and effective at least some of the time. A UN rapid-
intervention force of the kind that Genocide Watch advocates could

reduce the impunity of states to commit violence against their own subjects. The military defeat of perpetrator states has brought large-scale genocides to a halt: the Rwandan Patriotic Front's victory in Rwanda, the Indian army's intervention in East Pakistan (Chalk and Jonassohn 1990, 396–7), and of course the Allied victory against the Third Reich. But I would like to suggest that intervention is not an *unproblematic* solution to genocide, that it is not a *sufficient* solution, and that focusing too much on intervention impedes our efforts to understand the social roots of genocide. Conversely, looking critically at intervention raises questions that help to expose these roots and to bridge the theory gap.

What is problematic about intervention? I will not say that the agenda of Genocide Watch and of liberal scholars, who sincerely and earnestly desire to stop genocide as they understand it, is in itself a bad thing. But let's consider again the view of Amnesty International: "U.N. or regional military interventions invariably reflect the interests of politically and militarily powerful states ... If AI supported particular military interventions, prompted by the suffering of the victims, it might, over the longer term, find that it had inadvertently supported a global or regional concentration of power and in the short term had backed action that itself contributed to human rights abuses" (Sané 2000, 7–8). Sané's comment reflects an awareness of the immanence and reflexivity of struggles against state violence and of the contradictions with which these struggles grapple. Immanence and reflexivity mean that, for a system that has achieved globality as the nation-state system has done, there is no outside to the network of power relations that enable state violence. The contradictory quality of the state system means that it generates an opposition of interests between those who control the means of violence and those who do not. Mediating this oppositional relationship is the institution of "legitimacy," which makes certain forms of violence unacceptable at the price of accepting others and vice-versa. Legitimacy is always a contested or at least contestable institution, a battleground between what Antonio Gramsci – speaking about another contradiction, that between capital and labour – called hegemony and counterhegemony (Gramsci 1971, 12). Activists who attempt to use legitimacy to impede state violence run the risk of being co-opted (Powell 1999) and having their own claims work to the benefit of the dominant forces of the system. We can see this in the case of the American-led invasions of Iraq and of Afghanistan, both of which were partly justified on the grounds that overthrowing oppressive regimes would bring freedom to the citizens of these countries. We can also see it at work in the Canadian government's use of the Responsibility to Protect doctrine (ICISS 2001) to justify participating in the overthrow of a democratically elected government in Haiti (Engler and Fenton 2005). Cases like these do not necessarily mean that the push for a UN-based intervention capacity is nothing more than a foil for imperialism. They do suggest that the call for intervention needs to be coupled with a critical analysis of global geopolitics.

Focusing on armed intervention is also insufficient as a general solution to genocide either because it cannot always be used or because, when it can be used, it cannot in itself resolve the social tensions that produce genocidal violence. The former condition applies when genocide is committed by militarily and diplomatically powerful nation-states, or even under the auspices of the United Nations itself. A possible example of this is the program of economic sanctions applied to Iraq between 1991 and 2003 (Jones 2006a, 25–6). In 1999 a UNICEF report held the sanctions responsible for the deaths of 500,000 children (UNICEF 1999). Former assistant secretary general and United Nations humanitarian coordinator for Iraq, Denis Halliday, has claimed that these sanctions amounted to genocide (Edwards 2000); both he and his successor, Hans von Sponeck, resigned from the United Nations in protest against the sanctions regime and the intentional failures of the Oil-for-Food program (von Sponeck 2006). Even where it is possible to use armed intervention to overthrow authoritarian regimes and replace them with liberal-democratic ones, the experience of Afghanistan (see Jones 2004a) and of Iraq again suggest that this is not a sufficient solution. In both countries, formal legal entitlements have not automatically translated into practical improvements in security of person, social entitlement, or other human rights, especially for vulnerable groups like women and religious or ethnic minorities. In Afghanistan violence against women remained endemic for years after the overthrow of the Taliban. Although these forms of persecution and oppression do not amount to genocide, they suggest that the forces that make possible systematic violence against social groups are not confined to the central institutions of the state. Examining these kinds of forces helps us to move beyond thinking that genocide is unique and also helps us to conceive of strategies other than intervention that could prevent genocides from occurring.

BRIDGING THE GAP: CRITICAL THEORIES OF GENOCIDE

Bridging the genocide theory gap means explaining genocide in terms that also explain normal social relations. In this section, I review the work of a number of theorists who, between them, contribute several important ideas that help us to do just that. Zygmunt Bauman and Michel Foucault emphasize, in different ways, the *rationality* of genocide. Bauman explains the Nazi holocaust as the product of bureaucratic and scientific rationalities that understood society as a passive object to be acted upon, a garden that needed tending and weeding. Foucault proposes that biopower – a power-knowledge formation that addresses human groups as biological populations – explains both innocuous projects like public sanitation and evils like modern racism and the Nazi genocides. Jean-Paul Sartre, building on Karl Marx, emphasizes the importance of *class* to understanding genocide; he explains American genocide in Vietnam as the logical extension of imperialism in an age of total war. Patricia Marchak foregrounds the role of the *state* in maintaining systems of social inequality; when these systems are radically threatened, genocide is the state's last-ditch effort to maintain them. And the work of Mary Ann Warren, Adam Jones, and R. Charli Carpenter highlights the *gendered* quality of genocidal violence. Carpenter argues that gender is a modality of genocide, and Jones links gender and sexuality by exploring the heteronormative dimensions of genocidal violence. These various theoretical projects each contribute a piece to the puzzle of a critical sociology of genocide. However, the puzzle remains unfinished. Each of these projects has its own limitations, and taken together they still do not explain in a fundamental way how state power, identity, and violence come together to systematically produce genocide as a recurring feature of the modern world. I contribute this final piece of the puzzle in the next chapter, on civilization and genocide.

Rationality

BUREAUCRACY

In *Modernity and the Holocaust*, Zygmunt Bauman refutes the idea that the Nazi holocaust was a breakdown of social relations, of Western civilization, or of modernity. The "breakdown thesis" is, Bauman says, just another way of maintaining our denial. The deep roots of the Holocaust in the fundamental characteristics of modern society mean that it can "provide an insight into the otherwise unnoticed 'other aspects' of the societal principles enshrined in modern history" and can expose the "hidden possibilities of modern society" (Bauman 1991b, 11–12). His argument has two main aspects. First, he establishes the distinctly modern quality of Nazi anti-Semitism. Bauman distinguishes between "heterophobia" (or hostility toward and fear of difference) in general and racism in particular. Racism is a modern invention, arising from the modern state's unprecedented ability to intervene in ordinary social relations, to establish social control, and hence to engage in social engineering. Jews presented an anomaly to modern dreams of social engineering: capable of assimilating the cultural practices of their Christian neighbours (German Jews were among the most assimilated in Europe) while maintaining a core of distinctiveness, their identity as Jews, they were "the opacity of the world fighting for clarity, the ambiguity of the world lusting for certainty" (Bauman 1991b, 56). Dispelling this uncertainty required fixing and essentializing Jewish difference, pinning it down once and for all. So it was in the modern period that anti-Semitic thinking shifted from locating this difference in cultural and religious practices to locating it in individual bodies. Once the source of Jewish difference was located eternally and ahistorically in the body, the stage was set for genocide: "Racism ... combines strategies of architecture and gardening with that of medicine – in the service of the construction of an artificial social order, through cutting out of the elements of the present reality that neither fit the visualized perfect reality nor can be changed so that they do" (Bauman 1991b, 64). Unlike older forms of heterophobia, racism fixes difference in the body. Scientific rationality made possible the shift, in the anti-Semitic imagination, from Jews as killers of Christ to Jews as a disease in the social body.

The second aspect of Bauman's argument concerns the development of modern bureaucracy, which enabled a dispassionate calculation of the most efficient means to a predetermined end and which separated individuals from the moral consequences of their decisions. The cold, calculating quality of the Holocaust, the remorseless bureaucratic procedure, including meticulous documentation, that pursued the victims from their homes and workplaces to the crematoria, is one of its most distinguishing – and horrifying – aspects. Bauman adds to this the rational conduct of the executioners themselves: "special care was taken to weed out – bar or discharge – all particularly keen, emotionally charged, ideologically over-zealous individuals. We know that individual initiatives were discouraged, and much effort was made to keep the whole task in a businesslike and strictly impersonal framework ... On more than one occasion Himmler expressed deep, and in all likelihood genuine, concern with maintaining the mental sanity and upholding the moral standards of his many subordinates engaged daily in inhuman activity" (Bauman 1991b, 20). This rationality was not incidental but necessary to the Nazi holocaust. The sheer scale of the genocides, the resources they demanded, and the potential logistical complexity of their implementation necessitated the techniques of modern bureaucracy. Killing by "spontaneous" mob violence could not have worked; the Kristallnächte had failed to incite the German people to rise up and kill their neighbour Jews (Bauman 1991b, 89–90). The Final Solution "was neither conceived in a single vision of a mad monster, nor was a considered choice made at the start of the 'problem-solving process' by the ideologically motivated leaders" (Bauman 1991b, 15); rather, it emerged gradually in the course of bureaucratically organized attempts to achieve Adolf Hitler's objective of making the Reich "judenfrei, i.e., clear of Jews."[15] As means shaped ends,[16] "the very idea of the Endlösung was an outcome of the bureaucratic culture" (Bauman 1991b, 15).

---

15 This objective was first pursued through the forced deportation of Germany's Jewish subjects, but as the territory of the Reich expanded to include those spaces to which the Jews had been expelled, this tactic became insufficient. Exportation to Madagascar was seriously considered (Bauman 1991b, 16), but logistical considerations of a wartime context made this unfeasible, so physical extermination was eventually chosen as the most efficient resolution to the problem.

16 This quality comes through more clearly when Bauman discusses the extent to which the genocidal program fell victim to "the tendency of all bureaucracies to lose sight of the original goal and to concentrate on the means instead," even to the extent of undermining the German war effort: "But nowhere was the morbid tendency of substituting the means for the ends more visible than in the uncanny and macabre episode of the murder of Romanian and Hungarian Jews, perpetrated with the Eastern Front just a few miles away, and at an enormous cost to the war effort: priceless rail carriages and engines, troops and administrative resources were diverted from military tasks in order to cleanse distant parts of Europe for the German habitat which was never to be" (Bauman 1991b, 106).

Bureaucratic social structures also produced the moral indifference necessary to mass extermination. Bureaucracy provided the
means of and the impetus for this production; "the space extending
between the idea and its execution was filled wall-to-wall with
bureaucratic action" (Bauman 1991b, 105). This process began
with the expulsion of Jews from ordinary social life by taking away
their citizenship, their employment, and their property and by their
physical separation from their non-Jewish neighbours, their concentration in ghettoes, and their expulsion beyond the boundaries of
Germany (Bauman 1991b, 189). The perpetration of the Shoah involved the construction of a vast social machine in which most of
those responsible for violence were separated from the consequences
of their actions; genocide was accomplished through mundane activities such as filling out reports, procuring supplies, planning rail
shipments, modifying and repairing vehicles, and so on, all of which
were performed by functional specialists who could concentrate
only on the task at hand and who would be disciplined or replaced
if they refused (Bauman 1991b, 98). Moral considerations were
excised from the performance of technical tasks; moral responsibility gave way to technical responsibility; ordinary individuals
participated willingly and even enthusiastically in atrocity. The end
result of one's daily labour disappeared – as did its victims, not only
through the social distance that separated a clerk in Berlin from
an inmate at Birkenau but also through the dehumanization that
ensued from this inmate's being inscribed into the quality-free technical language of bureaucratic discourses (Bauman 1991b, 102). This
bureaucratic negation of moral affect extended to the choice of means
of execution and was necessary for killing to take place on an exterminatory scale: "The Germans employed the phrase Seelenbelastung
('burdening of the soul') with reference to machine-gun fire ...
directed at men, women, and children in prepared ditches. After all,
the men that were firing these weapons were themselves fathers.
How could they do this day after day? It was then that the techni-
cians developed a gas van designed to lessen the suffering of the
perpetrator" (Hilberg 1980, 90–1). Even in the death camps, the
technology of gas chambers facilitated the dissociation of moral responsibility from the performance of technical tasks. In his famous
experiments, the psychologist Stanley Milgram (1974) showed that
ordinary Americans could be induced to apply electric shocks at
seemingly painful and even life-threatening levels if they were asked

to do so by a technical expert in a situation framed as a scientific experiment. They did so even when face-to-face with their victims' suffering. In Auschwitz, and throughout the Reich, the same technical authority and even greater social distance allowed ordinary people to be enrolled in atrocity.

Bauman's account explains genocide as the product of social relations that are present in ordinary society and that come together in an unusual way to make genocide possible: "When the modernist dream is embraced by an absolute power able to monopolize modern vehicles of rational action, and when that power attains freedom from effective social control, genocide follows. A modern genocide – like the Holocaust" (Bauman 1991b, 93–4). The chilling implication of Bauman's analysis is that the mechanisms that made the Nazi holocaust possible, mechanisms through which instrumental rationality silenced the voice of moral responsibility, are still embedded components of contemporary modernity. If anything, their potential virulence is greater; the progress from the firebombing of Dresden to the high-altitude carpet-bombing practised during the Vietnam War to the cruise missiles and laser-guided cluster bombs of the second Gulf War has dramatized the ongoing refinement of social technologies that produce social distance, substitute technical for moral responsibility, and segregate and separate populations. All of these these effects of rationalization are "further strengthened by the principle of sovereignty of state powers usurping supreme ethical authority on behalf of the societies they rule" (Bauman 1991b, 199). Bauman's analysis connects genocide to features of ordinary social life in contemporary societies. This makes it easier to explain genocide and also suggests what can be done to prevent genocides before they occur. Constructing a "non-genocidal society," to use Leo Kuper's phrase (Kuper 1981, 186), requires that we reign in those social practices that separate technical from moral responsibility and that we work to overcome social distances that make violence possible.

Nevertheless, Bauman's sociology of genocide suffers from three major limitations. First, it is too narrow in its explanatory focus. As Mahmood Mamdani points out, "Unlike the Nazi Holocaust, the Rwandan genocide was not carried out from a distance, in remote concentration camps beyond national borders, in industrial killing camps operated by agents who often did no more than drop Zyklon B crystals into gas chambers from above. The Rwandan genocide was executed with the slash of machetes rather than the drop of crystals, with all the gruesome detail of a street murder rather than the bureaucratic efficiency of a mass extermination" (Mamdani 2001, 5). And yet the Rwandan genocide killed people at three times the rate of the Nazi holocaust (Gourevitch 1998, 3). The bureaucratic production of social distance can explain only some genocides. The same is true of bureaucratic impersonality. Whereas the Nazis took care to weed out "all particularly keen, emotionally charged, ideologically over-zealous individuals" from the killing process, this is not true for the 1992 Bosnian genocide of the Serbs: "At Omarska such men would have been cherished; the out-and-out passion with which a guard administered beatings and devised tortures could greatly bolster his prestige. Acts of flamboyant violence, publicly performed, made of some men celebrities of sadism" (Danner 1997). Second, Bauman's emphasis on the modernity of the Holocaust is Eurocentric. He ignores altogether the precedent for genocide set by colonial genocides from Christopher Columbus's encounter with the Americas to German South Africa. It is also Eurocentric because it asserts a universal moral framework from which "various moral systems can be compared and differentially evaluated" (Bauman 1991b, 172), a moral framework that not co-incidentally happens to be Bauman's own. Third, Bauman explains genocide sociologically only to essentialize morality: "Moral duty has to count on its pristine source: the essential human responsibility for the Other" (Bauman 1991b, 199). Bauman claims that "the Holocaust could be accomplished only on the condition of neutralizing the impact of primeval moral drives" (Bauman 1991b, 188) and claims that "it is therefore the incidence of immoral, *rather than moral*, behaviour which calls for the investigation of the social administration of intersubjectivity" (Bauman 1991b, 183, emphasis added). As I have already argued in chapter 1, we need to understand how both moral and immoral behaviour are socially produced, and we need to face up to the fact that genocide was institutionalized as a moral obligation for loyal subjects of the Third Reich. Bauman's sociology of genocide is partial, asymmetrical – a sociology of moral error rather than a sociology of morality per se.

BIOPOWER

Michel Foucault provides an account of the rationality of genocide that complements and extends Bauman's insights. In this theory, genocide is an expression of *biopower*, which is a form or an outgrowth of disciplinary power. Biopower is the art of governing populations; it is concerned with "the problems of birthrate, longevity, public health, housing, and migration" (Foucault 1990, 140). It relies on many of the same technologies that characterize disciplinary power, such as medicine, sanitation, mental health, surveillance, spatial distributions, and so on. It also operates through some of the same forms of subjectivity, especially sexuality. But whereas disciplinary power is concerned to individualize the mass of subjects, biopower carries discipline through its inversion, treating individuals as "a global mass that is affected by overall processes characteristic of birth, deaths, production, illnesses, and so on"; it is "not individualizing but, if you like, massifying, that is directed not at man-as-body but at man-as-species" (Foucault 1990, 242–3). Through this use of disciplinary power *en masse* to constrain the harmful and costly effects of disease, madness, criminality, and so on, the state acquires the power to produce health, produce sanity, produce safety. A shift occurs in the nature of the sovereign's right over the life and death of subjects: whereas up to the time of the absolutist kings in France this right had been only a negative right, the right to kill, symbolized by the sword (Foucault 1990, 136), after that time the state had also the power to give life, "the right to make live and let die" (Foucault 2003, 241).

This new right of life and death connects with what Foucault calls "reason of state" and with a transition in the nature of sovereignty: "the aim of this new art of governing is precisely not to reinforce the power of the prince. Its aim is to reinforce the state itself" (Foucault 1988, 150). This shift of attention from the prince to the state involved a reification of the state, an assumption that "the state is something that exists per se," "a kind of natural object" (Foucault 2003, 151). In combination with the massifying effects of biopower, this means that governments no longer have to worry about individuals,

> or government has to worry about them only insofar as they are somehow relevant for the reinforcement of the state's strength: what they do, their life, their death, their activity, their individual behavior, their work, and so on ... From the state's point of view, the individual exists insofar as what he does is able to introduce even a minimal change in the strength of the state, either in a positive or in a negative direction ... And sometimes what he has

to do for the state is to live, to work, to produce, to consume;
and sometimes what he has to do is die. (Foucault 2003, 152)

The individual may have to die in war, which is no longer waged in
the name of the sovereign but is waged "on behalf of the existence of
everyone," or more precisely on behalf of the organization of the
forces of life and death that biopower produces. This is the case because the modern state, whether capitalist or socialist, dictatorial or
liberal-democratic, has, through the operation of biopower, become
fundamentally informed by and dependent on racism. This racism
does not simply take "the traditional form of mutual contempt or
hatred between races"; nor is it simply an ideological operation
through which hostility toward a class or the state is diverted, trans-
ferred onto a "mythical adversary" (Foucault 2003, 258). Rather, it
is primarily a way of dividing populations, of introducing breaks
within "the biological continuum addressed by biopower" (Foucault
2003, 255). It is secondarily a way of justifying the state's continued
exercise of the traditional right of princes to take life, both by
its own direct action and by requiring its subjects to sacrifice their
own lives in its service. "Once the state functions in the biopower
mode, racism alone can justify the murderous function of the state"
(Foucault 2003, 256).

Foucault identifies the origins of this historically novel form of
racism with colonization and colonizing genocide. In the mode
of biopower, only the quasi-Darwinian notions of racial hierarchy,
of more and less fit races, and of the need to weed out the less fit can
justify the murder of populations, the destruction of civilizations
(Foucault 2003, 257). But this same racism can also be applied to
criminality, to mental illness, to class antagonisms, and so on.
Socialist states on the Soviet model, which took over wholesale "the
idea that the essential function of society or the State ... is to take
control of life, to manage it, to compensate for its aleatory nature,"
reproduced this racism not on ethnic terms but in their orientation
to the ongoing "internal" dimension of the class struggle, in their
way of dealing with "the mentally ill, criminals, political adversaries,
and so on" (Foucault 2003, 261–2). The virulence of genocide in the
twentieth century resulted not from the utopian ideologies of totalitarian regimes but from the intrinsic momentum of the state's cease-
less taking-into-itself of the forces of the life and death of human
populations: "If genocide is indeed the dream of modern powers,

this is not because of a recent return of the ancient right to kill; it is because power is situated and exercised at the level of life, the species, the race, and the large-scale phenomena of population" (Foucault 1990, 137). Nor is genocide the end point or natural limit at which biopower exhausts itself in its own profusion. The exist-ence of nuclear weaponry – and, one might add, other weapons of mass destruction – creates a problem of altogether unprecedented scale: "as the technology of wars has caused them to tend increas-ingly toward all-out destruction, the decision that initiates them and the one that terminates them are in fact increasingly informed by the naked question of survival. The atomic situation is now at the end point of this process: the power to expose a whole population to death is the underside of the power to guarantee an individual's con-tinued existence" (Foucault 1990, 137). To the three forms in which violence can be codified – politics, war, and genocide – a fourth must be added: omnicide (Goodman and Hoff 1990). One might say that domination, amplified beyond all measure by the proliferating tech-nologies of destruction and given impetus by the political rationality of biopower, reaches its culmination only in the negation of human life itself.

Foucault brings out more clearly than Bauman the *practical* aspect of forms of rationality. Read on his own, Bauman seems to treat bureaucratic and scientific rationalities as ways of thinking that legitimate certain practices, but read through Foucault, these ration-alities emerge as ways of acting concretely. Rationalities structure the efficient application of force to bodies, producing a knowledge that is inseparable from power and that enables new intensities of power. But Foucault also provides only a piece of the puzzle. His theory is limited in three ways. First, Foucault's historical framework is too narrow to explain even contemporary genocide. Genocide against Indigenous peoples in the Americas, which is still ongoing, precedes the emergence of biopower or reason of state by several centuries.[17] Like Bauman, Foucault overemphasizes the modernity of genocide. Second, by explaining genocide in terms of biologically conceived racism and the physical liquidation of racialized popula-tions, Foucault equates genocide with physical extermination. This is a mistake, as I have argued in chapter 2; we should understand

---

17 Foucault does acknowledge the contribution of colonialism to the emer-gence of biopower (Foucault 2003, 257), but this only reinforces my point.

genocide as involving a broader logic of identity that does not always reduce to biological populations. Third, Foucault's historical analyses are focused on the operation of expert knowledges rather than on the formation of state power as such; he sees state power from the perspective of his concern with knowledge and with subjectivity. We need to analyze force relations in themselves, which I do in chapter 4.

Class and Imperialism

The work of Bauman and Foucault shows us how we can begin to understand genocide as an extraordinary product of social relations that in themselves are quite ordinary. In addition, whereas I have argued in chapter 1 that genocide can be institutionalized as moral, Bauman and Foucault also show us that it can be institutionalized as rational. When we dispense with unprovable essentializing claims and look critically at morality and rationality as social practices immanent to the natural world, we find that neither morality nor rationality is a safe protection against genocide. We begin to understand how individuals can participate in genocide without any sense of wrongness to impede their actions. But we still have not begun to explain in an adequate way what kinds of social forces are likely to make genocide moral and rational in a given figurational context. What drives a society toward genocide? Karl Marx's class analysis and Jean-Paul Sartre's application of it to American genocide in Vietnam give us the next piece of our puzzle.

I have argued in chapter 1 that Marx's social theory is one of contradiction rather than conflict. The contradiction generated by the relation of alienated labour generates the classes of workers and capitalists (and other classes in between), with their necessary and irreconcilable conflict of interests. The very means by which workers seek to produce their own wealth and freedom produce the social forces that impoverish and enslave them. But this relationship is not static; it is fundamentally a dynamic, process-generating relation, a dialectic, in which the production of contradiction generates new forms of social life until the contradiction exhausts all its possible forms and breaks down, opening the possibility of a new social relation entirely – ultimately, for Marx, a society without class contradictions and hence a genuinely free society. Marx thought that class relations were fundamental to all other social relations and that the class contradiction generated all other contradictions. I think there is a difference between accepting that class contradictions are *omnipresent* (i.e., that they inform and condition all other social relations) and accepting that they are *foundational*. Treating class relations as omnipresent allows us to ask whose *interest* genocide serves. For if genocide is functional, this does not mean that it benefits all members of its perpetrator group, either equally or at all.

In *The 18th Brumaire of Louis Bonaparte*, Marx provides a kind of general template for the process by which, in a modern democratic state, power devolves into the hands of a dictator as political violence becomes widespread. Marx shows how the collapse of French democracy can be understood as a historically contingent inflection of class struggle. Various factions of the bourgeoisie and petit-bourgeoisie, facing the erosion of their political legitimacy and the demand for more genuine political enfranchisement by the working masses, decided that it was in their own interests to restrict political liberties progressively and to curtail the authority of the legislative branches of government in favour of the executive. Doing this, they painted themselves into a corner where even the narrowest forms of republicanism gave way to the authority concentrated in the president. Marx's analysis shows brilliantly how an elite class may undermine the conditions of its own political rule, with political terror as the outcome:

> Society is saved just as often as the circle of rulers contracts, as a more exclusive interest is maintained against a wider one. Every demand of the simplest bourgeois financial reform, of the most ordinary liberalism, of the most formal republicanism, of the most shallow democracy, is simultaneously castigated as an "attempt on society" and stigmatized as "socialism." And finally the high priests of "religion and order" themselves are driven with kicks from their Pythian tripods, hauled out of their beds in the darkness of night, put in prison-vans, thrown into dungeons or sent into exile; their temple is razed to the ground, their mouths are sealed, their pens broken, their law torn to pieces in the name of religion, of property, of the family, of order. (Marx 1979, III-12)

Marx could have been writing as easily of Idi Amin's Uganda, of Guatemala under the generals, or of Nazi Germany as of France under Louis Napoleon Bonaparte. Although he was not writing about a genocide per se, the parallels with genocidal events are striking. These include: the state's infiltration of the economy (Marx 1979, 139), the important role of militia recruited from the underclasses (Marx 1979, 148–51), the decision of the "finance aristocracy" to view the dictator as the "guardian of order" (Marx 1979, 170–1), the special relationship between peasants and the army (Marx 1979, 192), and so on. If not quite a general template for the analysis of genocide, *The 18th Brumaire* is at least an extraordinarily fertile launching-point. And in fact, the kind of detailed, historically specific class analysis that Marx performs in *The 18th Brumaire* is employed to great effect by some genocide scholars today, notably in the literature on the Rwandan genocide (e.g., Prunier 1995; Uvin 1998; Melvern 2000; Mamdani 2001; Jeffremovas 2002).

For a Marxian explanation of a particular genocide, we can turn to Arlette El-Kaïm-Sartre and Jean-Paul Sartre's essay *On Genocide*. In 1966, at the initiation of Bertrand Russell, a collection of "personalities of various political convictions from different countries" (El-Kaïm-Sartre and Sartre 1968, 3) met in London to form an International War Crimes Tribunal. Without any formal political authority, this tribunal attempted to mobilize the moral authority of its members, and of its claim to be an impartial body operating from within civil society, in order to examine whether the United States was guilty of violations of international law in its conduct of the war in Vietnam. The tribunal found the United States guilty of several war crimes; this finding included a unanimous decision that it had committed genocide under the terms of the UNCG (El-Kaïm-Sartre and Sartre 1968, 50–3).[18] Jean-Paul Sartre, who had written the text of the decision, further analyzes the relation between genocide and imperialism in *On Genocide*, which claims that genocide is inherent to the totalizing mode of war that has been made necessary by the logic of bourgeois nationalism since the beginning of the twentieth century (El-Kaïm-Sartre and Sartre 1968, 61). The inherently genocidal tendencies of this mode of war are held in check only by locally contingent infrastructural conditions: within Europe, by the deterrent potential each nation-state possesses, that of "the power of

---

18 The United States had not ratified the UNCG at this time; see Churchill (1998, 363ff).

applying the law of 'an eye for an eye'" (El-Kaïm-Sartre and Sartre 1968, 62); outside Europe, by the value of Indigenous populations as "an almost unpaid labour force" (El-Kaïm-Sartre and Sartre 1968, 64) or, occasionally and temporarily, by logistical obstacles to its implementation (El-Kaïm-Sartre and Sartre 1968, 77). Therefore, when colonial or neocolonial subjects attempt to refuse their labour to imperialist capital – for example, by socialist revolution – they are threatened with a choice between extermination and capitulation (El-Kaïm-Sartre and Sartre 1968, 75). The war in Vietnam involved "the greatest power on earth against a poor peasant people. Those who fight it are *living out* the only possible relationship between an overindustrialized country and an underdeveloped country, that is to say, a genocidal relationship implemented through racism – the only relationship, short of picking up and pulling out" (El-Kaïm-Sartre and Sartre 1968, 82, original emphasis). Imperialist capitalism is inherently prone to genocide, and on a global scale: "little by little the whole human race is being subjected to this genocidal blackmail piled on top of atomic blackmail, that is, to absolute, total war" (El-Kaïm-Sartre and Sartre 1968, 84).

In a Marxian analysis, genocide is one of the many tactics that the dominant class in society may use to maintain its privileged position. When faced with a choice between losing its privilege and implementing genocide, the dominant class will choose genocide unless some other contingent factors make this impossible or undesirable. We could say that genocide results when a perpetrator has both an *interest* in its effects and the *impunity* to commit it. Class analysis explains the incentive to commit genocide: the achievement of particular interests of the dominant class. Through *praxis* (world-creating activity), alienated relations of production inform all other social relations, and so too does the contradiction generated by the production relation. Class interest is more than a set of ideas or motivations in people's minds: it is an exigent figurational tendency built into ongoing production and reproduction of society. Morality and rationality, like other social institutions, are imbued with the contradictions of class and shaped by the interests that class generates. The quasi-objective moralization and rationalization of genocide expresses the quasi-objective interest in genocide that, in turn, is produced by the everyday/everynight relations of production, consumption, and exchange in which we all participate.

Marxian theory contributes an indispensable piece to our puzzle, but taken by itself it is not a *sufficient* basis for explaining genocide, for three reasons. First, Marx does not theorize any relation of difference or process of differentiation as fundamental, except that of alienated labour and class domination. Political contradictions within the nondominant production class disappear from view. We can see this in El-Kaïm-Sartre and Sartre's tendency to homogenize what they call "the Vietnamese people," to gloss over the distinctions between political and military leaders, rank-and-file combatants, peasants not directly involved in military activity, and so on. As feminist, antiracist, and Indigenous rights activists, among others, have already observed, historical capitalism has not eliminated gender, the nation, religion, race, and the other forms of identity-difference that cross class lines.

Second, the omnipresence of class contradictions does not imply class determinism. Marx argues that class relations are foundational because material production is an inescapable precondition of human existence: people must eat and drink before they can philosophize. But I can think of at least two other kinds of practice that set inescapable limits on human existence, one negatively and the other positively. *Relations of force* include the capacity to destroy the material infrastructure of life and to take life directly. *Relations of reproduction* include what in patriarchal societies is considered women's work: the bearing and raising of children, keeping house, washing clothes, preparing food, and the "logistics of bodily existence" that Dorothy Smith refers to (Smith 1990, 18). These and other material social relations generate their own contradictions, which do not reduce to the contradictions of production relations.[19]

And third, although the struggle to supercede capitalism and the struggle to end genocide may be inseparably connected, this connection is a complex one; the former struggle does not simply determine the latter. For one thing, genocide can be used effectively as a counterrevolutionary technique. Friedrich Engels naively writes that

19 As Foucault (1980, 88, 101) points out, the interests of the capitalist class can often be compatible with two or more antithetical rationalities for the use of power. As Stephen Resnick and Richard Wolff (1995) observe of the Soviet Union, and Charles Tilly (1985) of late medieval Europe, control of the means of violence can serve as a precondition for, rather than a consequence of, control of the means of production. And as Chalk and Jonassohn (1990, 417–20) point out, genocide can be economically destructive for its perpetrators.

"to shoot out of the world a party which numbers in the millions – all the magazine rifles of Europe and America are not enough for this" (Engels 1988b, 73). But history has proven otherwise – most conspicuously in 1965 in Indonesia, where the Indonesian state with the support of the United States (Keefer 2001) eliminated the Indonesian Communist Party through the slaughter of 500,000 people and the arrest of another 500,000 (Chalk and Jonassohn 1990, 381). And of course, nationalist movements wrapped in the mantle of communist revolution have been notoriously willing to practise genocide – in the Soviet Union, in the People's Republic of China, in Cambodia under the Khmer Rouge, and so on. Solving the problem of genocide requires that we focus on the quasi-objective dynamics of force relations in themselves, without reducing them to production relations.

The State and Inequality

Within sociology, the tradition of neo-Weberian, or *analytic conflict,* theory comes closest to focusing on force relations in themselves. I say "comes closest" because conflict theorists tend to practise a methodological individualism that sees the social world as being made up of individuals and groups rather than relationships. Despite this limitation, conflict theory adds to a critical sociology of genocide because it considers force relations focally and because it abstains from reducing group differences to any one specific relation. However, its strength is connected to its weakness; conflict theorists do not explain the deep connections between identity-difference and the state's monopoly of military force, as we shall see.

"The attempt to locate 'bad' practices in bad states is as flawed an approach as is the attempt to locate 'good' practices in good states," says Irving Louis Horowitz (2002, 297), who looks at practices of repression and tolerance toward dissent and deviance and correlates them with the practice of genocide. And yet Horowitz agrees with Rudy Rummel that "anti-democratic states are the unique carrier of the poison of genocide [and] conversely, that democratic states are the societies that embody anti-genocide premises and principles" (Horowitz 2002, 399). Rummel, who analyzes the sheer number of noncombatant individuals killed by their own governments, reaches a similar conclusion: "the way to end war and virtually eliminate democide appears to be through restricting and checking Power, i.e., through *fostering democratic freedom*" (Rummel 1994, 27). Strictly speaking, they are both mistaken. Their preoccupation with numbers of people killed leads them to underestimate the significance of colonial genocides (Rummel 1994, 57–60; Horowitz 2002, 154–5), and they ignore altogether how Western liberal democracies provide support and assistance to repressive regimes engaged in genocide or democide (Alvarez 2001, 45–6). But they do raise an important tautological point: by definition, subjects with meaningful democratic enfranchisement, in practice and not just formally, cannot easily be made victims of genocide. That is, genocide involves questions of the *balance of power between states and subjects.*

Leo Kuper points out that the capacity to commit genocide is a fundamental feature of state sovereignty. Writing in outrage over the persistent failures of the United Nations to act effectively against genocide, even diplomatically, he claims that "the sovereign territorial state claims, as an integral part of its sovereignty, the right to commit genocide, or engage in genocidal massacres, against peoples under its rule, and ... the United Nations, for all practical purposes, defends this right" (Kuper 1981, 161).[20] Kuper connects the state's sovereign right to commit genocide with structures of inequality and identity in the society that the state wishes to govern. He specifically claims that genocides are a product of what he calls "plural societies," which are characterized by "persistent and pervasive cleavages" between identifiable social groups, particularly by cleavages that are also the fault lines of "superimposed" social inequalities (Kuper 1981, 57–8). Plural societies set the structural preconditions for genocide, which is then triggered by more contingent factors. Kuper's thesis tends toward an oversimplification: the idea that genocide is the product of social difference as such. But he succeeds in reversing the usual question and asks, given the existence of difference, what *prevents* genocide. His answer is complex; nongenocidal societies may be ethnically homogeneous, may guarantee effective collective or individual rights of their subjects, or may have established settled and relatively uncontested divisions among the groups (Kuper 1981, 187–9). Kuper also points to the question of impunity by positing four factors that can mitigate against it: the ability of potential victims to conduct reprisals against their tormentors, the interdependence of the differing groups within an

---

20 For an updated argument accusing the United Nations of complicity in an international regime that enables genocide, see Lebor (2006). For an early account of the connection between international diplomacy, international finance, and genocidal impunity, see Simpson (1993).

advanced industrial economy, the involvement of the parties in inter-national economic or political networks that inhibit the extreme polarization of identity within the nation, and the existence of strong centrist movements that seek reconciliation between the opposed parties (Kuper 1981, 204–5). Kuper takes the existence of "groups" for granted, without inquiring into the forces that generate relations of identity-difference. But he does point out the *radical* link between state sovereignty and genocide, draw connections between *sovereign power and social inequality*, and cast the problem of genocide in terms of *impunity*.

Robert Melson, like Zygmunt Bauman, links genocide to the uto-pian aspirations of states engaged in social reconstruction, but he associates this connection more explicitly with revolution and war. "Revolutionary governments that come to power after the break-down of old regimes need to create a new order that will support the revolutionary state" (Melson 1992, xvi). To accomplish this, such regimes construct a category of mutual identification (e.g., the people, the nation, the class, or some such) that can be opposed to an Other – the enemies of the people or the revolution. The outbreak of war increases the likelihood of genocide because these enemies can be identified with the external foes of the regime. Like Horowitz and Rummel, Melson ignores the perpetration of genocide by estab-lished, nonrevolutionary governments, such as the United States' ac-tions in Vietnam. But he does show one way that genocide can be *productive*: it can be used to produce a collective solidarity that re-inforces the political power of an otherwise vulnerable regime.

Like Bauman, Michael Mann emphasizes that genocide – or, in his case, ethnic cleansing – is a thoroughly modern phenomenon, not to be understood as a breakdown of society but as the "dark side of democracy." The movement toward ethnic cleansing begins when ethnic citizenship displaces civic citizenship as the basis of social solidarity and specifically when "ethnicity trumps class as the main form of social stratification" (Mann 2005, 6), channelling class hostilities into an exclusionary ethnic nationalism. Mann describes the series of steps that leads toward ethnic cleansing: the formation of large movements representing two ethnic groups claiming the ancientness of both their identities and their grievances, the initia-tion of violence by either the weaker or the stronger party, and the subsumption of the state into one or more of the ethnic factions. Mann claims that ethnic cleansing is rarely the initial intention of the movements that end up perpetuating it but emerges as a "Plan C"

after other strategies for achieving ethnic dominance fail. He distinguishes between three levels of perpetrators: party elites, paramilitary-
forming militants, and core constituencies of supporters. And he
observes that "ordinary people" are brought by "normal" social
structures into committing murderous ethnic cleansing. We need a
"sociology of power" to explain how this happens, not a "special
psychology of perpetrators as disturbed or psychotic people" (Mann
2005, 12). Mann's own complex and nuanced theory of the socio-
genesis of ethnic cleansing in formally democratic states makes a
substantial contribution to this sociology of power. However, his
model does not address forms of genocide other than ethnic cleansing or the relations between colonialism and genocide on a world
scale. Focusing on genocide as a particular outcome of dynamics
mainly located within individual states, his otherwise formidable
contribution drifts toward the "breakdown hypothesis" that I criticize in chapter 4.

Some historians have begun the massive task of tracing, on a
global scale, the connection between Western imperialism and
genocide without recourse to a specifically Marxian mode of analysis. Ben Kiernan provides a mostly descriptive account of imperialist and colonial genocides from 1492 onward. He offers little
theorization of the systemic roots of genocides, beyond a five-part
typology of their ideological features (Kiernan 2007, 21–33) and
beyond postulating racism, expansionism, agrarianism, and the attempt to resurrect a lost antiquity as the four principle "obsessions"
motivating perpetrators of genocide (Kiernan 2007, 38). Mark
Levene stakes a more theoretically ambitious claim, asserting that
the process of formation of the international system of sovereign
states provides "both the primary well-springs and continuing
motor to genocide":

At the outset it was the avant-garde modernizing states, usually
in their colonial or imperial guise, who were its prime exponents.
Later it was primarily their foremost global challengers, later on
still, all manner of post-colonial polities as the system itself became truly globalized. Genocide as such is a systemic dysfunction
and cannot be simply or solely dismissed as the aberrant or devi-
ant behaviour of rogue, revolutionary or "totalitarian" egimes or
for that matter ones with particular, one might say peculiar, types
of political culture or social and ethnic configuration. On the

contrary, the very fact that genocide is the by-product of such states' drives towards development and/or empowerment only makes proper sense within the context of the system's fundamental disequilibrium as determined by a hegemonic leadership which either abets, ignores or anathematizes breaches of its rulebook. (Levene 2005a, 205)

Like Kiernan's account, however, Levene's is more descriptive than explanatory. For instance, Levene notes the paradoxical relationship between instrumental interests and emotive group identifications as forces motivating genocide, but he cannot resolve this paradox by commensurating these two types of forces. Doing so requires a social theory that analyzes the emergence of identity and of interests from the play of force relations.

Patricia Marchak's *Reigns of Terror* offers perhaps the most supple and generalizable account of genocide among conflict theorists. Marchak builds on the conventional Weberian definition of the state – as the institution with a monopoly of the legitimate use of force (Weber 1978, 56) – and adds a twist: "The state is an organization with a monopoly of the legitimate use of armed force in a given territory and with the mandate to reproduce a system that always involves relationships of dominance and subordination. States that cannot reproduce the system have a high probability of committing human rights crimes" (Marchak 2003, 131). In her account, it is struggles for power, rather than racist ideologies or authoritarian cultures, that directly produce the conditions under which crimes against humanity take place. Struggles over control of state power are bound up with, but do not reduce to, class struggles in the Marxian sense; conflicts between elite groups and dominated populations are complicated by the power strategies of nondominant elites within the state, by the semi-autonomous role of national militaries, and by powerful political and economic interests originating outside the state. Culture and ideology facilitate popular involvement in crimes against humanity by producing moral codes that authorize or even obligate individuals to commit violence against other human beings; bureaucratic and scientific rationalities do the same by producing social distance between killers and victims. However, the primary impetus behind crimes against humanity is generated by something general to the modern state as such, namely the intimate involvement between state institutions and the power strategies of social elites: "State-sponsored crimes against humanity occur when those in control of state institutions are unable to sustain the existing system, with its embedded inequalities" (Marchak 2003, 274). Marchak also discusses some of the problems associated with intervention as a solution to genocide and human rights abuses, situating the politics of intervention within structures of global inequality (Marchak 2003, 148–52), and she is pessimistic about the potential for armed humanitarian intervention organized by bystander states, under UN auspices or otherwise, to provide an effective solution to genocidal violence. The solutions she recommends concentrate more on measures to reduce social inequalities within and between nations than on global policing.

Marchak's work goes a long way toward providing a general theory of why genocides happen. One specific disadvantage of her account is that it focuses on breakdown situations; like Melson, she doesn't account for genocide committed by imperial powers in the process of their expansion. But she is on the right track – it's not much of a stretch to go from thinking of genocide as a tactic for maintaining a faltering system of inequality to thinking of it as also a tactic for constructing new systems of inequality. A more general limitation of her thinking, and of the work of all of the authors I've discussed in this section, is twofold. First, she tends to treat "social groups" as though they just exist in society, in and of themselves, without accounting either for the relational or for the processual character of their existence. I have argued that groups exist as the manifestation of relations of identity-difference, relations that are generated historically, such that the formation of social groups and the formation of distributions of power are differing aspects of a common process. This points to the second limitation of Marchak's work, and of analytic conflict theory in general: it treats "social identity," "power," "wealth," "ideology," "culture," and so on as though these were all things that exist independently of one another and that come together in complex ways to produce genocide – much as rainfall and anthropogenic deforestation exist independently of one another and come together to produce soil erosion. The advantage of Marxian sociology is its account of how relations of identity-difference are generated by relations of inequality and in a sense are the same thing. If this kind of insight could be joined to the focal attention that conflict theory gives to the state and force relations, and also joined to its refusal to treat one identity as the foundation of all others, we would have taken a large step forward in our formulation of a critical sociology of genocide.

Gender and Heteronormativity

In my discussion of Marxian theory, I have drawn a distinction between a relation's being foundational and a relation's being omnipresent. If a social relation is omnipresent throughout a figuration, and thus informs all other relations in the figuration, it will always be possible to analyze any event in the figuration as an expression of this relation – that is, to produce a *radical* theory of this relation for the figuration. If there is more than one type of relation that is operative throughout the entire figuration, then more than one radical theory will be possible.[21] The work of feminist theorists such as Shulamith Firestone (1970) and Catharine MacKinnon (1989), who articulate a radical theory of sexual inequality, suggests that sex-gender, like class, can be understood as an omnipresent relation of identity-difference, at least in contemporary societies. This means that genocide will always have gendered dynamics. Genocide scholars have only recently begun to investigate these dynamics, but they have already produced some important insights.

In her 1985 book *Gendercide: The Implications of Sex Selection*, Mary Anne Warren coined the term "gendercide" to refer to "the deliberate extermination of persons of a particular sex (or gender)"; the term "calls attention to the fact that gender roles have often had lethal consequences, and that these are in important respects analogous to the lethal consequences of racial, religious, and class prejudice" (Warren 1985, 22). Although Warren's concept of gendercide is designed to supplant concepts like "gynocide" and "femicide," which designate gender-specific killing of female persons only, her discussion of gendercide focuses on violence against women: female

---

21 This is one manifestation of the epistemological challenges posed by *complex systems*, which figurations inevitably are. Paul Cilliers expresses this challenge in these terms: "We cannot have complete knowledge of complex systems; we can only have knowledge in terms of a certain framework. There is no stepping outside of complexity (we are finite beings), thus there is no framework for frameworks. We *choose* our frameworks. This choice need not be arbitrary in any way, but it does mean that the status of the framework (and the framework itself) will have to be continually revised. Our knowledge of complex systems is always provisional" (Cilliers 2005, 258–9).

infanticide, witch-killing, suttee, female genital mutilation, denial of women's reproductive freedom, and misogynist ideologies. In an article first published in 2000, and republished in the 2004 collection *Gendercide and Genocide*,[22] Adam Jones modifies Warren's concept to mean "gender-selective mass killing" (Jones 2004b, 2). Jones rounds out Warren's discussion with an examination of how genocide has affected both men and women. In particular, Jones foregrounds violence against noncombatant men, observing that "the mass killing of males, particularly of 'battle-age' men, has roots deep in the history of conflict between human communities" (Jones 2004b, 3). He proposes three reasons for this: to exterminate potential combatants, to decapitate social elites (who happen to be men), and to spare the lives of women for the purpose of enslavement. Jones notes that men are disproportionately likely to be killed by mass murder, become prisoners of war, or be pressed into corvée labour (Jones 2004b, 14–15). He also discusses gendercide against women in the form of combined rape and murder on a mass scale (including the use of rape to deliberately infect women with HIV), female infanticide, and witch-hunts (Jones 2004b, 11–13).

As R. Charli Carpenter observes, however, Jones tends to conflate sex with gender, such that his conception of gendercide equates with sex-selective killing (Carpenter 2004, 231). This is a fraught issue in social theory. Social scientists often distinguish between sex, understood as the biological fact of being male or female, and gender, understood as the social norms and roles that particular cultures attach to male and female persons. Femininity and masculinity are not the same as maleness and femaleness.[23] On this basis, Carpenter

---

22 This collection contains many interesting articles that I do not have space to cover here and forms a good entry point into the efforts of genocide scholars to engage with gender.

23 The full picture is more complex still. The social lives of full and partial hermaphrodites (Fausto-Sterling 1993; Kessler 1990) and of transgendered persons (Star 1991, 45; Garfinkel 1967) point to the role of gender performance, social classification, and technological intervention in maintaining a strict dichotomy between the male and female sexes. Monique Wittig (1992, 9–20) and Judith Butler (1990) argue that sex as well as gender should be understood as social, rather than nonsocial and natural, categories. For this reason, I follow the practice of some other feminist authors in modifying Gayle Rubin's 1975 term "sex/gender system" (see Rubin 1997) with a hyphen, to speak of sex-gender relations.

makes six critical points (Carpenter 2004, 243–7). First, not all gendered outcomes result from intentional sex selection. Gendered outcomes may result from pre-existing gender structures; for example, that the massacre of POWs mostly victimizes men results from the pre-existing fact that it is men who are soldiers and that it is soldiers who become POWs. Second, patterns of abuse may be sex-distinctive even when abuse leads to death in equal numbers for both sexes: for example, women may be systematically raped before death, whereas men may be sexually mutilated. Third, even the same treatment – rape, for example – is experienced differently by men and women because of its gendered meanings. Fourth, some gendered practices have the same effects on both sexes: for example, both male and female children born to victims of forced maternity share the same stigma. Fifth, not all sex-selective outcomes are gendered: only women can be made victims of forced maternity, not because of social gender but because of their biological sex. Finally, not all gendered aspects of genocide are mass killing: genocidal rape,[24] for example, "may not involve killing of rape victims. What makes rape of women genocidal is the cultural effect it has on a target community's ability to reproduce" (Carpenter 2004, 246). Although Carpenter encourages researchers to study sex-selective massacres, she emphasizes that the gendered aspects of genocide extend far beyond such massacres. Carpenter proposes that gender is a *modality of all genocides* rather than only a basis for one type of genocide.

Perhaps in response to this critique, Jones (2006b) has offered a more complex analysis of the importance of gender to genocide through an investigation of genocide's relation to heteronormativity. The concept of "heteronormativity" reflects the inseparability of gender and sexuality, including the fact that compulsory heterosexuality is an important dimension of masculinity. Jones begins with the observation that "one of the most lethal gender roles in modern times is that of the 'feminized' male – by which I mean the male who has adopted or had imposed on him a cultural identification with traditionally feminine roles and behaviour" (Jones 2006b, 453). Heteronormativity thus connects gendered violence in genocide to commonplace practices in normal societies, such as "the relentless hounding of perceived 'geeks,' 'faggots,' 'pansies,' 'wimps,' and the

---

24 For a germinal discussion and application of the concept of genocidal rape, see Allen (1996).

like in schoolyards worldwide" (Jones 2006b, 453), and also to gay-bashing by adults. Jones makes four basic points about the effects of heteronormativity in militarized situations. First, and most obviously, militarism plays a crucial part in the construction of contemporary forms of masculinity. This tends to feminize noncombatant men relative to men involved in violence. Second, the militaristic component of masculinity is designed to prepare men for action in the supremely terrifying situation of armed combat. This makes noncombatant men into "gender traitors," who are liable to a severe punishment in proportion to combatant men's emotional investment in their own readiness to violence. Third, hegemonic masculinity is competitive and aims for victory. Defeat, therefore, is inherently feminizing. Fourth, hegemonic masculinity is militarily active, such that enemy soldiers may be accorded respect as fellow men, with deep homosocial and even homoerotic overtones. Noncombatants are excluded from this form of respect. On the basis of these points, Jones analyzes the use of sexual violence, including rape and castration, committed by men against men during genocides. Under these conditions, not only are men who rape men doubly masculine, but men raped by men are doubly feminized. Building on Beverly Allen's (1996) account of genocidal rape against women, Jones proposes that genocidal rape against men has three genocidal functions: first, like group rape of women, group rape of men may build solidarity among the perpetrators; second, by obliterating the masculinity of the victim, it "threatens the masculine group cohesion that is essential [sic] for military action"; and third, damage to genitals may prevent physical reproduction (Jones 2006b, 461).

These observations only begin to explore the radically gendered quality of genocidal violence. Gender is such a familiar and taken-for-granted part of everyday/everynight life that understanding genocide as an expression of gender relations makes a crucial contribution to closing the genocide theory gap – that is, to explaining genocide in the same terms that are used to explain ordinary social phenomena. By concluding this chapter on the topic of gender, I have tried to emphasize the relational quality of identity-difference and the potential uses of violence to intensify this relation.

In the next chapter I offer a fully relational conception of the state and explain genocide as a product of contradictions in this relation. Whereas "capitalism" is Marx's name for the figuration produced by contradictory relations of (modern industrial) production and "patriarchy" is the name feminists give to those figurations produced by contradictory relations of sex-gender, I borrow Norbert Elias's notion of "the civilizing process" to designate the figuration produced by contradictory force relations. In the next chapter I show how civilization produces genocides.

4

Civilizing Genocides
and Barbaric Civilization

Whoever has emerged victorious participates to this day in the triumphal procession in which the present rulers step over those who are lying prostrate. According to traditional practice, the spoils are carried along in the procession. They are called cultural treasures, and a historical materialist views them with cautious detachment. For without exception the cultural treasures he surveys have an origin which he cannot contemplate without horror. They owe their existence not only to the efforts of the great minds and talents who have created them, but also to the anonymous toil of their contemporaries. There is no document of civilization which is not at the same time a document of barbarism. And just as such a document is not free of barbarism, barbarism taints also the manner in which it was transmitted from one owner to another. A historical materialist therefore dissociates himself from it as far as possible. He regards it as his task to brush history against the grain.

Benjamin, 256–7

INTRODUCTION

In this chapter, I argue that there are such things as "civilizing genocides" – that is, genocides produced through the advance of Western civilization itself – and that these have been so integral to our civilization that we should stop thinking of civilization as an unproblematic good and start thinking of it as fundamentally contradictory: not as "civilization" but as "barbaric civilization." This is a large claim, so before making it, I should pause to review the claims that I have made so far, claims that I hope have brought the reader to a point of readiness to take this next and most important step.

In the first chapter, I have argued for a critical sociology of genocide that treats genocide as a relational social phenomenon. This critical sociology is guided by three rules: it explains social phenomena in terms of factors *immanent* to the natural universe, takes account of its own *reflexive* situation within social relations, and is alert to *contradictions* in social relations that make value-neutral knowledge impossible. A critical sociology of genocide shows us that, contrary to common sense and to what we wish were the case, genocide can be institutionalized as moral and can be functional. We have to confront the normalcy of genocide if we wish to understand its causes and how to prevent it. In the second chapter, I have explored the intractable debates over the proper meaning of the term "genocide." Genocide is an essentially contested concept; conflicts over its proper meaning cannot be settled by force of reason alone, but its socio-political stakes can be clarified by a historical analysis that situates it within the rise of nationalism and of the transformation of states into nation-states. The early framers of the concept assumed that nations were natural or essential forms of social organization, but treating them as historically specific figurations allows us to adopt a definition of "genocide" that is both broader and more robust than previous uses: genocide is *an identity-difference relation of violent obliteration.* In the third chapter, I have explored why sociologists have not been able to close the "sociological theory gap," the inability to explain genocide in the same terms that are used to explain ordinary social phenomena. The obstacles to bridging this gap include treating either the Shoah in particular or genocide in general as unique and thus separate from other historical social phenomena. But drawing from more critical work on genocide, we can begin to overcome these obstacles by understanding the rationality of genocide, how it expresses class and gender relations, and how the potential for it is built into the dynamic relation between state power and social inequality. Still missing from this account, however, is a relational understanding of state power that systematically connects sovereignty to the production and destruction of identity-difference relations. This chapter supplies this missing piece.

CIVILIZATION: CONSCIOUSNESS AND PRACTICE

Civilization produces genocides. To justify this claim, I have to treat "civilization" as a definite thing, a social figuration. But as it is used in ordinary language, "civilization" is a very slippery term.

It conflates facts and values, practices and community. Samuel
Huntington writes about a "clash of civilizations" (Huntington
1996) and takes for granted that people ought to fight, kill, and die
for their civilization. Civilization is several things: a socio-political
community larger than a single state (something like an empire but
without one central government), an ensemble of cultural achievements and monuments, a way of being (the condition of being
civilized), and a process (the condition of becoming more and more
civilized). To be "civilized" is to be culturally advanced, sophisticated, highly developed, and at the same time humane, peaceful,
and law-abiding (as in, "let's deal with our problems in a civilized
manner").[1] The term carries two very large sociological assumptions: that one culture can be said to be more or less advanced than
another *as a whole*, not just in terms of any one practice; and that
more advanced cultures are also more peaceful and humane. These
assumptions are both *ethnocentric*. They can be sustained only if we
judge the achievements of other cultures by our own familiar standards of normal and aberrant, justified and unjustified violence; but
since all such standards are themselves a part of culture, the judgments they produce are circular and have little or no descriptive
utility. More strongly, we can say that ethnocentric judgments perpetuate stereotypes and express an imperialist mentality. Claiming
an abstract or metaphysical superiority for our own civilization is a
political act that works to justify or advance its dominance on this
earth. This is the extended sense of the term *Eurocentrism* (Amin
1989). Eurocentrism couples ethnocentric thinking with imperialist
action; it asserts Western dominance both abstractly and in practice.
To speak about civilization in a non-Eurocentric way, I need to strip
the term of its universalizing and metaphysical connotations. I need
to treat civilization as a definite thing, which we may judge good or
bad in whole or in its parts, but which is not understood to be good
by definition. This means analyzing civilization critically – that is,
immanently, reflexively, and in terms of its contradictions.

---

1 Raphaël Lemkin's earlier term for genocide was "barbarism" (Lemkin
1947), and in his notebooks he stated that the crime of genocide would serve as
an "index of civilization" (quoted in Power 2002, 42); as Alexander Hinton
notes, "his signifier would index a type of 'modern' morality – and a type of
'civil' society governed by international law – by marking its binary opposite"
(Hinton 2005, 5).

At the opening of *The Civilizing Process*, Norbert Elias claims that the concept of "civilization" expresses "the self-consciousness of the West": "It sums up everything in which Western society of the last two or three centuries believes itself superior to earlier societies or 'more primitive' contemporary ones. By this term Western society seeks to describe what constitutes its special character and what it is proud of: the level of *its* technology, the nature of *its* manners, the development of *its* scientific knowledge or view of the world, and much more" (Elias 2000, 5, original emphasis). But having introduced us to civilization by way of its *self-consciousness*, Elias immediately directs our attention to *history* and to *practice*. He explains the civilizing process in terms of the dual reconfiguration of force relations and bodily dispositions. Does the mention of consciousness serve only as an incidental gesture, a point taken en passant? Or does Elias, with these few words on the "self-consciousness of the West," set the scene for a *critique* of this self-consciousness through his exploration of its troubled embodiment? And, if so, what kind of critique?

In their account of the "materialist method of history," Karl Marx and Friedrich Engels (1976) assert that human beings produce all of the forms of their life only through concrete, practical social relations, such that we can properly understand these relations only in connection with the material conditions of their generation and, concomitantly, in their historical specificity. If we read Marx in dualist terms that separate "the material" and "the ideal," then his "historical materialism" implies that material relations exert some ultimately determining causal effect on consciousness and ideation, an assertion that has led to intractable difficulties. However, if we read Marx relationally (Ollman 1976), then we get a different Marx, one who treats consciousness and the phenomena distinct to it as material, produced through labour, one form of practical life-activity among others. The separation of consciousness and materiality, assumed by dualist metaphysics, appears for the relational materialist as a historical consequence of a particular configuration of social relations.

Elias makes this very point in his analysis of the historical constitution of individuality and of the egoistic separation between self and society (Elias 1978; 2001), and his investigation of the history of the Western subject in terms of the historical dynamics of practical social relations has much in common with Marx's "materialist method of history." Elias's materialism differs from Marx's in that Elias treats *force* relations as irreducible to production relations and makes the economy of force relations a primary, rather than a secondary, matrix of historical explanation. However, we could treat this simply as an expansion of the relational historical materialism initiated by Marx and could situate both authors comfortably within the wider field of relational sociology (Ball 1978; Bates and Peacock 1989; Breslau 2000; Dépelteau 2008; Emirbayer 1997; Latour 1993 and 2005; Ollman 1976; Powell 2007; Sewell 1992; Wellman 1988). But a more crucial difference sets Marx apart from Elias. In Marx's analysis of capitalism, the distinction between consciousness and its material basis occasions a radical critique of the exigencies of capitalist social relations. This critique is occasioned because, in opposition to all claims that society constitutes an organically integrated whole or some approximation thereof, Marx understands capitalist society in terms of a contradiction inherent to its very logic, and this critique is radical because Marx locates the contradiction not in a consciousness that could be revised by thinking differently but in the material social relations out of which consciousness emerges, practical relations necessary and integral to the ongoing reproduction of the social order. Elias does not pursue a comparable critique of the civilizing process. However, his work does provide the sociological material that could serve as a basis for such a critique; he opens the door, even if he does not choose to step through it.

Elias's Historical Materialism

Having introduced civilization as an expression of the West's self-consciousness, a more typical sociologist of Elias's era might well have explained this consciousness in terms of the dynamics of consciousness (a history of ideas), or else in terms of the synchronic social functions of the values denoted by the term "civilization." Iconoclastically, Elias chooses a more laborious and rewarding path. Words like "civilization" and "culture," he writes, have emerged through historical practices: "They were tossed back and forth until they became efficient instruments for expressing what people had jointly experienced and wanted to communicate ... The shared history has crystallized in them and resonates in them" (Elias 2000, 8).

And to explain this emergence, Elias investigates practices of the body: of violence, of etiquette.

Taking France as his case study, Elias observes that the word "civilization" developed from *civilité*, which takes much of its meaning from *courtoisie*. Conveniently, the documentary tradition of manuals in civility and courtesy, written for the upper classes, provides evidence regarding the changing standards of polite conduct. These standards show a gradual historical progression from rudimentary to complex. If we look back far enough, we find injunctions against actions the mere mention of which we ourselves find disgusting: do not smear snot on your clothes or on tablecloths; do not urinate or defecate in the staircases, corridors, or closets of someone else's home; do not slurp from a spoon that someone else uses; and so on (Elias 2000, 51–2, 122, 111–12, 173). Elias notes that "in medieval society people generally blew their noses into their hands, just as they ate with their hands" and that "the distasteful feeling frequently aroused today by the mere thought of soiling the fingers in this way was at first entirely absent" (Elias 2000, 126). This absence extends to other encounters with the body that middle-class Westerners today find intuitively repugnant. The depth of our feelings does not make them natural. Elias identifies the movement of historical practice that cultivates these feelings – first, in the elite class and, eventually, in society at large. Not only our actions but also our very feelings change historically.

What changes them? According to Elias, the necessary factor is a change in the *configuration of distributed force relations*. At the start of the twelfth century, in the western remnants of the Holy Roman Empire, a "loosely integrated secular upper class of warriors, with its symbol, the castle on the autarkic estate" (Elias 2000, 256), monopolized means of military force; kings acted primarily as war leaders without substantial mechanisms of permanent centralized government at their disposal (Elias 2000, 198–202, 236). Under these conditions, knights and commoners alike freely laughed, cried, shouted, and embraced immediately as they felt moved to do so (Elias 2000, 180, 374). But from the eleventh to the thirteenth century the centrifugal dispersion of military dominance reversed; a few knights achieved regional monopolies of force, subjecting the others to their dominance (Elias 2000, 237). This monopolization and subordination imposed constraints on knights, especially at court. In the company of their equals and betters, knights found themselves in competition with each other to win by charm the esteem and the practical assistance that they could no longer compel by force (Elias 2000, 245–50, 389–97, 405–6). Courts made it tactically advantageous for knights to apply to themselves, pre-emptively, the judgments and reactions of others. External rules engendered internalized habits; the courts fostered a "social constraint to self-constraint" (Elias 2000, 365).

Elias uses the term "habitus" to designate the practical and taken-for-granted set of skills, attitudes, and understandings by which one conducts one's life. In the late Middle Ages, the word "courtoisie" expressed "aristocratic self-consciousness and socially acceptable behaviour" (Elias 2000, 53–4), but the *practice* of courtoisie involved an ongoing transformation of habitus that both derived from and contributed to the ongoing monopolization of violence by sovereigns. At the time of the Renaissance, with the aid of manuals of civilité like *De civilitate morum puerilium* by Desiderius Erasmus (Elias 2000, 47), this habitus spread to the urban bourgeoisie, the upper segments of which competed with the aristocracy for royal favour and social distinction. In the great social transformations driven by the Industrial Revolution, by nationalism, and by imperialism, this habitus spread downward through the class and gender structures in the social spaces enclosed by sovereign power and outward to every corner of the earth as European sovereignty globalized itself (Elias 2000, 35–43, 142–60, 382–7, 427–8, 431–2).

Sovereignty and civility – that is, the Western system of centralized monopolies of military force and the Western type of habitus formed through the social constraint to self-constraint – have conditioned and reinforced each other and make up the two components, distinguishable but inseparable, of what Elias calls *the civilizing process*. "When a monopoly of force is formed, pacified social spaces are created which are normally free from acts of violence" (Elias 2000, 369). In such spaces, people develop an increasing sensitivity to one another's reactions, feelings, and needs; they repress in ever more refined ways their impulses toward violence and, by extension, all potentially offensive emotional outbursts, and so they elaborate ever more complex and nuanced codes of social intercourse. And the acquisition of these habitual ways of feeling and acting strengthens, in turn, the demilitarization of quotidian life and hence the sovereign's monopolization of military force.[2] As the civilizing process advances, violence recedes from everyday/everynight life, breaking out only in times of war or in other situations where sovereignty fails.

On the one hand, then, we have civilization as the self-consciousness of the West and, on the other, the material social relations that produce and sustain this self-consciousness. How closely do the two cohere?

THE PERSISTENCE OF GENOCIDE: BREAKDOWN VS PRODUCTION

Few acts, if any, more thoroughly violate the self-consciousness of the West, or its claims to superiority, than genocide. But genocide takes place even in social spaces organized by the civilizing process.[3] A *teleological* reading of Elias seems unable to account for this. The movement of the civilizing process should prevent such barbarities as genocide or reduce their incidence and severity; the Armenian holocaust, Joseph Stalin's atrocities, and the genocides of the Nazis falsify this expectation.

---

2 Elias often writes as though the sovereign monopolizes force per se, but we can perceive on inspection that there are significant and systematic exceptions to this monopoly: every social space where men have had the freedom to assault or murder their wives or other women, along with their children; where men racialized as "white" have had the freedom to assault or murder persons racialized as "black"; where nominally heterosexual men have had the freedom to physically and sexually assault gay men, lesbians, and transgendered individuals; and so on. These exceptions to the sovereign's monopoly on physical force deserve more attention than I can given them here as part of a systematic theorization of force within the civilizing process. On the other hand, sovereigns have not systematically even claimed to monopolize forms of violence other than direct physical force, such as economic violence or symbolic violence, as Elias has recognized (Burkitt 1996, 138; Elias 2000, 369).

3 As Mahmood Mamdani writes of the 1994 genocide in Rwanda, "genocide was not a collapse of power and authority, a free for all in which everyone turned against their neighbor and all were thrown into some sort of a Hobbesian state of nature" (Mamdani 2001, 202).

Eliasian Functionalism

One can find the teleological reading among Elias's critics (e.g., Bauman 1991a, 12) but not actually among the proponents of his work. Elias, a German of Jewish descent, wrote *The Civilizing Process* amid the unfolding Nazi catastrophe, lost his parents to the Holocaust, and knew full well the atrocities that civilized Western subjects could commit. In the essays published in *The Germans* (Elias 1996), especially "The Breakdown of Civilization," he explains such atrocities as products of local and temporary reversals in the overall forward motion of the civilizing process, reversals produced by this forward motion just as the flow of a river produces eddies. Subsequent figurational sociologists have built on this analysis to develop theories of "decivilizing processes" (Fletcher 1997, 2–4; Mennell 1989, 247–8, and 1992, 227–50; Mennell and Dunning 1996, xv; van Krieken 1998, 70–71) or of "dyscivilizing processes" (de Swaan 2001, 269). Eliasians have taken genocide very seriously. They propose a complex relationship between civilization and violence, in which the institutional capacities developed through the civilizing process can, under contingent circumstances, reverse their usual operation and flood society with the destructive forces that it normally keeps dammed up behind the sovereign's monopoly of force and the social constraint to self-constraint. We could call this conception *functionalist* because, implicitly or explicitly, it contrasts the normal and healthy operation of the civilizing process with its pathological opposite.

Accounts of the civilizing process that associate its normal operation with the pacification of social life and that explain genocide as a pathology or dysfunction of this process require us to treat genocide as an abnormal phenomenon. However, one can perceive three major objections to doing this. First, "abnormal" implies "unusual" and "marginal," but the scale of genocide and democide in modern times defies such expectations. Rudy Rummel (1994), for example, estimates that states murdered nearly 170 million of their own subjects in the twentieth century alone,[4] and his tabulation lacks

---

4 Rummel defines "democide" as "the murder of any person or people by a government" (Rummel 1994, 31, 34), excluding the killing of combatants in wartime. Democide does not equate with genocide: not all state killings of civilians count as genocide, and not all genocidal actions involve killing.

important cases.[5] For their combination of scale, intensity, and efficiency, some genocides of the past 100 years far outdo anything from
previous, less civilized eras. Second, treating irruptions of violence
into social life as abnormal ignores the twentieth-century resurgence
of total war (El-Kaïm-Sartre and Sartre 1968, 60–1) and its logical
extension, the possibility of global human omnicide through nuclear
war (Goodman and Hoff 1990), which emerge directly from the competition for territorial military dominance that drives the civilizing
process.[6] Third, and most important, explaining genocide as an aberration from the overall pacifying tendency of the civilizing process
ignores entirely the central part that genocide has played in European
colonialism. As I have discussed in the Introduction, globally expanding European civilization has brought systematic destruction to
Indigenous societies through massacre, enslavement, dispossession,
forced migration, confinement to marginal living conditions, abduction of children, and suppression of language, religion, cultural practice, and political and economic institutions. The partial or near-total
destruction of Indigenous cultures has been integral to the formation
and global dissemination of modern Western civilization.

Normativity and Ambivalence

Robert van Krieken (1999) and Ian Burkitt (1996; 2006) offer
nonfunctionalist readings of Elias, based on two different trains of
investigation. Van Krieken recognizes the productive relationship
between civilization and genocide in the formation of white-settler
society in Australia:

the barbarism identified in this case was attempted, not only
within a society whose members regarded themselves as civilized,
but in the name of civilization. This was no "dark underbelly" of
modernity, state formation or civilization, it was an explicit and
central part of all three projects. It was integral to processes of

---

5 He omits, for example, the estimated 500,000 persons killed by the
Indonesian state in the anticommunist purge of 1965–66 (Chalk and Jonassohn
1990, 380–3).

6 Elias recognized and expressed grave concern for the threat of war between
the American and Soviet sides of the Cold War (Elias 1987, lxx-lxxii, 24–5,
93–115; 2000, 462). I discuss his response to this threat in more detail below.

civilization, not the result of some other process of decivilization or barbarization ... These policies and events were not the result of the disintegration of society and state, but precisely part and parcel of processes of integration. (van Krieken 1999, 299)

The genocides of Aboriginal groups in Australia constituted "civilizing offensives," "a particular form of barbarism explicitly within civilization and the formation of modern citizenship rather than opposed to, 'outside' or 'beneath' them." Barbarism persists "contained within our current concept of civilization" (van Krieken 1999, 311). Burkitt uses Zygmunt Bauman's notion of "ambivalence" to characterize the civilizing process, reading Elias closely to bring out the ambivalences Elias recognized and those at play in Elias's own theorizing. Burkitt observes that the sovereign monopoly of violence "allows for the means of violence and coercion to be built up to a level never known before" (Burkitt 1996, 144); the removal of violence behind the scenes of everyday/everynight life can allow this violence to take place offstage and unimpeded; and, as Bauman observes in *Modernity and the Holocaust*, the lengthening of chains of interdependence can involve a contraction of the scope for mutual identification, leaving "some groups of human beings ... excluded from mutual identification and moral recognition" (Burkitt 1996, 148). Van Krieken and Burkitt both show how the institutional resources generated by the civilizing process work to produce genocide, without the civilizing process as a whole breaking down or going into reverse.

The greater the historical importance of genocide within the civilizing process, the greater the tension between descriptive and normative uses of the terms "civilized" and "barbaric." Descriptively, these words can refer to particular social formations that are defined by their empirical features and about which one makes no particular evaluative comment; normatively, they by definition express approval or disapproval, based on consistency or inconsistency with a taken-for-granted set of values. If we investigate genocide seriously and non-Eurocentrically, we find ourselves confronted by a very great inconsistency between the self-image of the West and the actual performance of its institutions, between the values and the practices generated by the civilizing process. If this inconsistency did not obtain, one could use the term "civilized" both normatively and descriptively at the same time to refer to two classes of action: on the one hand, action organized by the dual process of the monopolization of violence and the social constraint to self-constraint as it emerged in western Europe and has spread across the earth; and on the other hand, action of which we approve[7] because we consider it humane, peaceful, just, and so on. Given the inconsistency, however, we must decide which connotation of the word to take as primary and which as secondary. This decision instantiates the larger question of what relative importance one attributes to conscious and nonconscious forces in the organization of social practices.

Van Krieken takes the normative use as primary: he calls racism and genocide "barbaric" even when in practice they form part of a "civilizing offensive." This normative use of the word "civilization" has a powerful advantage: it allows those who employ it to go on using the words "civilized" and "barbaric" to praise and disparage, respectively, and so to condemn the atrocities of civilization in the name of its ideal. However, thinking of civilization primarily as a normative ideal leaves us still with the questions of why the practice of civilization can so entirely contradict this ideal and of why the practice of genocide, for all its atrocity, is such a useful tool for those who act in the name of civilization.

Burkitt's analysis also escapes "the self-definition of the West" by understanding the normative uses of "civilized" and "barbaric" as a mutually entailing binary classification scheme produced by social forces that ambivalently resist any stable identification with either of these terms. And yet "ambivalence" seems a mild term to connote the intense extremes of safety and danger that the civilizing process can engender. Actors involved in the civilizing process may experience it as pacifying or violent, humanizing or dehumanizing, depending on their relation to it – on what Dorothy Smith (1990) would call their standpoint within relations of rule. So I would like to travel past ambivalence, through aporia and deconstruction, to an understanding of the civilizing process as contradictory.

TWO CONFLATIONS

The ambivalence of civilization lies in Elias's account of it, not in the civilizing process itself. Elias conflates the practice and the self-image

---

7 Or disapprove, if – like the Nazis, for example – we reject humanistic values.

of civilization on two questions. First, does the violence that the civilizing process represses derive from innate human nature or from social forces? Second, does civilization as such constitute a moral good or merely a social object without intrinsic value, onto which humans project value-judgments?[8] The two questions go together, and on both questions Elias tries to have it both ways.

On the one hand, Elias often describes the civilizing process as repressing innate, natural human dispositions and also often uses the terms "civilized" and "barbaric" to express positive and negative moral judgments. "The moderation of spontaneous emotions," says Elias, "the tempering of affects, the extension of mental space beyond the moment into the past and future, the habit of connecting events in terms of chains of cause and effect – all of these are different aspects of the same transformation of conduct which necessarily takes place with the monopolization of physical violence, and the lengthening of the chains of social action and interdependence. It is a 'civilizing' change of behaviour" (Elias 2000, 370). This change superimposes itself on and represses for the autarkic knight the "savage joys, the uninhibited satisfaction of pleasure from women, or of hatred in destroying and tormenting anything hostile" (Elias 2000, 371). Those passions that the civilizing process suppresses, Elias calls "spontaneous," "uninhibited," "immediate," "uncalculated," "unrestrained," and so on. He praises Sigmund Freud's *Civilization and Its Discontents* (van Krieken 1998, 19), in which the socially produced superego imposes itself on the primal passions of the id, and he makes substantial use of Freudian concepts throughout *The Civilizing Process*. He also claims, without evidence, that European imperial colonialism produced in non-Europeans "the same constant foresight and affect-control as in the West itself," "the habituation to foresight," "the stricter control of behaviour and the affects," and "the cultivation of the super-ego" (Elias 2000, 384–5) – as though colonized peoples entirely lacked their own Indigenous forms of foresight or affect control. And, despite the hundreds of years of the advance of the civilizing process, the impulses it

---

8 Roland Robertson claims that Elias fails to recognize that "what came by the end of the 19th century to be called the standard of civilization was a relatively autonomous, transnational norm" (Robertson 2006, 421). I think that, on the contrary, Elias takes the normativity of the concept of civilization too much for granted.

constrains remain powerfully threatening, ready at any moment to unseat their master: "the civilization of which I speak is never completed and constantly endangered. It is endangered because the safeguarding of more civilized standards of behaviour and feeling in society depends on specific conditions" (Elias 1996, 173). In these ways, Elias writes as though "barbaric" actions express innate human nature.

In keeping with this essentialism, Elias frequently uses the words "civilized" and "civilization" normatively or conflates their descriptive and normative uses. This occurs most often in *The Germans*, especially in "The Breakdown of Civilization," where Elias conflates civilization with pacification (Elias 1996, 173, 279, 302, 308), occasionally with humanism (417), and sometimes with a specifically compassionate conscience in particular (139–40, 158, 365),[9] and where he conflates barbarism with brutality and cruelty in social relations (302–4, 308–10, 314–15, 330, 345–6, 355, 359, 381, 402). In *The Symbol Theory*, Elias suggests that future societies will regard contemporary westerners as "late barbarians" (Elias 1991, 146–7); elsewhere, he states directly that civilization does not inhere to Western culture,[10] that the West has not always enjoyed a greater degree of civilization than other cultures and likely will not always in the future. Elias problematizes the *extent* of Western culture's civilization but not the *value* of civilization, and he problematizes the *basis* of its superiority but not the *fact* of this superiority. And at the close of *The Civilizing Process*, Elias identifies civilization with the possibility of future human happiness and freedom, saying: "Only when these tensions between and

---

9 This point requires care. For the most part, Elias uses the term "conscience" nonjudgmentally to indicate the type of self-constraint associated with an individual's we-identity (as opposed to his or her I-identity) (Elias 1996, 379). Sometimes, therefore, he explains the Germans' obedience to Adolf Hitler as the result of particular features of Prussian conscience-formation, which included, for example, intense loyalty to the state (Elias 1996, 415, 419). At other times, however, he describes the process by which Germans handed over decision-making authority to the Fuhrer as the breakdown of conscience (Elias 1996, 383–6). Different essays in *The Germans* take different positions on whether to treat humanistic values as one form of conscience among others or to equate them with moral conscience as such.

10 See also, for example, his comments on Chinese civilization (Elias 2000, 107, 410, 540n179).

within states have been mastered can we expect to become more truly civilized" (Elias 2000, 446).

Taken together, these two conflations echo Emile Durkheim's account of society as the source of all morality (1984; 1992; 1997; 2002): the civilizing process enables qualitative increases in the length and complexity of chains of social interdependency that integrate individuals into functional wholes, such that social forces external to the individual tame the unruly and anomic forces intrinsic to human nature and generate morally superior forms of social life. And yet one can also read, in Elias's work, an entirely opposite position. "It is difficult to see," says Elias,

> whether the radical contraposition of 'civilization' and 'nature' is more than an expression of the tensions of the 'civilized' psyche itself ... At any rate, the psychic life of 'primitive' peoples is no less historically (i.e., socially) stamped than that of 'civilized' peoples, even if the former are scarcely aware of their own history. There is no zero point in the historicity of human development, just as there is none in the sociality, the social interdependence among people. In both 'primitive' and 'civilized' peoples, there are socially induced prohibitions and restrictions, together with their psychological counterparts, socially induced anxieties, pleasure and displeasure, distaste and delight. It is, therefore, at least not entirely clear what is meant when the former standard, that of so-called 'primitives,' is contrasted simply as 'natural' to the historical-social standard of 'civilized' people. So far as the psychological functions of humans are concerned, natural and historical processes work indissolubly together. (Elias 2000, 135)

In this way, Elias argues that no social practice could derive entirely from biological human nature; all social practices depend on the relational context generated over time by the interactions of biological individuals. Society does not act on individuals from outside of themselves, shaping their psyches the way a pair of hands shapes a ball of clay; *society and individuals do not exist separately from one another* (Elias 1978, 13–18, 118–28; 2000, 473–4, 455–6, 470–1, 481–2). Social relations produce historically particular "affect-structures" (Elias 2000, 161) or "drive economies" (Elias 2000, 372) through which individuals come to experience particular impulses as "spontaneous" or "innate." Both the inclination and the disinclination to, for example, blow snot in one's own palm depend equally on a specific social context. Talking of persons or of practices as more or less socially shaped *in general* does not make any sense. One can say only that a *particular figurational pattern* has shaped them more or less strongly (Elias 2000, 374, 411). Neither does it make sense to talk of people behaving in a more spontaneous or more socially constrained way, a more uninhibited or more restrained way – except relative to the standards of spontaneity and constraint that prevail within a *particular* social context.

Throughout *The Civilizing Process*, Elias carefully places the words "civilized," "barbaric," "primitive," and "savage" in ironic quotations. In this passage he explains why:

> The greater or lesser discomfort we feel towards people who discuss or mention their bodily functions more openly, who conceal and restrain these functions less than we do, is one of the dominant feelings expressed in the judgment 'barbaric' or 'uncivilized.' Such, then, is the nature of 'barbarism and its discontents' or, in more precise and less evaluative terms, the discontent with the different structure of affects, the different standard of repugnance which is still to be found today in many societies which we term 'uncivilized,' the standard of repugnance which preceded our own and is its precondition. The question arises as to how and why Western society actually moved from one standard to the other, how it became 'civilized' ... It is necessary, at least while considering this process, to attempt to suspend all the feelings of embarrassment and superiority, all the value judgments and criticisms associated with the concept 'civilization' or 'uncivilized.' (Elias 2000, 51–2)

Explanation depends on suspending the conflation of difference and inferiority. Elias makes nonjudgmental detachment the cornerstone of his epistemology (Elias 1987, 1–38; 2000, xiv, 51–2). He presents, indirectly, two strong arguments against ethnocentrism: in his insistence on process and change, through which he criticizes Talcott Parsons for having taken Western nation-states as the universal model of social systems; and in his attacks on anthropocentric thinking, which warn that what an observer perceives as universal and unchanging may always appear local and transitory given a wider frame of reference (Elias 1978, 18–19; 2000, 463). His insistence that values and meanings do not inhere to natural phenomena in themselves but result from human social action (Elias 2001, 10) and that "the immanent regularities of social figurations are identical neither with regularities of the 'mind,' of individual reasoning, nor with regularities of what we like to call 'nature'" (Elias 2000, 366) mitigates against judging the civilizing process as good or bad in itself. And Elias recognizes that the normative value of terms like "civilized" and "barbaric" results from the workings of the civilizing process itself.

Elias's detached examination of the civilizing process allows him to make an almost dialectical gesture. Detachment differs from objectivity in leaving scientists embedded within the relations they study: Elias's parable of the fishers in the maelstrom suggests that the need for detachment arises from the subject's very involvement in a dangerous situation (Elias 1987, 45–6). Elias invokes this parable to illustrate the dangers facing humanity from the uncontrolled workings of social figurations, including the threat of nuclear omnicide generated by the competition for territorial dominance between the two world superpowers of the Cold War. He urges detachment as the attitude necessary to allow the influential middle classes of both sides of this conflict to see beyond the next step in the dance of escalation and to grasp the deadly nature of the overall pattern of action in which they find themselves embroiled (Elias 1987, 76, 108–11). The nuclear threat and the mania of identification with one side or the other resulted from the civilizing process (Elias 1987, 73–5). So, taking a detached view, and relative to a moral vision embracing the whole of humanity, we may say that the civilizing process has ambivalently produced certain goods and certain evils. But Elias indicates that detachment itself results from the workings of the civilizing process (Elias 1987, 55–73; 2000, 379–82). So, in effect, he advocates using one aspect of the civilizing process against another aspect of the civilizing process. And indeed he argues the *necessity* of this contradictory gesture (Elias 1987, xii–xv).

Although I prefer to discard the essentialist, moralistic Elias in favour of the relational, critical Elias, one question makes this difficult: why does Elias regard the centuries-old and globally dominant civilizing process as fragile, "constantly endangered"? If the habitus of barbarism resulted from definite social conditions, and if society has undergone a process of transformation away from these conditions for almost a thousand years, one would expect an equally great process of reverse transformation before barbarism could recur. But Elias warns that "the armor of civilized conduct" would crumble almost instantly if "danger became as incalculable as it once was" (Elias 2000, 532). This claim cannot fit within a thoroughly relational sociology of subjectivity – unless the civilizing process, in the course of its forward motion, somehow carries barbarism forward along with it.

FIGURATION AS DIFFÉRANCE

To read Elias deconstructively may seem perverse or simply destructive, but three lines of commonality allow one to graft deconstruction onto figurational sociology. First, deconstruction's insistence that texts produce effects that far exceed the intentions of their authors (Culler 1982, 110–28) accords with Elias's consistent interest in the unintended consequences of social action (Elias 2000, xiii, 215, 322, 348–9, 385). Second, the relational conception of meaning that Jacques Derrida adapts from the linguistics of Ferdinand de Saussure coheres with Elias's relational sociology. Third, deconstruction relies on a consideration of process and transformation, epitomized in the movement of "différance."

A brief review of Derrida's deconstructive reading of Saussure brings out the surprisingly figurational quality of deconstructionist thinking. Saussure, says Derrida, privileges speech over writing and treats the latter merely as a means of representing the former (Derrida 1976, 30). As Jonathan Culler explains, "Words issue from the speaker as the spontaneous and nearly transparent signs of his present thought, which the attendant listener hopes to grasp. Writing, on the other hand, consists of physical marks that are divorced from the thought that may have produced them" (Culler 1982, 100). Derrida finds this "phonocentrism" at odds with Saussure's own insistence on the arbitrariness of the signifier and the relationality of signification. Why should a scientist privilege utterances over inscriptions when both of these function as instruments of signification? Saussure's phonocentrism results from his logocentrism, his privileging of thought as the source of meaning, as well as its concomitant "metaphysics of presence," which regards thought as a presence inherent to meaningful speech and regards consciousness as present within the mind, or "self-present" (Culler 1982, 92;

Derrida 1976, 12). Yet Saussure's phonocentrism inverts itself in his demonstration of the relationality of signification. Saussure says that a given mark counts as the letter *t* (for example) not because of essential features that inhere to it in isolation but because one can distinguish it from *l, f, i, d*, and so on. A network of differences, not a collection of essences, makes signification possible. However, the phonocentric Saussure has used the properties of text to demonstrate this for all signification. The privilege of speech over text inverts itself. And yet this inversion reverts easily since it appears precisely as an effect of Saussure's phonocentric arguments (Derrida 1976, 56), such that we have an aporia on our hands in the form of an undecidable, perpetually unstable alternation between two opposed readings. Derrida displaces this aporia with the term "archi-écriture," which embraces both speech and writing. And archi-écriture instantiates "the movement of différance" (Derrida 1976, 60).

Derrida's untranslatable neologism "différance" puns on the established word "différence" (simply "difference" in English) by giving an *ing*-like suffix to the verb "différer," which in turn connotes (in English) both "to differ" and "to defer" (as in "postpone" or "temporize") (Derrida 1982, 3–9). So "différance" connotes both differing and deferring, as both verb and gerund in the manner of English words like "spacing." As Kanakis Leledakis states, "To the differential definition of structure – structure as a system of differences – a temporal difference is added. Structure is seen as deferring itself, opening itself in time" (Leledakis 2000, 176). And by curious coincidence, "to defer" in English connotes both "to postpone" and "to submit or give way, as to an authority,"[11] so an English reader of "différance" might reasonably add "deferring/deference" to its connotations. So, although French- and English-speaking authors alike have treated "différance" as untranslatable, I propose a new neologism to serve as its translation: *deferentiation*. I use the concept of deferentiation below in my discussion of habitus.[12]

---

11 I would like to thank Sheryl Peters for this observation.

12 Following Elias's use of the term "habitus," I use it applying much the same grammatical conventions that govern the use of the word "consciousness." So although I sometimes write expressions like "a subject's habitus" and "the habitus of Western civilization" and so on, I also often write expressions like "civilized habitus" (not "the civilized habitus") or simply "habitus" (not "the habitus"), as in "the effects of state formation on habitus" and so on.

Figure 4.1   Two visual aporias: Faces/vase and duck/rabbit

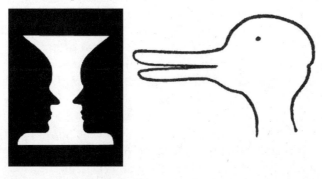

Sources: The faces/vase image, called Rubin's Vase, first appeared in the Danish psychologist Edgar Rubin's 1915 book *Synsoplevede Figurer* (see Shipley 1995, 134). This particular version of the image is taken from http://www.uic.edu/com/eye/LearningAboutVision/EyeSite/OpticalIllustions/FaceVase.shtml. The duck/rabbit image is from Wittgenstein (2001, 166).

Différance as Productive Labour

There is a possible objection to this line of thought: how can deconstruction, with its obsessive focus on texts, contribute to a sociology of practice such as Elias's? Using a relational materialism, we can reconcile the two by treating texts as machines and writing as productive labour. Although Derrida treats the social primarily as a "field of meaning" (Leledakis 2000, 178) rather than as a field of practical relations, his account of meaning privileges embodied meaning (inscriptions and utterances) over disembodied meaning (*logos*). One could say that texts, as congealed expended labour-power, operate as tools for the production of readings through the labour of reading. Treating texts as machines built by labour makes sense of two important deconstructionist claims: social institutions use texts to fix relations of domination, and deconstruction works as a political tactic for disrupting these relations. "What is somewhat hastily called deconstruction is not, if it is of any consequence, a specialized set of discursive procedures, still less the rules of a new hermeneutic method that works on texts or utterances in the shelter of a given and stable institution. It is also, at the very least, a way of taking a position, in its work of analysis, concerning the political and institutional structures that make possible and govern our practices, our competencies, our performances" (Derrida, quoted in Culler 1982, 156).

Derrida claims that deconstruction works not merely as a textual or hermeneutic operation but also as a form of practical action, a way of mounting a critique of relations of domination inscribed into the categories of our thought and action. In a dualist metaphysics, this would imply idealism: only if consciousness determines our social being would the labour of exposing the contingency of our categories *in itself* suffice to undermine relations of domination. For relational materialism, however, texts work materially as part of the invisible, taken-for-granted, practical knowledge of how to act efficaciously in the world – in other words, as part of habitus. As a labour of disrupting the operation of machines that reinscribe habitus, deconstruction can produce dramatic changes in some social situations.

Despite Derrida's claim that "différance is literally neither a word nor a concept" (Derrida 1982, 3), one can use différance precisely as a sociological concept: "Derrida reaffirms the role of *différance*, this time squarely on the level of the social. The social – society in general, language, a small community, etc. – is, like the text, a system of differences, a 'system of referral' and thus a domain of the play of différance" (Leledakis 2000, 178). If we treat the social as a field of material relations, and not only as a field of meaning, then "différance" connotes the movement that produces not only semantic differences among units of meaning but also concrete and practical differences among people. For example, in Marx's account of alienation, labour and capital appear not as separate social groups that come together as if by accident but as opposite poles of the relation of alienated production, and the movement of this relation produces not only commodities but also labour and capital themselves as definite forms of activity, as definite locations in a social structure, and hence as definite types of people capable of forming social groups with opposed interests (Marx 2000a, 93; Marx and Engels 1976; Marx 2000c, 281, 284; Ollman 1976, 204–7). Alienated labour produces a complex ensemble of material differences between workers and owners. These differences include what workers eat, under what conditions they labour, and how long they live; they also include material textual differences established through utterances and inscriptions, differences in what it means to live as a worker or as an owner. I propose that we regard the civilizing process as a similar movement of différance, in which the performance of relations of force produces an ensemble of social differences and deferences – and that this production works specifically through the *deferral* of violence.

THE DEFERRAL OF VIOLENCE

At its core, Elias's account of the civilizing process depends on two distinguishable but inseparable mechanisms: the formation of monopolies of military force, or *state formation*; and the transformation of habitus toward the particular forms of self-constraint that the term "civilized" valorizes. (Elias often speaks as though the latter equates with self-constraint per se, but we may take exception to this Eurocentrism.) Sociological convention would assign these two transformations, of the state and of subjects' habitus, to the "macro" and "micro" levels of analysis; Elias rejects this opposition, however, and treats the two as distinguishable but inseparable aspects of the same process (Elias 1978, 41; 2000, xi, 407, 411). If the civilizing process produces social differentiation through a deferral of violence, we should find this deferral evident in both state formation and subjectification.

Deferral in State Formation: Reproduction on an Expanding Scale

State formation proceeds through the establishment of territorial monopolies of military force. Elias asserts that "when a monopoly of force is formed, pacified social spaces are created which are normally free from acts of violence" (Elias 2000, 369). The growth of these monopolies, therefore, implies a growth in these pacified social spaces, which tends progressively toward the complete pacification of global social life:

> We see the following movement: first one castle stands against another, then territory against territory, then state against state, and appearing on the historical horizon today are the first signs of struggles for an integration of regions and masses of people on a still larger scale. We may surmise that with continuing integration even larger units will gradually be assembled under a stable government and internally pacified, and that they in turn will turn their weapons outwards against human aggregates of the same size until ... world society is pacified. (Elias 2000, 254)

Thus far, violence and civilization seem opposed to each other, the former receding with the advance of the latter.

On closer inspection, however, state formation does not do away with violence but reorganizes it. Competition among many small knights transmutes itself into competition among a few big knights. Large, organized armies replace small, local bands of warriors. Powerful lords, and later sovereigns, use their taxation privileges to hire ever-larger armies, to maintain permanent military institutions, and to develop intensified military techniques (Elias 2000, 192). The sovereign disarms the knightly class but arms himself.[13] This process displaces violence spatially, concentrating it in the sites of sovereign military power, and also disperses it outward beyond Europe, in the Crusades and in colonialism, to cover the face of the earth and to enrol all human beings in a single network of force relations. The same process defers violence temporally: wars and civil terrors happen less often but on larger scales. The "pacified social spaces," which are "normally free from acts of violence," expand relative to the spatial and temporal references of individual human perception. But from a longer-term, less egocentric perspective, we can perceive that the capacity for violence in the figuration as a whole actually *increases* with the advance of the civilizing process, reaching unprecedented heights in the twentieth century, which saw two world wars, genocidal slaughters in the millions, and the possibility of nuclear omnicide.

The disarmament of the autarkic warlords of eleventh-century France happened through force of arms and produced a new class of warlords, fewer in number but with larger resources at their disposal. If we take as our problem the practical vulnerability of unarmed subjects to the violence of those who control the means of force, we can perceive that the civilizing process does not abolish this problem but solves it in such a way as to reproduce it on a larger scale. In this sense, barbarism serves as the motor of the civilizing process, as Elias recognizes: "What finally meets its end in such conflicts or merges into new formations ... is no less indispensable to these new formations than the victorious opponent. Without violent

---

13 The gender pronoun in this case reflects the masculine-gendered quality of knighthood and of sovereignty, which a gender-neutral pronoun would only disguise.

actions, without the motive forces of free competition, there would be no monopoly of force, and thus no pacification, no suppression and control of violence over large areas" (Elias 2000, 311). So at each turn of the cycle, civilization must reproduce this same barbarism. If we liken the civilizing process to a dance (Elias 2000, 482–3), then as the dance proceeds the dancers find themselves returning again and again to their starting positions but with the stakes of the dance raised ever higher at each return. The capacity for violence increases through the effects of social organization, greater fiscal expenditures, economies of scale, discipline, and technology. States, in their competition with each other, *reproduce the means of violence on an expanding scale*. This reproduction defers violence into the future rather than dissolving it. In an arms race, actors seek to secure peace by raising the costs of war. When this tactic fails, for whatever reason, deferral stops and the deferred violence of civilization manifests itself concretely.

Deferral in Habitus: Deferentiation

The civilizing process imposes a social constraint to self-constraint on subjects otherwise disposed to act suddenly and "spontaneously" on their emotions, whether in anger or in joy; most especially it constrains the spontaneous use of violence. Where does this "barbaric" disposition come from? Elias often writes as though it derives from some presocial human nature, and just as often he rules out the theoretical possibility of any such nature. If we wish to construe barbarism as the product of social relations, we can piece together an account from Elias's observations.

"The majority of the secular ruling class of the Middle Ages lived the life of leaders of armed bands. This formed the tastes and habits of individuals" (Elias 2000, 164). This situation placed each knight in relations of perpetual tension with various types of persons he dominated, who surrounded him every day and over whom he had constantly to assert a superiority that ultimately depended on his mastery of the force of arms. Thus we can understand knighthood as a class relation defined by control of the means of bodily violence. This military class relation enabled other types of class relation: economic relations, as the knight lived off of the surplus of agricultural labour, expropriated as tribute (Amin 1989, 3; Elias

2000, 303); and, we may infer, gender relations[14] since the knight operated literally as patriarch. Force, class, and gender relations were intertwined, distinguishable but inseparable, and constituted through conflict:

> There was mistrust towards women – who were essentially objects of sensual satisfaction – delight in plundering and rape, desire to acknowledge no master, servility among the peasants on whom they lived, and behind all this the impalpable pressures that could not be met with weapons or physical violence: debt, the cramped, impoverished mode of life contrasting sharply with their larger aspirations, and mistrust of money whether in the hands of the masters or the peasants. (Elias 2000, 242)

And this same knight faced worse dangers from the other members of his own class, those who most resembled him in their subject position and with whom he might have most identified. Other knights posed a constant threat to him; they coveted his lands, as he coveted theirs (Elias 2000, 219):

> In the struggles in both these periods, the actual social existence of all the participants is at stake. That is the compulsion behind these struggles ... Either they can be conquered ... In extreme cases this means: imprisonment, violent death or material distress, perhaps starvation. In the mildest cases it means social decline, loss of independence, absorption by a larger social complex, and thereby the destruction of what gave their lives meaning ... Or they may repel and conquer their nearest rivals ... The mere preservation of their social existence demands, in the situation of free competition, this constant enlargement. (Elias 2000, 305)

A knight's ability to defend his holdings or to enlarge them depended on his ability to summon, on or off the battlefield, the ferocity to inspire his followers and intimidate his foes, as Elias describes in his portrait of Henri II de Montmorency: "To give way directly to impulses and not to take thought of the further consequences was ... a mode of behaviour which – even if it led to the downfall of the individual – was adequate to the social structure as a whole and

---

14 I base this notion of gender as class on Wittig (1992).

therefore to 'reality.' Martial fervour was a necessary precondition of success and prestige for a man of the nobility" (Elias 2000, 405). The "uninhibited" and "spontaneous" emotional behaviour of the knight, therefore, derives from a definite figurational situation. The civilizing process advances not by superimposing socially produced constraints on essential human drives but by reorganizing relations of violence and affect from one figurational movement to another.

If what civilized people call "barbarism" is not a natural or primitive condition but a particular social figuration, and if this figuration operates as the condition of possibility, indeed as the very engine, of the civilizing process, then *the civilizing process must reproduce barbarism in order to advance*. I've already shown that this happens in processes of state formation: sovereign power both depends on and reproduces the social capacity for violence; through the formation of greater and greater military capacity, the system of sovereign states continually reproduces on an ever-expanding scale the very problem that we expect it to solve. How does this happen at the level of habitus? To understand this, we need to look at the importance of *shame* in the formation of subjectivity.

The monopolization of military force by sovereign lords transmuted the life-or-death struggles among knights into the life-or-death struggles among states. But it also failed to extinguish the same struggle among the knights-turned-courtiers themselves. If the actual *social* existence of the feudal knight was at stake in his competitive struggles with others of his own class, the same was true for the civilized aristocrat: "Only life at court opened to individual nobles within this social field access to economic and prestige opportunities that could in any way satisfy their claims to an existence of upper-class distinction ... only life amid courtly society could maintain the distance from others and the prestige on which depended their salvation, their existence as members of the upper class, the establishment or the 'Society' of the country" (Elias 2000, 395). Expulsion from court society (from "Society" in an older sense of the term) constituted a serious, if not fatal, blow to one's social existence. It meant a loss of social standing, economic privilege, personal networks, and opportunities for performance of self that distinguished aristocrats from common people. Since social identity depends on relations of difference, exclusion from "Society," the "obliteration of social distinction" (Elias 2000, 395), meant, for aristocrats, the obliteration of their identity – that is, of *who they were* to themselves as well as to others. Loss of quasi-objective social status entailed a loss of quasi-subjective self-identity: "The conflict expressed in shame-fear is not merely a conflict of the individual with prevalent social opinion; the individual's behaviour has brought him into conflict with the part of himself that represents this social opinion. It is a conflict within his own personality; he recognizes himself as inferior. He fears the loss of the love or respect of others ... Their attitude has precipitated an attitude within him that he automatically adopts towards himself" (Elias 2000, 415). Hence the double meaning of the word "shame," which connotes both "disgrace, ignominy, loss of esteem or reputation" and "the painful emotion arising from the consciousness of something dishonouring" (Oxford English Dictionary 2010); where these meanings join and commingle, "shame" becomes not only a psychological concept but also a sociological one.

And precisely this notion of shame defines what was at stake in the performance of courtesy or civility. Successful or unsuccessful adherence to courteous conduct meant a real gain or loss in social standing, bringing with it symbolic and material gains or losses that became more and more important as the knights lost their autonomy and became dependent on the sovereign. Under these circumstances, charging others with a breach of courtesy or civility or civilized behaviour could inflict real harm on them, or at least threaten to. It was, in effect, a form of violence. For identities constituted through relations of hierarchical difference, shame could effect the *destruction of one's social self*.

Any process that threatens to destroy an individual's self constitutes a form of violence. So in the context of court society, any deployment of shame by which one subject could threaten another with exclusion from this society constituted a form of nonphysical violence, or what Pierre Bourdieu calls "symbolic violence" (Bourdieu 1990, 127; Bourdieu 2001; Bourdieu and Wacquant 1992, 167–8). Elias recognizes that monopolies of force make forms of nonphysical violence more important, especially economic violence (Elias 2000, 369), and he also recognizes the immense importance to individuals of preserving not just their physical lives but also their meaningful social existence (Elias 1996, 237ff, 351–3, 357–9). Through the transmutation of direct physical violence into symbolic violence, the feudal figuration of life-or-death struggle among autarkic subjects *persisted* in the "pacified" social spaces of court society; "it is just that conflict is now settled in a different way, one that has come to be labeled – by those who practice it – as more 'civilized'" (Burkitt 1996, 139). And this struggle propelled the development of increasingly sophisticated forms of self-regulation of bodily conduct.

Like state formation, the formation of civilized habitus has the formal properties of an arms race. Faced with the task of winning by charm and esteem privileges that they could not compel by force, knights innovated performances of the body to distinguish themselves from others, to win esteem for themselves, and by implication, to lessen the relative esteem of others. But knights also copied each other's performances, and in this way tactical advantages that distinguished one knight from his peers turned into general standards of acceptable conduct that distinguished the nobility from their inferiors. Where innovations of conduct conferred social advantage, others copied them until they ceased to function as advantages and functioned as minima. We can understand this as a process of fetishization (Marx 1990, 163), through which the practices of courtesy "transcended sensuousness" and confronted the knight as something outside of himself, even while the meaning of these practices constituted a part of the civilized subject's own sense of self. "Physical clashes, wars and feuds diminish," and anything recalling them disappeared from view. But "at the same time the battlefield is, in a sense, moved within. Part of the tensions and passions that were earlier directly released in the struggle of man and man, must now be worked out within the human being" (Elias 2000, 375; see also 424). As sovereigns reduced knights to dependency, and as other classes challenged the aristocratic monopoly on symbolic violence, the standards of civilized conduct progressively escalated. Each turn of the dance brought the dancers to a higher pitch of intensity.

Once this increasingly elaborate complex of bodily practices functions as a necessary condition of social inclusion, the performance of courtesy – or civility, or civilized behaviour – functions to *defer* the violence of social exclusion. Just as sovereigns arm themselves with the means of physical violence, so too do civilized subjects arm themselves with the means of symbolic violence to deter others similarly armed. This process produces and maintains distinction, *difference* marked by *deference*; hence it produces difference at the same time that it imbues difference with the danger of violence on which class privilege depends. The success of this deferral, differentiation, or *deferentiation* depends on the continuous activation of the threat of violence and hence on the possible application of shame to those who fail in their performances and to those classes of persons who lack civilization – which, over time, have included variously commoners, women, Jews, ethnic minorities, the racialized subjects of empire, and so on. So those persons, too, develop techniques for deferring violence, through the deferential performance of their differential subjugation, and so, in this way among others, acquire civilization. All civilized subjects obtain for themselves a *conditional* protection from the stored-up deferred violence of civilization, a conditional inclusion in what Helen Fein calls "the universe of obligation" (Fein 1979, 169; 1993, 36), exclusion from which serves as a precondition for genocide.

If sovereignty accumulates the deferred violence of the civilizing process in its institutional military and police capacities, where does deferred violence accumulate at the level of habitus? In the relation of individuals to themselves. Elias repeatedly emphasizes how the civilizing process constitutes an expanding network of relations of interdependence (Elias 2000, 128–9, 180, 231–8, 253–4, 326, 368, 370, 379–82, 481–2, and elsewhere). But this network also functions as a grid of differences or differentiations that stabilizes the identities of all involved – both their "we-identities" and their "I-identities." Consequently, deferred violence of the civilizing process operates within the structure of individual and collective identity. The "structure of social tensions" that martial competition had produced lives on in pacified society "as a continuous pressure that each individual member of the nobility must absorb within him or herself," turning a flame that could flare up and die away quickly into a "permanently smouldering fire whose flame is hidden and seldom breaks out directly" (Elias 2000, 423). The battlefield, Elias says, moves within (Elias 2000, 375, 424), as all individuals struggle to maintain their social standing and, with it, their sense of self under the constant and only partially calculable threat of shame. But successful performance of civilized conduct is always temporary, subject to failure at the next performance or at the next after that (Goffman 1959). As a result, social inclusion is always conditional and unstable. For civilized subjects, this conditional inclusion entails a correspondingly conditional self-acceptance and a habitual readiness to inflict violence on one's own self. And this in turn implies a conditional acceptance of others, a readiness to commit, or at least to condone, violence against those who count as Other because they have no secure place within the network of difference-deference-deferral that the civilizing process generates. So even in areas thoroughly pacified by the sovereign monopoly of force, "physical violence and the threat emanating from it have a determining influence on individuals in society, whether they know it or not ... [A] continuous, uniform pressure is exerted on individual life by the physical violence stored behind the scenes of everyday/everyday life, a pressure totally familiar and hardly perceived, conduct and drive economy having been adjusted from earliest youth to this social structure" (Elias 2000, 372). The deferral of physical violence produces ever-more elaborate and extensive structures of symbolic violence, which produce powerful but *conditional* mutual identification. This explains why civilized subjects can fail to recognize the humanity of others. It explains also why the armour of civilized conduct can crumble so speedily in the face of incalculable danger: in these moments, symbolic violence transforms back into physical violence. Through a *practical* process of différance as deferentiation, civilization reproduces barbarism within itself. Hence the *contradiction* of the civilizing process: seeking to produce our own security, we as subjects reproduce – both in the world around us and in our very selves, and on an ever-expanding scale – the conditions that threaten us with violence.

IDENTITY, IMPUNITY, AND INTEREST: THE ROOTS OF CIVILIZING GENOCIDES

The forward motion of the civilizing process reproduces the very barbarism that serves as its necessary precondition. The term "barbarizing-civilizing process" encompasses this dual movement, and thereby includes the history of colonial genocide, without reducing the figuration only to its negative aspects. Moreover, following Samir Amin's (1989, xii–xiii) use of the concept of Eurocentrism, we could usefully qualify the figuration in question as the "Eurocentric barbarizing-civilizing process," or "Eurocentric barbarization-civilization," to indicate the network of global relations through which the former European colonial powers and their settler-society offshoots have imposed the "self-image of the West" on the earth as a whole.

Reframing civilization as barbarization-civilization transforms the question "why does genocide happen despite civilization?" by opening it up to include also the question "why does genocide not happen everywhere within civilization?" Eurocentric barbarization-civilization produces *both* forces that enable genocide *and* forces that inhibit it. These forces operate along three axes: identity-difference, impunity-interdependence, and interest-indifference.

Through the movement of deferentiation, Eurocentric barbaric civilization produces hierarchical relations of identity-difference that entail a conditional inclusion in networks of moral obligation. Deferentiation inscribes these relations into the habitus of subjects, making them manifest and recognizable. Consider, for example, the differing bodily performances of gender (Bourdieu 2001; Garfinkel 1967; Young 2005) among white men and women or the minutiae of posture, eye contact, and gait through which black subjects negotiated their relationships with whites in the segregationist United States (e.g., Griffin 1977). In colonizers' accounts of their encounters with Indigenous peoples of the Americas, differences in dress, eating habits, and even smiling and laughing occasioned a gulf of incomprehension. Under conditions of Eurocentric barbaric civilization, habitus functions to indicate the social groups that others belong to, their relative power within the figuration, and hence the extent of one's practical moral obligation to them or impunity over them. Within force relations, superiority to another consists of having the liberty to treat that other as one wishes, without prohibitive repercussions. Thus relations of identity-difference also constitute relations of impunity-interdependence.[15] Habitus makes both of these types of relation evident to the observer who knows how to read its codes – but only imperfectly.

In Elias's account of the pacification of the warrior class, sovereign monopolies achieve pacification by altering the power balance within the figuration, depriving the knights of the impunity they enjoy over their subjects without entirely transferring that impunity to the sovereign. Nobles depend on the sovereign, but sovereigns also depend to varying degrees on the various classes of their subjects, increasingly as chains of functional interdependency within the figuration grow longer: "As the interdependence of people increases with the increasing division of labour, everyone becomes increasingly dependent on everyone else, even those of high social rank on those people who are socially inferior and weaker" (Elias 2000, 117). Elias's notion of function connotes not the service that each

---

15 For a more detailed examination of this relation, see Bowman (2001).

part contributes to an organically integrated whole but a particular kind of power relationship: "when one person (or a group of persons) lacks something which another person or group has the power to withhold, the latter has a function for the other" (Elias 1978, 78). So in what Elias calls the "primal contest," when two opposed groups with no mutual identification to each other compete for scarce resources, each group fulfils the function of enemy to the other so long as neither side has the power either to eliminate the other or to do without the goods that the other holds. Functional interdependency, then, expresses a power relation. Or rather, it expresses one pole of a continuum of balances of power, with impunity at the other pole. Thus one can conceptualize, for example, the variable role of violence and genocide in colonialism in terms of contingent local variations in the impunity-interdependency relation between colonizers and colonized. Colonized groups escaped genocide to the extent that they could fulfil a function for their colonizer, through some combination of resistance and service, securing a relatively protected space for themselves within the growing network of Eurocentric barbaric civilization. Pacification results from the loss of power to treat others merely as objects, the loss of impunity. The constraint to treat others as subjects can flow downward from the top of a social hierarchy, but it can also flow laterally and from the bottom up.

Eurocentric barbaric civilization produces simultaneously, but not at the same rate, both the relations of functional interdependency that reduce impunity and the deferral of violence on an expanding scale. Elias (1998, 180) characterizes this in terms of competing functions that the monopoly of force serves for sovereigns and for their subjects. As Burkitt explains, "if the balance of power relations move too far in favour of those who control the monopoly of violence it can be used for their own purposes, without the consent of the people and even against certain sections of the people" (Burkitt 1996, 140). But in the historical practice of genocide, many more oppositions come into play than only that between states and subjects. Settlers in a colonial society, dominant ethnicities in a multi-ethnic state, privileged economic classes faced with structural transformation, religious movements, gender groups, and so on – each can enjoy the impunity to perpetrate genocide. And the co-production of interdependency and impunity can generate complex situations in which a vulnerable identity-group loses its function because of events elsewhere in the figuration.

For example, consider the obliteration of the Ottoman Armenian community in the last years of the empire. Why only then, and not at the height of its power, did the Ottoman Empire perpetrate this holocaust? Vahakn Dadrian's (1997) account suggests that as long as the Ottoman state remained a multi-ethnic, cosmopolitan empire, the Armenians served a function as loyal servants of the empire, helping to maintain through their loyalty the legitimacy of Ottoman rule against separatist threats based on nation self-assertion. When the various other national minorities within the empire broke away to form their own nation-states, Armenian loyalty lost its function and the state acquired the impunity to commit genocide. The partly imaginary figure of Armenian disloyalty, inflated by the architects of the genocide, served a function by providing a radical Other to reinforce collective Turkish identity. This example shows how genocide can seem to result from social breakdown, even as it enables a productive process: the Armenian holocaust facilitated the emergence of the modern nation-state of Turkey based on ethnic solidarity. It represents, unfortunately, a successful genocide.

This example also points to the importance of *interest*, which serves as the third necessary condition for genocide. The interests that benefit from genocide and make it rational for some actors can vary enormously, which substantially accounts for the very wide range of genocidal practices. Genocide can obtain for its perpetrators wealth, territory, ideological homogeneity, intimidation of enemies, solidarity among members of the perpetrator identity, removal of a threat or obstacle to other strategic goals, or other benefits. All of these may contribute to the extension and intensification of Eurocentric barbaric civilization, both in terms of the formation of territorially sovereign states and in terms of the formation of the habitus that distinguishes civilized subjects from their barbarized Others. The interests that a given genocide serves partially determine the means its perpetrators use to accomplish it, the energy and resources they invest in it, the consistency with which they pursue it, and so on. Frank Chalk and Kurt Jonassohn's claim (1990, 416–21) that genocide produces more harm than good for the perpetrator does not apply universally: some genocides succeed. To work effectively toward the prevention of genocide, we must examine the diverse range of interests that draw different actors into genocide and consider what genocides produce as well as what they destroy.

CONCLUSION

How do identity, impunity, and interest come together to produce genocides within the barbarizing- civilizing process? I first want to say a word about the specificity of this question. The barbarizing-civilizing process that I have been talking about, and that Elias analyzes in so much detail, emerged in western Europe in the late Middle Ages and has become truly global only in the past few centuries. It is not the only figuration to combine the centralized monopolization of military force with the formation of a specific social constraint to self-constraint. These other civilizations need to be examined in their own specificity, not treated as earlier and more rudimentary versions of the one that is currently dominant. So to recognize this, we should call this figuration something more specific. The usual terms – European or Western or modern Western civilization – underestimate the globality of this figuration, which no longer has any outside, no matter what Samuel Huntington (1996) might imagine. To reflect its particular historical origins while allowing for its global scope, I have suggested that we follow Amin's terminology and call it *Eurocentric* barbaric civilization.

Second, not all genocides, historically or today, can be explained as products of this figuration. Such is the case because, obviously, the figuration has not always existed everywhere and, less obviously, because it is perhaps still possible that some genocides even today really do result from the sheer breakdown of monopolies of military force and of the specific forms of self-constraint centred on these monopolies. So I propose the term *civilizing genocides* to refer to genocides that happen in the course of an expansion or intensification of the civilizing process. Civilizing genocides happen as a consequence of or as a means to the expansion of a state's monopoly of force, and also as an expansion of the specific habitus that enables and is enabled by this monopoly. We can recognize a civilizing genocide when its aim or its practical result is the consolidation of state power. But we can also recognize it when victims are targeted based on their actual or attributed way of life, on their practices of the body, on their form of self-control (the balance of what they restrain and what they express, what they calculate and what they perform spontaneously), or even on features of their bodies as such that are construed as different from those of the perpetrator's habitus, whether this flies under the flag of "civilized behaviour" or whether it goes by some other name.

The expansion of Eurocentric barbaric civilization produces relations of identity-difference that are defined by differential relations
to the means of violence and constituted through habitus. So far I've
tended to follow Elias in speaking of this habitus as if it were singular, a single standard of conduct to which all subjects aspire. But the
contradiction of deferentiation, the differential and deferential deferral of violence, generates multiple forms of habitus, each according to the subject's location in the relations of violence. The habit of
downcast eyes and a humble tone of voice when addressing one's
betters is as much a feature of civilized behaviour as is the haughti-
ness of aristocrats. Specific forms of habitus develop in accordance
with specific balances of power relation. As Bourdieu observes in
Distinction and in *Masculine Domination*, the appropriation of
upper-class habitus by those who aspire to upward mobility is only
one feature of a system that also includes forms of habitus that sig-
nal and reinforce the inequality or asymmetry of social interdependencies. The deference of women to men in a sexist milieu, or of black
folk to white folk in a racist one, and the specific forms of conduct
by which women or black folk or working-class people relax among
others of their own kind – all are various aspects of the same network of relations. Any form of habitus that does not obey the logic
of deference, that is not smoothly incorporated into this network,
threatens its hierarchies. So the habitus of Aboriginal people who
have not yet been colonized stands, in the eyes of their would-be
colonizers, as a living refutation of the emotional investments of
civilized subjects – of the violences civilized persons have suffered
and out of which they have built their selves. So too does the habitus
of the worker or negro or woman or of the Jew or Armenian or
colonized Indigenous person who drops the habit of deference and
behaves as the equal of his or her "betters." Such persons become
Other because their actions place them outside of the network of
deferrals, deferences, and differentiations that tie them to the force
of the sovereign.

Eurocentric barbaric civilization produces interdependencies among
social superiors and inferiors, but these are unequal or asymmetrical
interdependencies. Masters depend on subjects, or else they would
not be masters, but what they depend on is not a concrete person but
the *figure* of the subject (or figurational position of the subject), the
fact of a person performing the subject end of the subject-master
relation, and individual people can come and go from this position

with great ease (just as subjects are dominated by the figure of the master more than by the concrete person who occupies that figure). We can explain this by analogy to workers and capitalists. If you are a capitalist and I am a worker, then as long as I work for you, I perform a function for you; that is, I have the capacity to keep from you something that you need or want. So I am relatively safe from violence at your hands (as long as you know your own interests). But if I go on strike, then by withdrawing my labour I leave myself without a function for you, and you have nothing to lose by hiring a gang of thugs to beat me and my fellows back into submission, or even to kill some of us to frighten the rest. This situation describes a transition from asymmetrical interdependence to impunity. This transition can happen for a variety of reasons: because those of the subordinate party exercise their function by withdrawing what they have to withdraw and so lose this function; because they lose it for some other reason; because something happens elsewhere, outside of the relationship, to render this function irrelevant; because something happens to make possible the invention of a new identity whose only function is to make subordinates into the Other, the ones who are to die, in order to produce or intensify the solidarity of a Self among those of the dominant party. All of these conditions are relational, as are the identities that define who is dominant and who is subordinate. The Indigenous peoples of the Americas were not Indians until Europeans encountered them and incorporated them, suddenly and violently, as objects of impunity in relations of deferentiation.

Within Eurocentric barbaric civilization, asymmetry of interdependencies and the potential for impunity are constantly shifting. The contradiction of deferentiation is expressed in the tension between the production of impunity and the production of interdependency. Through the struggles of the dominant to secure their dominance, the capacity for socially organized violence is produced and reproduced on an ever-expanding scale; through the struggles of the dominated to make their superiors dependent on them, this violence is deferred. When the latter process falls too far behind the former, the deferral of violence stops, and one pole of an identity-difference relation becomes the object of violent categorical obliteration. The process is comparable to what happens when the weaker partner in an arms race falls too far behind the other. But we can also say, contradictions being what they are, that through their struggles for security the dominated unintentionally reproduce their own insecurity, and through their struggles for dominance those who hold mastery unintentionally make themselves dependent on their inferiors. Again, when the latter process falls too far behind the former, deferral stops and violence is instantiated. I don't know whether there is any general indicator for when this happens. Genocide results from local and contingent turns in the power struggles among groups that constitute each other as groups through the process of struggle. Eurocentric barbaric civilization provides the matrix that ties together interest, identity, and impunity in an inexhaustible variety of permutations. In some of these permutations, genocide becomes rational, moral, and functional.

At this point, given the current state of our knowledge, we can learn to identify these permutations only by empirical historical study.

PART TWO

5

Genocides of Ideological Others
in Languedoc and Guatemala

INTRODUCTION

The next three chapters illustrate the uses of the theoretical frame-work I have developed by applying it to a series of historical examples drawn from the course of the expansion of Western civilization. Each chapter considers a pair of examples linked by a common structural factor. This chapter analyzes two instances in which state authorities, goaded and supported by a transnational power, used massacre, execution, torture, and other instruments of political terror to destroy a network of people defined by their actual or supposed opposition to the dominant ideology of their society. These instances are the extermination of the Cathars of Languedoc by the Catholic Church and its secular allies, including the king of France, in the thirteenth and fourteenth centuries and the mass murder and political terrorization of Mayans and supposed communists between 1980 and 1983 by the Guatemalan government with support from the United States of America. For each example, I show how genocide acted as an instrument for extending or consolidating both axes of the civilizing process: on the one hand, the state's sovereign monopoly on military force; and on the other, the forms of distinction that define relations between dominant and subordinated subjects – between, one might say, sovereign subjects and shameful, abject Others.

As it happens, these two cases inspired the line of empirical historical inquiry that led to this book. When I first read about the persecution of the Cathars, I was surprised by its similarity to political persecution in Central America during the 1980s: the use of guilt by suspicion, the solicitation of denunciations, secret interrogations, the extensive use of torture, and a preoccupation with extracting confessions and the names of co-conspirators. In both cases, the perpetrators of violence sought to find and destroy an Other defined not by skin tone or facial features or family lineage but by thoughts, convictions, and practices carried out in secret. In both cases, perpetrators sought to destroy a social movement that had both military and civilian expressions, such that defeat on the battlefield did not immediately mean defeat of the movement. Both sets of perpetrators understood themselves to be fighting something more than a group of individuals; they knew they were up against a collective identity sustained by practice, a "way of life," as one American official put it (Fred Sherwood, quoted in Fuentes and Ehrenreich 1983, 43). To destroy a way of life, violence attacked not only individual human lives but also the relational bonds between individuals in the effort to reinscribe the form of relations that benefitted the dominant subjects of sovereign power. From the massacre of whole towns and villages to the intimate and liminal space of the torture chambers, both of these genocides worked to define the right way to be a person, the right way to be-with-others.

PART ONE: LANGUEDOC

Introduction

From 1209 to 1321 the Catholic Church waged a campaign of extermination against the Cathars of Languedoc. This campaign took the lives of an estimated two hundred thousand men, women, and even children (Rummel 1994, 70, 234). They died in public executions, burned alive for heresy; they died at the swords of marauding crusader armies from the north, who sacked whole cities and held mass executions; they died after these armies destroyed their wells and villages, burned their crops and orchards; they died in prison, after torture, sent there by a neighbour's malicious testimony, or by an inquisitor's zealous use of hearsay, or by some other poor wretch's tortured "confession." Many died not for having practised heresy but for having known and associated with heretics – an unexceptional condition in the densely populated and comparatively tolerant lands of Languedoc. They died, unwilling sacrifices, to re-establish the ecclesiastical dominance of the Roman Catholic Church so that *its* doctrines, *its* practices, and no others would define Christianity in western Europe, and on this score at least they did not die for nothing. When Guillaume Bélibaste, the last Cathar "Perfect," was burned alive in 1321, Cathar practice disappeared from western Europe, "leaving not a wraith behind" (Lambert 1998, 314).

Who were the Cathars that the holy see and the kings of Paris should seek their destruction so zealously? The brief answer is that they were heretics, practitioners of a version of Christianity fundamentally opposed to the Catholic Church in crucial matters of doctrine, ritual, and spiritual authority. In Frank Chalk and Kurt Jonassohn's terms, their extermination counts as an ideological genocide, committed "to implement a belief, a theory, or an ideology" (Chalk and Jonassohn 1990, 29). That the church, faced with a challenge to its ideological dominance, should seek to destroy this threat might appear self-evident. But this self-evidence assumes that difference equals danger – the very assumption that I seek to interrogate. Why and how, in the thirteenth century, in the territory that would become southern France, did religious difference give rise to exterminatory religious violence?

The very phrase "religious violence" contains its own problematic self-evidence. It suggests, for many, that something in the nature of religious doctrines leads to intolerance and violence – because of the absolute truth accorded these doctrines, for instance, or because of the emotional and irrational nature of religious experience. Again, we must question this self-evidence if we want to understand the historical dynamics of religious persecution. Even a brief look at Christian doctrines shows their complexity and potential ambivalence. The Gospels, for instance, report Jesus of Nazareth as teaching that "whosoever shall deny me before men, him will I also deny before my Father which is in heaven. Think not that I came to send peace on earth: I came not to send peace but a sword" (Matthew 11:34–5, King James Version). But they also report him as saying, "Resist not evil: but whosoever shall smite thee on thy right cheek, turn to him the other also" and "Love your enemies, bless them that curse you, do good to them that hate you, and pray for them which despitefully use you, and persecute you" (Matthew 5:39, 44). Or again: "If any man come to me, and hate not his father, and mother, and wife, and children, and bretheren, and sisters, yea, and his own life also, he cannot be my disciple" (Luke 15:26) but also "Thou shalt love thy neighbour as thyself" (Mark 12:31) and "A new commandment I give unto you, That ye love one another; as I have loved

you, that ye also love one another. By this shall all men know that
ye are my disciples, if ye have love one to another" (John 13:34–5).
Diligent readers of the Bible can resolve these contradictions for
themselves, and they have done so in widely varying ways over the
history of Christian practice. This variability makes the Gospels a
polysemous text, capable of multiple meanings and multiple messa-
ges. And if the Gospels are polysemous, the Christian Bible as a whole
is even more so – and the long and complex tradition of Christian
thought from the first through the thirteenth centuries is even more
so than the Bible alone. Indeed, we can understand the enormous
effort of the Catholic Church to suppress heresy as a great labour of
suppressing the polysemy of its founding texts, a Herculean effort to
make them say one thing and one thing only. Or, rather, a Sisyphean
effort given how easily a text again becomes polyvocal as soon as the
effort of suppressing alternate meanings begins to weaken.

In other words, we should be wary of two familiar and commonplace essentialisms that distract from historical explanation: treating
religious difference as a sufficient cause for religious violence; and
treating abstract doctrines as a sufficient explanation for actual
practices. Whether difference occasions violence and how believers
put their doctrines into practice depend on the concrete social relations that connect people to one another. These connective relations,
whether peaceful or agonistic, define the contours and the stakes of
identity and difference.

Who Were the Cathars?

The precise origins of Catharism are still obscure, but its dualist
doctrines were influenced by those of the Bogomil Church, which
emerged in Bulgaria in the tenth century (Barber 2000, 2, 12–21;
Burl 2002, 9; Lambert 1998, 23–32). The Cathars practised a version of Christianity fundamentally opposed to Roman Catholicism
in crucial matters of doctrine and ritual. They believed that the material world had been created not by the good God of the spirit and
of light but by an evil being of darkness who was either co-divine
with the God of light or a fallen angelic being (Barber 2000, 1).
The good God regarded all things material as equally corrupt and
had never materially incarnated as the Christ. The teachings of the
Roman Church with regard to bodily practices such as sexual chastity had no spiritual value; nor did any of its rituals and sacraments.

Committed Cathars sought to unify themselves with God and free themselves from the otherwise eternal cycle of reincarnation in the corrupt world by renouncing all things material and pursuing a life of ascetic self-denial that included strict poverty, chastity, and abstention from "eating any products of coition: meat, milk, cheese, and eggs" (Shahar 2009, 16). The only Cathar sacrament, called the *consolamentum*, marked a person's entry onto this strict path of renunciation. Persons who chose this path were called "good men" or "good women," and those who accepted Cathar doctrine without passing through the consolamentum were called *credentes* (believers). The Cathars collectively called themselves only "good Christians"; the name "Cathars," from Greek *katharos*, meaning "pure," emerged as a sneering epithet, coined by the German monk Ekbert von Schönau in the twelfth century (Burl 2002, 9). Likewise, those who had received the consolamentum were called the "Perfect" by orthodox Christians,[1] in the sense of perfect or complete heretics (O'Shea 2000, 21). The Cathars had no ecclesiastical hierarchy and a minimal, decentralized institutional structure, and they regarded the temporal wealth and power of the church as a sign of its corruption (Barber 2000, 1).

Differences of theological doctrine gain their impact on lived experience through their connection to concrete practices. Catholic religious practice, in the thirteenth century as now, involved sacred acts, or sacraments, many of them marking crucial moments in the life cycle: baptism of infants, confirmation of adults, marriage, eucharist, confession and penance, and funerals. It also involved minor but habitual acts of devotion, such as reverence for the cross and for images of the saints (Rubin 2009a). Cathars rejected each of these practices as corrupt (Barber 2000, 101–2). This practical rejection had potentially major implications for the structure of western European society. Catholic religious practice engendered a network of relations of identity: people's repetition of the same gestures and same words and their profession of the same doctrines produced, concretely, a community of faith. At the same time,

---

1 Strictly speaking, a male initiate was called a *Perfectus* and a female initiate a *Perfecta*; the plural terms were *Perfecti* and *Perfectae*. I have chosen to use the English term because it lends itself more readily to gender-inclusiveness. This is especially important given the exceptionally prominent role that women played alongside men in the Cathar movement.

through these same actions, Catholics produced and reproduced the temporal power of the church over spiritual practice. Cathars, rejecting these practices and implementing their own, made themselves different from other Christians in a way that the devout Catholic and the committed Cathar alike would have felt intuitively, in the gut. This practical work of making-different also defined a new social identity, a network of like practitioners for which terms like "good Christians" and "Cathars" served as labels of convenience. And because this network, or community, was generated though practices not governed from Rome, it existed outside of and yet in relation to the network of Catholic identity. Relationally speaking, Cathars lived outside of Catholicism but close by; Catharism constituted a relational space whose expansion could only diminish that of Catholicism – a space into which the church could expand as an act of reconquest. To the Catholic Church, Cathars represented both a threat and an opportunity – a threat to the church's claim to ecclesiastical dominion over a unified Christian identity and an opportunity for the church to re-establish this dominion and this identity by redefining it in opposition to the abjection of the heretic.

State Formation in Languedoc

Catharism flourished primarily in the region of Languedoc and also in parts of northern Italy (see Lansing 1998). Before the devastation of the Crusades and the Inquisition, Languedoc enjoyed a "flourishing, cosmopolitan culture" (Chalk and Jonassohn 1990, 114). Language defined the region, literally as the area where Occitan was spoken. It was "a rich province" (Sumption 1978, 24) thanks to commercial trade on the Mediterranean and was more urbanized and densely populated than northern France (Sumption 1978, 25). It served as home to the culture of troubadours (Sumption 1978, 29–30), whose songs romanticizing court life bear witness to the refinement of manners and social graces among the aristocracy. The counts of Languedoc owed no substantial allegiance to the Capetian kings, although they paid them nominal homage (Sumption 1978, 17–18). The centrifugal break-up of the Holy Roman Empire, which Norbert Elias discusses in *The Civilizing Process*, had left Languedoc a patchwork of noncontiguous family holdings dotted with tiny independent fiefdoms. This centrifugal tendency had been somewhat reversed by the steady growth of the power of the county of Toulouse since the successes of Raymond IV in the eleventh century (Sumption 1978, 18). However, the Albigensian Crusade would completely overshadow locally centripetal tendencies through the sudden and violent incorporation of Languedoc into the Kingdom of France.

Elias's historical account of the civilizing process opens with France of the twelfth century, at the time in which the decentralization of the control of military force began to reverse itself. The centripetal accretion of military power in this period marked the beginning of a process that would eventually produce territorially sovereign nation-states. This state formation process had two crucial effects: it served as a material precondition for the cultural accomplishments that would define European civilization, and it engendered a gradual transformation of the subjectivities of members of the warrior class toward the particular forms of habitual self-regulation conveyed by the term "civilized behaviour." How did the extermination of the Cathars figure in this civilizing process?

Elias mentions the conquest of Languedoc only in passing, in the context of his discussion of the territorial accretion through which the noncontiguous holdings of the Capetian house morphed into the integrated territory of France. Elias notes that this transformation was not specifically planned or foreseen by those who brought it about and that even Philip II Augustus, for instance, "did not yet have 'France' in our sense in view." What Philip Augustus aimed at was "the territorial, military, and economic expansion of his family power and the subjugation of its most dangerous competitors, the Plantagenets" (Elias 2000, 285). Following Philip Augustus's success in achieving these goals, his successors simply carried the process further. The holocaust in Languedoc contributed to this process: "Louis VIII, Philip Augustus' son, secured this region [Poitou] afresh for his own dominion, as he did Saintonge, Anis and Languedoc, part of Picardy and the county of Perche. Partly in the form of a religious war, the struggle against the Albigensian heretics, the Capetian house began to advance south into the sphere of the only great territorial lord in that part who could, beside the Plantagenets, rival the power of the Capetians, the domain of the counts of Toulouse" (Elias 2000, 286). This brief discussion locates the Albigensian Crusade firmly within the state-formation process that partially defines civilization. But more can be said.

For one thing, a centripetal accretion of power was already taking place in Languedoc before the crusaders made their appearance.[2] In Eliasian terms, state formation was already incipient in Languedoc. Count Raymond V (1148–94) had enjoyed considerable success in expanding the family domains (Sumption 1978, 18), as had the rival viscounts of Béziers and Carcassonne (Barber 2000, 46). In other words, by the time that Pope Innocent III began pressuring Raymond VI to suppress heresy in Toulouse, the nadir of state formation in Languedoc lay well in the past, and the competition for regional sovereignty had begun.

Furthermore, the importance of troubadours in Occitan society suggests that another key aspect of the civilizing process had already established itself in Languedoc: the constraint to self-restraint imposed on otherwise habitually violent knights by the codes of *courtoisie*. Elias gives considerable attention to the relationship between the civilizing process and the music of the troubadours (Elias 2000, 236–56). Not only did courts provide the economic basis of support for the troubadours themselves, and not only did the knightly, or noble, troubadours come mainly from the ranks of the knights with little or no land who placed themselves in the service of greater ones, but the social relations at court also provided the lyrical content of the minstrels' songs. In part, these songs paid political homage to the singer's patron (Elias 2000, 245). But another major, and famous, staple for the troubadour was the love song, the song expressing tender affection and unconsummated yearning toward an idealized beloved. This type of song could emerge because of two effects of court society. By imposing a relative inhibition on the use of violence against women, court society gave noblewomen a relatively greater degree of freedom and power than they could enjoy outside of it (Elias 2000, 246–9). As a result of this situation, a male knight might find himself desiring a woman who was his social superior, a woman whom he could not simply take by force, whom he would be unwise

---

2 Jonathan Sumption states otherwise. Noting the continuing subdivision of property that had deprived the troubadours of many of their patrons, Sumption claims that "what the crusaders encountered in Languedoc was a society in an advanced stage of disintegration which still clung to the husk of a civilization that had all but disappeared" (Sumption 1978, 30–1). However, this claim ignores what Sumption himself mentions earlier in his account: the ongoing success of the counts of Toulouse in accreting power to themselves (Sumption 1978, 18).

even to offend; this knight would have to restrain his desires in an otherwise unaccustomed way (Elias 2000, 249–50, 255–6). This improved position of women, their small but substantial freedom from masculine impunity, provides one indication of the civilizing process beginning to take hold.

In these two definitive aspects, state formation and the constraint to self-constraint, Languedoc in the early thirteenth century had already begun to undergo its own process of barbaric civilization. Conquest by the Capetian monarchy did not involve simply an expansion of barbaric civilization into an uncivilized social space but also the destruction of one civilizing figuration and the superimposition of another.

As it happened, the extermination of the Cathars unfolded in two phases: first, through open warfare in the Albigensian Crusade from 1209 to 1228; second, through the operations of the Inquisition from 1229 to 1321. During the years leading up to 1208, Pope Innocent III, keen to regain the ecclesiastical ground lost to various heretical movements, put increasing pressure on the lords of Languedoc, especially Raymond VI, the count of Toulouse, to suppress heresy within their domains; they complied, but too slowly and inconsistently for the pope's liking (O'Shea 2000, 53–4). On 13 January 1208 the papal legate Peter of Castelnau died at the hands of an unknown assassin, and the pope immediately suspected Raymond VI (Sumption 1978, 76; Wakefield 1974, 92–3). Convinced that Languedoc was too tainted by heresy to cleanse itself, the pope called on 10 March 1208 for a crusade to purge Languedoc of heretics and their supporters. In June and July 1209 the crusading army assembled at Lyons and invaded the territory of Raymond Roger Trencavel, the viscount of Albi, Béziers, and Carcassonne (Barber 2000, 254).

On 22 July 1209 the most famous massacre of the war occurred when the crusading army unexpectedly gained entry to the city of Béziers and butchered its inhabitants indiscriminately before putting the city itself to the torch. Between 8,000 and 9,000 men, women, and children died violently, many of them crowded into churches and "huddled by the altars" seeking sanctuary (Burl 2002), although at most only about 700 were heretics (Barber 2000, 65). In mid-August 1209 crusaders occupied the city of Carcassonne after a siege, evacuated its inhabitants, and resettled the city (O'Shea 2000, 100–1; Wakefield 1974, 103). In April 1210 about 100 surviving defenders of the city of Bram suffered mutilation by having their

eyes gouged out and nose and upper lip cut off, before being delivered to Cabaret to intimidate the defenders there (O'Shea 2000, 106;
Barber 2000, 132; Burl 2002, 69). Other massacres occurred in April
1211 at Montgey, where the forces of Raymond Roger surprised
and slaughtered a group of several hundred crusaders and their
noncombatant followers (Burl 2002, 92–3; Barber 2000, 254); on
12 September 1213 at Muret, where at least 7,000 of the routed
civilian militia were butchered by the crusaders (O'Shea 2000, 142,
148–9); in June 1219 at Marmande, where crusaders under Prince
Louis methodically slaughtered "every man, woman, and child" in
"a cold-blooded massacre that mystified even their supporters,"
about 5,000 persons in total (O'Shea 2000, 169; Burl 2002, 159;
see also Wakefield 1974, 99); and in other places. Crusaders performed mass executions, burning at the stake, for example, 140
Cathar Perfect at Minerve on 22 July 1210, 300 to 400 Cathar
Perfect at Lavaur on 3 May 1211, and 50 to 60 Cathar Perfect at Les
Cassès in May 1211 (Barber 2000, 256).

In June 1226 the Capetian king Louis VIII took over leadership of
the crusade, having already fought in it since 1215 as Prince Louis
(Barber 2000, 139, 255). Louis died later in 1225, but in the summer
of 1228 a force raised by his widow, Blanche of Castille, waged a
devastating scorched-earth war on the countryside of Toulouse, destroying not only crops but also villages, wells, and orchards. Count
Raymond VII sued for peace, and in Paris on 12 April 1229 the
Albigensian Crusade was formally ended (O'Shea 2000, 182–7;
Barber 2000, 139–40, 255). From then on, Cathars suffered persecution without recourse to military resistance, with one exception.
Cathars and sympathizers staged a rebellion at Montségur in 1242.
They held out against siege for two years but fell in March 1244;
after the defeat, 200 Cathar Perfect burned at the stake (Sumption
1978, 236–41).

Inquisition

In 1229 Cardinal-Legate Romanus of St Angelo established at
Toulouse the first investigations into heresy after the crusade
(Ruthven 1978, 90; Barber 2000, 144–5; Mundy 2006). Investigators
had the authority to systematically search all homes, barns, caves,
and so on that might serve as hiding places for Cathars. Any persons
convicted of sheltering a Cathar would lose all of their property;

bailiffs negligent in the pursuit of heretics would lose their goods and posts. Since Cathars forbade themselves the swearing of oaths, each person over fourteen years of age had to do just that; each local parish kept a register of who had sworn. Heretics who recanted could resettle; those who did not, including even the infirm who sought the consolamentum on their deathbeds, were burned alive (Ruthven 1978, 90–1; Barber 2000, 145). However, because many Cathars had strong ties to the local community, and because inquisitors could be construed as seeking to destroy orthodox Christians for their own benefit, these measures met with considerable local opposition (Ruthven 1978, 90–1; Lambert 1998, 125–7). Once the military conquest of Languedoc was complete, therefore, the church faced the task of rooting out an invisible network of heretics with whom the local population covertly collaborated.

In the spring of 1233, Pope Gregory IX appointed inquisitors at Toulouse, Albi, and Carcassonne (O'Shea 2000, x, 196; Lambert 1998, 125). As Stephen O'Shea points out, "they would have successors in different parts of Europe and Latin America for more than 600 years" (O'Shea 2000, 196). In each district they visited, the inquisitors began by encouraging anyone who wished to do so to come forward confidentially and reveal any information that might incriminate anyone else as "a heretic, a defender of heretics, or in any way unusual or unconventional in his behaviour" (Ruthven 1978, 92). Heretics themselves were given a grace period in which to recant their beliefs and denounce their co-religionaries in exchange for lighter penalties. This tactic created a tremendous incentive to come forward, to confess, and especially to denounce others. "In a community that had had frequent contact with heretics ... nobody was likely to be innocent in the eyes of the Church, and therefore anybody could have been written into the inquisitors' copious records" (Barber 2000, 148). Suspects under interrogation could not know how much information the inquisitors possessed; in some districts they could not even know who had denounced them.

Interrogations took place under oath, which automatically exposed the committed Perfect; accordingly, actual interrogation procedures aimed at rooting out the *credentes* (believers) and *fautores* (protectors). Although the inquisitors could convict on the testimony of two witnesses, in practice they preferred to obtain a confession (Given 1997, 54; Ruthven 1978, 92). Interrogations focused less on heretical beliefs than on practices, on participation in rituals, and especially on obtaining the names of others complicit in heresy. When more clever credentes gave the names of dead persons to satisfy their interrogators, the inquisitors dug up corpses from cemeteries and burned them as if they were living heretics, disinherited their descendants, and burnt houses they had lived in without regard to the rights of the current inhabitants (O'Shea 2000, 199–200). Popular repute and hearsay evidence counted heavily as evidence of guilt. Even casual social exchange between unwitting persons and persons who later turned out to be Cathars formed sufficient grounds for guilt. The overall effect was to "attack any form of intercourse between the heretics and the Catholic population" (Ruthven 1978, 93).

Over time, the inquisitors developed a wide array of punishments of varying severity. The register of Bernard Gui, inquisitor of Toulouse, contains 633 penalties, ranging from milder penalties such as penitential pilgrimages and the wearing of crosses sewn into one's clothing (a stigma that barred the wearer from any participation in public life), through imprisonments of varying severity and duration, to burning alive and even the burning of corpses of those convicted posthumously (Given 1997, 67–71). The most common penalty that Gui recorded applying was lifetime imprisonment.

In 1252 torture made its formal appearance among the legitimate tools of inquisitorial technique (Ruthven 1978, 94). Even before this development, inquisitors could use a variety of coercive measures: "prolonged solitary confinement in dark, festering cells, a starvation diet, the use of 'stool-pigeons' (fellow prisoners posing as heretic sympathizers)" as well as "the torture of delay," the drawing-out of legal proceedings for months or years (Ruthven 1978, 94), although these techniques were not applied to all prisoners (Given 1997, 62). Even after their formal legitimation, the more direct forms of torture and execution were practised only by secular authorities working on behalf of the inquisitors (Burl 2002, 213). Torture began with the act of displaying the implements of torture to the suspect, followed by removal of clothing, followed by the torture itself: by stretching of the spine on the rack, dislocation of the shoulders on the *strappado*, burning of feet, immersion in water, "anything that hurt as long as bones were not broken and blood was not drawn, always stopping a few agonizing, semi-conscious seconds short of 'mutilation and danger of death'" (Burl 2002, 213).

At its peak the Inquisition operated as "a proficient bureaucracy employing hundreds and interrogating thousands" (O'Shea 2000, 225). The inquisition at Toulouse "had more or less completed its work" in 1271, and in 1279 "it unofficially suspended its activities"; after this time, the main victims of the Albi and Carcassonne tribunals were political opponents of the Inquisition itself (Sumption 1978, 242). Its success was briefly reversed by a revival led in 1300 by Pierre Autier, aided by his brother Guillaume (O'Shea 2000, 233–8). In villages in the hills of the Sabartès near Foix, the Autier brothers gathered about a dozen collaborators and succeeded in winning about 1,000 households back to Catharism. The revival faltered in 1305 with the betrayal and capture of two Perfect, and by 1310 all the leaders of the revival, including Pierre Autier himself, had been captured and burned. The last Cathar Perfect in Languedoc, Guillaume Bélibaste, fell captive in the spring or summer of 1321 and burned at the stake in the autumn of that year in Villerouge-Terménès (Burl 2002, 231; Lambert 1998, 258).[3]

What did the Inquisition have to do with the civilizing process? At first look, the connection seems tenuous. On the one hand, the Inquisition did not directly reinforce military sovereignty: except for the brief rebellion at Montségur from 1242 to 1244, the Cathars did not have the means to challenge Capetian sovereignty in Languedoc after 1228. On the other hand, Elias conceives of the social constraint to self-constraint engendered by court society as an explicitly *secular* process. The very title of volume 1 of *The Civilizing Process*,[4] "Changes in the Behaviour of the Secular Upper Classes in the West," makes this plain (see also Mennell 1992, 37). The Catholic Church attacked one of Desiderius Erasmus's early texts on civility, the *Colloquies*, because of its nonconformity with clerical standards (Elias 2000, 143–4), and not until the eighteenth century did the church play a major role in the dissemination of civility (Elias 2000, 86–7). Elias describes the church as having presented a challenge to the particular figurational tendencies of state formation, offering a failed alternative to statehood as the dominant social organization in European life (e.g., Elias 2000, 328–9).

And yet it would be deeply counterintuitive to leave Christianity out of the ensemble of institutions that make up European civilization. Even if the secular state ultimately thwarted the church's

---

3 Interestingly enough, a version of Catharism survived in Bosnia, beyond the reach of the Roman Church, even becoming the state religion for a time. It eventually faded away in the late fifteenth century (Lambert 1998, 297–313).

4 Contemporary editions include both "volumes" in one book but reproduce the original volume names in the table of contents (Elias 2000).

aspirations to dominance, could we not still find specific techniques or tactics of power developed by the church that have made their way into the enduring figurational ensemble of barbarous civilization?

Historian R.I. Moore argues that practices of persecution developed by the church have drifted loose from their ecclesiastical origins to become an integral feature of contemporary Western societies. Briefly,

> the eleventh and twelfth centuries saw what has turned out to be a permanent change in Western society. Persecution became habitual. That is to say not simply that individuals were subject to violence, but that deliberate and socially sanctioned violence began to be directed, through established governmental, judicial and social institutions, against groups of people defined by general characteristics such as race, religion or way of life; and that membership of such groups in itself came to be regarded as justifying these attacks. (Moore 1990, 5)

Moore claims that religious persecution had "faded away with the Roman Empire, and did not reappear until the eleventh century" (Moore 1990, 4) and that, even then, it did not become regular and systematic for another century afterward. This persecution did not reflect merely the formalization and rationalization of popular attitudes toward difference: secular and ecclesiastical authorities also used persecution, with varying degrees of success, to strengthen their own temporal power. In effect, Moore chronicles the growth of a figurational tendency that extends continuously from the era of the Crusades and the Inquisition to that of modern totalitarian and authoritarian states. The formation of this persecuting society involved the construction of social categories or identities, such that "heresy, leprosy and Jewishness lay with beauty in the eyes of the beholders, and that their distinctiveness was not the cause but the result of persecution" (Moore 1990, 67). Heresy, in particular, "exists only in so far as authority chooses to declare its existence" (Moore 1990, 68). The persecution of heresy served the interests of both the church and the state: it enabled the church to overcome tendencies toward its own decentralization and dissolution, tendencies well advanced by the eleventh century (Moore 1990, 69); and perhaps even more important, it enabled sovereigns to construct an ensemble of ongoing practices that furthered their control over the populations they dominated.

The most crucial of these ongoing social technologies of persecution were surveillance and the spatial exercise of power (Moore 1990, 106, 109–10). By about the middle of the twelfth century, the great danger of heretics derived not from their open opposition to the church but from the very invisibility of their existence. In seeking to reveal an enemy whose existence lacked outward evidence, the Inquisition created mechanisms for exposing the remotest corners of social life to the gaze of a central authority. Over time, secular authorities took over from ecclesiastical agents the task of operating this mechanism and documenting its findings. Literate clerks replaced warriors "as the agents of government and confidants of princes" (Moore 1990, 136). Law, which had formerly operated on mediatory principles, seeking agreement or compromise among dissenting parties, took on a new coercive function, imposing guilt or innocence from above, even for crimes that had no tangible victims (Moore 1990, 109–10). State institutions used moral repression to legitimate themselves (Moore 1990, 135). Accusations of heresy served not just to resolve local grievances but also to suppress resistance to the exercise of centralized power over the population (Moore 1990, 144). States concerned themselves with heresy because it constituted, at best, a communal autonomy from seigniorial and bureaucratic power and, at worst, open rebellion against this power (Moore 1990, 133).

Moore's account puts into a different light Elias's account of the decline of the warrior class and the concomitant muting of the use of direct violence in governing. What Elias glosses over as the pacification of everyday/everynight life, Moore analyzes as a transformation in the mode of governance through which violence is exercised. If a deconstructive reading of Elias brings out in the abstract the crucial and continuing importance of violence in civilization, Moore fills in some of the concrete details. Admittedly, persecution is not the same thing as genocide; a persecuting society is not quite a genocidal civilization. But the two are closely related: persecution excludes subjects partly or conditionally from the community of obligation, from which genocide excludes them completely. In figurational terms, persecution and genocide operate as different instantiations of civilizing *différance*.

The Anachronism of "Genocide"

The extermination of the Cathars of Languedoc easily fits within the terms of the 1948 United Nations Convention on the Prevention and

Punishment of the Crime of Genocide (UNCG). Religious and secular authorities collaborated with the explicit intent of destroying a religious group by killing members of the group; therefore, crusaders and inquisitors together committed genocide in Languedoc. Yet beneath this surface simplicity, the extermination of the Cathars exposes some deeper complexities involved in the concept of "genocide."

As I have discussed in chapter 2, the definition of "genocide" presented in the UNCG belongs in the context of Raphaël Lemkin's lifetime work of scholarly and legal activism. This trajectory of activism, which began in Lemkin's childhood (Elder 2005, 473) and continued up until his death in 1959 (McDonnell and Moses 2005; Schaller 2005), expresses, in terms that became richer and more complex over time, a consistent concern with the unique cultural life of distinct social collectivities. That is to say, Lemkin did not frame his conception of genocide in terms of an individual's right to freedom of conscience; for him, the atrocity of genocide did not lie primarily in its radical violation of individual autonomy. Rather, by defining and then criminalizing genocide, Lemkin aimed to protect a kind of life in which the individual plays only a part, a life that Emile Durkheim calls the reality *sui generis* of society:

> [The criminalization of genocide] is quite natural, when we conceive that nations are essential elements of the world community ... Essentially the idea of a nation signifies constructive cooperation and original contributions, based upon genuine traditions, genuine culture, and a well-developed national psychology. The destruction of a nation, therefore, results in the loss of its future contributions to the world. Moreover, such a destruction offends our feelings of morality and justice in much the same way as does the criminal killing of a human being: the crime in the one case as in the other is murder, though on a vastly greater scale. (Lemkin 1944, 91)

As I have argued in chapter 2, statements like these express Lemkin's primordialist understanding of society as an organic whole. Lemkin's writings on genocide express not a concern to protect individuals from the unjust imposition of a collective identification but a concern to protect the life of nations.

This raises problems for treating the Languedoc example as a genocide: the Cathars formed a distinct religious group but were not by any means a national group (not even, for instance, in the sense that European Jews in the 1930s could be called a national group). Rather, Catharism operated as a widely tolerated and influential social movement within the Occitan cultural sphere and, more peripherally, within a few areas outside of it. Languedoc, for its part, had not yet achieved the political or social unity to constitute anything like a national identity in modern terms. In general, to speak of "national" identities in the Middle Ages risks an inaccurate and anachronistic comparison to the kind of nationalist movements that would not emerge in Europe until the nineteenth century. The extermination of the Cathars resembles the destruction of a social or political group more than the murder of a nationality. So including the extermination of the Cathars in Lemkin's category of "genocide" strains or straddles the boundaries of the category, falling within it in some respects and outside of it in others.

By design, neither Lemkin's *Axis Rule* nor the UNCG defines the destruction of political groups per se as genocidal. Its inclusion was proposed during the drafting of the UNCG, but Lemkin did not favour this (Lippman 1984, 11), and the representatives of the Soviet Union opposed such inclusion for the obvious reason that actions in its own recent past would meet such a definition. Since then, however, genocide scholars have vigorously debated this exclusion of political groups from the definition of genocide. Leo Kuper argues at length against it (Kuper 1981, 24–30). Several authors have proposed their own expanded definitions that specifically include political groups among the possible victims: Churchill (1998, 432), Katz (surprisingly) (1994, 131), Porter (1982, 12), and Totten and Parsons (2009, 4–5). Chalk and Jonassohn take a slightly different approach by defining genocide in terms of intent to destroy "a group, as that group and membership in it are defined by the perpetrator" (Chalk and Jonassohn 1990, 23; Chalk 1994, 52; Jonassohn and Björnson 1998, 10); Fein (1984, 4), Thompson and Quets (1990, 248), and Charny (1994, 75) all take similar approaches. Barbara Harff and Ted Gurr instead propose the separate concept of "politicide" (Harff and Gurr 1988, 360; see also Mann 2005, 16), and Rudy Rummel (1994, 31) does the same. For Harff and Gurr, "genocide" and "politicide" are separate categories with no master category; for Rummel, they are separate subcategories of the master category "democide"; for Patricia Marchak (2003, 3), they are separate subcategories of the master category "crimes against humanity." Martin Shaw (2007, 70–1) argues for treating "politicide" as a subcategory of "genocide."

Contrasting politicide with genocide, as do Harff, Gurr, Rummel, and Michael Mann, makes an important, commonsensical, but very problematic assumption: that an observer not only can distinguish between the dynamics of cultural and political identities but also can analytically separate them. Harff and Gurr say that "in genocides the victimized groups are defined primarily in terms of their communal characteristics, i.e., ethnicity, religion, or nationality. In politicides the victim groups are defined primarily in terms of their hierarchical position or political opposition to the regime" (Harff and Gurr 1988, 360). Echoing Lemkin's own organicism, Rummel defines genocide as, "among other things, the killing of people by a government because of their indelible group membership (race, ethnicity, religion, language)," and he defines politicide as "the murder of any person or people by a government because of their politics or for political purposes" (Rummel 1994, 31). In the instance of the Cathars, however, as for other heretical groups, their communal characteristics and their opposition to the church's hegemony were inseparable. The very system of beliefs and practices that bound them together as a community *necessarily* implied political opposition both to the church's claim to totality and to its temporal power. Given the totalizing ambitions of the church, *any* communality organized on principles other than its own constituted a political opposition. In other words, the doctrines and practices that made up the Cathars' indelible group identity were also what put them in political opposition to the church.

In short, the example of the Cathars shows the instability of attempts to define genocide narrowly in terms of nationality: either such attempts arbitrarily privilege nationality over other forms of collective identity or they assert a false separation between relations of collective identity and relations of politics – that is, a separation between social relations and power relations. Recognizing the immanence of power in all social relations implies that all collective identification is political and that all genocides attack the relations of power that make identity-difference possible.

Civilizing Genocide in Languedoc

In sum, genocide in Languedoc was not simply a destructive act. It enabled the dramatic extension of the sovereignty of the Capetian kings and consequently of the Kingdom of France, and it simultaneously helped to reconsolidate the ecclesiastical hegemony of the

Roman Catholic Church in western Europe. Within the emerging framework of barbaric civilization, the institutionalization of the category of "heretic" and the techniques of the Inquisition produced a zone of active negation into which almost anyone potentially could fall. The possibility of guilt by suspicion created an onus on the visible, active, ongoing demonstration of one's conformity. If anyone could be a heretic, one's safety depended not only on adherence to a set of negative proscriptions or even definite positive prescriptions but also on the visible, active, ongoing demonstration of one's orthodoxy. This onus is equivalent to what Michel Foucault, writing about a different yet not altogether separate historical context, calls "normalization" (Foucault 1995, 183). In both examples, power attends not only to specific rules broken but also to deviation from an ideal standard, one that is open to an indefinite intensification. This mode of the operation of power is a central feature of barbaric civilization, where the civilized subject is one who adheres to an ever more intense code of conduct enforced by a broad continuum of great and small acts of violence. Genocidal inquisition has, in a more rudimentary form, several things in common with barbaric civilization: investment in a recognizable social hierarchy (violent différance, or deferentiation); the possibility of radical exclusion accompanied by the threat of active negation; the indeterminacy of what will bring about this negation, and hence the indeterminacy of what will count as sufficient conformity; the opportunity for competition and innovation regarding the practices of conformity; and the investment of individual subjects, through the very acts with which they protect themselves, in the maintenance and reproduction of the very figuration that threatens them. That is to say, the exterminatory persecution of the Cathars helped to make difference dangerous at the very outset of the Western civilizing process.

PART TWO: GUATEMALA

Introduction

The Guatemalan civil war began with the formation of the Rebel Armed Forces (Fuerzas Armadas Rebeldes, FAR) in December 1962 (CEH 1999, 71; REMHI 1999, 193) and formally ended with the signing of the Accord for Firm and Lasting Peace in December 1996 (CEH 1999, 77; REMHI 1999, 284). In this span of time, the war claimed the lives of over 200,000 noncombatants. Many of those who died underwent "forced disappearance"; abducted suddenly during a covert action, executed in secret, these victims simply disappeared without a trace, never to be heard from again, leaving families and loved ones to agonize over their fate (REMHI 1999, 159). Others suffered torture, rape, assault, irregular detention, or threats (REMHI 1999, 302). Although rebel forces committed some atrocities, the government forces perpetrated the overwhelming majority of these offences (CEH 1999, 44, 86; REMHI 1999, 302, 304–5). A continual low rumble of terror pervaded Guatemalan society from the war's beginning to its end, but killings spiked sharply from 1980 to 1983, as the government intensified its efforts to quell the insurgency. In these few years, army and paramilitary forces massacred an estimated 75,000 people. The UN-sponsored Comisión para el Esclarecimiento Histórico (Commission for Historical Clarification, CEH) identified the 1981–83 massacres of rural Mayans as genocidal under the terms of articles II.a, II.b, and II.c of the UNCG, arguing that these acts "were committed with intent to destroy, in whole or in part, groups identified by their common ethnicity, by reason thereof, whatever the cause, motive or final objective of these acts may have been" (CEH 1999, 41). In this same period, however, government forces also targeted non-Mayan political dissidents in an attempt to silence all opposition to the regime by liquidating all political leadership not strongly allied with itself (CEH 1999, 20, 34). In the analysis below, I treat both of these exterminatory campaigns as genocidal. I argue that the 1981–83 period constituted, for Mayans, a "hot genocide" that followed a long "cold genocide" ongoing since colonization. For Ladino political dissidents, genocidal state terror in the 1980s intensified the protogenocidal tendencies of US-supported anticommunism, tendencies that had established themselves in the events surrounding the 1954 overthrow of Guatemala's first democratic government. The coming together of the (post)colonial cold genocide and protogenocidal geopolitics tipped social dominance into outright impunity, unleashing hell in the Land of Eternal Spring.

The First Figuration: Cold Genocide under Colonial Rule

"For the Maya," writes Eduardo Galeano, "time was born and had a name when the sky didn't exist and the earth had not yet awakened" (Galeano 1985, 3). Twelve days created the world, and the thirteenth day put its hands in the soil and kneaded the mud into a human body. By the classic period of their society (200–900), the descendants of that moulded clay had produced "achievements in art, writing, architecture, astronomy, and mathematics [that] rivaled those of ancient Egypt or Classical Europe" (Wright 1992, 50). Mayans achieved these things without iron or bronze, and without any practical use of the wheel, using complex social organization, intellectual sophistication, and sheer patience, whereas Europeans relied on "gadgetry." "Their astronomical discoveries, for example, were made without telescopes of any kind, but they had the mathematical theory, the record keeping, and the perseverance to refine naked-eye sightings in the crucible of time" (Wright 1992, 50–1). A network of canals and raised fields sustained dense populations in the jungle. For reasons that scholars continue to debate, central government collapsed in the ninth and tenth centuries. Decentralization reversed temporarily in the fifteenth century, as kings of the Quiché nation "subdued several of their highland neighbours. But the Maya genius, like the Athenian, was not to be empire builders; the Quiché dominions soon began to drift apart" into something more like a plurality of small kingdoms than a unified empire (Wright 1992, 52). But no amount of centralization could have prepared the Mayans for the atrocities of Spanish conquest.

When the Spanish conquistadors first arrived in Mesoamerica, they exterminated by direct massacre, pillage, vandalism, and enslavement a large part of whatever Indigenous populations had survived the wave of introduced diseases that came before them (Stannard 1992, 69, 78–82, 86). Pedro de Alvarado alone claimed that he, his brothers, and his followers had killed "more than four or five million people in fifteen or sixteen years, from the year 1525 until 1540" (Las Casas, quoted in Stannard 1992, 18). Extreme cruelty accompanied the slaughter: for example, reports indicate killing by slow dismemberment or by having people, including children and infants, torn apart by dogs specially trained for the task (Stannard 1992, 71–2, 83–4). Dreams of easy riches fired the dreams of conquistadors, who treated villages "as little more than bivouacs and their inhabitants as forced conscripts" (Grandin 2000, 26). A stream of gold and silver did flow to Europe from the Mayan homelands (Galeano 1997, 19), joining the vast river of wealth that fed Europe's global colonial expansion and, with it, European modernity itself (Wallerstein 1983).

After Alvarado's death in 1541, Spanish rule shifted from conquest to permanent colonial administration (Grandin 2000, 27). The *encomienda* system entitled Spanish overlords to control not only the land but also the labour of the Indigenous persons living on it. This entitlement, combined with the *repartimiento* system of forced labour and the Catholic Church's project of *reducción* (by which scattered Mayans were sought out and brought into the towns), alienated Mayans from the lands they had occupied, which had religious and cultural significance to them, and forcibly integrated them into the colonial social and economic system as racialized subjects and as an unskilled labour force (Handy 1984, 22–3; Loucky 2001, 158). Dominican priests enforced conversion to Christianity, "often ruthlessly," and continually attempted to stamp out the pagan beliefs of the Mayans throughout the colonial period (Handy 1984, 27–9; Loucky 2001, 158). The Guatemalan historian Severo Martínez Paláez characterized the period of direct colonial rule as "a regimen of terror for the Indians" (quoted in Handy 1984, 14), directed at maximizing the appropriation of Indigenous land and the exploitation of Indigenous labour.

Independence changed the terms of this inequality but not its basic form. A "profound, vicious racism" emerged as a central element of Guatemalan nationalism (Grandin 2000, 98): "In a society sustained by the forced labor of the indigenous, obscurantism began with a contempt towards them that combined racism and a fear that bordered on paranoia. Since colonial society, the Creole proverb that roughly says, 'We are one thing and the natives quite another' ('aparte somos nosotros y aparte los naturales') expresses the segregationist premise that ruled Guatemalan society. The indigenous person was viewed as lazy, vicious, conformist, distrustful, reluctant to be civilized, and abusive" (Figueroa Ibarra 2006, 196). Circumstances improved somewhat from the late 1830s to the 1860s, as the newly independent Guatemalan state found itself too weak to enforce its will strongly against rural peoples in the highlands (McCreery 1990, 101). This situation changed, however, with the expansion of commercial coffee production and with the Liberal Revolution of 1871 (McCreery 1990, 104–12). Although the Liberals did not abolish community property, they did subject it to relentless pressure, seeking to individualize, commodify, and capitalize the rural economy. But communal land ownership and noncommodified (or weakly commodifed) agricultural labour formed the practical basis of Mayan community and identity in the countryside (Grandin 2000, 34–8). Appropriation of Mayan lands has continued up to the present era, such that in Guatemala today, 1 per cent of the population owns 65 per cent of the land, while 40 per cent of the rural population are landless (Loucky 2001, 159). Mayans in Guatemala have also suffered the damaging conditions of life resulting from severe poverty, recently exacerbated by ecological degradation stimulated by reliance on smaller and smaller landholdings (Loucky 2001, 153–61).

Taken together, the racism of Guatemalan nationalism and the policy of economic liberalization worked to build a postcolonial society that made no room for Mayans as such. This systematic pressure on the Mayan social institutions and collective life constituted Guatemala's cold genocide, similar to other cold genocides of Indigenous peoples in settler societies. Linda Tuhiwai Smith notes that, in the history of colonialism since the nineteenth century, "processes of dehumanization" have often been "clothed within an ideology of humanism and liberalism and the assertion of moral claims which related to a concept of civilized 'man'" (Tuhiwai Smith 1999, 26). In Guatemala the moral superiority of Western civilization helped to justify a permanent culture of state terror (Martinez Salazar 2008, 203–4). Mayans, however, have resisted this slow genocidal pressure, adapting to the capitalist mode of production and to the shifting currents of power in the modern nation-state. They have resisted the shameful abjection assigned to them by the settler society. The figure of the "sanctioned Mayan" described in government pamphlets dropped from military helicopters after the scorched-earth campaigns of the early 1980s epitomizes this abjection:

A man caricatured as a boy named 'Polainas' was depicted as the ideal genderless Maya: quiet, obedient, walking with his head down, clean but proud of wearing torn clothes, and smiling while saying that he was defended by the friendly army. 'Polainas' – a derogatory Spanish term meaning 'rotten shoes' – was also a good Christian and father ... The sanctioned Maya woman had to be an extremely mute and passive being; a stoic prototype of caring and nurturing. She also had to be an extremely content and obedient servant who was ever so grateful to her masters for leaving her 'alive' ... As such, she had to maintain her existence as invisibly as possible while ready to render her sexuality as a 'patriotic' duty to please the military and bourgeois phallus.

In 'peacetime' Guatemala, the sanctioned woman is before anything else 'decent, polite, docile, submissive' and always grateful
for all the benefits peace has brought to her. If she is impoverished, she must be patient because she will benefit from the new
free trade and from neoliberal development. (Martinez Salazar
2008, 213–14)

The choice implied in this propaganda, between life as a degraded
caricature and rape or death as an enemy of the state, paralleled the
practical choice that Mayans faced between "governmental expropriation of their lands and consignment of their families to forced
labour under *criollo* and *ladino* overlords, or ... the violence of military death squads" (Stannard 1992, 258). Both the symbolic and the
practical aspects of this Catch-22 merely intensified, compressed,
and accelerated the relation of genocide that had been playing out in
slow motion for centuries.

The Second Figuration: Protogenocidal Anticommunism

Mayans were not the only subjects to suffer exploitation and oppression in Guatemala; nicknamed the Land of Eternal Spring for
the temperate climate of its highlands, Guatemala has also been "the
land of eternal impunity" (Molina Mejía 1999, 56) since colonization. The 1871 Liberal Revolution, which ended the instability that
had followed on independence, also established the basic form
of Guatemalan authoritarianism that would persist through most
of the twentieth century: political dictatorships "run by and for the
coffee oligarchs" (LaFeber 1993, 77). A handful of wealthy families
and multinational corporations – most prominently, the United Fruit
Company (UFCO) – owned vast plantations, producing crops for
export, and paid off governments while rural families struggled on
ever-smaller holdings or went landless altogether, and workers in
town and country groaned under debt while facing layoffs and violence for any attempt to form labour unions.

In other words, political power – control of the state's monopoly
of military force and its taxation function – was very highly concentrated in Guatemala, and this very concentration enabled sovereign
authority to serve the interests of a small national elite and foreign
capital, at the expense of the great majority of the state's subjects.
The oligarchs' interest in exploiting land and labour controlled by

rural peasants and landless workers made for the kind of functional interdependency between enemies that Elias describes in *What Is Sociology?* (1978, 76–80), but this interdependency did not translate into growing mutual accountability. On the contrary, centralization of sovereign power combined with unequal functional interdependency to fuel Guatemala's "eternal impunity" and its "culture of terror" (Figueroa Ibarra 2006, 196).

In network terms, the Guatemalan state resembled a wheel with many spokes and, at its hub, a dense web of steel threads. At the rim stood those who were subject to state power but had little reciprocal influence on its exercise, the targets of impunity: Mayans, workers, and others with little or no effective enfranchisement. At the centre stood a small but highly interconnected network of rich families, military leaders, foreign capitalists, and American diplomats. This structure operated symbiotically with a parallel structure of economic relations connecting exploiters to exploited. Guatemalan nationalism articulated this combined structure of force and production relations, working to make the economy of right and wrong, of pride and shame, map cleanly onto the economy of sovereigns and subjects. Any communal organization that did not culminate, practically and symbolically, in the state and the Ladino elite, respectively, would destabilize the hub-and-spokes structure through which this elite maintained its dominance. So too would the growth of a middle class too large to enfranchise without diluting the authority of the elites.

Precisely this latter development came about during the 1931–44 dictatorship of Jorge Ubico. Ubico's government engaged in "a massive development of governmental activities (especially the building of infrastructure, such as roads) that created a new, nationalistic middle class and pulled some Indians out of their political isolation" (LaFeber 1993, 113). In 1944 university students and other middle-class professionals led a wave of public protests that pressured Ubico into resigning (LaFeber 1993, 114). When a new military junta led by General Federico Ponce Vaides attempted to succeed him, continuing protest enabled a group of young army officers led by Jacobo Arbenz Guzmán and Major Carlos Aldana Sandoval to stage a coup and hold the first democratic elections in Guatemala's history (Gleijeses 1992, 26–9; LaFeber 1993, 114), bringing Juan José Arévalo to the presidency. The governments of Arévalo and of Arbenz pursued measures that, also for the first time in Guatemalan history, aimed deliberately at reducing social inequality. New legislative measures blunted the power of landed oligarchs in the countryside while offering social security and labour rights to workers in the cities (LaFeber 1993, 114).

In figurational terms, a new alliance of class fractions took control of the mechanisms of the Guatemalan state and began to use the state's policing and taxation powers to benefit itself and its allies, who constituted a broader segment of Guatemalan society than the former rulers. If the Guatemalan state had enjoyed complete sovereignty, this partially equalizing tendency might have continued for some time, producing a different and happier transformation in Guatemalan society than the one that was to come. In the event, however, the sovereignty of the Guatemalan state was limited by its vulnerable location within the global system of states and specifically by the power and the interests of the United States in its geopolitical struggles with the Soviet Union. In 1953, partly encouraged by lobbying from the United Fruit Company but primarily on the grounds that the Arbenz government had come under communist influence (LaFeber 1993, 121; Figueroa Ibarra 2006, 193), the United States, through the Central Intelligence Agency, began organizing and paying for an armed counterrevolution (Blum 1998, 75–7). For its part, the Canadian government helped contribute to the diplomatic weakness of the Arbenz government and to allegations that it took orders from Moscow (Engler 2009, 88–9). In 1954 a coup led by Colonel Carlos Castillo Armas, supplied by the CIA with money, arms, and even aerial bombardment support, overthrew the Arbenz government and reinstated oligarchic rule in Guatemala (LaFeber 1993, 125; see also Blum 1998, 78–83).

After the coup, the culture of terror set in even more deeply than before. In the immediate term, the victorious Armas regime arrested an estimated 9,000 to 14,000 people and executed between 2,000 and 5,000 (Figueroa Ibarra 2006, 194). More fundamentally, however,

Cold War anticommunism revitalized nationalist racism against Maya Indians and reinvigorated old forms and justifications of domination. A racially divided and economically stratified Guatemala was a tinderbox; anticommunism was the match ... In the past, the state responded to demands made by political movements not only with repression, but with concessions and negotiations as well. The triumph of the 1944 revolution was the highpoint of this pattern. Following 1954 and intensifying after the 1959 Cuban Revolution, Guatemalan elites increasingly turned to the United States for technical support in order to crush domestic threats to their power. The balance tipped in the state's favour and repression gave way to full-scale terror. (Grandin 2009, 4)

The imagined figure of communism as a form of "negative otherness" emerged to complement the longstanding negative otherness of Indigeneity:

According to the predominant view, the new "betraying beast," seen as hypocritical and devious, sought to rob honorable citizens of the products of their labor in order to benefit the state; it intended to seize their houses and install in them multiple families, to dissolve matrimony and family, and even to snatch children from their parents and hand their guardianship over to the state. In this context, indigenous people continued to be seen as the black beasts of society, but were simultaneously viewed as easily manipulated because of their supposed stupidity and ignorance, so they could be turned into instruments of another even more dangerous black beast, the communists. (Figueroa Ibarra 2006, 195)

The roots of this fearful anticommunism go back to the early 1930s, but 1953–54 marked their decisive emergence onto the centre stage of Guatemalan political discourse. From this time forth, the oligarchic elite of Guatemala knew that it could count on abundant foreign support for the repression of its internal competitors, as long as it could justify this repression in the name of the struggle against communism. As the Cold War set in, unequal interdependency slid into ever greater impunity.

Guatemalan anticommunism thrived within the larger milieu of US-supported anticommunism. Intervention by the United States in the domestic politics of nominally sovereign nations throughout the Americas has a long history; the 1823 Monroe Doctrine, which "warned European colonial powers to keep hands off the Western Hemisphere," articulated the Jeffersonian intuition that "America has a hemisphere to itself" (LaFeber 1993, 23). But after 1945 the

struggle for geopolitical dominance between the United States and
the Soviet Union provided the former with a flexible and useful
ideological tool. Once the Cold War set in, anticommunism helped
to justify measures – ranging from diplomatic support, to financial
and military aid, to covert and not-so-covert military intervention –
aimed at bolstering regimes that deployed political terror against
their own subjects to protect oligarchic interests – or even, as
in Guatemala's case, to re-establish these regimes after their re-
placement with a more democratic structure (Blum 1998; Chomsky
and Herman 1979; Grandin 2004; LaFeber 1993; Porpora 1990).
Anticommunism justified the support of local tyrants in the name of
the all-or-nothing struggle between American-style freedom and
democracy, on the one hand, and Soviet totalitarianism, on the other,
even when the concrete issues at stake had more to do with US geopolitical influence or even American corporate profits. In these policies, the United States has enjoyed ongoing – yet often quiet – support
and assistance from lesser powers such as Canada (Engler 2009).

   In the name of anticommunism, the United States not only
supported political murder, disappearance, and torture by foreign
governments but also trained Latin American military officers in
precisely these techniques. At the infamous School of the Americas
(renamed in 2001 the Western Hemisphere Institute for Security
Cooperation), US military officers trained their Latin American
counterparts in conventional warfare and, increasingly, in counterinsurgency techniques, including "fear, beatings, the payments of
bounties for enemy dead, false imprisonment, executions, and truth
serum" as well as "extortion as a method of interrogation" and
"execution, or 'neutralization' of enemies" (Gill 2004, 49). From its
establishment in 1949 to 1964, less than two years after the outbreak of the civil war, the School of the Americas graduated 958
Guatemalan officers (LaFeber 1993, 111). "Forty per cent of the
cabinet ministers who served the genocidal regimes of Lucas Garcia,
Rios Montt and Mejia Victores studied at the School of the Americas"
(Monbiot 2001).

   Harff and Gurr have proposed the category "politicide" to refer to
"the promotion and execution of policies by a state or its agents
which result in the deaths of a substantial portion of a group ...
defined primarily in terms of [its] hierarchical position or political
opposition to the regime" (Harff and Gurr 1988, 360). For these
authors, genocide and politicide are forms of mass murder,

distinguished by the criteria defining the victims. However, if we conceive of genocide as a relation of violent categorical obliteration, politicide appears as one form of genocide among others – that is, as a phenomenon instantiated by a relation in which the relevant category of identity-difference takes its substance from political struggle and its imagery from political ideology. In this respect, communists in Latin America were like Cathars in Languedoc, an Other whose heterodox cosmological and normative ideals operated as the vestments of a practical opposition to concrete relations of hierarchy. But communists in Cold War – era Latin America were also like Jews in Nazi Germany, in that they were defined by their enemies in ways that had little necessary relation to how they were defined by themselves and those who knew them. By the 1980s in Guatemala, almost anyone who did not demonstrate unwavering loyalty to the regime could be labelled a communist and treated as one.

Fuelled by US foreign policy, applauded by multinational corporations, and implemented by local elites, hemisphere-wide anticommunism intensified throughout the postwar decades and climaxed in the 1980s, "the bloodiest, most violent, and most destructive era in Central America's post-1820 history" (LaFeber 1993, 362). A cautious estimate indicates that at least 200,000 civilians suffered murder or disappearance during this period: 40,000 in Nicaragua, 75,000 in El Salvador, 75,000 in Guatemala, and 10,000 in Honduras. Genocidal anticommunism worked to eliminate communism by exterminating communists, deploying murder and terror against persons to destroy a social institution. In this respect, it shared an objective with its nongenocidal forms, which worked to destroy communism by fostering social development. Not until the crisis of the early 1980s did this protogenocidal ambivalence resolve itself, in Guatemala, into outright genocide, in the form of Ríos Montt's vicious attempt to end the civil war and re-establish state sovereignty by eliminating the opposition root and branch.

The Civil War and Hot Genocide

Throughout the Guatemalan civil war, both global superpowers involved themselves in the combat, at a distance: insurgent forces received "political, logistic, instructional and training support from Cuba" (CEH 1999, 20), and the Guatemalan state received direct financial and military assistance from the United States, aimed especially at supporting intelligence and counterinsurgency forces (CEH 1999, 19). American policymakers rationalized their contribution to the hostilities in terms of preventing the spread of Cuban-inspired Marxist revolution to mainland Latin America, and not only agents of the US state but also private American intellectuals promoted anticommunist discourse in Guatemala. As part of its counterinsurgency policy, the Guatemalan state worked to militarize the daily life of ordinary civilians through the formation of Civilian Self-Defense Patrols (PACs) in rural communities. Villagers found themselves obliged to participate in the PACs, under direct army control (REMHI 1999, 45–6, 115–25). In the course of the war, members of the PACs were forced to participate in killing, rape, torture, and mutilation of corpses (CEH 1999, 27).

Between 1962 and 1996 over 200,000 noncombatant persons suffered murder or forced disappearance (CEH 1999, 17). Everyday/everynight life in Guatemala took place against a constant background rumble of human rights violations, ranging from direct killing, disappearance, torture, rape, and assault to irregular detention and threats against individuals (REMHI 1999, 302). Government forces, including the army and paramilitaries, accounted for the large majority of these offences, but the insurgent forces also contributed to the steady stream of offences (REMHI 1999, 304–5). So too did private individuals, especially large landowners, who either collaborated with agents of the state for counterinsurgency purposes or acted independently in their own direct self-interests (CEH 1999, 44). The CEH concludes that responsibility for 93 per cent of documented human rights violations rests with the state, "including in this category the Army, security forces, Civil Patrols, military commissioners and death squads," and that responsibility for 3 per cent of violations rests with guerrilla forces and 4 per cent with "other unidentified armed groups, civilian elements and other public officials" (CEH 1999, 86).

From 1980 to 1983 the steady stream became a noisy rush and then, in 1981, a roaring flood: offences during this period outnumber those for all other war years combined (REMHI 1999, 302). This peak of terror spans three governments: the latter part of the elected tenure of General Romeo Lucas García; the military junta of General Efraín Ríos Montt, General Horacio Egberto Maldonado Schaad, and Colonel Francisco Luis Gordillo Martínez; and the de facto presidency of General Ríos Montt. Under the rule of these generals, murder and assassination gave way to outright massacre. Following the largest guerrilla offensive to date in early 1981, and seeking a conclusive end to the guerrilla threat, the army pursued a scorched-earth policy in the countryside, moving into the areas where the guerrillas operated, slaughtering the men, women, and children of one entire village after another, burning houses and crops, and killing livestock – "a strategy that Ríos Montt called 'draining the sea that the fish swim in'" (Ball, Kobrak, and Spirer 1999, 26–7).

In this same period, government forces also escalated their tactics in the cities, directing violence widely throughout Guatemalan society in the name of anticommunism and the National Security Doctrine. The definition of "communist" and of derivative categories such as "subversive" and "the internal enemy" expanded readily to include "political activists, students, trade unionists, and human rights advocates," as well as "political and social leaders," who experienced kidnapping, murder, and forced disappearances (CEH 1999, 20, 34).[5] The army and allied death squads used murder, forced disappearance, and torture so broadly as to decapitate systematically all elements of Guatemalan civil society that did not strongly support the government. Soldiers themselves faced violence from their own comrades if they appeared to lack dedication to the task of suppressing subversion.

Women made up one-quarter of "direct victims of human rights violations and acts of violence," through murder, torture, and rape, perpetrated either for their own actions or in "massacres and other indiscriminate actions" (CEH 1999, 23). According to Michele Leiby, "it appears that sexual violence played an integral role in the Guatemalan state's overall counterinsurgency strategy" (Leiby 2009, 460). Like murders, most rapes occurred during the pacification campaigns of 1981 to 1983. Government soldiers used rape to terrorize entire communities, both raping women and girls in front of the entire village and mutilating the victims to leave behind permanent markers of the rape on their bodies (Leiby 2009, 461). Although Leiby could not find direct evidence of a policy to use rape for genocidal purposes, the scale of rape, its indiscriminateness, and the fact that 90 per cent of sexual violence victims were Mayans are all

---

5 "Communist" has been a strikingly flexible label in Guatemalan history. The CEH notes that up to the 1950s, the Catholic Church "qualified as communist any position that contradicted its philosophy" (CEH 1999, 20).

consistent with the use of rape as a means to destroy a group through the physical and psychological harm that rape inflicts, forms of harm that the International Criminal Tribunal for Rwanda argued should count among the means by which genocide may be perpetrated (Leiby 2009, 455, 462, 450–1). In addition to rapes committed by soldiers and paramilitaries, government officials in the cities used family planning programs grounded in an ideology of eugenics to encourage or coerce Mayan women into undergoing sterilization procedures (Fabri 2003). In addition to direct killing and sexual violence, state terror affected women by turning them into widows and single parents through the killing or forced disappearance of their husbands (CEH 1999, 23). However, women also took a leadership role in struggles for human rights, notably through new organizations such as the Association of Families of the Disappeared and Detained of Guatemala (REMHI 1999, 85)

Mayan Guatemalans formed the largest single category of victims of violence. The CEH reports that 83.33 per cent of identified victims of human rights violations and acts of violence were Mayan (CEH 1999, 85). During the period 1978–83, the army identified the Mayans as natural allies of the insurgents, and the state used this identification in combination with racism to authorize "massive and indiscriminate aggression directed against communities ... massacres, scorched earth operations, forced disappearances and executions of Mayan authorities, leaders and spiritual guides." These actions aimed "not only ... to destroy the social base of the guerrillas, but above all, to destroy the cultural values that ensured cohesion and collective action in Mayan communities" (CEH 1999, 23). Violence was directed against Mayan religion, language, cultural practices, and traditional authorities (REMHI 1999, 46–9). Massacres committed as part of the scorched-earth policy in the early 1980s resulted in the "complete extermination of many Mayan communities, along with their homes, cattle, crops and other elements essential to survival" (CEH 1999, 34). The army also systematically attacked children and pregnant women through direct and indirect killing, assault, and rape (especially of young girls) (REMHI 1999, 29–34). Testimonies of "soldiers or patrollers frequently refer to the killing of children as a way of eliminating the possibility of rebuilding the community and of circumventing the victims' efforts to attain justice" (REMHI 1999, 31).

Aftermath

Even before the formal end of the civil war, the Oslo Accord of June 1994 established Guatemala's own truth and reconciliation commission, the Comisión para el Esclarecimiento Histórico (Commission for Historical Clarification, CEH). In February 1999, after hearing testimony from thousands of survivors, interviewing high-ranking government officials and military officers, and attending exhumations of clandestine graves, the CEH delivered its report, which accounted for 42,275 named victims of human rights abuses (CEH 1999). The CEH built upon the work of the Informe Proyecto Interdiocesano de Recuperación de la Memoria Histórica (Recovery of Historical Memory Project, REMHI), conducted by the Human Rights Office of the Archdiocese of Guatemala, which had presented its findings in 1994 (REMHI 1999; Beristain 1998). These projects used the conceptual and legal framework of human rights to document the suffering of the victims of violence in Guatemala and to identify the agents responsible. The CEH made systematic recommendations for the reform of Guatemalan state and military institutions. However, the postwar government did not move to implement the CEH report's recommendations (Tomuschat 1999) and still had not done so six years later (Corntassel and Holder 2008, 378).

Although the civil war and systematic mass murder ended, the impunity of the genocidaires did not. Efraín Ríos Montt returned to politics as head of the Guatemalan Republican Front party, which won a congressional majority in 1999. Not surprisingly, the governing elite in Guatemala did not support the CEH findings. For the victims of violence, especially Mayan communities, the effects of the civil war included not only loss of life but also disintegration of social ties and destruction of economic productivity (Manz 2008, 157–9; Esparza 2005, 386–7). Meanwhile, although state killings declined, in peacetime impunity has found new expressions, as "paramilitary groups and former members of the military are actively engaged in criminal activities, ranging from personal vendettas and settling scores to corruption, kidnappings, rapes, thefts, shootings, and drug trafficking" (Manz 2008, 157). Perhaps even more significant, however, "persisting militarization continues the genocidal destruction of indigenous peoples' traditional communal bonds by setting army loyalists against human rights workers and the left-oriented wing of the Catholic Church." As a result, "the genocide has extended the divide that existed between wealthy, powerful elites and indigenous groups, into the hearts of indigenous communities themselves" (Esparza 2005, 378). Egla Martinez Salazar has analyzed the effects of the culture of terror in terms of "lifelong teaching-learning," a concept usually associated with more benign processes. In these terms, violence during the civil war worked in tandem with government education programs to teach a love of obedience as "the love of and obedience to those who govern and as the unconditional respect for patriotic symbols such as the national flag" (Martinez Salazar 2008). This teaching has succeeded in no small part, as "neighbors still use the now-normalized concept of the internal enemy to criminalize grassroots organizations" (Esparza 2005, 386), turning communities against themselves in ways that sabotage efforts for local revitalization.

However, struggle against impunity also continues and has taken new forms in response to the genocide. Among these are Guatemala's human rights movement itself. Although few perpetrators have been made to face justice, the movement has achieved important victories in transforming relations of impunity at the local level. It has brought about the exhumation and burial of victims of disappearances, en-abling relatives and loved ones to grieve and seek closure; it has helped survivors to keep alive the memory of the genocide and to express their outrage, putting Montt and other perpetrators on the defensive; and it has helped to "forge a collective identity that inspires action" (Stewart 2008, 246). Indeed, army massacres have provoked a reassertion of Mayan collective identity in some communities (Loucky and Carlsen 1991). The atrocities of the civil war have prompted Mayans to pursue collective revitalization along multiple axes (Fischer and Brown 1996). Mayan political self-assertion has exceeded the individualistic framework of convention-al human rights and demanded recognition of traditional communal relationships to land (Rostica 2007).

Civilizing Genocide in Guatemala

In a broad sense of the term "civilization" – for example, as "large, complex societies based on the domestication of plants, animals, and human beings" (Wright 2004, 33) – Mayan society of the third through tenth centuries qualifies as one of the great classical civilizations along with those of the Romans, Incas, Egyptians, and Chinese. The expansion of Western civilization into Mezoamerica in the sixteenth century brought hot genocide for Mayans during the immediate onslaught of colonial conquest, then cold genocide for centuries to follow, as colonial and postcolonial governments sought to exploit Mayan lands and labour while undermining the social institutions that sustained Mayan collective identity. These institutions and this identity did survive and adapt, in varying ways, to the pressures of the settler society. Partly the colonizers lacked the means, especially in impoverished rural areas, to enforce the Ladino form of civilization on the inheritors of a different figuration; partly they lacked sufficient motive. Oppressed Indians contributed to the Ladino Guatemalan social identity, both through their economic production and through countless public and private acts of self-distinction derived from denigration of the Other. And through the continuing vitality (however troubled) of their relations with each other, Mayans had the strength to withhold their own ultimate shaming from their colonizers. During the US-Soviet Cold War, this Guatemalan cold genocide intersected with the civilizing struggle for global hegemony between the two superpower states – a "civilizing struggle" because it involved the subordination of local sovereignties to globe-spanning supersovereignties, the direct long-term extension of the subordination of local knights to regional lords begun in western Europe's twelfth century (Elias 1987). In this perspective, colonized Guatemala exists as an offshoot of Europe's civilizing process, given formal sovereignty in 1821 but never truly autonomous because of its location within the imperializing project of the United States. This wider figurational tendency, intensifying during the Cold War, gave Guatemalan elites the impunity to turn cold genocide into hot genocide in the early 1980s. Indigeneity and communism as forms of Otherness overlapped to constitute a subjectivity radically outside the community of obligation, establishing an impunity whose violent effects ranged across the whole of Guatemalan society.

In Guatemala the self-image of Ladino elites as bringers of civilization to jungle savages masked, as in Joseph Conrad's *Heart of Darkness*, the opposite relation: the torchbearers of civilization brought violence and terror beyond comprehension to the jungle, and to their own cities as well. But "masked" is the wrong word, for the very distinction between civilized Ladinos and savage Indians depended on, and contributed to, the practical, material process of deferentiation that established Ladino dominance. Likewise, the self-perception of anticommunists as guardians of freedom against the totalitarian menace articulated and reinforced the polarizing us-them dialectic that legitimated political terror. The simultaneous hot genocide of Mayans and dissidents aimed to resecure the dominance of a threatened elite. In figurational terms, this amounted to something more complex than a simple "decivilizing process." It worked as a kind of "recivilizing process," aiming to re-establish the self-identity of the network of power relations that defined subjectivity and sovereign authority in the postcolonial state.

The insecure elite using genocide to consolidate its dominance is a figure common to civilizing genocides. Sometimes these projects succeed; sometimes they fail. In Guatemala genocidal violence against opponents of the regime did not prevent a return to multiparty democracy and the emergence of civil society organizations that could at least document and publicize the government's atrocities, but neither has formal democracy ended the impunity of the oligarchic elite, and the American policymakers implicated in the genocide have yet to be held accountable for their complicity. Whether Guatemala's recivilizing genocide succeeded or failed remains to be seen.

6

Genocides of Colonized Others in Tasmania and India

INTRODUCTION

The two historical episodes in this chapter offer contrasting examples of British colonialism turned genocidal. The first concerns the almost total annihilation of Aboriginal Tasmanian culture and lineage over the course of the nineteenth century. Initially through sporadic acts of theft, rape, and murder, then through territorial dispossession and an increasingly organized settler war, and finally through internment in inhospitable conditions, British colonists in Tasmania reduced the precolonial Indigenous population from about five thousand to almost nothing; the only survivors were descendants of Tasmanian women who had married European men. Just as the genocide of the Tasmanians wound down to its conclusion, a different kind of genocide broke loose in India, where, from 1876 to 1879 and again from 1896 to 1902, liberal economic policies combined with drought-induced crop failures to deny food to tens of millions of Indian peasants, producing massive famines that claimed between 12 million and 29 million lives.

These two genocides, one total and one partial, express different degrees of impunity and different qualities of interdependency in the relations between colonizer and colonized, based on the relative ease or difficulty of removing the Indigenous peoples from their land and replacing them with settlers versus incorporating them into the colonizer's political and economic institutions. However, the two examples resemble each other in how they differ from the popular image of genocide as a deliberate and purposeful campaign of extermination signalled by declarations to this effect. In both of these genocides, the colonial authorities claimed that they acted to save lives and prevent genocide. In both instances, I argue, genocide emerged as a by-product of the pursuit of larger goals rather than as an end in itself. And in both of these examples, genocide resulted from programs of action carried out explicitly in the name of civilization.

Civilization as Colonialism

Like capitalism, civilization needs to grow. It can grow in depth, producing greater concentrations of force, establishing more elaborate and subtle social hierarchies, and demanding more complex refinements of conduct. But it can also grow in breadth, incorporating new territories and new peoples into its figurational matrix. As it grows in breadth and depth, the Eurocentric barbarizing-civilizing process both produces and reduces social difference. On the one hand, civilized conduct (re)produces social distinction and, thereby, social privilege. On the other hand, the validity of the normative standards of civilization, their ability to confer distinction, depends partly on their universality, on the idea that everyone can and should conform to them. So within the national society of each sovereign state, standards of civilization both enhance class distinctions and gradually efface them as civility spreads, via upwardly ambitious individuals and groups, into the lower strata of the class structure (Elias 2000, 386, 432–3). By implication, this double motion means that barbaric civilization *depreciates*. As a result, the renewal of civilizing distinction requires the expansion of the civilizing-barbarizing process into new social spaces and the constitution of new uncivilized subjects. Colonialism provides these spaces in abundance, at least for a while.

This maintenance of social distinction by the discovery or production of new social differences articulates with the geopolitical and economic gains from colonization (Elias 2000, 431–2). In other words, these "subjective" and "objective" processes feed into each other (from a relational perspective, both types of processes happen in the relations between actors, appearing to have both subjective and objective qualities in varying degrees, and both types of processes transpire both in face-to-face interactions between individuals and in the aggregate across macroscopic figurational networks). But the duplicity of its movement, the tendency of civilization to depreciate, repeats itself in the relationship between colonizer and colonized: "This civilization is the characteristic which confers distinction and superiority on Occidentals. But at the same time Western people, under the pressure of their own competitive struggle, are bringing about in large areas of the world a change in human relationships and functions in line with their own standards ... Largely without deliberate intent, they work in a direction which sooner or later leads to a reduction in the differences both of social power and of conduct between colonists and colonized" (Elias 2000, 385). The imperative of maintaining the colonizer-colonized distinction helps to account not only for the fact of colonization but also for the particular form of its legitimation: the myth of "the white man's burden" fervently subscribed to by so many colonizers and not a few of the colonized.

"It is not a little characteristic," writes Norbert Elias, "of the structure of Western society that the watchword of its colonizing movement is 'civilization.'" It is not enough "simply to rule subject people and countries by force of arms like a warrior caste," although this plays "no small part" in colonization. Rather, the subject peoples "must be integrated, whether as workers or consumers, into the web of the hegemonial, upper-class country, with its highly developed differentiation of functions." This process demands that material living standards must be Europeanized – Elias says "raised," but the historical evidence suggests otherwise. It also demands that the colonizers transform the mode of self-control, the "super-ego functions" in the subject peoples, toward the Western model (Elias 2000, 431). In other words, to integrate the colonized people into the Western civilizing process, the colonizer must *reconfigure* the entire figurational structure of the colonized society, the dynamic network of relations through which people organize both their "objective" material lives and their "subjective" emotional and intellectual lives. Colonization tears apart established relations in order to establish new ones; it disrupts established flows – of goods, of force, of social esteem – in order to redirect them to its own ends. In historical perspective, we can picture this radical reconfiguration as a kind of event-horizon sweeping through the social figurations of the colonized subjects, a moving boundary between two social universes (Powell 2009). This event-horizon brings tremendous destruction as well as production; as the examples in this chapter show, many cannot survive its passage.

The self-descriptions of the colonizers and supporters at home tend to represent this process as a simply positive process of building something new over something older and less developed – a representation that Elias never explicitly refutes – or else as a merely natural process not worth questioning (e.g., Brantlinger 2003; Fanon 2008; Memmi 1965). To proceed otherwise would contradict the idealized self-image of the West, calling into question the very value of civilization. If the word "civilization" expresses the idealized self-image of the West, then, like any self-image, it requires validation from Others. A self-image has meaning only in relation to what Others think of the Self – or, more precisely, in relation to what the Self imagines Others to think of it (Cooley 2004). Colonialism provided an excellent vehicle for European societies to see themselves reflected in the eyes of Others – excellent because the impunity of the colonial relationship guaranteed that the image so perceived would come more from the colonizers themselves than from the colonized (e.g., Said 1978). In this way, the transformation occasioned by colonialism exceeded the revolutionary demands of capitalism that Karl Marx and Friedrich Engels write about so eloquently in the *The Communist Manifesto*, saying that "all that is solid melts into air, all that is holy is profaned." It did so because, rather than replacing "exploitation, veiled by religious and political illusions" with "naked, shameless, direct, brutal exploitation" (Marx and Engels 1988a, 23), it replaced old religious and political images with new ones, specifically with doctrines of the superiority of the colonizers to the colonized, individually and collectively, and with the claim that colonization benefited the colonized themselves, or would if they would only accept it. And the social force that guaranteed this claim flowed less from the means of production than from the means of violence. As Mary Wollstonecraft points out, power creates a kind of blindness in the powerful, a lack of self-awareness produced by the inability of the inferior to call their betters to account (Wollstonecraft 1997, 122–3, 156). Impunity made civilization irrefutable.

PART ONE: THE ABORIGINAL TASMANIANS

Introduction

The island of Tasmania sits off the southeast corner of Australia, divided from the mainland by the relatively shallow Bass Strait.

During the last ice age, when great polar glaciers locked enough water out of the seas to lower their level, the strait formed a land bridge, across which human beings migrated at least 36,000 years ago (Ryan 1996, xxii). As this ice age ended, rising sea levels turned Tasmania into an island and left its inhabitants cut off from all other human contact for the next 12,000 years (Clark 1986, 8). Boomerangs, hafting stone tools, and other technological developments on the Australian mainland never reached the island. But in this intervening time, the Tasmanians "led complex economic and cultural lives and responded in different ways in different parts of the country to changing climatic conditions" (Ryan 1996, xxii). About 4,000 years ago, they ceased to catch scale fish, possibly because a rise in sea levels made abalone and crayfish easier to obtain (Clark 1986, 19); over the past 2,000 years, bands in the northwest, southwest, and southeast parts of the island developed boats for hunting seals (Ryan 1996, 9). Inland, the Tasmanians used fires to clear areas in order to encourage the growth of food plants, and they developed roads through the forest for ease of travel (Clark 1986, 19; Ryan 1996, 17, 21). Throughout the island, they managed their land and food resources carefully, setting limits on the duration and intensity of the use of any one food source to prevent their depletion.

The 3,000 to 4,000 people who inhabited the island organized themselves into nine tribes and at least fifty bands (possibly as many as seventy to eighty-five), each with its own territory (Clark 1986, 24; Ryan 1996, 14; see also Markus 1982–83, 468). Bands consisted of a number of hearth groups, each centred around a husband and wife and their children. Different bands feuded with one another, sometimes murderously, and war could break out between entire tribes over trespassing on tribal lands or broken trade agreements. Nothing indicates, however, that the image of "savage" peoples as especially cruel or violent applied in fact to the Tasmanians. Bands and tribes traded with one another and sometimes allowed each other to use their lands and resources (Clark 1986, 31; Ryan 1996, 13–14). Early European visitors found them friendly, generous, and inquisitive (Clark 1986, 12).

Tasmanians spoke two languages, one of which had four dialects (Clark 1986, 36; Ryan 1996, 11), and they produced a rich oral culture. This included an animist religion in which good and bad spirits inhabited fire, rivers, trees, and other features of the natural universe and in which totems, taboos, and myths communicated normative rules governing relations among people and between people and the natural world (Clark 1986, 28; Ryan 1996, 11). Tasmanians believed that people had a spirit, which, after death, went elsewhere in the world. They also prohibited speaking the names of the dead. Along with their stories, rituals, and technology, they produced and passed on songs, dances, styles of self-decoration, bark-hut architecture, and complex charcoal drawings, and both petroglyphs and stencil paintings have been found in protected sites on the island (Clark 1986, 14, 25–6, 36).

In this thumbnail sketch, I have tried to indicate some of the richness, complexity, and adaptive sophistication of Aboriginal Tasmanian culture. I want to emphasize this richness emphatically in order to counter the deep and stubborn tendency of Eurocentric thought to categorize forager societies in stigmatized terms as "savage," "primitive," "less evolved," or even as "simpler" – where "simplicity" connotes a culture that offers its members fewer and poorer opportunities for social interaction and personal experience than our own. It's especially important to combat this kind of stereotypical thought for two reasons. First, the English colonists' own discourses about themselves and their relations with the Aboriginal Tasmanians are full of explicit references to the Tasmanians as primitive savages and to themselves as carriers or builders of civilization. If the word "civilization" expresses the self-consciousness of the West, "savage" is one word for its antithesis, and the English in Tasmania had the impunity to project onto the Aborigines whatever varying connotations this antithesis conjured up for them. Second, stereotyped images of the Aboriginal Tasmanians as primitive, hence lacking in culture, hence incomplete as human beings, have persisted into relatively recent scholarship on their genocide. Most conspicuously, Frank Chalk and Kurt Jonassohn's major work relies, for its chapter on the Tasmanians, on a 1972 article by James Morris titled "The Final Solution Down Under," which patronizingly depicts the Tasmanians as "naive," as "children," as resembling "elves" or even "hobbits," and as merely "puzzled" by the holocaust that overtook them after colonization (Chalk and Jonassohn 1990; Morris 1972). The image of Tasmanians as innocent children of the forest – or, for that matter, as Rousseauian noble savages – dehumanizes them as much as does the image of degraded primitives.

Writing about genocide in *Axis Rule in Occupied Europe*, Raphaël Lemkin expresses the conviction that "the world represents only so much culture and intellectual vigor as are created by its component national groups ... The destruction of a nation, therefore, results in the loss of its future contributions to the world" (Lemkin 1944, 91). But if some societies, by virtue of their "simplicity" and "primitiveness," simply had less culture to offer, their loss would be the lesser and might even be justifiable. And in terms of the centralization of the means of violence and the expression in quotidian etiquette of social distinctions based in status hierarchies – the central mechanisms of the civilizing process as Elias conceives it – the Aboriginal Tasmanians had no civilization. They also lacked the other accoutrements of "civilization" in the broad sense of the term. They had no cities, no technology not made from organic materials, and no written language. They did not exploit their ecosystem to a level that could support a permanent surplus and, with it, nonlabouring classes. However, they did achieve what seems to have been an indefinitely sustainable relationship between the needs of their society and the resources of their natural environment. They produced a dynamic system of relations and symbolizations that made their lives meaningful. Like other human beings, Aboriginal Tasmanians built cooperative as well as antagonistic relationships, produced meaning and beauty as well as violence and destruction, established enduring institutions, and made fluid adaptations; in short, they engaged in a wide range of divergent forms of self-realization, which resists forming any neat and easily characterizable package. If we could measure the richness of a society by the potential complexity of the social relationships and personal experiences that it makes available to its members, would precolonial Tasmanian society appear any less rich than our own? The shame of genocide is that we can never properly address this question; too much knowledge of the Tasmanians' everyday/everynight life has been irretrievably lost.

Dispossession

In 1642 the Dutch explorer and entrepreneur Abel Tasman, looking for new sea routes to Chile and Spanish America, "saw fires and heard human sounds, but saw no one" on the island he named "Van Diemen's Land" (Clark 1986, 12; Ryan 1996, 47). From then until 1802, contact between Europeans and Tasmanians involved only brief encounters between European explorers and would-be scientists, mostly French, and small coastal bands (Ryan 1996, 47–65).

Early explorers, such as Nicholas Marion du Fresne in 1771, saw the Tasmanians through the lens of Jean-Jacques Rousseau's claims about the condition of noble savagery, and inquired with them about the "state of nature" (Ryan 1996, 49). But European ideas about the "noble savage" contained an implicit ethnocentric bias, conceiving of Aboriginal peoples as merely underdeveloped Europeans, essentially the same as Westerners but lacking in the accoutrements of culture, and hence ready to be filled up with it, rather than as people with a highly developed and specialized culture of their own. This ethnocentrism had negative consequences when such people showed no interest in, or showed outright resistance to, the fruits of European culture. The members of François Péron's 1802 expedition failed to see past the strangeness of Aboriginal culture to its intelligibility. Delighted by their friendliness and generosity, but finding the Aboriginals "'strangers to every principle of social order' and without any apparent rulers, or laws, clothing, or cultivation of any kind," Peron concluded that, of all human beings, the Tasmanians were the most savage and most remote from European civilization (Ryan 1996, 62–3). The trajectory of European scientific attitudes formed a descending arc from the idealized conception of the "noble savage," through the "ignoble savage" (Ryan 1996, 50), and on downward. By the 1860s, there had emerged "a renewed interest in the Aboriginal Tasmanians from the scientific world, based upon the conviction that they were the missing link between ape and man" (Ryan 1996, 214).

In 1803 the British imperial government established its first permanent settlement on Tasmania, at Risdon Cove in the southeast corner of the island (Robson 1983, 35). This colonization "began initially, as in so much of their empire-making, to keep out another potential contender – the French" (Levene 2005b, 38; see also Robson 1983, 32–3). In other words, the same struggle for territorial sovereignty that fuelled the civilizing process in Europe also fuelled its colonization efforts. Arriving in Tasmania, the civilizing process established new relations of social interconnectedness, those between colonists and Natives. But the colonizers commanded such overwhelming means of violence that these relations could not take the form of functional interdependence, which requires that "one person (or a group of persons) lacks something which another person or group has the power to withhold" (Elias 1978, 78). Instead, they took the form of almost total impunity. Over the next three-quarters of the century, this impunity produced a civilizing genocide that nearly extinguished Aboriginal Tasmanian identity altogether.

This near-extinction unfolded in three phases: a period of mostly one-sided colonial dispossession of and violence against the Tasmanians, a mutually violent war between colonists and Natives culminating in the Black Line operation of 1830, and the internments at Flinders Island and Oyster Cove afterward. In 1803, before having actually seen any Tasmanians, the colony's founder, John Bowen, doubted that they would be "of any use to us" (Kiernan 2007, 265). Troops surveying the island opened fire on groups of Tasmanians that they encountered, and the first massacre of the colony took place in May 1804, when Royal Marines opened fire with muskets and cannon on a hunting party of 300 Aborigines, which included men, women, children, and elders, killing at least three and possibly as many as forty (Kiernan 2007, 265). However, the loss of their hunting grounds cost many more Tasmanians their lives than gunfire did directly. From 1803 to 1818 the European population of Tasmania grew to over 3,000 persons, while the Aboriginal population fell by over half, "from an estimated four thousand to somewhere under two thousand" (Ryan 1996, 79). Colonists converted to sheep pasture the unforested plains that the Tasmanians had used for hunting kangaroo, closing off a crucial Aboriginal food source. Colonists also tortured and killed Aboriginal Tasmanians on or near their lands and foraged in parties to kidnap and rape Aboriginal women and to steal Aboriginal children (Madley 2004, 171–2; Sousa 2004, 199; Elder 1988, 28–30; Robson 1983, 231–2, 239; Ryan 1996, 78). Although many early colonists were convicts serving sentences, free settlers came to take advantage of surging profits in wool production, especially after the 1822 British reduction of duties on Australian wool exports (Levene 2005b, 39). By 1830 the colonists numbered 23,500, including 6,000 free settlers and a larger number of convicts who provided the settlers with cheap labour (Ryan 1996, 83).

War

War began in 1824, when Aboriginal Tasmanians began to use force in an effort to slow the encroachment on their lands. In November 1823 members of the Oyster Bay tribe, led by Musquito and Black Jack, killed two stock-keepers in a raid at Grindstone Bay and two more in a second raid four months later. Colonial authorities captured, tried, and hanged the leaders of the raid, who pleaded not guilty to the murders but could not legally give evidence in their own defence because they were not Christians.[1] From this point on, "the Tasmanians began to fight back in fairly concerted ways. Between 1824 and 1830, approximately 170 whites were killed, some 200 wounded, and another 200 or so harassed or threatened" (Brantlinger 2003, 124). In 1826 the British brought military forces to defend the colonists and officially gave colonists the *de jure* right to use force against Aboriginals, which they had enjoyed unofficially until then (Ryan 1996, 90; 2008, 485). In November of that year, the Hobart Town *Colonial Times*, the island's principal newspaper, issued this demand, in boldface capital letters: "THE GOVERNMENT MUST REMOVE THE NATIVES – IF NOT, THEY WILL BE HUNTED DOWN LIKE WILD BEASTS AND DESTROYED!" (quoted in Sousa 2004, 202). Sporadic killings on both sides proceeded, with Aboriginal deaths outnumbering those of colonists by nearly three to one, until Lieutenant Governor George Arthur declared martial law against the so-called "bushrangers" on 1 November 1828 (Ryan 1996, 99; 2008, 485–6). Given total impunity, military forces and colonists foraged widely, seeking to capture, kill, or drive away all Aborigines in the settled southern portion of the island. Of the 1,500 Tasmanians alive in 1824, fewer than 300 survivors would remain by 1835 (Plomley 1992, 29). In 1830, bowing to pressure from his Executive Council, Arthur organized the infamous Black Line operation (Ryan 1996, 110–13). Two thousand men assembled to form a line stretching clear across the southern end of the island, and then they moved southward, hoping to drive the Indigenous population south and east toward a concentrated area where they could be taken into captivity. Superficially, the operation failed, with only two Tasmanians captured. In actuality, however, it accomplished its objective; Tasmanians escaping through the gaps in the line fled the area, moving northeast beyond the frontier. The densely settled districts were free of Aborigines by January 1832.

To resolve the issue of Aborigines living in the unsettled central and northern interior of the island, Lieutenant Governor Arthur appointed George Augustus Robinson to act as missionary and

---

[1] During the whole of colonial rule, "no European was ever charged, let alone committed for trial, for assaulting or killing an Aboriginal" (Ryan 1996, 88).

conciliator. Robinson had already achieved some repute in the Tasmanian colony by acting as what Howard Becker (1973) would call a "moral entrepreneur" in the service of the civilizing process, and he would enjoy a measure of celebrity for his role in the events to come (Johnston 2009). In 1829–30 Robinson travelled throughout the island, making contact with every surviving tribe and negotiating a cessation of Aboriginal attacks on colonists. Aboriginal collaborators, including a young Truganini, acted as ambassadors to facilitate his contact with new groups. In 1831 Robinson estimated that only 700 Aboriginal Tasmanians remained alive, although the real number turned out to be much lower (Robson 1983, 239). In that year, Robinson met with Arthur to discuss plans for the future of the Tasmanians (Ryan 1996, 151–2). The two agreed on a plan to remove Aborigines, purportedly for their own welfare, to Flinders Island, in the Bass Strait off the northeast coast of Tasmania. Chief Justice John Lewes Pedder objected to this plan on the grounds that the Tasmanians would wither away in an environment to which they were so unaccustomed, and he advocated instead the formation of a territorial reservation on Tasmania itself, modelled on those in the United States. Robinson disagreed, arguing that he could Christianize the Tasmanians only if their land and culture were stripped away. Despite the failure of two previous such civilizing efforts on the Australian mainland, Arthur agreed with Robinson's position.

Internment

From 1831 to 1834, therefore, Robinson travelled again throughout the island, persuading, and in some cases compelling, Tasmanians to surrender themselves, and promising them safety from the depredations of colonists. He succeeded completely, transporting all remaining Tasmanians to the Flinders Island Aboriginal Establishment between 1832 and 1835, except for one family that eluded capture until 1842 (Ryan 1996, 170; Robson 1983, 253). Historian Loyd Robson has described the establishment as the world's first concentration camp (Robson 1983, 220; see also Reynolds 1995, 159); its inmates named it "Wybalenna," usually translated as "black men's houses" (Ryan 1996, 183). Robinson hoped the establishment would serve as "the prototype of the multi-purposed institution, asylum, hospital, training centre, school, agricultural institution, rationing centre, pensioners' home, prison" (Rowley 1970, 52). For although

Robinson had promised to allow the Tasmanians to keep their culture, he actually believed that the only way to save them was to civilize them (Barta 2008b, 529). Indeed, from the early encounters of explorers and would-be anthropologists, through settlement, war, and captivity, Europeans chronically framed their understanding of the Aboriginal Tasmanians in terms of their savagery and their capacity, or lack thereof, for civilization. Colonial observers assumed the opposition of savagery and civilization and disagreed only about whether the former condition could be remedied:

> On paper Robinson was committed to allow the Aborigines to pursue their own culture, but in practice he intended to use the artificial environment of Flinders Island to prove that his captives wished to advance towards civilization, which consisted of an appreciation of the main tenets of Christianity and a disposition to adopt European standards of personal cleanliness, dress, and housing, develop a desire to accumulate money and material possessions, and pursue agriculture ... Robinson was determined to prove wrong the natural inference drawn by the colonists that the Aborigines possessed certain 'anti-civilizing properties' which prevented change. (Ryan 1996, 183)

The capacity for and disposition toward work – specifically, European modes of agriculture and industry – formed a central component of the image of the civilized subject, not only in Tasmania but also for English colonial discourse around the globe. The word "savage" "derives from *silvaticus*, a man of the woods, a forest dweller. Such people are judged as uncivilized barbarians for a range of reasons, of which perhaps the most emphatic is their failure to 'properly' work the land" (McVeigh and Rolston 2009, 7). Binary oppositions tend to polarize perceptions, becoming stereotypes that fix, essentialize, and naturalize difference (Hall 1997, 223ff). So the absence of European agriculture became, in the colonizers' imaginations, evidence of "an unbelievable laziness" (Memmi 1965, 79). Work, then, occupied a central place in Robinson's civilizing efforts. But since, in his civilized eye, everything about the Tasmanians that made them different from Europeans appeared as both a sign and a cause of their savagery, the effort of converting them into a reserve supply of alienated labour required nothing less than their total Anglicization; "what Robinson meant by civilizing the aboriginals involved the eradication of their beliefs, customs, and even identities" (Brantlinger 2003, 126). On this project, he staked his public reputation, making himself a celebrity of civilization (Johnston 2009). But civilized selfhood required this civilizing project in a more subtle way. Having undergone the civilizing process in their *own* lives, by which they had learned to define themselves as good or bad according to the fluid but remorseless standards of deferentiation, Robinson, Arthur, and other would-be protectors of the Tasmanians could not imagine that the latter could somehow remain outside of this process. Their understanding of themselves as civilized required that they civilize others. This accounts for Robinson's curious intransigence: "To achieve all this Robinson not only needed a willing Aboriginal community but also regular supplies of European food, reasonable living conditions, a sympathetic European staff, and an awareness of the psychological dislocation that this would create among his victims. That he had none of these did not deter him" (Ryan 1996, 183). As things turned out, the civilizing requirement would fulfil itself only in annihilation.

Like the Indian residential schools that the British government was to establish in Canada, the Flinders Island Aboriginal Establishment functioned as a total institution (Goffman 1961). Robinson took advantage of this to implement a thoroughgoing regime aimed at entirely abolishing the social identities of the Aboriginal Tasmanians (Ryan 1996, 183–9). He forbade all traditional dances and religious practices, urged men to cut their hair in European fashion, and encouraged the Tasmanians to take European names. Children, women, and men lived by a rigid daily routine, tightly regulated by the clock. Children learned Christianity, went to school, and studied gender-segregated occupations: trades for the boys and domestic skills for the girls. Women had to cook and clean in the fashion of European housewives, and they received English literacy training and Bible studies. Unmarried women could not cohabit with European men. Men enjoyed a less regimented life but were expected to "cultivate the gardens, build roads, clear forest land, erect fences, and shear sheep" (Ryan 1996, 185). Routine inspections enforced European dress for all, and administrators organized meals on the British model. In 1837 Robinson required the Tasmanians to build brick houses for themselves, and he started a weekly newsletter written by the boys. A weekly market involved the Tasmanians in the money economy. Robinson abstained from using physical force but used "moral and coercive force with devastating results" (Ryan 1996, 187), iso-lating groups, denying rations, prohibiting hunting, encouraging spies and informants, and appointing salaried constables among the men. The Tasmanians resisted this program, secretly engaging in traditional practices and refraining from more than superficial ad-herence to Christianity. After the nonarrival of supply ships in the winter of 1837, resistance became more overt. Robinson left in frus-tration in 1839 (Ryan 1996, 193).

While living as test subjects of this experiment in involuntary re-socialization, the Tasmanians faced death at a precipitous rate. When Robinson arrived at the Flinders Island Aboriginal Establishment in 1835, of the "three hundred he had originally captured," only 123 remained alive to meet him. "Most had died in the various transit camps set up to process them on capture" (Ryan 1996, 183, 193). Captives on Flinders initially lived in a penitentiary building and began "almost at once" to die of pulmonary disease (Robson 1983, 249). "In 1833, 43 Aborigines arrived at the establishment to join the 78 already there. But 37 died, leaving 84. In 1834, 42 arrived, but 14 died, leaving 112 ... several children were born, but most died within a few days" (Ryan 1996, 180). Flinders Island has a colder, rainier, and windier climate than the Tasmanians were used to. In 1835 the appointed surgeon reported to Robinson that the Aborigines lacked sufficient blankets and clothing, that the establishment sat exposed to prevailing cold winds, that it lacked "wholesome" water, and that the shelter was insufficient (Turnbull 1966, 176–7), but these warnings did not prompt an administrative response (Madley 2004, 175). Diet, too, was insufficient: in December 1834 daily ra-tions for each adult consisted of one pound of salt beef, one pound of flour, half a pound of biscuit, and one quarter ounce each of sugar, soap, and salt; child rations were half this. "Since the Aborigines would not eat salt meat, to stave off malnutrition they were forced to hunt, even though they were often too ill to hunt, or forbidden to hunt, or had nothing to hunt" (Ryan 1996, 180). Prior to contact, the Tasmanian diet had included high levels of vitamin C, iron, and thiamine (Ryan 1996, 175), but in captivity their intake of these nutrients was chronically insufficient. By 1837 the authorities had increased flour, sugar, and soap rations and had added tobacco and tea to the supplies; the Tasmanians had supplemented these with lo-cal cabbage and turnip and had begun eating the salt meat. But even after fresh mutton was added to their rations in 1838, the diet was still nutritionally inadequate (Ryan 1996, 186). Fatal epidemics of pulmonary disease swept the camp periodically. Between Robinson's arrival in 1835 and his departure in 1839, 59 of the original 123 Tasmanians died, 11 were born or arrived separately, and 15 left with him for the Australian mainland (Ryan 1996, 193). From 1839 to 1847, of the 60 who remained, 30 died, an additional 14 arrived from elsewhere, and "at least five children, all part-Aboriginal," were born (Ryan 1996, 203).

After Robinson's departure, the contradictions of the situation continued to intensify. Between 1839 and 1847, three boards of inquiry into living conditions at the establishment blamed the Aborigines for being ungrateful, lazy, and indolent (Ryan 1996, 195). Insubordination met with incarceration. The strict disciplinary regime relaxed for a while after Robinson's departure but reintensified in 1842 under Henry Jeanneret, who came to epitomize the coercive relationship between the Tasmanians and the colonial government. Jeanneret himself was suspended for insubordination in December 1843 (Ryan 1996, 200), and when he applied for reinstatement in 1845, the Aboriginal man Walter George Arthur, one of Robinson's original ambassadors, wrote to an influential Quaker in Hobart saying that his people could support themselves economically and wanted greater autonomy rather than another commandant. In 1846 the Tasmanians sent a petition to Queen Victoria asking that Jeanneret not be reinstated, accusing him of threatening to shoot them, putting them in jail, withholding rations, and forcing them to work without remuneration (Ryan 1996, 201). After Jeanneret was nevertheless reinstated that same year, the Tasmanians petitioned the lieutenant governor, complaining of ill-treatment and asking for their independence. The Colonial Office in London responded by ordering the removal of the Aborigines to a new colony at Oyster Cove on Tasmania in 1847 (Ryan 1996, 202–3).

The forty-seven Tasmanians who survived at Wybalenna hoped for a better life back on the mainland, but their situation deteriorated even further at Oyster Cove. Oyster Cove Aboriginal Station sat on a mudflat with poor drainage, flooded for much of each year by waste water from farms upland. The wooden buildings, damp and vermin-infested, offered insufficient protection from cold south winds (Ryan 1996, 205). Still, rations improved and the Tasmanians could find shellfish, a traditional staple, in abundance, so their health improved for a time. Christianization, especially of children, continued, but otherwise the Tasmanians enjoyed greater autonomy. "[A] visiting magistrate made weekly inspections of the Aborigines' clothes, houses, treatment and behaviour, and the quality and condition of their rations" (Ryan 1996, 205–7). Community leaders Walter George Arthur and Mary Ann Arthur bought land and tried to live as farmers. However, over the next two years morale declined and mortality rose. More deaths brought the population down to thirty in 1851, and then to seventeen in 1854 (Ryan 1996, 209). The colonial authority extended self-government to the settlement in 1855 and accompanied this with a 50 per cent cut in expenditure by reducing rations, reducing magistrates' visits from weekly to monthly, and ceasing all housing repairs. By 1859 the station had fallen into severe disrepair, its occupants afflicted with mental illness, senility, alcoholism, and severe respiratory complaints (Ryan 1996, 210). Community leaders like William George Arthur and later William Lanney complained to the authorities, but to no avail. Deaths continued to stalk the small community, claiming William George Arthur in a boating accident in 1861 (Ryan 1996, 212). The last male of the group, William Lanney, died in 1868. The following year, with only two residents remaining in the station, the colonial authority disbanded it. Mary Ann died in July 1871, and Truganini survived until 1876.

Abjection

To validate their own self-image as civilized peoples, the English colonial authorities wanted the Aboriginal Tasmanians to voluntarily collaborate in the active negation of their being – that is, in the radical shaming of precolonial identities. It is no wonder that the Tasmanians resisted for so long and never succeeded in taking it on. It was a negation that could never pay off: for one thing, Tasmanians were expected to adopt an English habitus but not to stand up for their rights like English subjects. Elias observes that as colonized groups succeed in adopting the habitus of the colonizer, the distance between colonizer and colonized shrinks, and so the system of difference that reinforces the civilized status of the colonizer is threatened (Elias 2000, 385). This happens at the same time that the civilizing process itself tends to reduce these differences through propagation of its own standards. So one can see that a contradiction is created for civilized persons at any given moment. Elias notes that colonizers may respond by increasing the refinement of their conduct; he does not consider what other methods they may adopt: refusing to provide the colonized with the means to civilize themselves successfully; and refusing to recognize civilized behaviour even when the colonized subject performs it consummately.

These refusals doomed Walter George Arthur, "the one 'fullblood' Aboriginal Tasmanian who tried to conform to European mores" (Ryan 1996, 212), to soul-wrenching failure. Kidnapped by colonists at the age of ten and raised in an orphanage before arriving at Wybalenna, he became one of the community leaders to regularly petition the colonial authorities for better treatment. He also worked hard and successfully to take on English modes of conduct and of economic productivity. This personal transformation came at a cost: "He had developed a schizophrenic personality: sometimes he was a resistance leader demanding better conditions for his people; at other times he was a desperate conformist aching for the acceptance of white society. But he was never 'good enough'" (Ryan 1996, 212). This "schizophrenia" that Walter George Arthur experienced from his position of poverty and marginality contains elements in common with the transformation of self experienced by the upper classes of colonized groups and upwardly mobile members of a class structure: "people in this situation acknowledge in one part of their consciousness the upper-class norms and manners as binding on themselves, without being able to adopt them with the same ease and matter-of-factness. It is this peculiar contradiction between the upper class within themselves ... and their incapacity of fulfilling its demands, it is this constant inner tension that gives their affective life and their conduct its particular character" (Elias 2000, 431). In his younger days, Walter George Arthur studied to become a catchetist, but his relationship with Mary Ann Cochran in 1838 ruled out this occupation for him because it did not meet Christian standards of chastity. He worked as a stockman and drover, and later he ran his own small farm (Turnbull 1966, 230). After the move to Oyster Cove, he and Mary Ann had lived independently in a three-room bush cottage "surrounded by the trappings of European civilization," but they "preferred the communal warmth of the [Oyster Cove] station, where they could relax and share a bottle with their own people" (Ryan 1996, 212). As Clive Turnbull puts it, "Walter George Arthur had attained a high degree of civilization, even by Mr. Robinson's standard. He was given the white man's learning and perhaps the white man's tastes, but not the white man's rights nor the white man's place in society. At Oyster Cove ... he saw his people sunk in despair, filth, and disease, all their old happiness and dignity gone from them" (Turnbull 1966, 231). Afflicted with alchoholism, Walter George Arthur died in a boating accident in 1861, a victim of the "constant inner tension" resulting from a self divided between identification with European civilization and with his "own people." It is small wonder that Robinson's project failed. The captured Aboriginal Tasmanians were literally civilized to death.

However, the incorporation of the Tasmanians into Western civilization did not stop even at the grave. The death of William Lanney, the last "full-blooded" Aboriginal man, aroused "great agitation among both the scientific community and the general public" because of the "inestimable significance" that his bones could have for scientific knowledge (Brantlinger 2003, 128; see also Bonwick 1970a, 395–400). Dr W.L. Crowther and Dr George Stokell, competing for this inestimable scientific capital, each stole part of his body after it had been buried. Crowther took Lanney's skull, which ended up in the possession of the Royal College of Surgeons in London; Stokell, a leading member of the Royal Society of Tasmania, took Lanney's hands and feet and then the rest of his body. Stokell "had a tobacco pouch made out of a portion of his skin, and other worthy scientists had possession of the ears, the nose, and a piece of Lanney's arm. The hands and feet were later found in the Royal Society's rooms in Argyle Street" (Ryan 1996, 217). As the last surviving recognized Tasmanian Aboriginal, Truganini feared that a similar fate awaited her and asked to be buried in the deepest part of D'Entrecasteaux Channel (Ryan 1996, 218). Truganini had been born in 1812 to Mangerner, chief of the Recherche Bay people. By the time that she met Robinson at the age of seventeen, "she had been raped, had seen her mother stabbed, her uncle shot, her step-mother kidnapped, her sisters captured and kidnapped," and her fi-ancée had drowned trying to rescue her from abduction by sawyers (Elder 1988, 31; see also Ryan 1996, 217). From 1832 to 1834 she accompanied Robinson on his missions to the Aborigines, but by the time she arrived on Flinders Island in 1835 she had become one of his firm critics. In 1839 she absconded from Port Phillip with four companions and began raiding and looting shepherds' huts. Acquitted, Truganini rejoined the interned Tasmanian community, and after the move to Oyster Bay she gradually withdrew from the civilizing project. When she died in 1876, at the age of sixty-four, the English believed her to be the last of her "race." Against her expressed wishes, and despite extraordinary precautions, scientists secretly exhumed her bones (Ryan 1996, 217–20; Brantlinger 2003, 129). They came into the possession of the Tasmanian Museum in Hobart, where they stood on public display from 1904 to 1947. The museum kept them tenaciously as long as it could, even after the Aboriginal Tasmanian university student Harry Penrith, writing on behalf of all surviving Tasmanians, requested their return (Cove 1995, 146–7). It did so partly on the grounds that scientific researchers might make use of them at some point (none ever did) and partly because it feared opening the door to requests for other human remains. Only in 1976 did Truganini finally find her rest; on 30 April her skeleton was cremated, and survivors of the Aboriginal Tasmanian community scattered her ashes the next day on the waters of D'Entrecasteaux Channel.

Survival and Recognition

However, the story, and the life, of the Aboriginal Tasmanians did not end with Truganini's death. The process that brought about their survival dates back to 1800, when Captain Charles Bishop discovered the abundant sealing grounds on the islands off the northeast corner of Tasmania. Following on this discovery, hundreds of sealers made seasonal settlements and harvested massive numbers of sealskins. Tasmanians entered into trade relations with the sealers and "offered women in an attempt to incorporate the visitors into their own society" (Ryan 1996, 67). Through their skills at survival in the local ecosystem, these women made a valuable contribution to the sealers' lives (Ryan 1996, 69). Historians disagree over the extent to which sealer-Aboriginal relations should be characterized as violent or mutually beneficial. Robson's account says, "the sealers in the north-east had already disrupted the Aborigines' lives by abducting or buying or securing loans of their women and murdering the men" (Robson 1983, 210). Lyndall Ryan frames this dynamic differently, claiming that sealers participated in pre-existing feuds between competing tribes (Ryan 1996, 69). Regarding the place of women in the sealer society, Ryan says, "their skills at first made them chattels in the exchange system devised by the Aboriginal men and the sealers but later proved a useful means with which to bargain for their independence" (Ryan 1996, 69). Either way, the appropriation or infiltration of Aboriginal women into the community of white seal-ers had the important long-term consequence of preventing the com-plete extinction of Aboriginal Tasmanian culture: "The sealers were instrumental in the destruction of a number of Aboriginal tribes on the north coast of Tasmania through exchange and abduction of women, but they also saved Aboriginal Tasmanian society from extinction because their economic activity enabled some of its traditions to continue" (Ryan 1996, 71). All surviving descendants of Aboriginal Tasmanians come from unions between Aboriginal women and European men.

This community practised a culture that mixed European and Aboriginal Tasmanian elements. Over the years, it resisted various attempts by the colonial government and by commercial interests to disintegrate it or to impede its economic self-sufficiency. By 1810 the seals had mostly perished, and only a few sealers stayed behind with their Aboriginal wives to found a permanent community. By 1820 the colonial government had begun to evict the sealers from the area; those who stayed behind shifted their economic activity from sealing to mutton-birding, at the initiative of the Aboriginal women. In 1847 this community consisted of thirteen families totalling about 50 people (Ryan 1996, 222). By 1908 the population had grown to about 200, incorporated into the new municipality of Flinders (Ryan 1996, 239). The Tasmanian Parliament created a reserve for them on Cape Barren Island in 1912 (Ryan 1996, 242). In 1951 the govern-ment terminated this reserve, hoping to assimilate the islanders into Australian society (Ryan 1996, 248). A small community remained, however, and those who relocated to Launceston also retained their sense of community, partly because they faced discrimination in Anglo-Tasmanian society. Struggle over ownership of land on Cape Barren Island continued through the 1960s, and in 1971 the federal government appointed a "community development officer" to assist in redevelopment of the island (Ryan 1996, 251). In 1973 the government established an Aboriginal legal service, which went on to operate as a vehicle for Aboriginal political and cultural self-assertion (Ryan 1996, 263). In 1993 the High Court of Australia ruled in favour of land rights for an Aboriginal group in the Murray Islands, abandoning the principle of *terra nullius*, which had been operative throughout Australian history (Ryan 1996, 292). This de-cision encouraged further activism by Aboriginals in Tasmania, leading to land claims negotiations between the federal government and the Aboriginal community in the mid-1990s, the passage of the Aboriginal Lands Act of 1995, and continuing struggles over the definition of "Aboriginal Tasmanian." Aboriginal Tasmanians have also featured in public debates, apologies, and reparations policies regarding the "Stolen Generations," Aboriginal children throughout Australia forcibly removed from their families (Human Rights and Equal Opportunity Commission 1997; BBC News 2006).

Genocide or Not?

After Truganini's death, Western commentators believed that they had witnessed the extinction of the Tasmanian "race." Operating on this assumption, scholars produced elegiatic works whose tone ranged from gentle regret to scathing condemnation (Bonwick 1970a, 1970b; Calder 1972; Plomley 1992; Roth 1899; Travers 1968). Raphaël Lemkin, also believing the Tasmanians to have suffered complete extinction, included them among his case studies of genocide in his massive and tragically uncompleted history of genocide (Curthoys 2005). Examining the killing of Tasmanians, the disruption of biological reproduction through the kidnapping of women and children, the fatal consequences of being driven away from the land on which they depended for their food, and the demoralizing effects of confinement on Gun Carriage, Bruny, and Flinders Islands, Lemkin found settlers responsible for genocide. He also assigned responsibility to the colonial government on the grounds that its officials, "while neither planning nor conducting genocide, failed in their basic duty of protection" (Curthoys 2005, 168). Half-way around the world, the anthropologist Clive Turnbull reached a similar conclusion: that the Aborigines of Tasmania were destroyed by "the ill-will of the usurpers of that race's [sic] land. When that ill-will was active it found expression in brutality. When passive it deplored extermination while condoning, and participating in the rewards of, a system which made extermination inevitable" (Turnbull 1966, 1). Leo Kuper, likewise, refers to the "systematic annihilation" of the Aboriginal Tasmanians (Kuper 1981, 40). These views have influenced much subsequent genocide scholarship (Barta 1987, 2008c, 2008a, 2008b; Chalk and Jonassohn 1990; Fein 1993; Jones 2006a; Kiernan 2007; Levene 2005b; Moses 2000).

Some recent work, however, has disputed this view, arguing that no genocide took place in Tasmania (Lewy 2007; Reynolds 2001; Windschuttle 2002). This work has appeared against the backdrop of public debates about Australia's genocidal history. In these so-called "history wars," prominent political leaders, including Prime Minister John Howard and Premier Ray Groom of Tasmania, have adamantly denied that the term "genocide" applies to Australia's past (Reynolds 2001, 49; Barta 2008a; MacIntyre and Clark 2003). Denials by scholars like Keith Windschuttle and Günter Lewy have articulated a wider reluctance in Australian society to accept the political and ethical implications of the nation's colonial atrocities. Some of this work has turned out to depend on faulty research methods and unsupported or mistaken empirical claims (Manne 2003; Ryan 2008), combined with stereotyped views of Indigenous societies as "wanting in pity and compassion" in contrast to "enlightened administrators" working toward "the advance of Christian civilization" (Bonnell and Crotty 2004, 429). However, even Henry Reynolds, whom Windschuttle attacks as one of the prime "fabricators" of history for having written abundantly on the colonial dispossession and massacre of Aboriginal peoples, argues that no genocide took place in Tasmania. His argument, like Lewy's, centres on intent: "In the draft convention put together by the UN secretary-general, it was determined that in cases where victims were placed in concentration camps with an annual death rate of 30 to 40 per cent, the intention to commit genocide was unquestionable. Clearly the death rate on Flinders Island puts it well within the range of such death camps, but there is no available evidence at all to suggest that it was the intention of the colonial government to affect the extinction of the Tasmanians" (Reynolds 2001, 85). Reynolds takes for evidence the statements by Lieutenant Governor George Arthur, George Augustus Robinson, Henry Jeanneret, and others expressing distress at the precipitous mortality of the Aborigines and the desire to prevent, or at least not to hasten, their extinction. For Reynolds and Lewy to find genocide in Tasmania, Arthur and his peers would have had to openly proclaim an exterminatory intent.

As I have discussed in chapter 2, arguments like these presume a strongly subjectivist conception of social life, in which actions derive their entire significance from the subjective meanings present in the mind of the actors who perform them. To subjectivist thinkers, the ways that actions exceed the intentions of their actors do not count as part of the action. Relational social theories like Elias's figurational sociology treat actors' subjective understandings as only one component of any given action, let alone of a large ensemble of interconnected actions. In the relational conception of genocide that I have proposed, genocide not only destroys individuals but also destroys figurations; acting through relations of identity-difference, genocide destroys collective identities by violently tearing apart or negating the relations that sustain identification. By this standard, the historical record shows overwhelmingly that Aboriginal Tasmanians experienced genocide. The English invasion and occupation involved murder, massacre, displacement from food sources, kidnapping of women, and internment in unsanitary conditions with inadequate food and shelter. These processes irrevocably destroyed the form of life practised before colonization and brought the Tasmanians to the very brink of cultural and physical annihilation.

However, we should also consider the protestations of Reynolds that Arthur and other responsible officials repeatedly expressed a concern for the Tasmanians' welfare and a desire to see them survive. Should we classify the events in Tasmania as an *accidental* genocide? Did the Tasmanians die despite the best efforts of the colonial authority to protect them? This interpretation glosses over the specific intentions at work on the scene. English authorities intentionally arranged for the settlement of Tasmania and intentionally appropriated the lands on which the Aboriginal Tasmanians depended for food. These actions had entirely foreseeable, and forseen, genocidal consequences: "the invaders from the other side of the world knew very well that they were causing the extinction of whole Aboriginal peoples even if they did not set out to exterminate them ... Taking land meant taking lives, immediately and in the succeeding years: the whole nature of the supplanting society was the creation of economic and cultural interests inimical to Aboriginal survival" (Barta 2008b, 521). These same authorities also intentionally refrained from ever sanctioning a European settler for violence against an Aborigine (Ryan 1996, 88). As the genocidal effects of colonization intensified, the colonial government increased settlement and land appropriations on the island. Some voices in the settler society did speak against the destruction of the Aborigines, among them Lieutenant Governor Arthur, who expressed his wish that the

Aborigines should survive and made some ineffectual gestures at opposing settler violence. But taking these minority voices as indicative of the intentions of the whole of settler society would mean naturalizing and making invisible the actively exterminatory forces that predominated in everyday/everynight life on Tasmania. That the best Arthur and Robinson could do to ensure the physical survival of the Aborigines was to relocate them to a remote and inhospitable bit of unused land, and that the Tasmanians themselves were desperate enough to agree to this, testifies to the extremity of the situation.

During and after the relocation to Flinders Island, several observers communicated the genocidal quality of the internment to the responsible authorities. Chief Justice Pedder objected to the relocation of the Tasmanians to Flinders Island on the grounds that confinement would demoralize them and cause them to "pine away" (Ryan 1996, 151). Major Thomas Ryan, who visited the settlement, reported that the Aborigines' living conditions were so poor as to be likely to bring about their extinction, and he recommended both a new site and "vastly improved rations" (Ryan 1996, 186). James Stephen, undersecretary in the Colonial Office in London, observed the population decline and recommended relocation back to the mainland, declaring that "why we should persevere in a policy at once so costly to the author, and so fatal to the objects of it, I cannot imagine" (quoted in Ryan 1996, 202). And in another sense, the internment on Flinders had an openly genocidal purpose from its very conception: to completely and forcibly eradicate the Tasmanians' own culture, converting the Aborigines themselves to the English mode of life (Ryan 1996, 152, 183, 196, 209). Robinson took a dim view of the Aborigines' savagery and had no use for them as they saw themselves; although he did not use the phrase "white men in brown skins," it applies to what he and Arthur hoped to achieve.

With the resettlement to Oyster Cove, the colonial authority did deliberately alter its policy in response to complaints from the Tasmanians themselves. At this moment, all the priorities that might have changed were instead reaffirmed: low expenditures for support of the Aboriginals; placing the interests of British settlers categorically ahead of Aboriginal well-being; and making Europeanization of the Tasmanians a precondition for their inclusion in colonial Tasmania. If Aboriginal survival had taken precedence over these other priorities, the colonial government would not have placed

Aborigines in inadequate housing on a cold, vermin-infested, and disease-ridden mudflat with an ever-decreasing budget devoted to their welfare.

From the outset, the project of colonizing Tasmania had no room in it for the Indigenous inhabitants of the island. The range of thinkable options ran from complete physical extermination to physical survival at the cost of cultural annihilation. Unwillingness to invest substantial resources in the latter ensured the predominance of the former. In this sense, genocide was *both* structurally embedded in the colonial project *and* intended by those who participated in it:

> Certainly, colonialism in Australia, as elsewhere, could not be halted in the manner of flicking a light switch ... But only a miserably attenuated concept of intention would absolve it in these circumstances. The rhetoric of inevitability also served to mask choices open to policymakers, choices they were not prepared to entertain because they fundamentally approved of the civilizing process in which they were engaged. The fact is that they did not take their own humanitarian convictions seriously enough to implement the radical measures necessary to prevent indigenous deaths, whether caused by massacre or disease, for it would entail relinquishing control of the land and jeopardizing the colonizing mission. (Moses 2002, 30)

Once the genocidal effects of settlement had become apparent, continuation of the colonial project in its current form involved a decision to accept these consequences. Discourses of the inevitability of Aboriginal extinction reflected the non-negotiability of a colonial vision that intentionally made no place for Aborigines *qua* Aborigines. Inside the boundaries of the Flinders Island and Oyster Cove settlements, the Aboriginal Tasmanians stood outside the community of obligation, where inexorably they died of attrition.

CIVILIZATION, DIFFERENCE, AND IMPUNITY

"It is not a little characteristic of the structure of Western society that the watchword of its colonizing movement is 'civilization'" (Elias 2000, 431). Colonialism involved the extension, through a process of competition between sovereign powers, of territorial monopolies of force – that is, the reproduction of sovereignty on an expanding scale, which burst the boundaries of Europe itself to colonize the rest of the world. And by the same gesture, colonialism entailed an expansion of specifically European forms of civilized habitus, of European ways of performing subjectivity. In the colonization of Tasmania, this expansion happened primarily through direct demographic transplant – British subjects arrived, displacing the Tasmanians from their land – and secondarily through the attempted resubjectification of the captive Aborigines. These violent processes did more than destroy Tasmanians' relationships to the land and to each other; they also produced new relationships, where none had existed, between the settlers and Natives. Just as there were no settlers in Tasmania before the British arrived, neither were there any "Natives," for the people who lived there became Natives – became Aboriginal Tasmanians – only in relation to their white colonizers. Unfortunately, this process had a fatal dynamic from its outset because the interests that drove the colonists, the coherence of their identification with each other, and the balance of force at their command completely overmatched the resistance that the Tasmanians could offer, producing the identity-difference relationship between settlers and Natives as one of impunity.

That the genocide of the Aboriginal Tasmanians resulted from intentional social action does not necessarily mean that a high priority was ever attached to this outcome or that it was ever pursued as an end in itself. We should not conflate the importance an event has for us as observers with the importance it has for its architects. Rather, in the history of the Aboriginal Tasmanians, the fact of genocide testifies to the unimportance of its victims. Or, more precisely, it attests to the unimportance of their physical and cultural survival. The Tasmanians were tremendously important to their colonizers as long as they served as an obstacle to the construction of a civilized, British Tasmania. Once interned, they lost this importance. Robinson and a few others found them important as a test case for the universal validity of Europe's defining cultural accomplishments, its civilization. Jeanneret seemed to find them important mainly as objects of domination and exploitation. At every turn, these various ways that they were important worked against the Tasmanians' survival; the nature of their importance placed them outside the community of obligation. Their physical extermination happened almost casually, as a by-product of the active negation of their political and cultural existence.

PART TWO: INDIA

Genocidal Famines

In the late nineteenth century India suffered two periods of enormous famine, "the worst famines in perhaps 500 years": 1876–79 and 1896–1902. Mortality for the first famine is estimated at 6.1 million to 10.3 million dead and for the second at 6.1 million to 19 million dead, for a total combined mortality of between 12.2 million and 29.3 million persons dead (Davis 2001, 7–8). These famines never threatened to destroy Indian society as a whole; indeed, they occurred while colonial occupation was fusing together the many diverse societies of South Asia to produce such a thing as "Indian society as a whole." But they did effect a very substantial destruction of it in part, and I argue below that they resulted from a *genocidal relation*, one expressed through commodity exchange relations and ultimately sanctioned by state force. But treating these events in this way raises the question: how can famine count as genocide?

THEORETICAL ISSUES

Doesn't famine result from natural events, mainly from drought, from too much sun and too little rain? Of contemporary events, we can say that even *weather* has been permeated by the effects of social action, thanks to anthropogenic global warming, but this had not begun to set in at the end of the nineteenth century. Classical sociologists drew a sharp and definite line between the realms of "society" and "nature"; both Max Weber (1978, 7–8) and Emile Durkheim (1982, 50) have defined natural events, such as variations in rainfall, as data that sociologists must consider but that do not form part of the subject matter of sociology. For Weber, rainfall does not count as a social action; for Durkheim, it does not count as a social fact. Writing in the middle of the twentieth century, Talcott Parsons (1951, 541–5; 1966) defined the natural world as one of the environments within which social systems operate. Famine can play a part in my account of civilizing genocides only if it can count as a social phenomenon.

Unlike Weber and Durkheim, Karl Marx did not draw a sharp line between the social and the natural. For Marx, natural objects become part of a society as soon as they are involved in human labour.

A stick, lying undisturbed in the forest, belongs to nature; this stick, picked up and used to dig for tubers, becomes a social artefact. The activity of labour connects human sociality intimately with the properties and the dynamics of natural phenomena. From this perspective, then, a term like "drought" refers not only to a natural event but also to its effects on socially organized food production (Davis 2001, 18–22).[2] These effects themselves have social as well as meteorological determinants. Inadequate or poorly timed rainfall will cause crop failure only if stored water is inadequate or inaccessible. Stored water can occur in naturally formed streams, lakes, and aquifers or in socially constructed reservoirs, wells, and canals, so the impact of deficient rainfall on food production depends, among other things, on whether artificial irrigation systems can distribute water to plots and – if water is commodified – on whether cultivators can afford to buy it. Similarly, whether crop failure or simple food availability decline leads to famine mortality depends on the availability of alternate sources of food and on whether affected people can secure access to them. In a commodified food economy, this depends not only on the local price of food but also on regional or global market conditions; if commodity traders find it more profitable to sell Bengal grain in Lancashire than in Bengal, Bengalese may starve. The likelihood of famine mortality also depends on political conditions: on public relief efforts or the lack thereof, on the effectiveness of protests and riots to appropriate food for the

---

2 In retelling the historical details of the six exemplary genocides that I use to illustrate my theory, I have usually drawn on multiple sources that corroborate and correct each other, partly to establish the validity of my empirical claims and partly to show interested readers where they can find histories that are more in-depth. However, for the Indian famines, I have relied almost exclusively on Mike Davis's outstanding *Late Victorian Holocausts*. In this work, his systemic historical account of how the production of hunger and of famine emerged in the nineteenth century to become an embedded, institutionalized feature of the modern world-system is uniquely suited to the needs of my figurational analysis of civilizing genocide. However, Davis's theoretical approach is far from unique; he draws on a well-established research program of the political economy of hunger influenced by Indian economist Amartya Sen (1981) that analyzes famine in terms of restricted social entitlements to food rather than absolute food scarcity. For a summary of this literature as it relates to India, see Drèze (1995); for a more recent assessment of the state of the art, see Rubin (2009b); and for a (somewhat humanistic) sociological appropriation of this literature, see Scanlan (2009).

nonentitled, on the willingness of state or private authorities to use force against such actions, and so on. In this respect, famine can operate as a form of upwardly redistributive class struggle. Finally, the definition of "famine" itself reflects power relations among social groups. Social power determines who gets to decide what counts as famine and who doesn't – and, for those who do, it determines whether they consider famine simply to comprise "mass starvation unto death" or also death from disease caused by malnutrition. Further, it determines whether they also consider chronic hunger, destitution, and social breakdown to be parts of famine. Treating drought and famine as simply natural events masks the operation of social relationships of production and distribution. A fuller account understands famine as a figurational event.

PRECEDENTS

In 1904 the German colonial army, seeking to establish sovereignty over present-day Namibia, faced a rebellion by the local Indigenous nation of the Herero (Bridgman and Worley 2009). To end this conflict, the German army organized a massive offensive that drove the entire Herero nation into the Omaheke Desert and trapped them there – 80,000 men, women, children, and elders – with no access to food or fresh water. Only one-quarter of this group survived; this massive population loss brought about a collapse of the Herero community and collective identity that lasted for decades. In 1915 the Turkish nationalist government of the Ottoman Empire "deported" hundreds of thousands of Armenian subjects by force-marching them through a desertic mountain route to Syria, beating or executing any who lagged behind, and exposing the deportees to robbery, extortion, and murder along the way (see chapter 7 for a more detailed account). Again, three-quarters of the deportees died, many from exhaustion and exposure (Hairapetian 1984), contributing to the near-total destruction of the Armenian community in Turkey. Genocide scholars have no difficulty recognizing these events as genocidal, and the 1948 United Nations Convention on the Prevention and Punishment of the Crime of Genocide, which regards "inflicting on the group conditions of life calculated to bring about its physical destruction in whole or in part" as one of the recognized means of genocide, explicitly includes these kinds of tactics. Likewise, scholars like David Stannard (1992), Ward Churchill (1998), and Tony Barta (1987) who investigate colonial genocides against Indigenous peoples in the Americas and Australia point out that driving people away from the food sources on which they depend causes deaths from malnutrition-related illnesses and that these deaths can severely damage or destroy the collective life of the group, causing or contributing to genocide.

These examples show how social action that removes people from their food sources can count as genocide. The opposite, removing food sources from people, also has precedents – most notably the Ukrainian famine of 1932–33, known as the Holodomor (murder by hunger) (see Conquest 1990; Mace 2009). Crop failure or food availability decline made only a minor and arguable contribution to this famine; rather, violent seizure of grain from independent farmers by state authorities caused millions to go hungry. At the end of the 1920s, about one-fifth of Ukraine's peasantry remained outside the Soviet Union–sponsored regime of collectivized farming. Joseph Stalin's government imposed a heavy quota on each of these households, partly to service the economic objectives of the Soviet Union as a whole, partly to suppress the formerly wealthy class of labour-employing independent farming families (or kulaks), and partly to cut the legs from under the burgeoning movement for Ukrainian national self-determination. An exceptionally large harvest in 1930 allowed most farmers to meet their quotas, but a mediocre harvests in 1931 and a poor one in 1932 made this impossible. In the winter of 1932–33, at Stalin's direct behest, tens of thousands of government employees (some of them corralled into the task by local authorities) swept through the countryside, seizing the stored remnants of the fall harvest and even seed grain necessary for the next season's crop. An estimated 5 million to 7 million persons died from outright starvation or from diseases brought on by malnutrition. Soviet authorities prohibited any publicity of these deaths and officially maintained that no famine was taking place. One outcome of this famine was the partial destruction of Ukrainian national identity. This included a loss of national leadership, especially in the countryside, where one out of every five people perished (Mace 2009, 105), and a reversal of the move toward using Ukrainian instead of Russian as the language of public life. Only the annexation of western Ukraine from Poland in 1939 restored the figurational vitality of the Ukrainian nation.

A few scholars have sided with a widespread current of public opinion that declares Ireland's Great Famine of 1846–52 (An Gorta

Mo'r, or the Great Hunger) to have been an English genocide against the Irish nation, or at least to have had genocidal outcomes (for summaries of public and scholarly contention, see Kinealy 2002, 10–13; McVeigh 2008, 549–50). The famine killed at least 1 million people, one-eighth of the population (Ó Gráda 2006, 16), and prompted another 1.5 million more to leave the country, producing an almost 25 per cent reduction in the national population (Kinealy 2002, 212). Although the fungus *Phytophthora infestans* (potato blight) provided the immediate cause of the famine by destroying entire potato harvests (Ó Gráda 2006, 7), proponents of the genocide thesis point to the general availability of food in Ireland and the continuation of food exports during the famine, ongoing evictions of poor peasants from their lands, inadequate and inhumane relief policies, expressions of racist sentiment by British officials and in the *Times* of London, and the broader dynamics of English settler colonialism in Ireland (see especially Mullin 1999; Rubenstein 1983). If the arguments in favour of classifying An Gorta Mo'r as a genocide bear the weight of serious scrutiny (and more work needs to be done to decide this question), then this event counts as an important precedent to the great Indian famines under colonialism.

SOCIAL FAMINE IN INDIA

Extreme drought and flooding that correlated with El Niño and La Niña weather events provided the ecological triggers for the Indian megafamines of the late nineteenth century.[3] The summer monsoons failed in south and central India in the summer of 1875, and the

---

3 El Niño and La Niña are effects of a climatic system with global effects called El Niño Southern Oscillation (ENSO): "Rapid warmings of the eastern tropical Pacific (called El Niño events), for example, are associated with weak monsoons and synchronous drought throughout vast parts of Asia, Africa and northeastern South America. When the eastern Pacific is unusually cool, on the other hand, the pattern reverses (called a La Niña event), and abnormal precipitation and flooding occur in the same 'teleconnected' regions. The entire vast see-saw of air mass and ocean temperature, which extends into the Indian Ocean as well, is formally known as 'El Niño-Southern Oscillation'" (Davis 2001, 13). However, this causal relationship is very complex and is masked by regional variations: "the devastating drought of 1896–97 in central India, for instance, is masked by positive rainfall anomalies elsewhere" (Davis 2001, 247). Major ENSO events took place from 1876 to 1878 and in 1891, 1896–97, and 1899–1900; all of these correlated with drought and famine in India (Davis 2001, 271).

winter rains failed even more precipitously in 1876. Severe and intense famine ensued, ravaging much of southern India in an area
fanning out widely west and northwest from Madras and also a
large area in central northern India east, west, and south of Delhi
(Davis 2001, 25–9). Heavy rain returned to southern India in the fall
of 1877, bringing a malaria epidemic that further disrupted agricultural production; dry weather continued in the North until 1878
(Davis 2001, 50–1). Again in 1896 the monsoons failed throughout
large areas of central and northern India (Davis 2001, 142), and
famine ensued over a huge swath of the country, from contemporary
Punjab to Bihar and south to Madhya Pradesh, Maharashtra, and
parts of Karnataka (Davis 2001, 145). Rains returned in 1898, only
to disappear again catastrophically in 1899, except in Assam, where
record rainfall caused widespread flooding (Davis 2001, 158).
Famine was intense in contemporary Gujarat, north into Rajasthan,
and east and south into Madhya Pradesh and Maharashtra; severe
famine struck the rest of central India and north into Punjab (Davis
2001, 163). Low rainfall persisted until late 1902 (Davis 2001, 170).
In the Gujarat district, an estimated one-sixth of the population died
(Davis 2001, 173); death rates reached as high as one-third for some
districts (Davis 2001, 171).

But El Niño Southern Oscillation was not the only global system
that interfered with food supply in India during this time. By the
1770s British imperialism had integrated India's agricultural economy into the global capitalist market. Imposed cash taxes and other
systematic measures induced peasant farmers to switch from producing locally consumed food crops like millet and rice to growing
wheat, cotton, opium, sugar, indigo, and other products for export
to foreign markets (Davis 2001, 312–24). In English markets, their
primary destination, Indian commodities competed on unfavour-
able terms with identical raw goods from other parts of the world,
such as cotton from the southern United States or wheat from the
Argentine pampas (Davis 2001, 319–20). Colonial authorities also
taxed local handicrafts to raise their cost and thereby encourage
Indians to consume imported English-manufactured goods (Davis
2001, 313–14). However, small producers could not sell directly to
the world markets, so throughout India local elites found a new role
as middlemen and moneylenders, able to control local markets, reap
the benefits of rising global prices, and pass on the costs of falling

prices to the direct producers (Davis 2001, 313, 320–3, 325–6). Since nonpayment of taxes meant loss of land ownership and since taxes were set at fixed amounts based on estimated market value of the land, economic downturns meant the expropriation of large numbers of small producers, to the benefit of wealthier landowners and merchants/moneylenders. Forest and pasture commons, formerly an integral source of free resources for the peasant economy, became taxable private property or revenue-generating state property (Davis 2001, 326). Water, another free commons, was also privatized (Davis 2001, 331). The colonial state reduced its investment in irrigation systems on the grounds that this investment did not generate revenue (Davis 2001, 334), while making massive investments in a national railway system. These changes combined to increase both the ecological and the economic vulnerability of the rural Indian population. On the one hand, hydrological reserves declined, forested areas were cleared, and agricultural soil was depleted through overuse. On the other hand, the conversion of a communal and subsistence-oriented agricultural economy into an individualist, cash-based economy meant that when markets fluctuated millions of people could find themselves unable to obtain food even if food was physically present nearby. These two global figurations – El Niño Southern Oscillation and imperialist capitalism – intersected with devastating effect in 1876, 1896, and 1899 to produce the famines of 1876–79 and 1896–1902.

British Civilization in India

In *Capital*, Marx uses the term "primitive accumulation" to refer to the process, like the Enclosure Movement in England, by which capital converted noncommodified social goods into commodities ripe for capitalization (Marx 1990, 873ff). Treating the state as a simple expression of dominant class interests, Marx pays descriptive attention to the violence of this process but gives it little theoretical analysis. In *The Accumulation of Capital*, Rosa Luxembourg shows how primitive accumulation required a substantially greater expenditure of physical force, and therefore substantially greater direct involvement by the state, than Marx recognizes (Luxemburg 2003). Her analysis treats primitive accumulation not only as an economic process but also as a political one that requires the deliberate exercise of

what Elias would call the policing function of the state and sometimes even the exercise of its military function. Although her analysis
still follows Marx in situating the dynamics of state power entirely
within those of class struggle, Luxembourg's insights into primitive
accumulation bring a more critical perspective to thinking about
colonialism than Elias ever entertained and open the door to thinking of colonialism as a product of two interconnected but mutually
irreducible figurations, capitalism and the civilizing process, each of
which facilitates the other's expansion.

Colonialism in India served the interests of British capital by providing exotic commodities, raw materials, cheap labour, and markets for finished goods. But it also fed the process of distinction/
differentiation/deferentiation that drives the civilizing process. The
Raj enabled an entire new class of British subjects to constitute
themselves as distinguished, by virtue of their privileged position in
the imperial regime, in relation to Indian subjects. David Cannadine
has documented this distinction, characterizing the British relation
to India in terms of "ornamentalism" rather than "orientalism."
Interestingly, the British in India identified themselves with India's
traditional rulers: "For ornamentalism was hierarchy made visible,
imminent and actual. And since the British conceived and understood their metropolis hierarchically, it was scarcely surprising that
they conceived and understood the periphery in the same way, and
that chivalry and ceremony, monarchy and majesty, were the means
by which this vast world was brought together, interconnected, unified and sacralized" (Cannadine 2001, 122). The British who could
participate in this process came from Britain's own aristocratic
caste. This caste faced the erosion of its caste privilege at home, and
so its members felt drawn to the opportunities for distinction that
empire provided. Identification ran along the lines of class caste;
differentiation separated the privileged agents of empire, whether
British or Indian, from common Indians in India, just as it separated the gentry from the commons in the imperial metropole.
India's colonial governors needed to maintain and extend or deep-
en imperial authority not only in order to serve the "objective" interests of British capital or the British imperial state but also, more
immediately and more viscerally, for "subjective" reasons: to preserve their own social identities, to protect themselves from shame
and abjection.

The First Famine, 1876–79

When the monsoons failed in 1876, drought turned immediately into famine as food prices rose above what agricultural labourers and small landowning peasants could afford. "The traditional system of household and village grain reserves regulated by complex networks of patrimonial obligation had been largely supplanted since the Mutiny by merchant inventories and the cash nexus" (Davis 2001, 26). The previous three years of above-average wheat and rice production counted for nothing, as these crops had been exported to England. In the absence of price controls, scarcity promoted speculation and hoarding (Davis 2001, 26–7, 51). New transportation infrastructure – the railways, expected to make famine impossible – served not to ship food into famine districts but to ship it away to central depots for hoarding and protection. Telegraph communication enabled local price hikes to translate regionally or nationally. Indian wheat exports to the United Kingdom actually rose during the famine, from 308,000 quarters in 1875 to 757,000 quarters in 1876 and to 1,409,000 quarters in 1877 (Davis 2001, 27). Meanwhile, the Indian viceroy, Lord Lytton, committed to other large expenditures that impeded the scope for food relief: a lavish celebration to honour Queen Victoria and a military campaign in Afghanistan (Davis 2001, 28). Relying on Adam Smith's claim that state intervention would only exacerbate famines, Lytton issued "strict, 'semi-theological' orders that 'there is to be no interference of any kind on the part of Government with the object of reducing the price of food'" (Davis 2001, 31).

The famine intensified in 1877, as families that had sold their tools to survive the drought could not sow emergency rape and *cumboo* crops when a little rain fell in April and May (Davis 2001, 33). As millions who did not simply starve to death reached a stage of acute malnutrition, cholera and dysentery became mass killers. Peasants fled the countryside en masse to large cities seeking work or food relief; some rural regions lost their entire populations. In February, Viceroy Lytton appointed Sir Richard Temple to clamp down on any relief efforts organized by local authorities (Davis 2001, 36). After organizing a successful relief effort during the 1873–74 drought and almost losing his career for it, Temple worked as an uncompromising enforcer of strict laissez-faire principles. Temple purged hundreds of thousands from relief work, required that relief be given only in exchange for heavy labour, further stipulated that this labour be performed in militarized work camps located outside a ten-mile radius of the homes of those requiring it, and set the relief ration at a mere one pound of rice per diem (Davis 2001, 38). This so-called "Temple wage" provided only 1,627 calories: fewer than the 1,750 calories of the ration at Nazi Germany's Buchenwald concentration camp, less than the traditional amount available to British prison inmates, and 40 per cent of a 1981 estimate of the caloric requirements for an adult performing heavy labour (Davis 2001, 39). It also completely lacked protein. By the summer of 1877, most of the inmates of the relief camps in Madras were dead. In addition, Temple implemented the Anti-Charitable Contributions Act of 1877, which imposed prison sentences for any private relief donations that could interfere with the market fixing of grain prices. He also took active measures to stop officials in Madras from remitting land taxes in the famine districts (Davis 2001, 40).

Indian resistance to the relief regime began with food riots in 1876 but intensified in January 1877 with a movement among relief camp inmates to protest the rice reduction and the distance tests. The movement employed passive resistance; starving peasants refused to perform labour or left the camps entirely (Davis 2001, 41). This relief strike stirred up "the broadest demonstration of Indian anger since the Mutiny" (Davis 2001, 42–3). Lytton came under attack from the Indian press and from British reformers (including Florence Nightingale) but ordered his subordinates to hold fast (Davis 2001, 43). Officials in Bombay refused to publish mortality estimates, and throughout the famine the official government line was to deny its very existence. One Indian civic association, however, compiled its own estimates in the Sholapur district, as did the governor of Madras. Reports indicate that by the summer of 1877, at least 1.5 million had already died in the Madras districts alone.

From within the colonial administration, the Temple wage immediately met with medical testimony to its insufficiency, which Temple chose to disregard. Officials in Madras reported that by May 1877 half of the inmates in relief camps (receiving the Temple ration) had become too weakened to carry out any physical labour. Soon thereafter, Dr William Robert Cornish observed that monthly mortality in the camps had risen to a rate equivalent to 94 per cent per annum. Temple responded only by blaming the victims, accusing them of laziness and of choosing starvation over "submission to even simple and reasonable orders" (Davis 2001, 38–41). After the relief strike, dissident journalists such as William Digby reported on conditions in the country, and "a group of old Indian hands and Radical reformers" in England "kept *The Times*'s letters column full of complaints about Calcutta's callous policies" (Davis 2001, 43). Viceroy Lytton dismissed these reports as hysterics, but the secretary of state for India wrote to Lytton advising him to loosen restrictions on the discretionary ability of local governments to provide relief. The Indian civil society organization Sarvajanik Sabha (Civic Association) and Lord Buckingham each published mortality estimates showing the extent of the famine. Residents of large cities such as Madras could see evidence of mass famine with their own eyes, as "famished peasants dropped dead in front of the troops guarding pyramids of imported rice" (Davis 2001, 45). In the Mysore countryside, where the famine was worst, women and children stealing grains from fields were tortured, disfigured, and sometimes killed, while rural mobs assaulted landowners, stealing their stores and sometimes burning them alive. There are reports of cannibalism, otherwise "extremely rare" in Indian history. In northern districts affected by famines, there were 150 grain riots in August and September 1877, to which the governor responded by filling the jails and prisons (Davis 2001, 52).

Viceroy Lytton "was kept well-informed of such grisly details" (Davis 2001, 47) and in August 1877 made a personal visit to inspect conditions in Madras. By this time, "relief" camps had turned into "fetid, disease-wracked boneyards where a majority of refugees quickly died" (Davis 2001, 46). However, neither public opposition, nor reports of the famine's effects, nor the entreaties of his subordinates, nor personal observation deterred the viceroy's policy. After the Madras visit, he took active measures to prevent Buckingham from raising relief funds in England (Davis 2001, 47–8). He rejected out of hand the request of Sir George Couper, the executive of the North Western Provinces, to remit land taxes during the famine and instead ordered his district officers to discourage relief works "in every possible way" and to "put the screw" on landowners who were slow to pay their taxes (Davis 2001, 52). Pleas for relief efforts from all levels of the civil service met with rebuke, and even civilians who opened private relief efforts faced sanctions (Davis 2001, 51–3). In 1879–80 the government conducted a "militarized campaign" in the

Deccan region to collect by force any tax arrears that had accumulated during the famine; the resulting wave of foreclosures on small holdings effected a substantial redistribution of land upward through the class structure (Davis 2001, 50).

At no time did genocidal famine constitute the purpose of the imperial government. Rather, as in Tasmania, the impunity of the imperial state grew so great that genocide could emerge as an incidental by-product of the pursuit of larger goals. These goals included the profitability for England of the occupation of India: "Both Calcutta and London feared that 'enthusiastic prodigality' like Buckingham's would become a Trojan horse for an Indian Poor Law ... None of the principle players on either side of the House of Commons disagreed with the supreme principle that India was to be governed as a revenue plantation, not an almshouse" (Davis 2001, 33). British authorities expressed concerns that "the embarrassment of debt and weight of taxation consequent on the expense" would have consequences "more fatal than the famine itself" (Davis 2001, 37). In 1876 Britain planned to invade Afghanistan in order to preempt Russian imperial aspirations there. Sir John Strachey, chief budgetary advisor to Viceroy Lytton, "constantly reminded" him that Indian taxpayers would have to bear the entire costs of the Afghanistan campaign. Expenditures for famine relief appeared to these officials as at best a distraction from, and at worst a drain on, the much more vital project of expanding the empire through further military conquest (Davis 2001, 28, 51). Malthusian ideas combined with liberal economics to legitimate this distribution of priorities by suggesting that even mass starvation averted some yet worse evil that feeding those who could not feed themselves would bring about. Sir Evelyn Baring, finance minister during the 1876–79 famine, said afterward: "every benevolent attempt made to mitigate the effects of famine and defective sanitation serves but to enhance the evils resulting from overpopulation" (Davis 2001, 32). Similarly, an 1881 report concluded that "80% of the famine mortality were drawn from the poorest 20% of the population, and if such deaths were prevented this stratum of the population would still be unable to adopt prudential restraint. Thus, if the government spent more of its revenue on famine relief, an even larger proportion of the population would become penurious" (Davis 2001, 32). These statements indicate an intentional willingness to withhold food from a portion of the population that policymakers considered to be congenitally unfit, lacking in the "prudential restraint" required by utilitarian political economy. India's starving found themselves in the wasteland outside the community of obligation, just as surely as the Tasmanians, the Ukrainian kulaks, and the Herero. The final report of the Famine Commission of 1878–80 affirmed that the correct course of action had been taken (Davis 2001, 57–8), and the government's antirelief policy would continue essentially unchanged under Lord Elgin and Lord Curzon during the famines of 1896–1902.

In September and October 1877, heavy rains eased the drought in southern India but brought a malaria epidemic that killed hundreds of thousands and was followed by great locust plagues that inflicted further devastation on crops (Davis 2001, 49). Prices remained high in early 1878. Drought continued for another season in the northern districts. There, ample food reserves would have existed if the export economy had not siphoned away the surplus crops of 1874–76. In the North Western Provinces it was most obvious that the "staggering death toll was the foreseeable and avoidable result of deliberate policy choices" (Davis 2001, 51).

The Second Famine, 1896–1902

Low rainfall translated into drought and famine again in 1889 and 1891–92, when again India's integration into global markets converted crop failures into rising food prices, entitlement scarcity, and starvation. But a far more severe catastrophe struck in the second half of the decade, when the monsoons "simply 'jammed'" in 1896 and again in 1899 (Davis 2001, 159). Although relief works were shut down temporarily in 1898 (Davis 2001, 158), the famine that had begun in 1896 did not abate until 1902.

After the 1876 famines, in response to public pressure, the government had established a Famine Relief and Insurance Fund to enable financing of relief efforts independently of the government's other financial commitments, and after the investigations of a Famine Commission in 1880, regional authorities had implemented famine codes to allow local relief efforts and also to restrict mass population movements during food crises. The government expected integration of Burma's rice production into the imperial system and the construction of 10,000 miles of new railway track to make absolute food scarcity impossible in India. However, all of these measures proved ineffective soon after the 1896 drought began. Again, large

exports depleted grain reserves; again, communications networks
translated high prices throughout the country rapidly and efficiently;
again, railways "could not bring grain into districts where mass
purchasing power was insufficient." The government diverted a substantial portion of the Famine Fund to another military campaign in
Afghanistan, eating up most of its reserve (Davis 2001, 141–2). And
just as military campaigns in Afghanistan affected government responses to both the 1876 and the 1896 famines, so too did large and
expensive celebrations of empire: in 1897 the British Empire celebrated the diamond jubilee of Queen Victoria, for which the colonial
administration of India sponsored a lavish festival, estimated by
Cosmopolitan magazine at the time to have cost over US$100 mil-
lion (Davis 2001, 150–1, 157–8). Less conspicuously but more ur-
gently, a large portion of the Indian population already suffered
from malnutrition before the rains failed in 1896.

"Acute distress was already visible in the North Western and
Central Provinces in August 1896; by October the police were opening fire on grain looters in Bihar and the Bombay Deccan" (Davis
2001, 143). Again in 1896 the colonial authorities considered prohibitive the possible expense of systematic poor relief in India (Davis
2001, 143). Davis's account of the 1896 famine brings out the
physical force used to maintain the existing food distribution system
and thereby keep food out of the mouths of the starving. When peasants in the Central Provinces assaulted grain depots, the Lancashire
Regiment moved in to reinforce native infantry (Davis 2001, 148).
When bubonic plague struck Bombay in the summer of 1896,
the governor's Plague Committee responded by sterilizing with fire,
lime, and carbolic acid the tenement neighbourhoods where the
plague spread most virulently, a measure that did not combat the
plague's true vector (rats) but did make thousands of people homeless. "In England, some of the press proposed the 'radical purifica-
tion' of burning the entire native city to the ground" (Davis 2001,
149). In the Deccan the Epidemic Disease Act authorized the use of
troops to raid slum neighbourhoods and forcibly detain suspected
plague carriers; a "huge number of people" entered the plague
camps apparently healthy and came out as corpses (Davis 2001,
150). During the second wave of famine in 1900, Viceroy Curzon
decided to deport refugees who had fled into British India from ad-
joining native states, a practice that was "virtually a death sentence
for hundreds of thousands of desperate people" (Davis 2001, 167).

In 1900–01 the government decided to redeploy militarized collection of land taxes, based on land value assessments inflated by the famine-induced spike in food prices, in hard-hit areas like Gujarat and the Central Provinces; those who could not make their payments had their land confiscated (Davis 2001, 172–3).

Beyond overt episodes like these, direct physical force played a more constant function of guaranteeing an economic order that inflicted massive economic violence on the starving. Throughout the entire course of the famines, the government determinedly abstained from any measures to control the price of grain (Davis 2001, 142–4, 162–4). Starvation resulted from rising prices rather than from absolute scarcity: in Bombay "immense grain stores" sat "piled up at the docks" while thousands of refugees from rural areas starved "openly in the streets"; one American missionary observed fat pigeons gorging themselves on open sacks of grain at railway stations "in the sight of scores of miserable, famine-stricken villagers crying aloud for food" (Davis 2001, 167–8). Near the outset of the famine, Viceroy Elgin created poorhouses for those too weak for heavy labour. The rations provided at these sites had even fewer calories than the Temple wage (Davis 2001, 166). Moreover, the poorhouses operated under lax regulations, such that administrators could confiscate food from its intended recipients and resell it for their own profit (Davis 2001, 154–7). In at least one case, a visiting American official observed that relief grain had been adulterated with earth before being ground into flour and distributed, and merchants sometimes adulterated the grain that they sold at inflated prices (Davis 2001, 147–8). Economic violence within India also connected up with the direct force of empire building elsewhere: during the first wave of famine in 1896–98, the secretary of state for India offered famine aid to Viceroy Elgin, but in the second wave of 1899–1902, the secretary took the opposite course, refusing appeals to organize a famine charity in England and urging Viceroy Curzon to launch a War Fund in India to help pay for the Boer War (Davis 2001, 164).

In 1901 the British medical journal the *Lancet* estimated that excess mortality in India over the previous decade had totalled at least 19 million, equal to half of the population of the United Kingdom at the time (Davis 2001, 174). The two great famines of 1876–79 and 1896–1902, along with another in 1907–08, "cast a long mortality shadow over the first decade of the twentieth century," contributing via weakened immune systems to epidemics of malaria, tuberculosis, and plague that claimed millions of lives. Productive forces in the countryside suffered severe damage, with great losses of plough cattle and declines in net cropped area in some provinces (Davis 2001, 175). Population growth for India declined appreciably and came to a standstill in some areas. The 1901 Famine Commission's report estimated that barely one-fifth of famine victims received any British assistance but nevertheless stated that the "relief distributed was excessive."

Accidental Genocide?

In *Late Victorian Holocausts*, Mike Davis enrols a systemic argument to make a moral point: "it is the burden of this book to show that imperial policies towards starving 'subjects' were often the exact moral equivalents of bombs dropped from 18,000 feet. The contemporary photographs used in this book are thus intended as accusation, not illustrations" (Davis 2001, 22). Concerned with the moral culpability of individuals, Davis focuses on such psychological details as Lytton's arrogance or his possible madness (Davis 2001, 30–1). My figurational analysis does not concern itself so much with moral accusation, partly because such accusation itself forms a part of the affective economy of shame that I seek to analyze and partly because – as I have argued elsewhere (Powell 2011) – genocide is, in a way, bigger than morality since genocidal figurations deploy morality in the service of annihilation. I would rather look at genocide the way one might look at a building on fire or the way that Elias's detached fisher (discussed in chapter 1) looks at the whirlpool. One does not need to blame a fire to feel the urgency of getting out of the building.

This detachment gets easier the more one moves beyond an individualistic notion of genocide that stresses the intentions of actors – in other words, the more one approaches "genocide" the way that one approaches other social scientific phenomena, like "social stratification": "A definition of stratification as constituted by actions committed with the intent to produce it would be quite inappropriate. It would mean that even where one social collectivity was known to have been systematically disadvantaged by the actions of another, if it could not be shown that these actions were committed with the intent of producing stratification as such, we would be unable even to claim that stratification had occurred" (Thompson and Quets

1990, 247). Tony Barta (1987; 2008c; 2008b) likewise stresses the need to understand genocide as a structured social relation rather than as a type of intention. One recognizes genocide as a type of consequence of social action rather than as a type of motive. Even more strongly than the Tasmanian genocide, the Indian famines raise an interesting and troubling possibility: can genocide happen *by accident*?

Viceroy Lytton, along with Finance Minister Sir Evelyn Baring and other senior officials, expressed total conviction in the objective correctness of Adam Smith's claim that interfering with market mechanisms would only worsen the famine and in Malthusian claims that famine in India resulted from sheer overpopulation (Davis 2001, 31-2): "Smith's injunction against state attempts to regulate the price of grain during famine had been taught for years in the East India Company's famous college at Haileybury. Thus the viceroy was only repeating orthodox curriculum when he lectured Buckingham that high prices, by stimulating imports and limiting consumption, were the 'natural saviours of the situation'" (Davis 2001, 31). The immediately precipitating condition for the famines – low rainfall – lay well outside the scope of human action to alter, and responsible officials like Lytton could only react to the chain of social events that the drought triggered, using the best knowledge available to them. Commodifying the rural subsistence economy, enforcing strict market rules that disadvantaged small farmers, enmeshing India's food economy in global markets, denying food relief to masses of destitute, starving people – could all of these add up to a well-intentioned, misguided, but at the time reasonable attempt to save as many human lives as possible?

We might answer in the affirmative if the colonizers had found themselves in possession of a country without social institutions capable of defending against famine and if they had been required to build these themselves from the ground up by trial and error. However, Davis claims that under the Moghul Empire northern India lived "generally free of famine until the 1770s" and that "food security was also probably better in the Deccan during the period of Maratha rule" (Davis 2001, 285–6). The Moguls regarded the protection of the peasant population as an obligation and "relied on a quartet of fundamental policies – embargoes on food exports, antispeculative price regulation, tax relief and distribution of free food without a forced-labour counterpart – that were anathema to later

British Utilitarians" (Davis 2001, 286). Both the Mogul and the Maratha regimes made a point of subsidizing the maintenance of irrigation systems and employed flexible laws that placed lower tax demands on peasants when crops were bad, taking account of "the crucial ecological relationships and unpredictable climate fluctuations of the subcontinent's drought-prone regions" (Davis 2001, 287). In short, the British colonizers in India took over control of societies that already had produced their own mechanisms for reducing the effects of famine and then proceeded to dismantle these mechanisms.

They did so because the mechanisms stood in the way of incorporating India into the Eurocentric system of globalizing capital. As Elias observes, "the transformation of the whole of social existence is the basic condition of the civilization of conduct" (Elias 2000, 384). In economic terms, this transformation involved the production of a commodified, export-oriented agricultural economy governed by unregulated capitalist markets. Capitalist agriculture placed Indian farmers in a relation of dependency with respect to the world markets, a dependency that persists to this day. The production of these relations incorporated Indians into the extended chains of interdependency that characterize the civilizing process.

The civilization of the Indian food economy also involved the production of new relations of impunity. Prior to the British transformation of rural life, large local landowners had operated within relations of patrimonial obligation with their social inferiors, relations that inhibited their ability to use famine as a vehicle for upward redistribution of wealth. Liberalizing reforms under British rule severed these obligations. The capitalist world-economy could provide benefits that outweighed the cost of breaking local ties. This meant that large landowners could combine the role of grain merchant and moneylender to their own profit; they could benefit by the default of smaller landowners; and they could hoard food grain speculatively or export it to foreign markets. For its own part, the colonial government depended on the agricultural population as a whole but did not depend on the short-term survival of any specific fraction of it. The death of millions of small farmers and agricultural labourers and their families, and even the depopulation of whole districts, would have been a severe blow to previous rulers but did not register as a prohibitive material loss in imperial calculations. Economic imperialism therefore brought the majority of Indians into a relation of asymmetrical dependence: they depended greatly on persons who depended very little on them. The production of these asymmetrical relations formed an integral part of the barbaric civilization of India. Indeed, Davis argues that the dependency cultivated in the Victorian period helps to explain food insecurity in contemporary India and around the world. The production and maintenance of the Third World is one of the effects of the figurational expansion of European barbaric civilization.

Neither government policymakers nor private commodities traders ever had as a goal of their actions the production of mass starvation. Rather, the extension of the civilizing process to colonial India generated enough impunity that mass death could emerge as a by-product of the pursuit of other goals without deterring the sovereign authority from continuing to pursue these goals. Through the confluence of economic and political interests in the imperialist project, the civilizing deferentiation that distinguishes sovereignty and subjection overlapped and resonated with the contradictory relations of capitalist commodity exchange, allowing the colonial government to implement a radical restructuring of Indian economic life. By continuing to push through this restructuring during severe food crises, British sovereign authority in India produced an identity-difference relation of violent obliteration that articulated itself through relations of commodity exchange, dividing those with the means to buy food from those without and excluding the latter from the community of moral obligation.

In the more familiar types of genocide, perpetrators commit mass murder or impose lethal conditions on a group in order to undermine its institutions, disrupt the collective life of the group, and sever the network of relations that holds a community together. In India under the viceroys, the converse happened: severing a particular cluster of relations – the moral economy that maintained food entitlements during relative shortages – had the structural consequence of producing mass death. These deaths were not intended, but neither did they persuade the architects of empire to alter their designs: "Even during the famines that ravaged India between 1860 and 1908, costing at least thirty million lives, humanity was sacrificed to economy – Lord Curzon later acknowledged that an Indian famine excited no more attention in Britain than a squall on the serpentine" (Brendon 2007, 231). Not an accidental genocide, precisely, but an incidental one.

7

Genocides of National Others in the Ottoman Empire and Rwanda

INTRODUCTION

This chapter examines two examples of genocide that appear in most anthologies of the subject and that fit comfortably into the notion of genocide as "events like the Nazi holocaust": mass murders of racial or ethnic minorities by authoritarian governments. These events also illustrate the contradictory quality of the civilizing process, which produces both genocidal and antigenocidal forces. The destruction of the Ottoman Armenian community inspired Raphaël Lemkin to submit to the International Conference for the Unification of Criminal Law, in Madrid in 1933, a proposal "to declare the destruction of racial, religious, or social collectivities a crime under the law of nations" (Lemkin 1947, 146) The 1933 proposal specified two new crimes: "barbarity," defined as "action against the life, bodily integrity, liberty, dignity, or economic existence" of a person, if performed "out of hatred towards a racial, religious, or social collectivity, or with a view to the extermination thereof"; and "vandalism," defined as destruction of cultural or artistic works for the same reason. The 1994 genocide in Rwanda marks a comparable turning point: along with similar events in Yugoslavia, the Rwandan genocide highlighted the failure of the United Nations to fulfil the mandate of the 1948 United Nations Convention on the Prevention and Punishment of the Crime of Genocide (UNCG) through effective genocide prevention. This failure, along with comparable failure in the former Yugoslavia, served as a catalyst for political processes that led in 2004 to the creation of the Office of the Special Advisor on the Prevention of Genocide (United Nations 2008) – although, like the UNCG itself, this new measure has yet to realize its full promise.

Both of the examples in this chapter involve a mix of civilizing processes that strengthen the relation between state sovereignty and individual subjectivity and decivilizing processes that disrupt this relation by undermining the state's sovereign monopoly of military force. In the Ottoman Empire this disruption happened because large parts of the empire broke away to join other states or to achieve their own sovereign independence and because military defeats in international wars obliged the empire to submit to treaties that gave foreign powers the right to intervene in its internal governance. In Rwanda a much more compressed decivilizing movement happened through civil war and an internationally brokered peace treaty. In both of these cases, dominant elites within the state, threatened by the prospect of a complete loss of their privileged relation to its sovereignty, used genocide as an extreme strategy for reconstituting the state on the basis of a strengthened collective identity that privileged themselves. Like the genocide in Guatemala, I call these "recivilizing" genocides because, in them, genocidal violence reverses or attempts to reverse a decoupling of identity and sovereignty – although, if successful, such genocides carry the civilizing process further than it has yet progressed in that locality. Ironically, genocides committed in the name of supposedly ancient enmities between peoples actually produce a qualitatively new intensity of ethnic or nationalist identification – and with it, a qualitatively new intensity of exclusion of the Other.

Civilization and Ethnic or Racial Nationalisms

Norbert Elias analyzes the civilizing process as a figuration comprised of two mutually reinforcing developments: the formation of territorially sovereign states through the institutional monopolization of the means of military violence; and the formation of civil and civilized subjects through the social constraint to self-constraint. In my deconstructive reading of Elias, I have used this same theoretical model to show how the civilizing process reproduces violence on an expanding scale and defers violence away from the civilized subject by displacing it through relations of differentiation that simultaneously operate as relations of deference. In concrete interactions between people, the civilizing process establishes individual and collective identity through an economy of symbolic violence. Elias's principle work on the subject focuses on etiquette as both the means and the manifestation of the formation of a civilized habitus. In more critical language, we can say that he (uncritically) examines the civilizing process in terms of the symbolic violence of class distinction. Part of my objective in this book has been to open up the formal structure of his theory in order to account for a wider range of substantive contents. If we understand the civilizing process in formal terms as a circulating system of micropractices of deferral/differentiation/deference – an economy of deferentiation – generated by, and generative of, relations of force centred in the sovereign state's monopolization of violence, then the specific content of these micropractices of deferentiation could include a range of types of social action, not just those designated by terms like "etiquette" or "civility." In chapter 5 I have explored how ideological identification/differentiation can operate as the currency of this economy, rendering "heretics" or "communists" into abject Others situated outside the community of moral obligation. In chapter 6 I likewise have explored how the relation of colonizer and colonized – often overtly a relation of civilized to savage – can provide this currency, making expendable both the physical lives of the colonized and their distinct social institutions. In this chapter, I investigate a third type of currency, that of ethnic nationalism.

In *Economy and Society*, Max Weber observes that the routine practices that constitute ethnic identity – dress, cuisine, folk art, vernacular language, and so on – do not naturally and automatically make the actors who share them into a "nation" or a "people" (Weber 1978, 385–98). Rather, it takes the mobilization of these attributes by political elites to constitute persons into a people, folk into a nation. Weber points out that the common attributes of a nation – its shared history, including its historical grievances – owe as much to the imagination of political entrepreneurs as to empirical fact. If nations live and breathe as "imagined communities" (Anderson 1991), they can do so because imagined representations of the national community circulate through the network of hierarchical power relations anchored in the sovereignty of the state. Ethnic nationalism in particular both enables and disguises this circulation by strengthening a particular formal property of this figuration: *self-similarity*.

Through the civilizing process, the same figurational movement shapes both the macroscopic form of state institutions and the microscopic form of individual subjectivity. Both are sovereign, at least in principle: both are supposed to be bounded, to control themselves within these bounds, hence to be internally self-sufficient, and hence also to be separate from those around them (Elshtain 1990–91; see also Cregan 2007). We can describe this particular isomorphism, in which the whole resembles its parts and vice versa, by borrowing a term from fractal geometry and saying that the civilizing process is "self-similar" (Pietgen, Jürgens, and Saupe 1992, 63–6, 75–6, 95). This self-similarity has an important political effect: it allows individual subjects to identify with the states to which they are subjects by perceiving the state as a person writ large and imagining that this person resembles themselves and therefore acts as they would themselves act and therefore acts in ways with which they themselves agree.

But the differentiation integral to the civilizing process works against this process of identification: the production of distinction through the innovation of more refined standards of conduct tends ceaselessly to differentiate the dominant and the privileged few from the great mass of the dominated. And for those in the middle of the spectrum of privilege, these contradictory tendencies toward identification and differentiation produce a "high-tension zone" (Star 1991) of partial and precarious privilege, which can manifest quasi-subjectively as intense anxiety.

Ethnic nationalism works to alleviate this contradiction by glossing over the differentiating qualities of the civilizing process. It does this by supplementing the formal isomorphism of the civilizing process with a substantive identification: subjects imagine the nation – and by extension, the nationalist state – to derive its properties from themselves. Not just the people as individuals but the nation as a collectivity speaks Turkish, prays to Allah, wears the fez, and so on. Racialization takes this process even further, replacing the similarity of ethnocultural performances, which operate visibly and so can visibly fail, with an invisible and putatively nonperformative sameness of lineage, of blood. Race turns out to demand its own performances capable of failure – and indeed, prone to failure, as the experience of Nazi race science has shown (Koonz 2003, 190ff), but what matters politically is its ability to foster a collective identity absorbed into the habitus – an identity that people not only imagine but also feel, that they know in their guts. Through nationhood or through race, the nation and myself become one, which means that I have nothing to fear from state power and must approve its judgments, for they are my own. But if my religion or my folk tradition or my lineage makes me Other to the idealized Self of the collectively sovereign nation, this same logic works against me, and I literally have everything to fear.

PART ONE: THE OTTOMAN EMPIRE

Folk tradition attributes the origin of Armenian identity to the landing of Noah's ark on Mount Ararat; historical scholarship traces its emergence to sometime around 600 BCE (Hovannisian 1990, 251–2). Armenians converted to Christianity at the turn of the fourth century CE, and the last Armenian kingdom collapsed at the end of the fourteenth century, after which the Armenian population was divided between the Ottoman, Russian, and Persian Empires. The Ottoman Empire, for its part, governed diverse ethnic and religious groups through multiple, hierarchically ordered categories of citizenship. Traditional Islamic law recognized non-Muslim monotheists, or *dhimmis*, as entitled to protection within the Islamic state. In the Ottoman Empire each religious community, or *millet*, had its own system of courts for administering ecclesiastical law, and up to 1856 these functioned as "little theocracies" (Bloxham 2007, 43; see also Melson 1992, 54–6). As part of this system, Armenians enjoyed a partial but limited political enfranchisement. They lived as a tolerated minority, subject to special taxes, prohibited from bearing arms, unable to give legal testimony, forbidden in some regions to use the Armenian language except in prayer, and occasionally subjected to the *devshirme*, or child levy. Most lived as tenant farmers or sharecroppers under the Muslim feudal-military elite, but some lived as merchants, traders, artisans, and professionals. Despite their partially underprivileged status, they lived in relative peace until the decline of the empire in the eighteenth and nineteenth centuries. Indeed, until the mid-nineteenth century, "Ottoman toleration of non-Muslims compared favourably with the record of many European states towards their religious minorities" (Bloxham 2007, 15). But in the second half of the nineteenth century, this arrangement broke down, leaving both urban and rural Armenians vulnerable to ongoing violent abuse and periodic massacres, before utter holocaust arrived in 1915 and again in 1920. How did the comparatively pluralistic and tolerant Ottoman state change into an institutional vehicle for persecution and genocide?

Civilization, Decivilization, and the Accretion of Potential Violence

If it's fair to say, as Elias does, that the sovereign kingdom of France emerged in the power vacuum left behind by the decline of the Holy Roman Empire, so too did the sovereign Ottoman Empire expand into the power vacuum left behind by the declining Byzantine Empire. But whereas the expansion of the kingdom of France involved also a violent reconsolidation of Catholic Church ecclesiastical authority over a population with a long Christian history, the expansion of the Ottoman Empire brought Christian populations under Muslim authority. Christians enjoyed a more fortunate relation to their Ottoman conquerors than did the Cathars to their Capetian conquerors because Islamic law, or *sharia*, recognized them as dhimmis and prescribed a limited tolerance and protection, which the Ottomans instantiated through the millet system. No doubt this difference between Ottoman and Capetian treatment of religious minorities owed as much or more to the differing interests and power relations at work in the two conquests as they did to differences in doctrinal traditions. But whatever the factors internal to the empire that made comparative tolerance more expedient than religious genocide, these would be mixed with external factors as the empire entered its long slow decline in the late seventeenth century.

The territorial scope and internal sovereignty of the Ottoman state reached its peak some time before its military defeat at Vienna in 1683. From that time forward, "the significant and growing differential in the ability of states to wage war, created by European technical and organizational superiority, grew stark" (Bloxham 2007, 29). To compensate for its lost military superiority, the Ottoman state began in the eighteenth century to offer political concessions to its European rivals, concessions that compromised its sovereignty by bending its domestic policies to suit the demands of the emerging Great Powers. After "humiliating" treaties in 1699 and 1718 (Kiernan 2007, 396), the Ottomans conceded to Russia, in the Treaty of Küçük Kaynarca of 1774, a right of humanitarian intervention on behalf of Orthodox Christians (Dadrian 1997, 8). In 1829 the Russo-Turkish Treaty of Adrianople gave Russia protectorship of an autonomous Serbia and the Danubian principalities (Bloxham 2007, 30). Russia and England jointly intervened in the struggle for Greek independence, which succeeded in 1830 (Dadrian 1997, 13–14). In 1833 Russia even temporarily gained a "privileged right of protectorship over Turkey" (Kiernan 2007, 396).

Russia's policy at this time "was to extend its influence into the Ottoman empire without destroying it" (Bloxham 2007, 30). Great Britain, for its part, pursued a symmetrically opposed policy, seeking to thwart the expansion of Russian influence by encouraging the liberalization and modernization of the Ottoman state, but also without any substantive concern for the well-being of Ottoman subjects, including its Christian minorities (Bloxham 2007, 31–6). Both states, however, found it expedient to mobilize a pan-Christian solidarity – Russia in order to strengthen its own appeal to Ottoman minorities and Britain in order to legitimate its policies to its own electorate. A discourse of civilization overtly facilitated this mobilization:

> Given the overtly racialized European portrayals of non-Europeans at the *fin de siècle*, we would not expect Armenians to be necessarily viewed by Westerners in admiring terms. The image of the male Armenian as an unscrupulous and cunning Levantine trader was certainly a common British and American stereotype of this period. The fact that some Armenians were also terrorists should also hardly have appealed to the respectable, middle-class, evangelical opinion from which, in these countries, the Armenian cause drew its most solid partisanship. Significantly, however, this potential blot on the copy book was largely overlooked, in favour of the more narcissistic notion that, as the Armenians were really 'Europeans of the East' – in other words a mirror image of themselves – their actions were clearly self-defensive and hence entirely justifiable ... Certainly, Gladstone on his accession to the British premiership, in 1880, made no bones about his feelings. 'To serve Armenia,' he said, 'is to serve civilisation.' (Levene 2005b, 320)

In an effort to appease both parties and regain some of its self-determination, the Ottoman state under Sultan Abdülmecid declared a major legislative reform in 1839 and again at the end of the Crimean War in 1856 (Dadrian 1997, 19; Bloxham 2007, 31). These reforms, called the *tanzimat* (reorganization), gave formal equality to non-Muslims within the empire and secularized the Ottoman state – in principle. Implemented partly to appease foreign powers, they also aimed to buy domestic social peace by tying "the aspirations of the large Christian communities with the future of the state." In practice, however, the structure of power relations both within and outside the empire ensured that the reforms had little positive effect. Domestically, the reforms "rankled the Ottoman elite," given their origin in foreign ideologies and the prominent role of the British in dictating the terms of the 1856 reforms in particular (Bloxham 2007, 33). Worse, the empire lacked the ability to enforce the reforms on the ground where they were needed most, namely in rural Anatolia close to the Russian border (Bloxham 2007, 40). There, Armenian peasants lived under the domination of Turkish and Kurdish landlords and nomadic tribal leaders (Bloxham 2007, 39–42; Kiernan 2007, 399; Dadrian 1997, 45–8). This hinterland, armed elite extorted a separate tax from that of the Ottoman state, could murder its peasants with impunity, and had a history of ignoring or rebelling against the authority of the Sultan. The situation grew still more tense from the late 1850s onward as *muhajirs*, Muslim refugees fleeing Christian persecution in Russia or the newly independent Balkan states, settled in Anatolia, bringing both resentment and a need for land. In eastern Anatolia, and to a lesser extent elsewhere throughout the empire, the tanzimat reforms actually brought worse conditions for Armenians, who were perceived as gaining disproportionately while ordinary Muslims suffered.

The tanzimat reforms may have slowed the decline of Ottoman sovereignty, but they did not halt it (Bloxham 2007, 30–1, 44–5; Kiernan 2007, 397). By 1829, in addition to Greece (and Egypt, in all but name), the empire had lost Bessarabia, Serbia, Abaza, and Mingrelia. By 1856 it had lost Moldavia and Wallachia. France invaded Beirut in 1860. After the disastrous Russo-Turkish War in 1877–78, it lost Bosnia, Herzegovina, Bulgaria, Kars, Ardahan, and Cyprus – one-third of its territory and 20 per cent of its inhabitants in a single year. The 1878 Berlin Treaty gave Britain the right to dispatch its own "military consuls" to the eastern provinces – in exchange for withdrawal of Russian forces, giving Britain the primary responsibility for foreign oversight of Armenian lives at a time when its interest in doing so effectively was waning (Bloxham 2007, 37–8). In 1879 England and France took control of Egypt. More insidiously, the empire lost control of its finances to foreign powers. One

measure of the tanzimat reforms that did get implemented effectively was economic liberalization, guaranteeing private property and
entwining the Ottoman economy more closely with global markets,
in which it occupied a dependent position (Bloxham 2007, 35).
Financial collapse in 1874 led to direct financial supervision of the
empire, beginning in 1881 (Hovannisian 1990, 252).

In 1876, "to forestall European control of the implementation of
reforms," the Ottoman state implemented a new, liberal constitution
(Dadrian 1997, 29), but this constitution produced no better results
for Armenians than had the tanzimat reforms. Given the internal
power dynamics of the empire, substantive change would have required the foreign powers to intervene forcefully on behalf of the
Armenians, but the international dynamics of power made this im-
practical. Gerard Libaridian characterizes the situation in this way:
"The game of musical chairs played by England, France, Germany,
Russia ... – alternating as 'defenders of Ottoman territorial integrity'
and 'protectors of Christian minorities' – allowed the Sultan's government to exchange its economic prerogatives and many of its
sovereign territorial rights in outlying areas for the license to resolve
domestic unrest in the core of the empire as it saw fit" (quoted in
Bloxham 2007, 54–5). In this "game of musical chairs," each power
was principally interested in expanding its own influence or neutralizing the interests of the others. Britain and Russia in particular
tended to cancel out each other's ability and willingness to intervene
effectively on behalf of Armenians. But even though the tanzimat
reforms and the Midhat Constitution lacked force, they still provoked resentment among Ottomans, for whom they symbolized the
humiliation of their empire by foreign and infidel Others. Public
declarations of concern for Armenian well-being, used as reasons
to exact humiliating diplomatic concessions, unsupported by any
substantive intervention or willingness to intervene, placed the
Armenians in an increasingly untenable situation. In addition to this
development, by the 1880s the gap between *de jure* rights and *de
facto* realities had impelled Armenians themselves to turn away from
the strategy of uncompromising loyalty to the state as a means to
improving their situation and to organize underground, local self-
defence groups, which evolved into secret political societies in the
1890s (Hovannisian 1990, 256; Dadrian 1997, 114–17; Bloxham
2007, 49–51). These parties, copying the tactics of earlier minority
groups in the empire, tried to appeal to the foreign powers and

leverage their nominal commitments into substantive intervention. The unfortunate result was that, to Muslim Ottomans, Armenians came to appear as "only the most obvious element of a link between external and internal Christian forces antithetical to the established order" (Bloxham 2007, 41).

In figurational terms, military weakness translated into ongoing symbolic violence in which Turkish Ottomans, identifying with the sovereign state to which they were subject, experienced diplomatic losses as personal humiliations. Discrepancy between reforms on paper and practice on the ground meant that "short-term stability was purchased at the expense of storing up grievances among the minorities ... and of grievances amongst Ottoman elites about repeated intervention in their internal affairs" (Bloxham 2007, 38). In the mid-1890s this stored-up, deferred violence began to instantiate itself.

The Accretion of Impunity

From 1894 to 1896 Ottoman Armenians suffered a series of massacres that foreshadowed the later genocide. In 1894 Armenian villagers in the Sassun district in Bitlis province refused to pay the protection tax being extorted from them by Kurdish chieftains (Hovannisian 1990, 256; Dadrian 1997, 114–17). The Kurds charged the villagers with sedition and obtained Turkish army support to lay siege to the village. The Turkish forces convinced the defenders to lay down their arms in exchange for a promise of amnesty, but once the defenders had given up their means of resistance, Turkish and Kurdish forces joined in plundering Sassun and indiscriminately massacring several thousand Armenians. Soldiers primarily used bayonets to kill their victims, but the British vice consul, Cecil M. Hallward, who conducted an investigation of the atrocities within a few weeks of its occurrence, reported that the soldiers had burned young men alive in mass pyres, torn children "by main force," torn pregnant women open, and committed mass rapes of women and girls. "The Sassoun massacre was the first instance of organized mass murder of Armenians in modern Ottoman history that was carried out in peace time and had no connection with any foreign war" (Dadrian 1997, 117). The government portrayed the event as an attempted coup, establishing a "legacy of denial" (Dadrian 1997, 117) that would provide useful service to Turkish nationalists after the 1915 genocide.

Paradoxically, foreign intervention on behalf of the Armenians triggered the next wave of atrocities. Between May and October 1895, British, French, and Russian diplomats negotiated with the government of Sultan Abdülhamid II for measures that would give physical security and greater political enfranchisement to Armenians within the empire. Encouraged by this show of foreign support, the Armenian nationalist party Hunchak ("clarion" or "bell") organized a demonstration aimed more at the international stage than at the national one. On 1 October a crowd of between two and four thousand Armenian demonstrators marched together in Constantinople, decrying the Sassun massacre and demanding equal rights (Dadrian 1997, 119–21, 153; Balakian 2003, 57–9; Bloxham 2007, 52). This demonstration constituted "the first time in Ottoman history that a non-Muslim, subject minority had dared to confront the central authorities in the very capital of the empire with a large protest that amounted to a challenge" (Dadrian 1997, 120). Police officers and an organized mob armed with cudgels met the demonstrators and, after an exchange of shots, proceeded to lay into the crowd, killing twenty and wounding hundreds (Balakian 2003, 58). Around the city, Islamic theological students "appeared on the streets and alleyways and boulevards and began massacring Armenians" while police stood by or joined in. Massacres continued in the city for the next two days, and "hundreds of small and large massacres throughout the length and breadth of the Ottoman Empire" continued for the next twelve months (Dadrian 1997, 152–6; Hovannisian 1990, 256; Balakian 2003, 59). Richard Hovannisian estimates that between 100,000 and 200,000 people died in these massacres; Dadrian estimates 80,000 to 100,000 killed by December 1895 and 200,000 to 250,000 killed by October 1896. Armenians put up military resistance – successfully at Zeitoun from 24 October 1895 to 2 February 1896 and unsuccessfully at Van from 15 to 23 June 1896 (where, again, the defenders were massacred after a negotiated ceasefire). An Armenian paramilitary cell staged a temporary occupation of the Ottoman Bank in Constantinople in August 1896 but could not hold out against government forces; this action provoked only further massacres in this city (Dadrian 1997, 127–9, 131–45). Crucially, the massacres revealed the unwillingness of foreign powers to intervene directly on behalf of the Armenians. While public sympathy for Ottoman Armenians was at its zenith in the mid-1890s, British foreign-policy interest in Ottoman affairs was at its nadir, and Russia, desiring stability in the Near East to facilitate its imperial expansion in the Far East, opposed any other Great Power intervention into Ottoman domestic affairs (Bloxham 2007, 54). Divided among themselves, and interested more in economic and territorial issues than in humanitarian ones, the foreign powers intervened only minimally and ineffectively.

In July 1908 the Ittihadist (Young Turk) movement came to power in a relatively bloodless coup that deposed Sultan Abdülhamid and installed its party, the Ittihad ve Terraki Cemiyeti (Committee of Union and Progress, CUP) (Dadrian 1997, 179; Bloxham 2007, 4, 57). The fall of the Sultanate precipitated the partial disintegration of the empire: Austria-Hungary annexed Bosnia-Herzegovina, Greece absorbed Crete, Bulgaria seceded and declared independence, and Italy threatened Ottoman control of Tripoli and Libya (Hovannisian 1990, 258; Bloxham 2007, 60). On 13 April 1909 "an assortment of Islamic fundamentalists, opponents of Ittihad, and Abdul Hamit loyalists" attempted a counterrevolution but failed (Dadrian 1997, 181). Alarmed or excited by this brief destabilization of the regime, civilians in the town of Adana, assisted by police and military officers, and partially instigated by local CUP officials, massacred between 20,000 and 25,000 Armenians in Adana and its environs from 14 to 27 April 1909 (Dadrian 1997, 182; Hovannisian 1990, 257; Bloxham 2007, 61). Anticipating the attacks, several hundred young Armenians had obtained weapons and engaged in a successful armed defence of the Armenian wards of the city. Eventually, their supplies ran out, and they agreed to a truce arranged by the British consul. By this time, however, new regular army contingents had arrived, ostensibly to restore order, and the attackers, supported by these new forces, "descended upon the totally disarmed and defenseless Armenians, butchering and burning them alive by the thousands" (Dadrian 1997, 183). Schools, hospitals, and churches served as preferred sites for mass killing – as they would again during the Rwandan genocide. Warships from England, France, Italy, Austria, Russia, Germany, and the United States entered nearby coastal waters but refrained from intervening in an internal affair of the Ottoman state. The massacres appear to have involved government functionaries in concert with Ottoman military authorities, who made use of the arsenals of local garrisons but without direct instigation from CUP leaders in Istanbul (Dadrian 1997, 182; Bloxham 2007, 61). However, on this occasion the central government publicly and officially recognized the Armenians as victims of wrongdoing, and local tribunals and military courts-martial convicted and executed 124 Turks, along with 7 Armenians, in connection with the attacks. The CUP officially repudiated the bloodshed and conducted a public memorial to Muslim and Christian sons of the fatherland.

Nevertheless, tendencies toward genocide intensified over the next few years. Later in 1909 the CUP cabinet declared a state of siege and issued a four-year suspension of normal constitutional rights (Hovannisian 1990, 258). During this period, exclusive nationalism grew to dominate in the CUP, sidelining more liberal elements (Bloxham 2007, 62). "The Ittihadist program of national renewal essentially aimed at discarding as useless, and even as pernicious, the traditional concept of multi-ethnic Ottomanism based on the premise of harmony among the various nationalities" (Dadrian 1997, 195). The Balkan War of 1912 went disastrously for the CUP regime, as Serbia, Bulgaria, and Greece captured all remaining Ottoman territory in the Balkan Peninsula (Dadrian 1997, 188–92). The disastrous outcome of the war "left the very survival of that empire hanging in the balance" (Dadrian 1997, 185). Ousted by a group of military officers in the summer of 1912, the CUP returned to power in another coup in January 1913, with its leadership firmly in the grip of its ultranationalist faction (Bloxham 2007, 60; Hovannisian 1990, 258). From then until 1918, a triumvirate of ministers divided among themselves the functions of head of state. Known as "the three Pashas," they were Enver Pasha, minister of defence; Talât Pasha, minister of the interior; and Cemal Pasha, military governor of Constantinople and minister of the marine. Despite the rise of these ultranationalist tendencies, the most influential Armenian political party, the Dashnaktsutiun, stayed allied to the CUP until the start of the First World War in another attempt to win security through loyalty (Hovannisian 1990, 258). Nevertheless, armed Kurdish bands given impunity by the state continued to maraud Armenian villages in the eastern provinces.

In February 1914 the European powers (Britain, France, Russia, Germany, Austria-Hungary, and Italy) agreed on a reform plan to combine six Armenian provinces in the Ottoman Empire into two regions with substantial local autonomy, thereby formulating the most comprehensive proposal for resolving the Armenian question yet put forward (Hovannisian 1990, 258–9). However, the Ottoman

Empire officially entered on the German side of the war on 14 November 1914 and officially annulled the agreement on 16 December 1914 (Dadrian 1997, 212). Armenian homelands lay on both sides of the Ottoman-Russian border, and the CUP government hoped to extend Ottoman territory into Russian Transcaucasia and central Asia. In the winter of 1914–15, Enver Pasha sacrificed an entire army in a failed attempt to break through to the Caspian Sea; in April 1915 the Allies landed at Gallipoli in a failed attempt to capture Constantinople (Hovannisian 1990, 259). Following these events, Young Turk extremists accused Armenians of treachery, making them scapegoats for the empire's military insecurity. However, observations by foreign diplomats suggest that the CUP may have decided some years before to take advantage of the next opportunity to eliminate finally the Armenian question (Dadrian 1997, 207–9).

The Great Crime

In August 1914, following a general mobilization, the Turkish armed forces inducted male Armenians between the ages of 15 and 60, organizing men under 45 into unarmed labour battalions and using men over 45 as "pack animals for the transport of military equipment" (Dadrian 1997, 221). After the Ottoman Empire entered the war in November, the ruling triumvirate empowered the military to make emergency war requisitions, which enabled it to strip provincial Armenians of most of their personal property. On the night of 23–24 April 1915, "scores of Armenian political, religious, educational, and intellectual leaders in Constantinople, many of them friends and acquaintances of the CUP leadership, were arrested, deported to Anatolia, and put to death" (Hovannisian 1990, 260); an estimated 2,345 leaders were arrested "in Istanbul alone in a matter of weeks" (Dadrian 1997, 221). The deportation program officially began on 26 May 1915, when Talât Pasha requested that cabinet enact a Temporary Law of Deportation, authorizing "Commanders of Armies, Army corps, Divisions, and commandants of local garrisons to order the deportation of population clusters on suspicion of espionage, treason, and on military necessity" (Dadrian 1997, 221).

However, deportations were already "well underway" by this time (Dadrian 1997, 235). Supplementary laws on 10 June and 26 September made provisions for the confiscation and handling of

property, debts, credits, and assets of deportees (Dadrian 1997, 222).
Between 4 October and 13 December 1915, a lone senator, Ahmed
Riza, opposed the measure, submitting a draft bill proposing to
postpone application of the Temporary Law until after the end of
the war, argued against the constitutionality of the law, and requested relief measures for the deportees – to no avail (Dadrian
1997, 222–5). The minister of the interior began by ordering the
deportation of all Armenians from war zones to the deserts of Syria
and Mesopotamia (Hovannisian 1990, 260; Melson 1992, 143).
As deportations unfolded, state authorities systematically expelled
Armenians from the whole of the empire, except for Constantinople
and Smyrna, where many foreign diplomats were stationed. On
8 April 1915 soldiers authorized by Enver Pasha's Ministry of War
massacred the unarmed labour battalions of Armenians serving in
the army (Hovannisian 1990, 260; Melson 1992, 144–5). Meanwhile,
during the deportation process, CUP officials and agents, the gen-
damerie, and bandit groups hired by the state systematically separated adult and teenage males from deportation caravans and executed
them. Women and children were then "driven for weeks over moun-
tains and deserts, often dehumanized by being stripped naked and
repeatedly preyed upon and abused" (Hovannisian 1990, 260).

In 1916 Arnold Toynbee estimated that the pre-genocide Armenian
population in the Ottoman Empire was 1.6 million, that 600,000
escaped the deportations or were spared, and that 400,000 persons
survived the deportations, meaning that mortality in 1915–16 was
600,000 (Melson 1992, 146–7). Three very large massacres took
place after 1916: at Res-ul-Ain, with 70,000 victims; at Intilli, with
50,000 victims; and at Der Zor, with 200,000 victims. In sum, Robert
Melson estimates that the total number of Armenians killed by genocide during the First World War was nearly 1 million. Dadrian states:
"By official Turkish accounts alone, those directly killed numbered
about 800,000, not counting the tens of thousands of wartime conscripts liquidated by the military" (Dadrian 1997, 225). In a foot-
note he adds: "Excluded from this figure [the 800,000] are all other
categories of victims such as those executed while serving in the
Turkish army, the multitudes of young females forced into concubin-
age, Muslim marriages, or adoption, victims of coercive religious
conversions, and countless others who eventually perished as a result of the extraordinary hardships of deportation" (Dadrian 1997,
233n240).

With the vast majority of the Ottoman Armenian population killed or deported, the CUP launched further waves of genocidal massacre in Russian territory. Following the collapse of the Russian Army after the Bolshevik Revolution, the Ottoman army crossed into Russian Armenia in the Transcaucasus and proceeded to massacre Armenians there (Dadrian 2001, 159). In September 1920 the Turkish army invaded the Republic of Armenia, and in five months of murder, rape, and destruction of economic infrastructure before the Red Army drove them out, Ottoman forces killed 200,000 Armenians in the region (Dadrian 2001, 161; 1997, 361). They did so partly to forestall implementation of the Sèvres Treaty of 10 August 1920, agreed to among the Allied forces, to establish an Armenian state "bestriding eastern Turkey and the Caucasus" (Dadrian 1997, 356). Contemporary estimates for the number of Armenians killed by Ottoman forces from 1915 to 1922 range from just over 1 million to 1.5 million (Balakian 2003, 180, 196; Adalian 2009, 71). Through murder, expulsion, and forced conversion, a prewar Armenian population estimated to be between 1.6 million and 2.1 million was reduced to a tiny vestige surviving only in Constantinople (Melson 1992, 146; Adalian 1992, 86), all but obliterating the Armenian cultural presence within the Ottoman Empire. The elimination of Ottoman Armenia averted continued European intervention into Turkish affairs over the Armenian question and removed an ethnic barrier between Ottoman Turks and Turkic peoples of the Caucasus and Transcaspia (Hovannisian 1990, 260). In these respects, the genocide succeeded in its aims.

Outcomes

DENIAL

After the defeat of the Axis powers at the end of the First World War, the postwar Ottoman government convened a series of military courts-martial "aimed at bringing the perpetrators of the Armenian Genocide to justice" (Balakian 2003, 331; see also Dadrian 1997, 317ff). These tribunals "prepared more than two hundred files to indict those in the military, in the CUP, and those at the top levels of the government" on the basis of municipal law and the Ottoman penal code (Balakian 2003, 334). The tribunals brought many details of the genocide into public knowledge and drew a connection between the aspirations to social revolution of the Ittihadist movement, the engineering of the empire's entry into the First World War, and the deliberate massacre of the Armenians. As well as convicting and imprisoning or executing other senior officials, the tribunals convicted in absentia "the three Pashas" – Talât, Enver, and Cemal, who had fled to Germany – and sentenced them to death.[1] In so doing, the courts and the postwar government responsible for them attempted to narrate the CUP era as an exception to and a violation of the proper traditions of Ottoman rule. That this happened draws our attention to the importance of contradiction and dissonance within any figuration as large and complex as the civilizing process. During the genocide, important Turkish political figures and senior members of the civil service and the military had objected to the annihilation of the Armenian millet: "The CUP discharged the Ankara province governor, Mazhar, for his refusal to carry out the orders to massacre the deportees. For similar reason the governor of Aleppo province, Celal, also lost his post, and two lower-ranking governors were reportedly murdered" (Kiernan 2007, 409). General Mehmet Vehip, in command of the Ottoman Third Army from early 1916, court-martialled one of his subordinates for having facilitated the murder of an Armenian labour battalion and attempted to arrest Dr Behaeddin Shakir, a CUP leader, who was organizing massacres in Vehip's area (Kiernan 2007, 413). Senator Ahmed Riza, former founding leader of the Young Turks, actively opposed the passage of laws authorizing the dispossession and maltreatment of Armenians (Kiernan 2007, 412, 414). In sum, genocidal Turkish nationalism was only one tendency among those that struggled for dominance over the Ottoman state in the years of its decline. Humiliating defeat in 1918 snatched this dominance from it, sending its most celebrated leaders into prison or exile. From 1918 to 1922 the bearers of a more civic patriotism attempted to reconstitute Ottoman sovereignty in the direction of the inclusive pluralism foreshadowed by the tanzimat reforms.

Sadly, they did not succeed. By 1922 the Turkish Resistance Movement, led by Mustafa Kemal Atatürk, had achieved military control over the territory of the empire, and on 24 July 1923 the Treaty of Lausanne formally recognized the Republic of Turkey. Despite

---

1 Armenian nationalists assassinated Talat in 1921 and Cemal in 1922; Enver, having returned to Turkey after the Kemalist revolution, died in battle with the Red Army in 1922.

adopting secular government and representative democracy, the Turkish state reproduced key aspects of the religious-ethnic nationalism of the CUP. Most important, it has denied – to this day – that a genocide took place (Balakian 2003, 374–5; Akçam 2004, 198–200, 208–9). The denial narrative asserts that the Armenian people conspired with the enemies of the Ottoman Empire, seeking its dissolution, and that this clandestine collaboration with enemy forces made the deportations necessary. Regarding the mass death of Armenians, the deniers assert that enemies of the Turkish people have inflated the numbers killed, that both the Turkish and Armenian sides of the struggle committed massacres, that the Turkish forces never intended to physically destroy the Armenian people as such, and that such massacres as did happen belong to the category of warfare rather than genocide (e.g., Republic of Turkey 1982, 1998; Lewy 2005).

Official denial began under Kemal and went largely unopposed by the international community (Bloxham 2007, 9). Since then, attempts within Turkey to discuss the genocide as such have met with "widespread, repressive sanction, that is to say a condemnation by public opinion which consists of avenging any violation of the precept," to borrow a phrase from Emile Durkheim (1982, 79–80). Since the introduction in 2005 of article 301 of the Turkish criminal code, which prohibits "insulting Turkishness," prosecutors have made several attempts to convict scholars and journalists for making public statements about the genocide. Even so, some Turkish scholars have fought this denial, organizing conferences and publishing historical works that examine the genocide and grapple with Turkish responsibility for atrocity (Akçam 2004; 2006). They do so in the face of public hostility and at some personal risk. On 19 January 2007 the seventeen-year-old radical Turkish nationalist Ogün Samast assassinated the Armenian-Turkish journalist Hrant Dink, who had been charged under article 301 for speaking out about the Armenian genocide (Freely 2007; Temelkuran 2008). Samast, who appears to have had support from an indeterminate network of highly placed nationalists, told police "I killed him because he insulted Turkishness." Reportedly, Dink had received some 26,000 death threats.

On the international stage, Turkey brings diplomatic reprisals against states that formally recognize the genocide. When France recognized the genocide in 2001, for example, Turkey temporarily blocked French companies from receiving defence contracts and suspended official visits to France (CBC News Online Staff 2004). When a private member's bill recognizing the genocide was passed in a free vote in the Canadian House of Commons in April 2004, the Turkish Foreign Ministry condemned the decision, the Canadian prime minister and other cabinet members absented themselves from the vote, and Foreign Minister Bill Graham felt it necessary to play down the significance of the resolution. Turkey's official denial has been an obstacle to its entry into the European Union (Rennie 2005), but the EU has stated that Turkish acceptance of the Armenian genocide is not a condition for Turkey's entry into the bloc (BBC News 2010).

A RECIVILIZING GENOCIDE[2]

After the territorial expansion of its sovereignty halted in 1683, the Ottoman Empire became an "empire in retreat" (Levene 2005b, 213) – slowly at first but precipitously by the second half of the nineteenth century. Intervention into its internal affairs by the Great Powers and the success of separatist movements meant that the Ottoman state's sovereign monopoly of the means of force leaked away above and below. As this happened, the complex web of interdependencies that protected religious minorities within the millet system unravelled, leaving Ottoman Christians exposed to murderous violence. This *decivilizing* process fostered the conditions for genocide. But the genocide itself reversed this decivilizing tendency, *recivilizing* the configuration of relations in the Ottoman state at the expense of Ottoman Armenians.

Why did secession, not reform, provide the "solution" to the demands of the empire's subject nationalities in its final century? And why did the separation of huge portions of its territory and population not simply destroy the Ottoman state entirely (as Turkish nationalists feared that it could)? The plural character of Ottoman identity provides the answer to both of these questions. A key aspect of the civilizing process – the alignment of the structure of individual subjectivities with the structure of sovereign power, generating an

---

2 Taner Akçam's use of Elias's theory to analyze the contribution of the genocide of Armenians to Turkish national identity provides an interesting parallel and counterpoint to my own (see Akçam 2004, 45–51).

isomorphism between subjectivity and sovereignty – happened in a far more complex way in Ottomania than it had in France, Elias's exemplary case. Rather than simply suppressing and assimilating different religious-ethnic communities, the Ottoman Empire in the course of its expansion had incorporated them into itself, whole and viable. In idealized terms, this made it more "civilized" than its Western counterparts – more tolerant and inclusive – but in practical terms this made it less "civilized" because less internally integrated. The logic of its internal integration allowed for a fundamentally different habitus – expressed in everyday/everynight practices of worship, of language, and so on – among subjects whom the French civilizing process would have rendered similar. These differences in habitus articulated with differences in legal norms – that is, in the manifest logic of the use of state force – as each millet lived partially under its own legal code, administered as "little theocracies" dependent on the sovereign. If we imagine the paradigmatic civilizing process as constituting its subjects in a network with a pyramidal shape that puts the sovereign at the top, Ottoman society resembled a pyramid made of smaller pyramids, each culminating at the sovereign, divided from each other by cleavages running from top to bottom. But these vertically divided subfigurations did not operate simply in parallel; the Muslim millet sat closer to the sovereign than all the others. And in practice, this millet consisted mainly of Sunni Muslim Turks. A more complete isomorphism obtained between the Ottoman sovereign and its Turkish subjects than between the sovereign and its non-Turkish subjects.

As the empire expanded, the millet system enabled it to absorb conquered peoples without assimilating them, economizing the use of force to the sovereign's advantage. Once established, the same economy of force made abolishing them cost-prohibitive. As long as a plurality of identity-groups coexisted within the empire, they acted as a check on Turkish dominance. Although the non-Muslim subjects of the empire depended on the sovereign for protection, the sovereign depended on them for their continued cooperation with the imperial project. As the various subject nationalities broke away from the empire, however, this balance of force and interdependencies dissolved, leaving the Armenians and a few other minorities virtually alone in a predominantly Turkish polity that had less to gain from multicultural tolerance and more to fear from minority self-assertiveness.

Competitive struggle with other sovereign powers fuelled these fears. If by "civilized" we mean tolerant and internally nonviolent, the Ottoman Empire became more civilized on paper and less civilized in practice the more that the Great Powers intervened in its internal affairs. Superficially, this intervention constituted the enmeshment of Ottoman power in a wider chain of interdependencies. Elias's account of how the civilizing process works leads us to expect that as the Ottoman state became more connected to wider networks of interdependency, social life within its domains would have become more nonviolent. The history of the nineteenth century showed the opposite: as the empire became more integrated into wider networks of international legal accountability, its social life became more violent, as evidenced by attacks on Armenians and other minorities. Social theorists from Henri de Saint-Simon to Durkheim had dreamed that international governance might one day supercede merely national governance, replacing the narrow parochialism of national patriotism with the universalizing humanism of world-patriotism (Saint-Simon 1975; Durkheim 1992, 75), and they might have mistaken the internationalization of Ottoman affairs for a move in this direction. In practice, however, intervention in Ottoman affairs expressed the impunity of particular nation-states over others, more than it expressed the genuine emergence of a supranational system of moral interdependency. Russia, Britain, and other Great Power states intervened in Ottoman affairs in their own interests, whereas the Sublime Porte could not respond in kind. Because of the isomorphic relationship between the Ottoman state and Turkish Ottoman subjects, the politico-military force that enabled foreign intervention translated into a symbolic violence experienced by individual subjects as a shameful loss of self (Akçam 2004, 87, 100). As the flow of this symbolic violence intensified, it was translated through the millet system, manifesting in ongoing persecution and occasional massacres of minorities and in a hardening, a raising of the stakes, of religious-ethnic identity.

Denied opportunities for military expansion at its borders, and also locked out of the European scramble for Africa and other opportunities for colonial expansion, the Ottoman Empire could not defer violence outside its borders. As a result, violence recirculated within the empire, and as it "heated up," its pluralistic internal structures lost their stability, gaining volatility. Religious-ethnic nationalism provided a resolution of sorts to this instability by establishing singular identities strongly identified with the sovereign, allowing violence to circulate downward and outward to abject or to foreign Others. The singular Ottoman plurality decayed into a plurality of singularities – separate nation-states – leaving the remnant of the empire internally off balance and politico-militarily vulnerable.

The genocide of the Armenians solved several problems at once. It eliminated Armenian nationalism as a real disruptive force within the Ottoman state and as an excuse for foreign intervention. It facilitated the militarization of Ottoman society (see Kiernan 2007, 407), thereby strengthening the Ottoman sovereign in its struggles with other sovereignties. And, perhaps most important, it affirmed – indeed, it helped to construct – a singular national identity. Nationalist ideologues like Ziya Gökalp (see the postscript to this part of the chapter below) dreamed of a moral unity for the Turkish nation, based on shared historical experience and shared collective emotions. Genocide realized this unity, enabling Turks to share in the active negation of Armenian identity, defining their collective selfhood through the vigorous expression of what that selfhood could not include.

Genocide emerged as a means to the production of a more integrated and sovereign – hence, in practical terms, more "civilized" – Turkish society: "the Turkish revolution initiated by the CUP was successful in creating a new Turkey, but it also came close to destroying an ancient people in the process" (Melson 1992, 170). The triumph of the nationalist movement even after the empire's abject defeat in the First World War points to the success of the genocide of the Armenians in achieving its monstrous social function. The official policy of denial, sanctioned by state force, echoes this monstrous function, even after the generation that committed the genocide, the CUP government, and the Ottoman Empire itself have all passed away.

GERMAN CONNECTIONS

A rope of entwined relational developments connects the Ottoman genocide to the Nazi holocaust. Contemporary historians debate precisely how direct and active or indirect and passive this connection was. During the First World War, Germany was the Ottoman Empire's strongest ally, German diplomats had close contact with the highest levels of the Ottoman government and substantial influence over its policies, and senior German military officials served as officers in the Ottoman army. Vahakn Dadrian argues that the German state implicated itself actively and directly in the genocide, as a matter of deliberate policy, through measures ranging from institutional support and the provision of intelligence to diplomatic and personal expressions of support for anti-Armenian violence (Dadrian 1997, 206, 237, 255–6, 268–77; 1996). Donald Bloxham, on the other hand, argues that, in the context of assumptions common to European statesmanship regarding "military necessity" and "ethnic insurrection," the Germans failed to perceive the specifically genocidal quality of Ottoman policy and rendered themselves complicit in holocaust more by passive acquiescence and self-serving wilful blindness than by shared genocidal intent (Bloxham 2007, 115–33). Figurational theory suggests not only that a specifically genocidal intent matters less than Bloxham implies it does but also that German complicity belongs to a wider civilizational context, one in which state actors normally made racist and primordialist assumptions about ethnic identity-difference and understood themselves as duty-bound to privilege the interests of sovereign states over the lives and personal security of politically impotent minority groups. In other words, if the German state made itself complicit in Ottoman genocide, its especially close relationship to this event resulted more from the contingencies of interstate power struggles than from any distinct cultural qualities of its own.

Nonetheless, this close relationship flowed both ways. The Ottoman holocaust helped to inspire Raphaël Lemkin to coin the legal concepts of "barbarism" and "vandalism," concepts that he consolidated into the term "genocide" during the Nazi holocaust. Ironically, the Ottoman genocide may also have inspired Lemkin's antithesis. Adolf Hitler appears to have known about the Turkish annihilation of the Armenians and to have derived from it the lesson that the international community would tolerate or even accept the destruction of a national minority. In a statement made during or prior to 1924, Hitler claimed that, unless Germany deals with its Jewish question, "the German people will end up becoming just like the Armenians" (Dadrian 1997, 402). Similarly, in 1943 he blamed the fate of the Armenians on pernicious Jewish influence. In 1933 he expressed great admiration for Turkish nationalism (Dadrian 1997, 402), and on another occasion he emphasized the urgency of "the task of protecting the German blood from contamination, not only

of the Jewish but also of the Armenian blood" (Dadrian 1997, 409).
Most famously, in 1939 in a speech to the chief commanders and
commanding generals, admonishing them to be brutal and merciless
in battle, Hitler is recorded as saying, "Who after all is today speaking of the destruction of the Armenians" (Dadrian 1997, 403;
Bloxham 2007, 111). In the same document he also says, "The world
believes only in success" (Dadrian 1997, 404) – echoing (perhaps
unknowingly) Talât Pasha's self-justifying statement, "I have the
conviction that as long as a nation does the best for its own interests,
and succeeds, the world admires it and thinks it moral" (Dadrian
1997, 383).

THE BIRTH OF "GENOCIDE"
The contradictory quality of the civilizing process manifests in this
way: an event that helped to inspire the most paradigmatic of all
genocides also helped to inspire the formation of a concept, a law,
and a movement to end genocides. In response to the obliteration
of Ottoman Armenians, Lemkin formulated the two concepts that
he later synthesized into the concept of "genocide": "barbarity, consisting in the extermination of racial, religious or social collectivities";
and "vandalism, consisting in the destruction of cultural and artistic
works of these groups" (Lemkin 1947, 146). Along with the Nazi
holocaust, therefore, the Ottoman atrocities serve as a prototype,
or exemplar, for the concept of "genocide." Both events involve a
state's calculated annihilation, on the basis of an enduring collective identity, of a portion of the population over which it enjoys
sovereignty. In some ways, the earlier event fits more closely with
Lemkin's concern for the protection of national groups since
Armenians perhaps more fully constituted a national group than
did German Jews. Much of the Ottoman Armenian population still
lived in eastern Anatolia, on or near the territory of the former
Armenian state. Under the millet system, Armenians preserved a
more distinct social and cultural life in Ottoman society than Jews
did in German society. The formation of an Armenian nation-state
out of a part of the territory of the Ottoman Empire was a possibility in a way that the formation of a Jewish nation-state out of
German territory was not. And the actions committed against
Ottoman Armenians amply satisfy the terms of the UNCG: the
Ittihadists and their agents killed, inflicted bodily and mental harm

on, and imposed destructive conditions of life on members of a group defined by its nationality, ethnicity, and religion.

Unlike the Nazis, however, the CUP did not pursue the complete physical extermination of Armenians as such on the basis of a racialist conception of difference. On this basis, the American scholar Steven T. Katz has tried to argue that the label "genocide" does not apply to the CUP's destruction of the Armenian millet (Katz 1994; 2001). Examining the failures of his argument helps to draw out a deeper sense of what the word "genocide" works to do. Katz argues that the Ottoman state did not pursue physical extermination as an end in itself but as the means to a political goal, namely the elimination of perceived threats to Turkish sovereignty. The deportation process, however murderous, aimed at the removal of a community, not the annihilation of a race. However, functionalist analyses of the Shoah reveal that, in its actual implementation (as distinct from the visions of ideologues), the genocide of Europe's Jews followed a comparable logic. German bureaucrats pursued the goal not of exterminating the Jewish race as such but of making the Third Reich *judenrein* ("clean of Jews"). In this respect, deportation to eastern Europe, concentration in ghettoes, and systematic mass slaughter all appeared over time as different expedient solutions to this problem. The combination of deportation and massacre presented a similarly expedient means to the goal of eliminating the Armenian question.

The status of the Armenian experience as a genocide has several implications for the concept. First, extermination does not have to constitute an end in itself. As a tactic in struggles for dominance within social formations, the practice of genocide aims to effect a transformation in relations of power and subjectivity. Second, perpetrators do not necessarily intend the total physical destruction of a group. Genocide involves the destruction of the social existence of an identity, which may or may not require the physical annihilation of the bearers of the identity. Third, genocide inflicts violence not only on concrete human beings but also on the relationships among them. A nation consists not only of persons but also of persons relating to each other in a particular type of figuration. Genocide takes varying forms, and uses varying principles of legitimation, according to the varying forms of interpersonal connection that its perpetrators seek to destroy – or, sometimes more saliently, the forms of connection that they seek to forge among themselves.

Postscript: Sociology's Complicity in Genocide[3]

One remarkable feature of the obliteration of the Armenians concerns the role that sociology, and specifically Durkheimian theory, has played in the legitimation of exclusionary nationalism and genocide.

Ziya Gökalp has been called "the father of Turkish nationalism" (Melson 1992, 164) and is regarded by many as "the pre-eminent Turkish thinker of the century" (Smith 1995, 46). He was also a sociologist who considered Durkheim to be his major intellectual influence. He rose to prominence in the wake of the 1908 revolution and was a member of the Central Committee of the CUP from 1911 to 1918 (Smith 1995, 46; Melson 1992, 165). In this capacity, he achieved recognition as "the leading intellectual of the new regime" (Smith 1995, 46) and influenced the ideas of both Talât Pasha and Enver Pasha. The CUP gave Gökalp the mandate of investigating the conditions of minorities, especially the Armenians. During the genocide, he wrote an internal party document titled "The Two Mistakes of the Tanzimat," lambasting the reform edicts of 1839 and 1856 and asserting that the empire should be a nation of overlords "with the watchword: 'Islam mandates domination'" (Dadrian 1997, 180). He participated, with Enver Pasha, in directing the Association for the Promotion of Turkish Strength and other Ottoman youth groups that combined paramilitary training and nationalist indoctrination (Dadrian 1997, 196). When the postwar regime decided to prosecute those responsible for taking the empire to war, Gökalp faced arrest on 21 September 1919, along with Enver Pasha and other senior CUP officials. During his trial, he admitted to having approved of the deportation of the Armenians but denied that massacres had taken place, stating

---

3 In *Sociology Responds to Fascism* (Turner and Käsler 1992), Stephen Turner comments on the myth of sociology as an inherently oppositional force whose power to reveal unpleasant truths frightened the Nazi ideologues. The essays in that volume provide an interesting complement to the story of complicity in Ottoman genocide.

instead that the Armenians had been "killed in a war between them and the Turks, whom they had stabbed in the back" (Uriel Heyd, quoted in Melson 1992, 165). Convicted, Gökalp was deported to Malta. After the war, he became an ardent supporter of the Atatürk regime. He published his most important work, *The Principles of Turkism*, in 1923 and died in 1924 (Smith 1995, 48).

But in addition to his political career, Gökalp helped to bring sociology as a discipline into Turkish society. In 1912 he established the first Ottoman chair of sociology, in the Department of Philosophy in Istanbul University (Ertürk 1990, 39). In 1915 he achieved the position of professor of sociology at Istanbul (Kahveci 1995, 52). He played an instrumental part in ensuring intermediary schools taught sociology. Even after his death, his work occupied a "dominant position within mainstream sociology" (Ertürk 1990, 40). This work entwined the doctrine of integral, or organic, nationalism with Durkheimian sociological theory. Gökalp's "National Sociology," symbolized by the slogan "Turkify, Islamize and modernize," at the theoretical level incorporated the organic and evolutionary assumptions of Auguste Comte, Charles Darwin, and Herbert Spencer within a nominally Durkheimian framework (Ertürk 1990, 39). Specifically, National Sociology justified an "ultra-nationalist perspective which left no room for individual liberties and initiative" (Smith 1995, 48) by appropriating Durkheim's ideas about social solidarity, moral unity, the division of labour, and corporatist political structures (Smith 1995, 47–9; Kahveci 1995, 52–5; Melson 1992, 164). In this process, Gökalp substantially modified Durkheim's ideas. As Robert Melson says, "it was Gökalp's *reading* of Durkheim and his *adaptation* of the French sociologist to the [Turkish] political landscape that proved to be seminal" (Melson 1992, 164, emphasis added). But this connection, however tenuous, raises an interesting question regarding the relationship between sociological theory and the genocide of the Armenians.

In Gökalp's vision, a nation exists as "a society consisting of people who speak the same language, have had the same education and are united in their religious and aesthetic ideals – in short those who have a common culture and religion" (Heyd 1950, 63). Nationalism depends on moral unity deriving from shared historical experience and collectively shared emotions (Kahveci 1995, 53). For Gökalp, nationality provided "the basic principle of moral action" (Melson 1992, 167). The life of the individual is therefore absolutely subordinate to that of the nation and to authority that acts in the name of the nation, as Gökalp expressed in a poem:

I am a soldier it [the nation] is my commander
I obey without question all its orders
With closed eyes I carry out my duty.
(Quoted in Heyd 1950, 124)

Gökalp's integral nationalism broke with the Ottoman tradition that "not only accorded minorities a place in the empire but also defined certain moral and political responsibilities of the state toward them and toward all millets" (Melson 1992, 167). It also broke with Islamic tradition that recognized Christian Armenians as people of the book (Melson 1992, 169). It sanctioned genocide in two ways: it implied that any action is good if carried out for the good of the nation, and it excluded the Armenians from the Turkish nation (and, by implication, from the community of obligation).

How much of this derives from Durkheimian thought properly so called? Certainly, Gökalp's militarism, ethnocentrism, and conformist nationalism contrast sharply with Durkheim's lifelong opposition to ethnically chauvinist tendencies in French nationalism, especially during the Dreyfus Affair and the First World War (Turner 1992). Gökalp's "writings show the influence of many Durkheimian texts, including essays and lectures that were quite obscure at the time" (Smith 1995, 49). But he seems to have ignored Durkheim's Montesquieuian insistence, in *Professional Ethics and Civic Morals* (based on a lecture series that Durkheim gave at Istanbul), that the power of the state be counterbalanced by the power of secondary institutions so that individual liberty is not stifled – an argument that also appears in the second preface to *The Division of Labour in Society*. Ethnically chauvinist nationalism also ignores Durkheim's arguments to the effect that solidarity based on sameness derives from and best suits societies with a low division of labour, whereas the complex division of labour of modern industrial societies requires an organic solidarity based on the recognition that difference implies mutually complementary interdependence (Durkheim 1984, 16–24). Overall, one may accuse Gökalp of perversely wanting to build a modern society on the basis of mechanical, not organic, solidarity.

And yet a nationalist celebration of the nation as the principle of moral action harmonizes with Durkheim's claim that social solidarity constitutes the essence of all morality (Durkheim 1984, 329–32), that society forms the ultimate object of moral action, and that the good of society is the basis of all morality (Durkheim 2002, 55–61). Durkheim advocated a "democracy" defined not by popular control over the mechanisms of government but by close communication between the state, as the organ of social thought, and the vague collective representations diffused throughout the social body (Durkheim 1992, 81–4). If Durkheim's work sometimes displays a concern to reconcile social solidarity with individual liberty, at other times it celebrates the insignificance of the individual in the face of the godlike magnificence of society (Durkheim 1995, 208–9). Writing on the division of labour, Durkheim argues that the question of which class controls the means of production matters less than the nature of the moral code that governs economic life (Durkheim 1992, 9–13). Taking all of these points together, one may read in Durkheim an analysis of power in which concrete human individuals disappear and only the objective functional needs of society (Durkheim 1982, 85–97) have any significance. In sum, Gökalp's attempt to appropriate Durkheim in the service of genocidal nationalism extends certain themes in Durkheim's writing at the expense of others rather than simply caricaturing his thought.

Deconstructive theory subverts the distinction between reading and misreading: in an important sense, all readings are misreadings. This notion denies any simple recourse to the claim that Gökalp misread Durkheim (or, comparably, that Joseph Stalin simply misread Karl Marx). Gökalp's reading synthesizes aspects of Durkheim with ideas quite foreign to Durkheim, although some very fruitful contemporary readings of Durkheim do that also. Gökalp's synthesis presents manifest liabilities and offers little or nothing of value to contemporary sociologists. But it does have some value as an object lesson in the limitations of Durkheimian theory taken on its own and uncritically.

Nicole Vartanian argues that "the danger lies in Durkheim's one-sided analysis of the power dynamic": "Durkheim simply offers no conceptual opportunity for this power dynamic to be abused or for the balance of power to be misappropriated ... Considering the context of his writing, at a time when he generally saw the modern French state as a manifestation of organic solidarity, perhaps this is reasonable. Nonetheless, for his theory of society to be fully developed, and for it to have applicability outside his particular moment and place in history, this seems to be a significant void"

(Vartanian 2000, 8). One of Elias's criticisms of Talcott Parsons (Elias 2000, 466–7) applies to Durkheim also: Durkheim's model of a functionally integrated organic society, in which the state *is* the organ of social thought and in which society *is* the foundation and object of morality, conflates an idealized version of the late Victorian French nation-state with the concrete actualities of modern nation-states in general. Durkheim does not clearly declare whether his description of state power in *The Division of Labour in Society* or in *Professional Ethics and Civic Morals* refers to any actually existing society or to one dimension of a hypothetical model of the perfectly functional society. At best, this ambivalence between the descriptive and normative connotations of statements like "the state is the very organ of social thought" (Durkheim 1992, 51) has provided an opportunity for ideologues like Gökalp to appropriate Durkheim in the service of authoritarianism and genocide.

PART TWO: RWANDA

The Meanings of Genocide

If the Armenian holocaust helped to inspire the formation of the very concept of genocide, and its criminalization in international criminal law, and the campaign to eliminate its practice, the Rwandan genocide of 1994 gave new life to this concept, law, and campaign by showing at a stroke the depth of their failure and the urgency of the need for them. For when the Rwandan state systematically murdered over half a million of its subjects, with the openly declared aim of exterminating all Tutsis in the country, interested observers around the world faced a genocide whose recognition did not require a deep appreciation of Lemkin's politico-cultural vision: an unambiguous and spectacular genocide, satisfying the most narrow definitions of the term, carried out in broad daylight. Even so, official recognition and intervention by the agents of international law came slowly, reluctantly, and too late to prevent hundreds of thousands of brutal rapes and murders. This failure, along with similar failures around the same time in the former Yugoslavia, had at least one salutary effect: the reinvigoration of the 1948 UNCG, which, after fifty years of near-inactivity, was enforced by the International Criminal Tribunal for Rwanda (ICTR), created by a resolution of the United Nations Security Council in 1998.

In scholarly discourse, too, Rwanda stands as a landmark that helps to define the term "genocide": if for half a century "genocide" meant "events like the Nazi holocaust," it now means also "events like the Rwandan massacres." Given its unusual status as an epitome of the type, I would like to open my examination of the Rwandan genocide by unpacking some of the different ways the event has been framed and the implications these frames have for understanding and preventing future genocides.

During and after the genocide, its senior leaders, when speaking to non-Rwandan audiences, tried to cover up their own responsibility for atrocity by claiming that the violence resulted not from deliberate state planning but from centuries-old tribal animosities. In making this claim, they played to their audiences' well-established tendencies to understand collective identity in *essentializing* terms: to regard the qualities of groups as belonging inherently to those groups, timelessly, naturally, and for all practical purposes irremediably. As we have seen in chapter 3, Lemkin's own conception of genocide has essentialist undertones due to its organic conception of nationality. Although Lemkin also expressed fundamental respect for the unique achievements of all cultures and wrote extensive (unpublished) analyses of the genocidal effects of Western colonialism, the essentialist elements of his conception of genocide lend themselves to a Eurocentric narrative of genocide prevention.

This Eurocentric narrative would go like this: genocides result from ancient and natural animosities between differing nations; more civilized and enlightened political communities can more readily overcome these ancient, primal feelings than can their less developed counterparts; therefore, the more advanced nation-states of the world have an obligation to protect the citizens of the weaker states and failed states from the violent manifestations of these primal hatreds, by armed intervention if necessary – to the extent that this intervention does not undermine the interests of the leaders of civilization, whose advancement serves after all as a precondition for the continuing enlightenment of humanity. In the terms of this narrative, genocide prevention grapples with deep atavistic passions intrinsic to the human psyche, inevitably requires force, and produces an irresolvable tension similar to the tension between the superego and the id within the civilized subject (Freud 2002).

Since 1945 most scholars of nationalism have moved away from the primordialist model in favour of varying accounts of how political struggles in the present construct and reconstruct national identities and "memories" of past history. But primordialism lingers on as a trope about genocide in media reportage, popular discourses, policy statements, and even some scholarship. Mahmood Mamdani takes time to point out its flaws, and also to rebut its opposite and twin, instrumentalism, which explains genocide as an outcome of rational actors pursuing their self-interest by unethical means (Mamdani 2001, 15). Instrumentalism takes for granted the boundaries of identity and the nature of difference – in effect, essentializing the identity-difference relation. Mamdani proposes instead a pluralistic model of the political construction of cultural identity, in which ethnic identity emerges as political force through struggles to define who will control the state and the resources at its command, struggles that define the membership and the attributes of the very groups that struggle. In addition, recent studies (Straus 2006; Lyons and Straus 2006; Mironko 2006) based on interviews with actual perpetrators convicted by the ICTR give extraordinary insights into what drove genocide on the ground for the ordinary men and women who perpetrated it. Taken together, studies of elite political culture and studies of ordinary perpetrators assemble into a revealing account of how deferentiation translates the violence between contenders for sovereign power into violence between ordinary people far removed from any substantial control over this power.

In what follows, I show how the Rwandan genocide emerged as an expression of the Eurocentric civilizing process and how the struggle to end genocide is not a struggle of enlightened civilization against primordial hatreds but a struggle between two contradictory tendencies of the civilizing process itself. But before the Eurocentric civilizing process arrived in central Africa, Rwanda had begun to move through a civilizing-barbarizing process of its own. New research on precolonial state formation and on the origins of "Hutu" and "Tutsi" as social categories illuminates the early wellsprings of the movement toward genocide.

State Formation and the Hutu-Tutsi Relation

Some time in the sixteenth century, Ruganzu Ndori founded the kingdom of Nyiginya in what is today central Rwanda (Vansinia

2004, 44).[4] Likely a great herder arriving from grasslands to the north, Ndori established his power by means of a new and unequal form of contract, *ubuhake*, through which he superseded the more reciprocal obligations of the older *ubugabire* contracts: "The patron (*shebuja*) gives one or more head of cattle in usufruct to the client (*umugaragu*) but maintains the ultimate ownership of these cattle. He assures his client of his protection. In return the client must help his patron whenever needed and becomes his servant or *umuhakwa*. The relation was hereditary and only the patron could dissolve it" (Vansinia 2004, 47). Ubuhake relations resembled the patron-client relations in early-modern northern England, in which "a relationship of a close collaboration between patron and client could be very strong, leading to a sense of family bonds and mutual cordiality" (Gasanabo 2006, 52). Through enduring military success against rival political regimes in raids of varying sizes,[5] Ndori and his heirs expanded the territory governed through their ubuhake contracts to include most, but not all, of the territory of modern Rwanda. During the reign of Rujugira (1756–65), this Nyiginyan kingdom developed a standing army and permanent administrative institutions (Mamdani 2001, 66–8). By the nineteenth century, the kingdom had developed "an organized and structured monarchy, semi-feudal with aristocrats and vassals, and an administrative structure that emanated from the court" (Melvern 2004, 5). Nyiginyan administration divided into four levels of government below the royal court: provinces, districts, hills, and villages (Prunier 1995, 11–12; Mamdani 2001, 68). An army chief (or "chief of men") governed each province; within each province, a "chief of landholding" (or "chief of the

---

4 As Jan Vansinia carefully points out, "the Nyiginya kingdom is not equivalent to Rwanda as a whole" (Vansinia 2004, 5). Indeed, the word "Rwanda" itself "literally means 'the surface occupied by a swarm or a scattering,'" and in precolonial times it referred to a territory, not to a nation per se, such that there is at least one instance in which the term is used to refer to foreign territory, to the country of the enemy (Vansinia 2004, 35). This means that the use of the word "Rwanda" to refer to a nation-state society is a product of colonialism. However, the institutional practices and the Hutu-Tutsi relations established by the kingdom of Nyiginya carried over into modern Rwanda in ways that proved crucial to the genocidal process.

5 The Rwandan language makes no distinction between "to defeat" and "to conquer," so to call them wars of conquest risks anachronism (Vansinia 2004, 51, 483).

earth") oversaw the agricultural economy, and a "chief of pastures" (or "chief of the long grass") administered the herding economy. Within each district, hill chiefs oversaw collections of villages, each of which had its own headman. In addition, complex networks of ubuhake relationships ran throughout Nyiginyan society from top to bottom (Prunier 1995, 13–14; Mamdani 2001, 64–6). From about 1870 onward, these networks involved a system of compulsory group work, *uburetwa*, paid to chiefs of the land by their farming tenants (Vansinia 2004, 134). This system required farmers to set aside two out of every four days for services to their chief. The requirement to perform uburetwa labour served to polarize the relationship between Hutus and Tutsis in ominous ways.

The racist imaginations of European colonizers, augmented by the self-serving mythmaking of Hutu Power extremists,[6] have firmly entrenched the story of Tutsis as foreigners in Rwanda. According to the Hamitic hypothesis, "Tutsi" herders arrived in Rwanda from the upper Nile region and established dominance over the "Hutu" farmers sometime just prior to the rise of the Nyiginyan kingdom, preserving a distinct identity despite intermarrying with and adopting the language and religion of their "Hutu" subjects (e.g., Sellström and Wohlgemuth 1996, 21–49; see also Uvin 1998, 13–14; Prunier 1995, 5; Des Forges 1999, 31; Mamdani 2001 41–75). But as early as 1981, dependency theorist Water Rodney argued that differences in diet account for the differences in stature between Hutus, Tutsis, and Twas: as cattle-herders, Tutsis enjoyed much more protein than the farming Hutus, who ate proportionately more grains, accounting for the taller, thinner frames of the former (whereas the foraging Twas, living in the forests and constituting 1 per cent of Rwanda's pre-genocide population, suffered chronic malnutrition, accounting for their exceptionally short stature) (Rodney 1981). In addition to diet, other scholars have suggested that physiological effects of social status and caste-selective breeding can account for differences between Hutu and Tutsi facial features, observing similar effects in nineteenth-century France (Mamdani 2001, 45). Some genetic research suggests that Tutsis did not arrive from north-eastern Africa at all (Luis et al. 2004).

---

6 "Hutu Power" designates a constellation of social, political, and paramilitary forces oriented toward preserving the racialization of Hutu and Tutsi identity and maintaining or intensifying Hutu supremacy (Melvern 2000, 13, 19).

Written records of oral history indicate that the word "Tutsi" in the seventeenth century, before Ndori's rise to power, most likely referred to a social elite among herders (Vansinia 2004, 37, 134). The terms "Hima" and "Tutsi" both referred to herders, but in areas where both terms were used, the latter referred to the elite as opposed to common herders (Vansinia 2004, 36). As it rose to regional dominance, the Nyiginyan dynasty abandoned its label as "Hima" in favour of "Tutsi" (Vansinia 2004, 37). Over the life of the kingsom, both the terms "Hutu" and "Tutsi" went through several transformations. As the political elite within Rwanda's herders came to refer to themselves as "Tutsi," the word "Hutu" designated rural boorishness or loutishness; masters at court called their servants "Hutu" even if they belonged to the Tutsi lineage group (Vansinia 2004, 134). The term applied generally to menials and servants, and also to foreigners, but not systematically to farmers. The formation of a permanent standing army by Rujugira added a new layer of distinction to the Hutu-Tutsi relation: members of the armed forces came from the herders, not from the farming families, so "the elite eventually began to call all farmers 'Hutu' and to oppose this word to 'Tutsi,' now applied to all herders, whether they were of Tutsi origin or not." This distinction spread as the political influence of the capital grew, establishing an absolute equivalence between "Hutu" and farmer. In the mid-nineteenth century, "the distinction between chief of the long grass and chief of the land again *institutionalized* a division between Tutsi herders and Hutu farmers" (Vansinia 2004, 135, original emphasis). This institutionalization set the stage for the introduction of uburetwa, which "aggravated that division and poisoned it. For only Hutu owed *uburetwa* because of their tenure of arable land, and only Hutu were obliged to perform the menial work required by the chief of the land in contrast to the less humiliating obligations of his Tutsi clients. *Uburetwa* seems to have provoked a new awareness across the whole society that resulted in the emergence of the two hierarchized social categories" (Vansinia 2004, 135–6). With this "humiliating" imposition, the Hutu-Tutsi distinction decisively became one of deferentiation. From the 1870s onward, this deferentiation spread throughout the kingdom, provoking resentment and resistance (Vansinia 2004, 136–8). Aristocrats began calling new men at court "Hutus" if they did not issue from an illustrious family and engaged in armed reprisals for any insults to "Tutsis," while in the countryside, farmers' revolts began to break out in 1885. A coup at court in 1896 invited overt expression of anti-Tutsi resentment, which gathered energy and became an armed anti-Tutsi movement from 1897 to 1899. German observers on the scene misattributed this social conflict to racial hatred, or "Rassenhaß" (Vansinia 2004, 138). This misrecognition foreshadowed the furious energy that Rwanda's deferentiating figuration was about to gain from its incorporation into the much larger Eurocentric civilizing process.

European colonization of Rwanda began in 1897 through the establishment of protectorate treaties with Germany (Sellström and Wohlgemuth 1996, 21–49). The Germans, and Belgians after them, subscribed to the "Hamitic hypothesis," which regarded Tutsis as racially superior to Hutus, even "white" in every characteristic save skin colour, and naturally suited to ruling: "Given that some Tutsi (a minority) ruled over a majority, they 'must' possess incongruous martial skill and intelligence, which, when combined with the observation that the Tutsi at the central court possessed a different physiology to that of Hutu, was taken to indicate Tutsi provenance outside Rwanda" (Eltringham 2006, 427). German indirect rule further centralized the state and stratified Hutu-Tutsi relationships dramatically. In 1916 the Belgians took Rwanda by force from the Germans; the League of Nations confirmed Belgian title to Rwanda in 1923, as did the United Nations in 1946. In 1926 the Belgians first introduced the identity card system designating each Rwandan as Hutu, Tutsi, or Twa – initially, on the basis of self-declaration. In the 1930s the colonial government engaged in the "Tutsification" of Rwandan state structures, removing Hutu chiefs and replacing them with Tutsis, abolishing the division between chiefs of men, landholding, and pastures, and establishing a Tutsi monopoly over all political positions under Belgian authority in Rwanda. After this reform, some Hutus sought and obtained redesignation as Tutsis even after the 1930s (Des Forges 1999, 37–8). In 1933 the identity cards became mandatory for all Rwandans; they would remain so until the 1994 genocide. In addition, Belgian policy further accentuated the hierarchical and coercive quality of the Hutu-Tutsi relation by imposing on all farmers a requirement of forced labour, *akazu* and *shiku*, enforced by a new and especially demeaning punishment – *ikiboko*, eight blows with a stick – and by requiring Tutsi aristocrats to implement this requirement (Gasanabo 2006, 53).

The identity card system and the enforced Tutsi monopoly on government positions, legitimated by the Hamitic hypothesis, both racialized the Hutu-Tutsi distinction and charged it with a deferentiating violence that the precolonial state-formation process had only begun to generate. "Social revolution" and formal decolonization failed to peacefully discharge this relation; indeed, by locating sovereignty within the Rwandan state and tying it even more firmly to Hutu-Tutsi difference, decolonization intensified the actual and deferred violence invested in this difference. In the years leading up to the 1962 Belgian withdrawal, Hutu "ethnic" nationalism – epitomized in the 1957 Bahutu Manifesto – emerged as a powerful force in Rwanda. From 1959 to 1961 Rwanda underwent a social revolution, in the course of which Belgium reversed its policy of Tutsi dominance within the colonial state and handed over all Tutsi-held positions to Hutus. During this time, Hutu nationalists murdered or expelled Tutsi chiefs. In 1961 the state abolished its monarchy and held elections that gave a 78 per cent Hutu majority the mandate to form Rwanda's first independent government. Following independence, Tutsi Rwandans suffered increasing persecution, which escalated in 1963 to mass killings of Tutsis and the dissolution of Tutsi political parties. Large numbers of Tutsis fled the country, primarily to Uganda, where they created a permanent exile community that would number 600,000 persons by 1990. Grégoire Kayibanda and his personal allies from Gitamara prefecture usurped complete power in Rwanda, making the country a one-party state by 1965.

The years 1962–73 are known as the years of the "first republic" in Rwanda and 1973–94 as the "second republic" (Sellström and Wohlgemuth 1996, 21–49). In 1972 and again in 1973 the Tutsi-dominated government in Burundi engaged in genocidal killings of Hutus in that country (Lemarchand 1998, 6–7). The spectacle of anti-Hutu genocide provoked civil unrest in Rwanda; anti-Tutsi violence broke out in schools, administrative offices, and businesses, spilling over to victimize many Hutus also. On 5 July 1973 a faction led by Defence Minister Juvénal Habyarimana staged a coup against the Kayibanda regime (afterward known as the "moral revolution") and established a new government that would last until the 1994 genocide. Initially fuelled by "majoritarian aspirations" (Mamdani 2001, 133), the revolution failed to reform the authoritarian character of Rwandan governance. It succeeded only in transferring power from one regionally derived elite, based in

Gitamara prefecture, to another, rooted in the northern prefectures of Gisenyi and Ruhengieri and articulated in Habyarimana's party, the Mouvement Républicain National pour la Démocratie et le Développement (National Republican Movement for Democracy and Development, MRND). The MRND regime did succeed nonetheless in modernizing Rwandan trade and infrastructure and in stimulating economic growth. The years of the "second republic" brought urbanization and relative prosperity to Rwanda, at least until 1989. However, corruption and embezzlement, supporting traditional ubuhake relationships, riddled the export-oriented economy. In the late 1980s the Rwandan economy declined, partly because of fluctuating coffee prices on international markets, and in 1990 the Rwandan state agreed to a Structural Adjustment Programme (SAP) sponsored by the International Monetary Fund and obtained US$260 million in balance of payments support (African Rights 1995, 68).

The Build-up to Genocide, 1990–94

All scholarly and nongovernmental organization (NGO) observers agree that the killings were highly organized. The stockpiling of weapons, the training of militias, the use of radio to disseminate an ideological framework, and, most of all, the speed and efficiency of the killing show the spuriousness of claims by Hutu Power leaders that the killings resulted from a spontaneous outbreak of popular anti-Tutsi passion and show that these leaders made extensive preparations for mass killing well before 6 April 1994. In addition, however, interviews with ordinary men and women convicted of having implemented the genocides cast further light on the complexity of the genocidal process (Hatzfeld 2005; Lyons and Straus 2006; Mironko 2006; Straus 2006). These interviews show a disconnect between the ideological and political motives that drove the leaders of the genocide and the more prosaic motives that drove the ordinary Rwandans who wielded machetes and killed face to face. This research suggests that although the leaders of the genocide *prepared for* it in advance, they may not have been able to *plan for* it specifically but instead were able to take advantage of pre-existing features of the Rwandan state to implement genocide as a tactic of desperation in order to prevent the imminent loss of their own dominance within the Rwandan state formation (see especially Straus 2006, 12,

225; Mironko 2006, 164). In other words, the highly civilized-barbarized quality of the Rwandan state enabled its dominant elite to extemporaneously choose genocide as a strategic response to crisis. This crisis drew its principal energies from Rwanda's connection to wider, global networks of interdependence: the global economy and its governing institutions, the geopolitical manoeuvrings of other sovereign powers, and, ironically, the liberal-democratizing efforts of an internationally organized peace process.

By "modernizing" Rwanda's economy, the Habyarimana regime had converted a large part of the countryside from production for local consumption to production for sale on the world market. In doing so, it followed the prevailing economic orthodoxy, which affirmed that national economies should specialize in the goods and services that give them a comparative advantage. But this strategy rendered millions of Rwandans intensely dependent on the world price of coffee. In 1989 the price of coffee declined precipitously, bringing poverty like a plague to the countryside (Mamdani 2001, 147–8). In 1990 the International Monetary Fund's imposed Structural Adjustment Programme cut government subsidies to coffee farmers as a deficit-cutting measure. The government raised military spending dramatically after the October 1990 outbreak of civil war. And, with calamitous timing, a disease affecting coffee trees began to spread in some parts of the country. Income from coffee sales declined by almost four-fifths between 1985 and 1993. Gross domestic product (GDP) per capita fell by 40 per cent from 1985 to 1989 and continued to drop sharply in the early 1990s. The government devalued the currency by 67 per cent in 1990. The effects of these developments fell primarily on working people and small producers. Some areas of the country suffered drought, and "for the first time since independence, people could not afford to buy food, emergency stocks were reduced, and people died of hunger" (Jeffremovas 2002, 110).

This economic crisis, common to many African economies at the time, intersected with Rwanda's political crisis, which also had significant international dimensions. On 1 October 1990 the armed forces of the Rwandan Patriotic Front (RPF), a political organization formed by Tutsis in exile but nominally committed to the equality of Hutus and Tutsis in Rwanda, invaded Rwanda from Uganda to the north. While the RPF received support from the Ugandan government, French troops provided training to the Rwandan Defense

Force and took part in actual fighting in 1990 and 1993 (Human Rights Watch Arms Project 1994, 6). The international community provided military aid to the Rwandan government with no effective conditionality, with the exception of a threat to cut aid in March 1993, which "is widely believed to have incited the Rwandese President to resume peace talks with the RPF" (Sellström and Wohlgemuth 1996, 41). From 1989 to 1992 military spending as a portion of the GDP quadrupled (Mamdani 2001, 148). In the context of the war, the government began accumulating weapons in 1990, and over the three years prior to the genocide spent US$112 million to arm the people of Rwanda (Melvern 2000, 66–7). It paid for arms out of foreign loans obtained under the auspices of the Structural Adjustment Programme, disguising arms expenditures through fraudulent accounting, while the SAP-mandated austerity measures masked the negative impact of arms expenditures on social spending (African Rights 1995, 68). Egypt, South Africa, and France made large arms deals with Rwanda, and France and the United States provided direct military aid (Melvern 2000, 65–6; Human Rights Watch Arms Project 1994, 14–17; African Rights 1995, 67).

Peace talks between the government and the RPF took place in two rounds, the Mwanza round from October 1990 to April 1992 and the Arusha talks between May 1992 and August 1993. The United States, France, and the Organization of African Unity organized the second round, which produced the Arusha Accords, signed 4 August 1993. The accords prescribed a major structural transformation of the Rwandan state: the government would shift from a presidential to a parliamentary form, multiparty politics would be established, and Hutu Power extremists would be excluded from the new regime. The Coalition pour la Défense de la République (CDR) was formed in March 1992 out of a hard-line faction of the MRND and led the development of Hutu Power infrastructure and ideology (Prunier 1995, 128). Aside from the CDR itself, the Hutu Power leadership excluded President Habyarimana himself but included his wife, Agathe Habyarimana, Colonel Théoniste Bagosora, and other members of the *akazu* ("little house"), a network of people close to the president but not entirely loyal to him (African Rights 1995, 100–12). That the Arusha Accords proposed to exclude the Hutu Power movement from the Rwandan state therefore implied the disenfranchisement of the most powerful clique within the state. But forseeing just such an eventuality, this clique had been building up a powerful social movement in the hope of establishing its own power once and for all.

Starting in 1992, Hutu Power leaders organized a paramilitary force drawn from the youth wings of the MRND and the CDR, namely the Interahamwe ("those who stand together") and the Impuzamugambi ("those who have the same goal"), respectively (Mamdani 2001, 204), and augmented these forces with "civilian self-defense groups" formed by the government independently of the party militias (Des Forges 1999, 102; Human Rights Watch Arms Project 1994, 27). Positions of Hutu Power leaders in the highest tiers of the state meant that the distinction between these movements was never very strong, and it collapsed once the genocide began (Des Forges 1999, 228). The CDR and the militias employed two major propaganda organs to disseminate Hutu Power ideology: the newspaper *Kangura*, which was launched in mid-1990, and Radio Télévision Libre des Milles Collines (Free Radio and Television of the Thousand Hills, "thousand hills" referring to Rwanda, abbreviated as RTLMC), which began broadcasting in June 1993. *Kangura* and RTLMC issued a steady stream of anti-Tutsi propaganda that referred to the Tutsis as *inyenzi*, or "cockroaches" (a term used to refer to Tutsi commandoes since 1960) (Prunier 1995, 54), portrayed Tutsis as wanting to commit a genocide of the Hutus like the one in Burundi, and warned Hutus to be vigilant against the enemy and ready for violence. Such claims gained credibility after the assassination by Tutsi soldiers, on 21 October 1993, of the first Hutu elected president of Burundi, Melchior Ndadaye, and the subsequent massacre of tens of thousands of Hutus in that country (see Lemarchand 1998; 1994). But the Hutu Power extremists did not trust only the power of words and personal loyalties to secure their hold on sovereign power: by April 1994, "85 million tons of munitions are thought to have been distributed," including 581,000 machetes (one machete for every third adult Hutu male in Rwanda), and hundreds of thousands of hoes, axes, hammers, and razor blades (Melvern 2000, 64–5; Des Forges 1999, 127). As early as September or October 1992, the army had begun to compile lists of people said to be accomplices of the RPF, and district prefects secretly ordered burgomasters to compile lists of those who had left the country surreptitiously (Des Forges 1999, 99–100). During the genocide, RTLMC "involved the public in hunting down named individuals, directed killers where to find them and then announced their murders" (Des

Forges 1999, 206; see also African Rights 1995, 71), which suggests that these lists may have been used in the genocide.

As early as the spring of 1992, the Belgian ambassador in Kigali, Johan Swinned, reported to Brussels, "This secret group is planning the extermination of the Tutsi of Rwanda to resolve once and for all, in their own way, the ethnic problem and to crush the internal Hutu opposition" (Melvern 2000, 43). The French government may have received a similar warning even earlier.

The Genocide, 6 April to 18 July 1994

The implementation of the Rwandan genocide reveals the complexity of the processes that link macrolevel institutions with microlevel interpersonal interactions and individual motivations within a state-formation figuration. As I mentioned earlier, interviews with ordinary men and women convicted of implementing the genocide on the ground – literally, hand to hand – show a cleavage between elite and grassroots motives for killing. Analyses of the interplay between cultural identity and sovereign power (Mamdani 2001; Prunier 1995) show that the high political stakes of Hutu-Tutsi difference in the colonial and postcolonial Rwandan state enabled cunning political entrepreneurs to articulate and disseminate a cultural identity, in the form of Hutu Power, that bundled together group solidarity, anti-Tutsi hatred, and a preoccupation with state power. As in the Ottoman Empire, the identity of the (Hutu) sovereign mapped isomorphically onto the identity of the Hutu Power factionalist. More specifically, what Elias calls the "we-identity" derived its substance from a Hutu-Tutsi relation of difference that became more polarized the more effectively Tutsis were excluded from the universe of obligation. And the direct concrete importance of the state to so many people's day-to-day lives as a provider of jobs, subsidies, and personal authority connected the "we-identity" to the "I-identity" in practical terms for anyone relatively privileged by the state institution: civil servants, prefects, burgomasters and local councillors, soldiers, and their extended families.

Peasant farmers, on the other hand, did not strongly identify with their Hutu status or with Hutu Power ideology (Straus 2006, 8–9; Mironko 2006, 164). The men and women who responded to the calls issued by RTLMC and by the local administrators of the genocide, which asked them to come out to kill Tutsis face to face, did so mainly from some combination of three types of motive. First, the assassination of President Habyarimana on 6 April 1994 and the resumption of the RPF invasion of the country generated the conditions of fear and uncertainty common to wartime. The calls to "work" in the extermination of Tutsis came as calls to participate in a war effort of national self-defence. Second, participation in killing offered ordinary genocidaires opportunities for personal gain through appropriation of the goods of the murdered and through status and material rewards received from the local authorities. Third, and most significant, the Rwandan state had an exceptional infrastructure of social coercion at its disposal. A meticulous and detailed apparatus of oversight kept all levels of the Rwandan state tightly integrated. This apparatus divided the nation into ten prefectures, each prefecture into several communes headed by their burgomasters, each commune into about eleven sectors headed by *conseillers* (councillors) and each sector into about four committee-run *cellules* (cells) (Straus 2006, 68, 203). In addition, some areas implemented "a sub-*cellule* stratum called *nyumbakumi*, which refers to a semi-formal policy of having one (unpaid) official for every ten households" (Straus 2006, 203). Combined with the density of settlement in Rwanda and the lack of open spaces in which to flee the authorities, this structure of surveillance and authority gave the Rwandan state almost total administrative closure over its population. This meant that its sovereign control of the means of force could be brought to bear effectively and efficiently on every individual Rwandan. As a result, organizers of the genocide could speak with the authority of the state, and those called upon to participate usually could not evade the order without being victimized themselves.

At about 8:30 PM on 6 April 1994, President Habyarimana's airplane, also containing President Cyprien Ntaryamira of Burundi, was shot down on its approach to Kigali airport. The identity of the assassins remains a mystery (Doyle 2006), but genocide followed the assassination so quickly that its leaders seem likely suspects (Prunier 1995, 213, 222–5). RTLMC broadcast news of the assassination within half an hour, and by 9:15 PM the army and militias had set up roadblocks and begun to search houses (Prunier 1995, 223). The roadblocks limited movement and made it more difficult for persons targeted for killing to flee to safety; they also made it difficult for United Nations forces, Médecins sans Frontières workers, and other third parties to interfere with the implementation of the genocide.

Almost immediately, state forces began a "selective assassination of opposition politicians, of which most were Hutu from parties opposing the party in power" (Sellström and Wohlgemuth 1996, 51). The assassins also targeted dissenting civilians, both Hutus and Tutsis. Once the political opposition was out of the way, the genocidaires moved on to the generalized massacre of Tutsis throughout the country.

The killers began by targeting Tutsi men and boys, including even infant male children, and also educated men and women, while inflicting torture and rape on women, including young girls. As the genocide progressed, killing expanded to include men and women alike (Jones 2002). As Alison Liebhafsky Des Forges documents, the mass killing itself unfolded in three stages. Starting from "the middle of the first week of the genocide," killers drove Tutsis out of their homes to public sites such as churches, schools, offices, and so on, where they were "massacred in large-scale operations." "Towards the end of April," authorities ordered the strategy of "pacification" in order to decrease the visibility of the genocide; large-scale killings halted in many areas, and perpetrators brought their victims into custody and then murdered them there. This also functioned as a way of luring Tutsis out of hiding. "By mid-May, the authorities ordered the final phase, that of tracking down the last surviving Tutsi" (Des Forges 1999, 9–10). These killings targeted those who had hidden successfully so far; those who had so far been spared because of age, gender, or status in their communities; and, in the face of the RPF advance, those who could testify about the genocide.

In the early days of the genocide, killers worked in small bands and killed their victims "where they found them" (Des Forges 1999, 209). But as potential victims fled to what they perceived as places of refuge, particularly churches, schools, hospitals, and government offices, the genocidaires used these as sites of mass killing. Beginning on 11 April, the government encouraged people to go to these places with the expectation of safety, while rounding up the unwilling and forcing them into these places of false refuge (Des Forges 1999, 210). In some cases, the genocidaires simply bulldozed these sites to kill the people inside (Des Forges 1999, 211). In some places the armed forces used artillery on crowds of people, as when a group of thousands gathered at Amahoro Stadium in Kigali under protection of the United Nations Assistance Mission in Rwanda (UNAMIR) (African Rights 1995, 724–5). Perpetrators assumed that anyone wounded was a Tutsi, so bands of executioners entered hospitals, shot patients, and massacred medical staff (Prunier 1995, 254).

The order of the genocide emanated from the central government in Kigali and travelled through all levels of the state administrative apparatus: "The killers were controlled and directed in their task by the civil servants in the central government, *préfets, bourgmestres* and local councilors, both in the capital and in the interior. It was they who received the orders from Kigali, mobilised the local *Gendarmerie* and *Interahamwe*, ordered the peasants to join in the man-hunts and called for FAR [Forces Armées Rwandaises, or Rwandan Armed Forces] support if the victims put up too much resistance" (Prunier 1995, 244). But despite the key role played by bureaucratic organization, the massacres in Rwanda bore little resemblance to the faceless and impersonal killings of the Nazi holocaust that Zygmunt Bauman analyzes. For example, in the case of the massacre at the École Technique Officielle at Kicukiro (in Kigali), soldiers initiated the killing by firing and throwing grenades into the crowd, then the militia "came in and started with the machetes, hammers, knives and spears" (Melvern 2000, 3–4). This pattern appeared in many of the large-scale massacres: soldiers from the army or the Presidential Guard would begin things by shooting and using grenades, militias armed with hand-to-hand weapons would carry out the bulk of the killing, and soldiers would reappear if the militias started to flag or encountered resistance. African Rights notes that "One of the most common methods of killing was hacking with a machete. The killers often wielded their weapons in ways designed to inflict the maximum pain on the victim before death ensued ... Such was the fear of the machete that many killers were able to extort money out of their victims-to-be by demanding payment for the privilege of being killed with a bullet – a much quicker and less painful way to die" (African Rights 1995, 629). Even considering the brutality of the routine killing practices, many perpetrators committed acts of astonishing cruelty, including systematically mutilating the face, limbs, and genitals of victims before killing them, burning victims alive, throwing people into pit latrines and burying them alive, and forcing people to kill their family members and loved ones (African Rights 1995, 624–41). One UNAMIR officer remarked: "I had seen war before, but I had never seen a woman carrying a baby on her back kill another woman with a baby on her back" (quoted in Des Forges 1999, 261). (Nevertheless, women and children more usually engaged in pillaging and destruction of property than in direct killing.) The genocidaires inflicted rape, torture, and sexual mutilation on women and girls and sometimes sold them into sexual slavery (African Rights 1995, 748ff; see also Totten 2009). At least 250,000 women suffered rape during the genocide (Amnesty International 2004, 3). Because at least 35 per cent of Rwanda's soldiers were HIV-positive before the genocide, an estimated 70 per cent of the survivors of genocidal rape have HIV/AIDS (Jones 2002, 82; Amnesty International 2004, 3).

At peak efficiency, the rate of killing by militias reached 1,000 persons every twenty minutes (Melvern 2000, 5). Philip Gourevitch claims that "the dead of Rwanda accumulated at nearly three times the rate of Jewish dead during the Holocaust. It was the most efficient mass killing since the atomic bombings of Hiroshima and Nagasaki" (Gourevitch 1998, 3). The number of persons killed is not easy to determine, partly because it is not clear how many Tutsis there were in Rwanda to begin with. Human Rights Watch conservatively estimates that "at least half a million persons were killed in the genocide, a loss that represented about three quarters of the Tutsi population of Rwanda" (Des Forges 1999, 16). Gérard Prunier estimates 800,000 to 850,000 killed, 86 per cent of the Tutsi population of Rwanda and 11 per cent of the total Rwandan population (Prunier 1995, 261–5).

All scholarly and NGO observers agree on the highly organized quality of the killings; Prunier (1995, 242) notes that the efficiency with which they were carried out testifies to careful advance preparation. Claims that killings were spontaneous, tribal, irrepressible, and chaotic came from the perpetrators themselves, being a deliberate tactic used to conceal what was going on, to forestall international involvement (African Rights 1995, 250–4), and to facilitate recruitment for the genocide within the Rwandan population (Des Forges 1999, 252–60).[7] At the same time, however, "the genocide was not a killing machine that rolled inexorably forward but rather a campaign to which participants were recruited over time and by the use of threat and incentives" (Des Forges 1999, 6). Among other devices, the genocidaires took advantage of the historical practice of compulsory collective labour, going back to the uburetwa tradition

---

7 These disinformation tactics resemble those used by Holocaust deniers (see Prunier 1995, 241).

in precolonial Rwanda, and of the postcolonial state's conduct of "campaigns of various kinds" that operated "through the existing administrative and political hierarchies, requiring agents to go beyond their usual duties for a limited period of time for some national goal of major importance" (Des Forges 1999, 222):

> In the past, the Rwandan government had often mobilized the population for campaigns of various kinds, such as to end illiteracy, to vaccinate children, or to improve the status of women ... The organizers of the genocide similarly exploited the structures that already existed – administrative, political, and military – and called upon personnel to execute a campaign to kill Tutsi and Hutu presumed to oppose Hutu Power. Through these three channels, the organizers were able to reach all Rwandans and to incite or force most Hutu into acquiescing in or participating in the slaughter. (Des Forges 1999, 222)

The genocidaires thereby used existing administrative, political, and military structures in order to pressure the entire Rwandan Hutu population either to participate actively or to acquiesce passively in the slaughter.

Every aspect of Rwandan society made active contributions to the genocide: the military and the National Police; political leaders at every level; civil servants in the central government, prefects, burgomasters, and local councillors; Radio Rwanda and RTLMC; the Anglican Church, from Archbishop Augustin Nshamihigo to local pastors; academics in the university system; private business owners; members of the militias; and ordinary Rwandans, mostly those living in poverty but also many who were not, including women and even children (Des Forges 1999, 223, 226–8, 231, 234–5, 241–2, 244, 246, 248, 261; Prunier 1995, 244; see also McCullum 1995; Rittner, Roth, and Whitworth 2004). These contributions included helping to legitimate killing, providing logistical and material support, helping to locate and identify victims, and direct killing. Although estimates of the number of perpetrators have ranged from tens of thousands to 3 million, a careful and empirically based investigation indicates that about two hundred thousand Rwandans participated in the genocide (Straus 2004).

Some Rwandans opposed the genocide, including the prefect of Butare, the Tutsi Jean-Baptiste Habyarimana (no relation to the president). Killing in Butare prefecture did not begin until 20 April, when the government removed Habyarimana from his office and replaced him with the extremist Sylvain Ndikumana (Prunier 1995, 244). Human Rights Watch notes that "Tens of thousands of Hutu refused to join the killing campaign and saved Tutsi lives. Hundreds of thousands more disapproved of the genocide but did nothing to oppose it or to help its victims. They did not answer the call of the local cell leader but neither did they respond to the cries of Tutsi in distress" (Des Forges 1999, 262). Indeed, in commune after commune, genocide happened only after "the president's assassination and the resumption of war ruptured the preexisting order, creating a feeling of intense crisis and uncertainty in local communities" and only after "a play for power *among Hutus*," in which Hutu Power extremists struggled against resistance, sometimes very determined, from Hutus opposed to committing genocide (Straus 2006, 65–6, original emphasis). In Giti commune, the burgomaster Eduard Sebushumba and his councillors agreed to oppose any escalation toward violence and on 8 April arrested youths who had slaughtered Tutsis' cattle, perceiving (correctly) that such acts left unpunished would serve as a step toward murderous violence (Straus 2006, 86–7). Giti commune held out against an external attack from neighbouring Murambi commune and was just starting to crumble when RPF soldiers arrived in the area on 9 April. Despite the manifold horrors of the genocide, "it was also a time of undisputed heroism by people who expected no reward but the satisfaction of a clear conscience" (Prunier 1995, 259).

Colonel Théoniste Bagosora, director of services in the Ministry of Defence and the architect of the provisional government that took power following the assassination of President Habyarimana, acted as the chief organizer of the genocide. Bagosora was a central figure in the Hutu Power movement and a founding member of the CDR (Prunier 1995, 240–2; Des Forges 1999, 223). Still, the genocide was not his brainchild, nor was he the sole instigator. African Rights, discussing those responsible for the genocide, spends twelve pages discussing other genocidaires before turning to Bagosora and other military figures, listing first the members of the akazu, especially Agathe Habyarimana, along with members of the interim government and other politicians (African Rights 1995, 100–12).

In sum, then, the Rwandan genocide did *not* result from ancient and primal tribal antagonisms, held in check by a fragile modern state, that had burst their bonds and run rampant when this state failed. Entirely the contrary: the strength of the Rwandan state, notably its power to transform individual subjectivity, produced for Hutu elites a strong sense of identity and solidarity and enabled these elites to efficiently mobilize a great mass of ordinary Hutus who had no direct say or stake in the exercise of sovereign authority. A faction of politicians, business owners, and military and administrative officials seized control of the state following the president's assassination. This faction implemented genocide as a strategy to prevent the power-sharing arrangement mandated by the Arusha Accords by eliminating the populations that stood to benefit the most from this arrangement. If the Rwandan state had not lost the civil war, it could have succeeded in establishing a new political culture based on Hutu nationalism, echoing the Ittihadists success in Turkey. Furthermore, sovereign authority provided the means for committing the genocide. The active participation of the civil service and official administrative structures at all levels of government resolved the immense logistical challenge of mounting a nationwide campaign of systematic massacre, and the coercive power of the state enabled the enrolment of masses of ordinary Hutu Rwandans who had not yet bought into Hutu Power ideology. We could say that in Rwanda the *regime* was weak even though the *state* was strong. This combination of a weak regime in a strong state may serve as one of the early warning signs of genocide in the making.

But what of the civilizing process as a whole – that is, the system of interrelated and interdependent sovereignties? How did the torchbearers of Western civilization respond to such a naked and bloodthirsty "barbarism"?

The UN, the RPF, and the End of the Genocide

In June 1993 the UN Security Council created the United Nations Observer Mission Uganda-Rwanda (UNOMUR), with General Roméo Dallaire of Canada as its commander (Melvern 2000, 243–8). Dallaire arrived in Kigali with a reconnaissance mission in August, roughly as the Arusha Accords were being signed. In October, Security Council resolution 872 upgraded the observer mission to the United Nations Assistance Mission in Rwanda. By November, UNAMIR was brought up to its mandated strength of 2,548 troops

(Melvern 2000, 89). Dallaire had asked for a minimum of 4,500. Linda Melvern says, "How half-hearted was the UN's effort for Rwanda was plain to see. Dallaire lacked the barest essentials. He was reduced to borrowing petty cash from another UN agency. He lacked everything from ammunition to sandbags, fuel, and barbed wire. The mission lacked essential personnel; there was no public affairs officer, legal adviser, humanitarian or human rights expert" (Melvern 2000, 85). In December, UNAMIR peacekeepers occupied their designated positions throughout Rwanda, with a contingent in Kigali, as per the Arusha Accords. On 11 January 1994 Dallaire informed UN headquarters in New York that an informant within the Hutu Power movement had warned him of preparations for genocide and had told him of the locations of hidden weapons stockpiles. Dallaire tried to persuade his superiors to allow him to conduct arms seizures, but the UN headquarters in New York denied his requests. On 5 April 1994 Security Council resolution 909 renewed the mandate for UNAMIR but with a threat to pull out in six weeks unless the Arusha Accords were obeyed. Until the genocide was well underway, the United Nations treated UNAMIR as a peacekeeping force intended to help facilitate the Arusha peace process, without significant consideration given to the possibility that Rwandan civilians needed protection from their own government.

On 7 April, the day after Habyarimana's assassination, Rwandan soldiers in Kigali captured and then executed ten Belgian peacekeeper soldiers. On 10 April, Dallaire requested a reinforcement of 5,000 soldiers, with which he believed he could put an end to the massacres (Melvern 2000, 146). The next day, Belgian peacekeepers withdrew from the École Technique Officielle at Kicukiro (in Kigali), leaving behind 2,000 defenseless civilians; within "literally two minutes," militias moved in and began killing (Melvern 2000, 1–4; African Rights 1995, 1113). The Belgian force, approximately 400 troops, left Rwanda by 20 April. Throughout the genocide, UNAMIR lacked essentials: water, fuel, ammunition, medical supplies, and so on. Only a few governments, including Canada's, provided very limited support, which enabled UNAMIR to keep from collapsing entirely (Melvern 2000, 233). On 22 April, Security Council resolution 912 ordered the withdrawal of all but 270 peacekeepers from Rwanda, mandating the remnant to secure a ceasefire between the Rwandan army and the RPF (Melvern 2000, 174).

Dallaire, with Brigadier Henry Kwami Anyidoho of Ghana and his troops, defied the order; 456 soldiers remained. On 4 May, nearly a month after mass killings began, UN Secretary General Boutros Boutros-Ghali made his first public use of the word "genocide" to refer to events in Rwanda. On 17 May, Security Council resolution 918 approved the deployment of 5,500 troops, but without making available any actual troops, transportation, or plan. In late May the United States, which owed the UN more than US$1 billion in back dues, charged US$4 million for the use of forty-eight armoured personnel carriers plus another US$6 million for transport; the vehicles arrived in Entebbe without radios or machineguns, making them useless (Melvern 2000, 196). On 6 June, Security Council resolution 925 extended UNAMIR's mandate until December. On 17 June, France announced a plan to deploy its own troops, free of charge, as an interim peacekeeping force. The United States and Boutros-Ghali supported the plan. Under the title Operation Turquoise, French troops entered Rwanda through Zaire on 21 June and by 5 July had established control of a "safe zone" in southwest Rwanda. However, by this time the RPF had conquered most of the country, and the most notable effect of the safe zone was to enable genocidaires, and Hutus afraid of the RPF, to flee into Zaire, with calamitous long-term consequences for the region. The Rwandan civil war ended with an RPF victory on 18 July, and on 16 August, Dallaire left Rwanda, succeeded by General Guy Tousignant of Canada. At this point, UNAMIR still had only 1,624 soldiers.

In a sense, the genocide was only an opening act for the much larger cataclysm that followed (Prunier 2009). The Rwandans who had fled into Zaire, some 2 million strong, formed expatriate communities from which Hutu Power leaders could launch attempts to destabilize the RPF government in postgenocide Rwanda in the hope of regaining control of Rwandan sovereignty. In 1996 the intervention in to Zairian territory by the Rwandan armed forces began a chain of events that would involve eight sovereign states and over twenty-five armed groups in "Africa's world war." This war lasted nearly eight years and claimed nearly 4 million lives, five times the number of the Rwandan genocide, partly through direct killing but mostly because of the destruction of people's homes, their crops, and the whole infrastructure of human survival (Prunier 2009, 338).

The Shame of the West

An assessment by the Carnegie Commission on Preventing Deadly Conflict, the Institute for the Study of Diplomacy at Georgetown University, and the United States Army found that "a force with air support, logistics and communications would have prevented the slaughter of half a million people" if deployed between 7 and 21 April and that "US forces, backed by air power, could have protected Rwandan civilians with little or no risk to US soldiers" (Melvern 2000, 147). In the actual course of events, the genocide ended only in territory occupied by the advancing armed forces of the RPF and, to a lesser extent, by Operation Turquoise. However, the RPF itself committed mass killings during its takeover of the country. These killings appear to have been serious, although less extensive and systematic than the state-perpetrated genocide. A 1999 Human Rights Watch report accuses the RPF of the "indiscriminate massacre of individuals and groups, bearing no arms, and posing no threat to them" and of the summary execution of selected individuals. The report estimates that these killings claimed between twenty-five and thirty thousand lives from April to July 1994 (Des Forges 1999, 734). In his memoir of the genocide, General Roméo Dallaire accuses Paul Kagame, leader of the RPF, of refusing to accelerate his own military campaign after the scale of the genocide had become clear (Dallaire and Beardsley 2003, 515).

Why did the United Nations and the international community fail so completely to prevent or halt the Rwandan genocide? Subsequent analyses have pointed to a range of particular interests that prevented each of the significantly involved nation-states from recognizing the genocide until too late: for Belgium, protecting and evacuating its own citizens in Rwanda; for both Belgium and France, maintaining the remnants of their neocolonial influence over African politics; for the United States, avoiding an entanglement like the one in Somalia that had recently cost nineteen American soldiers their lives at the Battle of Mogadishu; and so on (Melvern 2000; Power 2002; Ferroggiaro 2001). In addition, the bureaucratic structure of the United Nations worked against the swift fulfilment of moral responsibility by translating ethical issues into technical dilemmas, diluting personal responsibility, and establishing a great social distance between decision makers at the top of the hierarchy and Rwandans affected by UN action or inaction (Barnett 2002). Scott Straus suggests that clear evidence of planning for mass killing is rare and sets too high a threshold of recognition for genocides in the making (Straus 2006, 240); the evidence that Dallaire found and reported to his superiors clearly showed preparation for genocide but arguably did not show a specific purpose or intent. Dallaire himself observes that the official mandate of UNAMIR was to keep the peace established by the Arusha Accords and that after the assassination of Habyarimana and the outbreak of civil war, his superiors intimated that UNAMIR's mandate had evaporated (Dallaire and Beardsley 2003).

Taken together, these various factors highlight different aspects of a common problem: impunity in international relations. Like Ottoman Armenians, Rwandan Tutsis participated in a highly one-sided relation with an international network of sovereign powers (which in the Rwandan case also included the pseudo-meta-sovereign power of the United Nations). In both instances, the members of this network partly competed and partly cooperated with one another to enrol the concerns of a threatened minority for their own purposes, which centred on the question of Rwanda's own sovereign authority. Tutsis mattered to this network (the misleadingly designated "international community") because the fraught Hutu-Tutsi relationship threatened to destabilize the Rwandan state. With their attention focused squarely on the question of sovereignty, the interested foreign powers were blind to the intensifying movement toward genocide and remained wilfully blind to it even after the dam had burst. Like Ottoman Armenians, Rwandan Tutsis could not hold the other foreign powers – or, in the latter's case, the UN – accountable for failing to guarantee their safety.

Interdependence and Impunity in Rwanda

Posthumously, the unquiet dead of Rwanda's genocide have exacted a measure of accountability. The magnitude of the killing, its evident racialist logic, and its overt similarity to the events of the Nazi holocaust struck a severe blow to the moral legitimacy claimed by each of those parties that failed in Rwanda to fulfil the promise made after the Second World War, "never again." This failure wounded the idealized self-image of the West, which the term "civilization" expresses. Figurational theory suggests that such failures will produce a sense of shame for those subjects who both identify with the ideals of the West and face up to the discrepancy between these ideals and the actuality. Certainly, a strong note of shame runs through accounts of Rwanda written by figures such as Roméo Dallaire, Peter Uvin, or Linda Melvern, people heavily invested, in their differing ways, in the Sisyphean effort of making Western civilization live up to its ideals. Perhaps this kind of shame works, above and beyond the practical exigencies of establishing political stability and the opportunism of transnational governmental entrepreneurship, as a motive force behind the establishment of the International Criminal Tribunal for Rwanda. But if shame results from the internalization of an image of oneself that casts oneself in a negative light, then, tautologically, an entire collective subject cannot become ashamed of itself on the basis of norms that it itself has produced. In a dominant group, shame for the crimes and failures of the group can only move through circuits marginal or opposed to the main concentrations of power. Perhaps this is why the ICTR, despite the impressive resources behind it, has proven so profoundly inadequate to the task it has set itself (regarding these inadequacies, see for example Lemarchand 2009, 496), or why the UN's failure in Rwanda has helped to justify a very problematic enthusiasm for "armed humanitarian intervention," justified by the doctrine of Responsibility to Protect (ICISS 2001; see also Marchak 2008, 6, 33ff), with strong neoimperialist overtones (see for example Fenton 2005; Mégret 2009; Nicholls 2009).

In any case, the inability or unwillingness of the United Nations, and of the United States, France, and Belgium in particular, to intervene military to prevent or halt the killing in Rwanda constitutes only the most overt sense in which the Eurocentric civilizing process engendered this genocide. Likewise, the question of personal moral culpability only addresses a small part of the complex figurational dynamics that made genocide possible. Through colonialism, the forward movement of the civilizing process subsumed and greatly intensified processes of violent différance, or deferentiation, that Nyiginyan state formation had already set in motion by establishing "Hutu" and "Tutsi" as terms differentiating dominated from dominating subjects. To the differential honour, political power, economic wealth, and freedom from obligation to labour that distinguished Tutsis from Hutus on the basis of their location in the social order, European colonizers added the race privilege implied by the Hamitic hypothesis, bureaucratically codified by the Belgians in permanent records of identity and used to assign Tutsis to government positions while imposing forced labour on Hutus. Decolonization exchanged the places of Hutus and Tutsis but did little to mitigate either the symbolic or actual violence of the relation between them, as the post-colonial political elites invested heavily in the maintenance of Hutu-Tutsi distinction to secure their own continued dominance within the Rwandan state figuration. When civil war and internationally brokered peace negotiations threatened this dominance, a faction of Rwanda's governing party formed a broad social alliance capable of commanding or coercing grassroots participation in mass murder and used international aid money and arms deals to accumulate means of violence conducive to the task. The president's assassination provided the opportunity for the use of genocide as a partly planned, partly extemporaneous strategy of desperation. Even after the RPF victory and the end of the genocide within Rwanda, the solidarity engendered through shared participation in collective violence and shared exclusion from the new Rwandan polity kept Hutu Power alive as a political force, catalyzing a regional war that would eventually claim over five times as many lives as the genocide itself.

None of this resulted from a weakness or breakdown of state institutions; "'anarchy' and state collapse do not characterize what happened in Rwanda" (Straus 2006, 234). Rather, this course of events gained its energy from the centripetal accretion of force by sovereign states, including the competition between states for relative dominance, feeding back through the formation of individual subjectivity to invest identity-difference relations with partially deferred violence. The civilizing process in Rwanda produced both social interdependence and impunity. When faced with the loss of their political dominance, a social elite commanding the institutional and material means to ignite a holocaust perceived that they had more to gain than they had to lose from severing the last, weak ties of moral reciprocity that connected them to their Others. As the temptations of impunity overpowered the constraints of interdependence, deferred violence actualized itself as hell on earth.

Conclusion

Everywhere in the world where knowledge is being suppressed, knowledge
that, if it were made known, would shatter our image of the world and
force us to question ourselves – everywhere there, *Heart of Darkness*
is being enacted. You already know that. So do I. It is not knowledge we
lack. What is missing is the courage to understand what we know and
draw conclusions.

Lindqvist 1996, 179

CONTRADICTION AND HOPE

The advantage of a radical systemic explanation of genocide is that
it explains, without recourse to moralizing homilies about human
nature, why genocide is so widespread and why it can coalesce out
of a seemingly normal society like a summer thunderstorm out of a
clear blue sky. One disadvantage with this way of explaining, as of
all structural explanations of pernicious phenomena, is that the task
of change can seem impossibly discouraging. If the possibility of
genocide lies implicit in the very order of things, we would seem
fated to endure this possibility, for who has the strength to overturn
the order of the world? Against this pessimism, figurational sociology asserts that the one inevitability of human existence is change.
Social structures are themselves patterns of motion, not static things,
and visibly or invisibly they are always fluid, unstable, temporary.
The direction of change is not given, but the fact of it is. To this
circumstance, radical sociology adds that social contradictions generate the conditions of their own overcoming. If the genocidal
propensity of Western civilization seems to us an intolerable monstrosity, this reaction is also itself a product of the same civilization.
Norbert Elias (2000) was not wrong to perceive that the civilizing
process generates pacified social spaces and fosters opportunities for

humane, empathetic conduct between persons. Eurocentric barbaric civilization has generated colonialism and slavery but also movements to abolish these institutions; it produces genocide but also global human rights movements and the very concept of "genocide" as something criminal. "The strong *are* sometimes constrained from doing what they have the power to do – or at least from doing it as and when they wish" (Jones 2004a, 8, original emphasis). Elias failed only to perceive the awful connections between the pacification of the counts of Toulouse and the extermination of the Cathars, just as he would have failed to perceive the connections between the civility of British governors concerned to civilize the Natives and the violent erasure of Tasmanian identity, or between the modernization of Rwanda's economy through its incorporation into ever-lengthening chains of economic interdependence and the stockpiling of machetes in church basements. The freedom to be civil comes at a cost, and this cost is not paid by those who enjoy the benefit. Yet, knowing of these connections, a civil people cannot go on calling themselves civil without expanding the scope of their civility to include the Others of civilization. A sense of oneself as good, moral, and worthy might originate in relations of exclusion and deferentiation, and persist happily as long as this exclusion remains taken for granted as natural and inevitable, but once the contingency and ultimate arbitrariness of these relations become apparent, a civil subject has several choices: to retreat into denial, to abandon claims to worthiness, or to make good the claim by working to ensure that no person is left or pushed outside the universe of moral obligation – a work performed not out of altruism but as an authentic expression of the desire to realize one's self.

If and when the impulse to erase the limits of moral obligation finds its practical realization in a nongenocidal global society, fundamental changes will have taken place in the basic social relations that organize everyday/everynight life as well as in the centralized institutions of such a society. It is not as though one must revolutionize society, and *then* the problem of genocide will be solved. The work of preventing genocide entails a labour of social transformation, converting relations of deferentiation, in which the flow of power is fixed in one direction, into relations of reciprocal interdependence, in which power flows freely between both partners. Every social struggle that tends to this end – human rights, disarmament, feminism, anticolonialism, labour, ecology, queer liberation, antiracism, and countless other movements against oppression – helps to undermine the conditions that make genocide possible. Conversely, because genocide so viciously negates opportunities for egalitarian social transformation and entrenches local hierarchies, its effective prevention helps to secure the space for social justice and personal freedom.

The means by which this change will take place (if it takes place) are not something that can be predicted by science. As Bruno Latour writes, of quite another context, "If they were foreseeable, they would already have been used by an opposing power" (Latour 1988, 229). In social struggle, one cannot draw an objective map of the field because all such maps, if they are any good, immediately get incorporated into the field as a tool of struggle; the best one can hope for is to think one or two steps ahead of the social forces against which one contends. Any particular work of social science inevitably favours one side or another, depending on what it reveals and to whom.

UNANSWERED QUESTIONS

Among books written by academics, there are those that aim to cap off a line of inquiry and present the last word on its subject; there are those that aim to take an existing line of investigation and carry it ten yards farther down the field; there are those that aim to make known to many what is already well known to a few; and there are those that attempt to call into question existing categories of inquiry and raise entirely new questions. This book belongs in the first category not at all and in the second, third, and fourth to increasing degrees. I have attempted to advance the field of genocide studies by offering a theoretical framework for making comparisons among different genocides, connecting them to each other via a global but historically specific social figuration: the Western civilizing process. In making my case, I have presented narratives about some lesser-known episodes in the expansion of this process and retold the stories of some of the better-known. Most of all, I have wanted to call into question the automatic assumption that civilization is everywhere and always a good thing and to raise troubling questions about the connections between the centralization of the means of violence, the personal investment of civilized subjects in normative codes of conduct that anchor themselves in state sovereignty, and those moments when identity-difference relations become so intense and so dichotomized as to enable attempts at the organized or systematic obliteration of one group by another.

My argument remains partly speculative; although it is possible to document the correlations and connections between the expansion of the system of sovereign states and the near-obliteration of marginalized or colonized identity-groups, many unanswered questions remain about the specific dynamics of the various forms of habitus within this process. There are many questions about the sociology of the body that have not so far been investigated by genocide scholars: what effects does state formation have on people's ways of standing, of walking, of making or not making eye contact, on their smiles, their tears, their modes of dress, on the foods they eat, how they smell, their sense of time, on the rituals of greeting, conversation, and leave-taking? The observations that John Howard Griffin (1977) obtained by transforming himself from a white man into a black man in the American South under segregation only hint at the rich potential for empirical investigation into deferentiation as an embodied material relation. What effects do relations of deferentiation have on the pattern of people's emotions: their assertiveness and submissiveness, their pride and shame, their anxieties, angers, desires? How do these habits manifest in genocidal discourse, in the speech acts and gestures and practices through which victims are pushed outside the universe of moral obligation? How do stigma and stereotype express and reinforce something felt deeply in the body, felt differently by oppressor and oppressed? And how are such feelings sharpened, intensified, through rituals or rites of passage or acts of collective effervescence, to enable otherwise ordinary individuals to become killers, torturers, rapists, despoilers of culture, kidnappers of children, immune to the pleas and cries of victims? In sum, how are the habits and dispositions cultivated in ordinary life as part of civil behaviour mobilized in genocidal situations? Some of these questions have been investigated in genocide or human rights literature;[1] some have been studied but not connected to genocide; some remain open to inquiry. The prospects – for adding to our

---

1 The Recovery of Historical Memory Project (1999), for example, examines the rites of passage through which recruits to Guatemalan death squads were socialized in progressive stages to be able to commit ever-greater atrocities; this account shows how such rituals work on the body to change its habitual responses in order to make possible and easy actions that before were impossible or at least very difficult. Frantz Fanon's (1963) account of a torturer who believed in the appropriateness of his actions but was nevertheless haunted by them shows how such transformations can remain incomplete.

understanding of the mechanisms of genocide while adding to our
total stock of knowledge about human social life – are exciting.

RETHINKING RATIONALITY

Among books written by academics with an activist orientation,
most have one or both of two complementary aims: to raise consciousness about an issue and to prescribe a solution to a problem.
As efforts to contribute to egalitarian social change, these strategies
have a long and distinguished history, but they do have their limitations, and the analysis in this book suggests something about the
structural bases of these limitations. To seek to raise consciousness
as a means of change invites the questions: whose consciousness,
and why would a change in consciousness lead to a change in action? On the other hand, for a scientist to prescribe specific solutions
or to argue in favour of a specific program falls into the pattern of
"intellectual as legislator." Zygmunt Bauman (1987) has analyzed
this form of intellectual practice as belonging to a modernist ethos
that makes two very large assumptions: truth is ultimately the same
for everyone and reason operates in the same way everywhere.
Although I am not convinced of the strength of "modernity" and
"postmodernity" as sociological categories, I share postmodernists'
skepticism – or "incredulity," as Jean-François Lyotard puts it (1984)
– toward the assumption, so dear to Western civilization, that human
reason operates in such a way that truth can be established independently of local and contingent social relations. A critical figurational
analysis of the barbarizing-civilizing process suggests another, more
problematic view of reason, consciousness, and action.

If we think of social structures in terms of a vertically ordered
hierarchical scheme of emergence, then states exist as *macro* structures that determine the *micro* interactions *below* them. In such a
scheme, higher determines lower, and consciousness, being a higher-
order phenomenon, determines lower-order phenomena. In sociologies that treat consciousness as determinant, from Henri de Saint-Simon
and Auguste Comte through to Emile Durkheim, Talcott Parsons,
Jürgen Habermas, and beyond, the unity of truth can be understood
without recourse to metaphysics as deriving from the functional
unity of the social organism – and the universality of truth as deriving from the inevitable eventual formation of a functionally integrated world-society. Social institutions express the shared values

and ideas of society, and the best way to change society is by changing its consciousness – changing its mind, as it were. The state, being the one higher-order institution that encompasses the whole of social life, is the site par excellence for the functioning of this consciousness; Durkheim actually calls the state "the organ of social thought" (Durkheim 1992, 81–4). So to change the structures of a modern, democratic society, the best strategy would be to change the consciousness of the electorate, which is understood as not being differentiated by radical social contradictions; this electorate will empower the state to take action and implement the solution.

For activists whose vision of social freedom includes social equality, this approach made sense as long as Keynesian economics and welfare-state liberalism or social democracy were ascendant in the richest countries at the core of the world-system. Since the rise to dominance of neoliberalism, however, states have pursued policies that actively increase inequality between rich and poor both within and between countries; consequently, egalitarian-minded activists are increasingly interested in strategies that rely less heavily on state-based redistributive measures for their success. At the same time, social struggles have themselves become increasingly diverse. In feminism, for example, the rise since the 1970s of antiracist, queer, and Third World (or Majority World) feminisms have recontextualized supposedly universal truths about women as local and contingent truths about white, heterosexual, First World women. This increased complexity calls for visions of social transformation that do not rely on a consensus of values, tactics, or even objectives within the movement.

If, instead of thinking of social structures hierarchically, we think of them as a laterally ordered dynamic network of interpersonal relations, then states and the social hierarchies they involve appear not as emergent macrostructures looming above the microworld of individuals' interactions but as topological features of the network of these interactions: knots and nexuses and stable currents in the flow of social exchanges. If the sovereign state appears as a leviathan, as a figure-writ-large of the sovereign individual, it is because both are products of the same figuration. The figure of the individual human subject, possessing definite boundaries, conceived primarily in isolation and only secondarily in relation to others, engaged in endless struggles to preserve its integrity against centrifugal forces within it and invasive forces outside it, emerges through the same relational process of violent différance as do sovereign states. A relationship of isomorphism, or self-similarity, obtains between the two types of structures, which exist not at different vertical levels of analysis but at differing horizontal degrees of scale. And so it makes intuitive sense that the state, being an individual-writ-large, must have the sort of coherent mind that we attribute to individuals, must – if it works properly – express the collective thought and the collective will of its constituent members. Except that, in a radically critical relational view, neither individuals nor states have the coherence that functionalism attributes to them. They are fractured not only by endlessly various and contingent conflicts of interest but also by systemic and hence fundamental contradictions: of class, of sex-gender, of force. These contradictory relations mean that individuals produce their own oppression in the very practices by which they seek to realize their own freedom, and they engender latent but irreconcilable oppositions of interests within the social order. They produce their own fractured truths: with contradictory social relations, what is rational to believe and what can be socially established as true are not the same for everybody, not even under the best possible circumstances.

If we leave aside both metaphysical and functionalist conceptions of reason, what is there to go on? A relational sociology foregrounds the importance of *identification* to reasoning understood as a social process. A conspicuous feature of the process of rational persuasion is the identity that it establishes between interlocutors. Being persuaded by you, I come to think as you do; we come to be *of the same mind*, as the saying goes. Rationality means that, if we are both rational beings, the conclusion you have reached before we begin to argue is the same conclusion that I would have reached if I had been exposed to the same evidence you had; argument, especially scientific argument, involves sharing with me the experiences that led you to your conclusion, on the assumption that – everything else being equal – they will have the same effect on me. And if I come to trust that what you say is true without calling for proof in every instance, it is because I am convinced that you think as I do, that an identity obtains between the workings of our minds even though their contents are different, such that faced with information that I do not have access to and choices I am not empowered to make, you make those that I would make in your place. (So, for instance, it is not stupid for voters to demand that candidates for office should seem to be like themselves rather than merely experienced and capable; it is a rationally intelligible demand, even though it often leads to bad outcomes.)

This description refers to reason as it is idealized; in practice, it is a good deal more messy. If I have to convince someone without recourse to direct force, I depend on dynamic structures already operating "within" their subjectivity: words, concepts, prior knowledge, dispositions, as well as criteria for judging the rightness and wrongness of claims. If these a priori conditions are established through social relations, I cannot count on them to operate reliably in every instance. If I present an argument, for instance, that the earth is round or that Guaraní are human beings, and if this argument is perfect according to the locally established rules of rationality, even then what is there to prevent my interlocutor from ignoring these rules and refusing to be persuaded? This is a question for empirical research, but a few possibilities come to mind: the listener may have an interest in agreeing with the thesis of my argument; the listener may not have the impunity to disregard what I say but may depend on my goodwill in some respect; breaking the rules of rationality may entail too painful a violation of the listener's identity, of who one is to oneself and/or to some community of bystanders. These are social conditions and so subject to failure. This corresponds with historical experience: it is not possible rationally to persuade oppressors to abandon their oppression as long as the conditions of interest, impunity, and identity-difference continue to be met. Reason alone cannot overcome the contradictions that exist in practical social relations. If it could, it would not be necessary for oppressed peoples to engage in organized social struggle against relations of inequality.

GETTING OVER CIVILIZATION

Not legislating solutions is one thing; practical inapplicability is another. What does a critical figurational theory of Eurocentric barbaric civilization imply for a successful action to abolish genocide?

One immediate implication is a skepticism toward international law and armed humanitarian intervention as an effective and sufficient global remedy for genocide. As the history of the 1948 United Nations Convention on the Prevention and Punishment of the Crime of Genocide shows abundantly, states very often do not obey their own laws; in principle, we should expect that they do so when it serves their self-perceived interest to do so and not otherwise. Within the barbarizing-civilizing process, law emerges as an effect of sovereigns' dependence on their subjects, of sovereigns' lack of complete impunity. Law is always a site of contestation. Even when states do obey their own laws, they do not do so in the way that, for example, a computer obeys the instructions of its software. Laws must be interpreted to the specificities of particular cases, especially in novel areas of law, and this interpretation must be done in such a way that the specification it involves seems not like an active selection from a range of possibilities but like passive acquiescence to the one correct possibility. Law can be an important or even indispensable tool for mitigating the impunity of the powerful, but it can also be an instrument of this impunity; its valence shifts depending on forces in the wider social field within which it is embedded. Calls for armed humanitarian intervention likewise have a double-edged quality. Roméo Dallaire's claim that effective intervention could have saved hundreds of thousands of lives in Rwanda is compelling (Dallaire and Beardsley 2003), but it is also the case that Saddam Hussein's record of genocide in Iraq was used to help legitimate the UN sanctions regime and its genocidal consequences. A critical figurational view of barbaric civilization suggests that a deliberate effort to end genocide should engage with state power but not depend on it and that this effort must always remain alert to states' attempts to co-opt antigenocide discourse for their own ends.

Additionally, as I have already mentioned, the struggle to end genocide by constructing a nongenocidal society is inseparable from and complementary to other struggles to transform social relations in an egalitarian and noncoercive direction. Eurocentric barbaric civilization is a macroscopic network of force relations, global in extend and centuries old. Yet it is also a microscopic interpersonal relation of deferentiation. Local struggles for free and equal human relationships complement each other, while drawing energy away from civilization's escalating material and symbolic arms race. A critical figurational analysis of barbaric civilization has this curious implication: kindness, compassion, empathy, generosity, charity, and gentleness are more than just abstract moral virtues or personal idiosyncrasies; they are eminently pragmatic virtues. They put into practice that part of the civilized habitus that desires release from its barbarity, that yearns to be free from the ubiquitous and pointless struggle for social dominance and from the unacceptable choice between conformity and danger. The gentler virtues – revalued as mutuality rather than altruism, reciprocity rather than submissiveness – rewrite the genetic code, so to speak, of barbaric civilization. They effect a de-escalation of the symbolic struggles for dominance, a de-escalation that is the interpersonal counterpart and analogue of the de-escalation of struggles for state sovereignty, which is the most immediate macroscopic preventative for genocide. As with sovereignty, structures at the collective and individual scales have a degree of self-similarity and are mutually reinforcing. In the labour of constructing a nongenocidal society, the means and ends of struggle ultimately converge.

Appendix: Definitions of Genocide

UNITED NATIONS

Excerpted from the *Convention on the Prevention and Punishment of the Crime of Genocide*, 9 December 1948:

ARTICLE I
The Contracting parties confirm that genocide, whether committed in time of peace or in time of war, is a crime under international law which they undertake to prevent and to punish.

ARTICLE II
In the present Convention, genocide means any of the following acts committed with intent to destroy, in whole or in part, a national, ethnical, racial, or religious group, as such:
  (a) Killing members of the group;
  (b) Causing serious bodily or mental harm to members of the group;
  (c) Deliberately inflicting on the group conditions of life calculated to bring about its physical destruction in whole or in part;
  (d) Imposing measures intended to prevent births within the group;
  (e) Forcibly transferring children of the group to another group

ARTICLE III
    The following acts shall be punishable:

(a) Genocide;
(b) Conspiracy to commit genocide;
(c) Direct and public incitement to commit genocide;
(d) Attempt to commit genocide;
(e) Complicity in genocide.

                    (quoted in Chalk and Jonassohn 1990, 44–5)

OTHER DEFINITIONS

Barta, Tony

In Australia very few people are conscious of having any relationship at all with Aborigines. My thesis is that all white people
in Australia do have such a relationship; that in the key relation,
the appropriation of the land, it is fundamental to the history
of the society in which they live; and that implicitly rather than
explicitly, in ways which were inevitable rather than intentional,
it is a relationship of genocide ... My conception of a genocidal
society – as distinct from a genocidal state – is one in which the
bureaucratic apparatus might officially be directed to protect
innocent people but in which a whole race is nevertheless subject
to remorseless pressures of destruction inherent in the very
nature of the society. (Barta 1987, 239–40)

Chalk, Frank, and Kurt Jonassohn

Genocide is a form of one-sided mass killing in which a state or
other authority intends to destroy a group, as that group and
membership in it are defined by the perpetrator. (Chalk and
Jonassohn 1990, 23; Chalk 1994, 52; Jonassohn and Björnson
1998, 10)

We need to begin with a question: what elements do we look for
in evaluating situations and events before determining whether
we are dealing with a case of genocide? We used three major criteria: (1) there must be evidence, even if only circumstantial, of
the intent of the perpetrator; (2) there must be a group whose
victimization threatens its survival as a group; and (3) the victimization must be one-sided. We realized that these conditions can,
in some cases, be problematic; therefore we recognized as

"genocidal massacres" those events that violate one of our conditions. (Jonassohn and Björnson 1998, 10)

Charny, Israel W.

The generic definition of genocide:

> Genocide in the generic sense is the mass killing of substantial numbers of human beings, when not in the course of military action against the military forces of an avowed enemy, under conditions of the essential defenselessness and helplessness of the victims. (Charny 1994, 75)

Charny elaborates on this generic definition by including under it the following possible variants:

- Genocidal Massacre (mass killing "on a smaller scale");
- Intentional Genocide;
- Genocide in the Course of Colonization or Consolidation of Power;
- Genocide in the Course of Aggressive ("Unjust") War;
- War Crimes against Humanity;
- Genocide as a Result of Ecological Destruction and Abuse.

He also adds, parallel to the generic definition of genocide, the categories of "Accomplices to Genocide" and "Cultural Genocide," the latter of which includes the variant "Linguicide" (Charny 1994, 76–7).

He further adds, like Ward Churchill (see below), definitions of first, second, and third degrees of genocide, war crimes, and ethnocide (Charny 1994, 85).

Churchill, Ward

Proposed Convention on Prevention and Punishment of the Crime of Genocide (1997)

ARTICLE II
In the present convention, genocide means the destruction, entirely or in part, of any racial, ethnic, national, religious, cultural,

linguistic, political, economic, gender or other human group, however such groups may be defined by the perpetrator. It is understood that, historically, genocide has taken three (3) primary forms, usually, but not always, functioning in combination with one another.

(a) *Physical Genocide*, by which is meant killing members of the targeted group(s) either directly, by indirect means, or some combination ...

(b) *Biological Genocide*, by which is meant the prevention of births within the target group(s), either directly, indirectly, or both ...

(c) *Cultural Genocide*, by which is meant the destruction of the specific character of the targeted group(s) ...

ARTICLE IV
[I]t is understood that several degrees of culpability pertain to the commission of genocide. These may be taken into consideration for purposes of determining the appropriateness of punishment.

(a) *Genocide in the First Degree*, which consists of instances in which evidence of premeditated intent to commit genocide is present.

(b) *Genocide in the Second Degree*, which consists of instances in which evidence of premeditation is absent, but in which it can be reasonably argued that the perpetrator(s) acted with reckless disregard for the probability that genocide would result from their actions.

(c) *Genocide in the Third Degree*, which consists of instances in which genocide derives, however unintentionally, from other violations of international law engaged in by the perpetrator(s).[1]

(d) *Genocide in the Fourth Degree*, which consists of instances in which neither evidence of premeditation nor other criminal behavior is present, but in which the perpetrator(s) acted with depraved indifference to the possibility that

---

1 The analogous correspondent in US statutory codes would be "felony murder."

genocide would result from their actions and therefore to effect adequate safeguards to prevent it.[2]

(Churchill 1998, 432–5)

Fein, Helen

Genocide is the calculated murder of a segment or all of a group defined outside the universe of obligation of the perpetrator by a government, elite, staff or crowd representing the perpetrator in response to a crisis or opportunity perceived to be caused by or impeded by the victim. The universe of obligation is the range of people to whom the common conscience extends: the people toward whom rules and obligations are binding, who must be taken into account, and by whom we can be held responsible for our actions. (Fein 1984, 4)

Harff, Barbara, and Ted Gurr

By our definition, genocides and politicides are the promotion and execution of policies by a state or its agents which result in the deaths of a substantial portion of a group. The difference between genocide and politicide is in the characteristics by which members of a group are identified by the state. In genocides the victimized groups are defined primarily in terms of their communal characteristics, i.e., ethnicity, religion, or nationality. In politicides the victim groups are defined primarily in terms of their hierarchical position or political opposition to the regime. (Harff and Gurr 1988, 360)

Horowitz, Irving Louis

A formal distinction between genocide and assassination is also required. Genocide is herein defined as *a structural and systematic destruction of innocent people by a state bureaucratic apparatus*, whereas assassination designates random and sporadic efforts of people without power to illegally seize power and

---

2 The analogous correspondent in US statutory codes would be "negligent homicide."

liquidate paramount central figures in a given regime as a means
to that goal. (Horowitz 2002, 23)

Katz, Steven

On genocide:

I shall employ the notion of genocide as applying to, and only as
applying to, "the actualization of the intent, however successfully carried out, to murder in its totality any national, ethnic, racial, religious, political, social, gender or economic group, as
these groups are defined by the perpetrator, by whatever means."
(Katz 1994, 131)

On cultural genocide:

Cultural genocide being understood as "the actualization of the-
intent, however successfully carried out, to destroy the national,
ethnic, religious, political, social, or class *identity* of a group, as
these groups are defined by the perpetrators." (Katz 1994, 137)

Lemkin, Raphaël

By "genocide" we mean the destruction of a nation or of an ethnic group. This new word, coined by the author to denote an old
practice in its modern development, is made from the ancient
Greek word *genos* (race, tribe) and the Latin *cide* (killing), thus
corresponding in its formation to such words as tyrannicide,
homicide, infanticide, etc.[3] Generally speaking, genocide does not
necessarily mean the immediate destruction of a nation, except
when accomplished by mass killings of all members of a nation.
It is intended rather to signify a coordinated plan of different actions aiming at the destruction of essential foundations of the life
of national groups, with the aim of annihilating the groups themselves. The objectives of such a plan would be disintegration of
the political and social institutions, of culture, language, national

---

3 Note by Lemkin: "Another term could be used for the same idea, namely,
ethnocide, consisting of the Greek word 'ethnos' – nation – and the Latin word
'cide.'"

feelings, religion, and the economic existence of national groups, and the destruction of the personal security, liberty, health, dignity, and even the lives of the individuals belonging to such groups. Genocide is directed against the national group as an entity, and the actions involved are directed against individuals, not in their individual capacity, but as members of the national group. (Lemkin 1944, 79)

The crime of genocide involves a wide range of actions, including not only the deprivation of life but also the prevention of life (abortions, sterilizations) and also devices considerably endangering life and health (artificial infections, working to death in special camps, deliberate separation of families for depopulation purposes, and so forth). All these actions are subordinated to the criminal intent to destroy or to cripple permanently a human group. (Lemkin 1947, 147)

Porter, Jack Nusan

Genocide is the deliberate destruction, in whole or in part, by a government or its agents, of a racial, sexual, religious, tribal, ethnic, or political minority. It can involve not only mass murder, but also starvation, forced deportation, and political, economic, and biological subjugation. Genocide involves three major components: ideology, technology, and bureaucracy/organization. (Porter 1982, 12)

Rummel, R.J.

The short version:

Genocide: among other things, the killing of people by a government because of their indelible group membership (race, ethnicity, religion, language).

Politicide: the murder of any person or people by a government because of their politics or for political purposes.

Mass Murder: the indiscriminate killing of any person or people by a government.

Democide: The murder of any person or people by a government, including genocide, politicide, and mass murder. (Rummel 1994, 31)

The long version:

In detail, *democide* is any action by government:
(1)   designed to kill or cause the death of people
(1.1) because of their religion, race, language, ethnicity, national origin, class, politics, speech, actions construed as opposing the government or wrecking social policy, or by virtue of their relationship to such people;
(1.2) in order to fulfill a quota or requisition system;
(1.3) in furtherance of a system of forced labor or enslavement;
(1.4) by massacre;
(1.5) through imposition of lethal living conditions; or
(1.6) by directly targeting noncombatants during a war or violent conflict; or

(2)   that causes death by virtue of an intentionally or knowingly reckless and depraved disregard for life (which constitutes *practical* intentionality), as in
(2.1) deadly prison, concentration camp, forced labor, prisoner of war, or recruit camp conditions;
(2.2) murderous medical or scientific experiments on humans;
(2.3) torture or beatings;
(2.4) encouraged or condoned murder, or rape, looting, and pillage during which people are killed;
(2.5) a famine or epidemic during which government authorities withhold aid, or knowingly act in a way to make it more deadly;
(2.6) forced deportations and expulsions causing deaths.

...

(h)   Excluded from this definition are:
(h.1) execution for what are internationally considered capital crimes, such as murder, rape, spying, treason, and the like, so long as evidence does not exist that such allegations were invented by the government in order to execute the accused;

(h.2) actions taken against armed civilians during mob action or riot (e.g., killing people with weapons in their hands is not democide); and

(h.3) the death of noncombatants killed during attacks on military targets, so long as the primary target is military (e.g., during bombing of enemy logistics).

(Rummel 1994, 37–8)

Shaw, Martin

Genocide is

a form of violent social conflict, or war, between armed power organizations that aim to destroy civilian social groups and those groups and other actors who resist this destruction.

Genocidal action (or genocide *as action*, a sense closer to previous understandings) ... can be defined as

action in which armed power organizations treat civilian social groups as enemies and aim to destroy their real or putative social power, by means of killing, violence, and coercion against individuals whom they regard as members of the groups.

(Shaw 2007, 154)

Thompson, John L.P., and Gail A. Quets

In short, given the problems which arise from restrictions, we define genocide as the destruction of a group by purposive action. This allows the role of intentional action to be explored, different subtypes of genocide to be compared, and the impact of different factors on genocide to be examined empirically.
(Thompson and Quets 1990, 248)

References

American Association of Physical Anthropologists. 1996. AAPA Statement on Biological Aspects of Race. *American Journal of Physical Anthropology* 101, no. 4: 569–70.

Adalian, Rouben Paul. 1992. The Armenian Genocide: 1915–1923. In *Genocide in Our Time: An Annotated Bibliography with Analytical Introductions*, ed. M.N. Dobkowski and I. Wallimann, 86–8. Ann Arbor, MI: Pierian.

– 2009. The Armenian Genocide. In *Century of Genocide: Critical Essays and Eyewitness Accounts*, ed. S. Totten and W.S. Parsons, 55–92. New York: Routledge.

African Rights. 1995. *Rwanda: Death, Despair, and Defiance*. Rev. ed. London: African Rights.

Akçam, Taner. 2004. *From Empire to Republic: Turkish Nationalism and the Armenian Genocide*. London: Zed.

– 2006. *A Shameful Act: The Armenian Genocide and the Question of Turkish Responsibility*. New York: Metropolitan.

Alexander, Edward. 1980. Stealing the Holocaust. *Midstream*, November, 46–50.

– 1994. *The Holocaust and the War of Ideas*. New Brunswick, NJ: Transaction.

Alexander, Jeffrey C. 2002. On the Social Construction of Moral Universals: The "Holocaust" from War Crime to Trauma Drama. *European Journal of Social Theory* 5, no. 1: 5–85.

Allen, Beverly. 1996. *Rape Warfare: The Hidden Genocide in Bosnia-Herzegovina and Croatia*. Minneapolis: University of Minnesota Press.

Alvarez, Alex. 2001. *Governments, Citizens and Genocide: A Comparative and Interdisciplinary Approach*. Bloomington: Indiana University Press.

– and Ronet Bachman. 2008. *Violence: The Enduring Problem*. Los
    Angeles: Sage.
Amin, Samir. 1989. *Eurocentrism*. New York: Monthly Review Press.
Amnesty International. 2004 . Rwanda: "Marked for Death": Rape
    Survivors Living with HIV/AIDS in Rwanda. 5 April. http://www.
    amnesty.org/en/library/info/AFR47/007/2004 (accessed 11 June
    2010).
Anderson, Benedict. 1991. *Imagined Communities: Reflections on the
    Origins and Spread of Nationalism*. London: Verso.
Arendt, Hannah. 1994. *Eichmann in Jerusalem: A Report on the Banality
    of Evil*. Rev. ed. New York: Penguin.
– 2001. *The Origins of Totalitarianism*. New ed. San Diego: Harcourt.
Balakian, Peter. 2003. *The Burning Tigris: The Armenian Genocide and
    America's Response*. New York: Harper Collins.
Ball, Patrick, Paul Kobrak, and Herbert F. Spirer. 1999. *State Violence in
    Guatemala, 1960–1966: A Quantitative Reflection*. Washington, DC:
    American Association for the Advancement of Science.
Ball, Terence. 1978. Two Concepts of Coercion. *Theory and Society* 5,
    no. 1: 97–112.
Barber, Malcolm. 2000. *The Cathars: Dualist Heretics in Languedoc in the
    High Middle Ages*. Harlow, UK: Longman.
Barnett, Michael. 2002. *Eyewitness to a Genocide: The United Nations
    and Rwanda*. Ithaca, NY: Cornell University Press.
Barrett, Michele. 1996. *Women's Oppression Today: The Marxist Feminist
    Encounter*. Rev. ed. London: Verso.
Barta, Tony. 1987. Relations of Genocide: Land and Lives in the
    Colonization of Australia. In *Genocide and the Modern Age: Etiology
    and Case Studies of Mass Death*, ed. I. Wallimann and M.N.
    Dobkowski, 237–52. New York: Greenwood.
– 2008a. Sorry, and Not Sorry, in Australia: How the Apology to the
    Stolen Generations Buried a History of Genocide. *Journal of Genocide
    Research* 10, no. 2: 201–14.
– 2008b. "They Appear Actually to Vanish from the Face of the Earth":
    Aborigines and the European Project in Australia Felix. *Journal of
    Genocide Research* 10, no. 4: 519–39.
– 2008c. With Intent to Deny: On Colonial Intentions and Genocide
    Denial. *Journal of Genocide Research* 10, no. 1: 111–19.
Bates, Frederick L., and Walter Gillis Peacock. 1989. Conceptualizing
    Social Structure: The Misuse of Classification in Structural Modeling.
    American Sociological Review 54, no. 4, 565–77.

Bauer, Yehuda. 1978. *The Holocaust in Historical Perspective*. Seattle: University of Washington Press.

– 1980. Whose Holocaust? *Midstream*, November, 42–6.

– 1991. Holocaust and Genocide: Some Comparisons. In *Lessons and Legacies: The Meaning of the Holocaust in a Changing World*, ed. P. Hayes, 36–46. Evanston, IL: Northwestern University Press.

– 1998. A Past That Will Not Go Away. In *The Holocaust and History*, ed. M. Berenbaum and A.J. Peck, 12–22. Bloomington: Indiana University Press.

– 2001. *Rethinking the Holocaust*. New Haven, CT: Yale University Press.

Bauman, Zygmunt. 1987. *Legislators and Interpreters: On Modernity, Post-Modernity, and Intellectuals*. Cambridge, UK: Polity Press.

– 1991a. *Modernity and Ambivalence*. Ithaca, NY: Cornell University Press.

– 1991b. *Modernity and the Holocaust*. Ithaca, NY: Cornell University Press.

BBC News. 2006. Pay-out for Tasmania's Aborigines. 18 October. http://news.bbc.co.uk/2/hi/asia-pacific/6063146.stm (accessed 6 April 2010).

– 2010. Q&A: Armenian Genocide Dispute. 5 March. http://news.bbc.co.uk/2/hi/europe/6045182.stm (accessed 22 May 2010).

Becker, Howard S. 1973. *Outsiders: Studies in the Sociology of Deviance*. New York: Free Press.

Benedict, Ruth. 1934. *Patterns of Culture*. New York: Houghton Mifflin.

Benjamin, Walter. 1969. Theses on the Philosophy of History. In *Illuminations*, ed. H. Arendt, 253–64. New York: Schocken.

Beristain, Carlos Martín. 1998. Guatemala: *Nunca Más. Forced Migration Review* 3: 23–6.

Bloxham, Donald. 2007. *The Great Game of Genocide: Imperialism, Nationalism, and the Destruction of the Ottoman Armenians*. Oxford, UK: Oxford University Press.

Blum, William. 1998. *Killing Hope: U.S. Military and CIA Interventions since World War II*. Montreal: Black Rose.

Boas, Frank. 1940. *Race, Language, and Culture*. Chicago: University of Chicago Press.

Bonnell, Andrew G., and Martin Crotty. 2004. An Australian "Historikerstreit"? Review article. *Australian Journal of Politics and History* 50, no. 3: 425–33.

Bonwick, James. 1970a. *The Last of the Tasmanians, or The Black War of Van Diemen's Land*. New York: Johnson Reprint Corporation.

– 1970b. *The Lost Tasmanian Race*. New York: Johnson Reprint Corporation.

Bourdieu, Pierre. 1984. *Distinction: A Social Critique of the Judgment of Taste*. Trans. R. Nice. Cambridge, MA: Harvard University Press.

– 1990. *The Logic of Practice*. Trans. R. Nice. Stanford, CA: Stanford University Press.

– 2001. *Masculine Domination*. Trans. R. Nice. Stanford, CA: Stanford University Press.

– and Loïc J.D. Wacquant. 1992. *An Invitation to Reflexive Sociology*. Chicago: University of Chicago Press.

Bowman, Glenn. 2001. The Violence in Identity. In *Anthropology of Violence and Conflict*, ed. B.E. Schmidt and I.W. Schröder, 25–46. London: Routledge.

Boyko, John. 1995. Native Canadians, 1867–1991: Attempted Cultural Genocide. In *The Last Steps to Freedom: The Evolution of Canadian Racism*. Winnipeg: Watson and Dwyer.

Brantlinger, Patrick. 2003. *Dark Vanishings: Discourse on the Extinction of Primitive Races, 1800–1930*. Ithaca, NY: Cornell University Press.

Brendon, Piers. 2007. *The Decline and Fall of the British Empire, 1781–1997*. London: Jonathan Cape.

Breslau, Daniel. 2000. Sociology after Humanism: A Lesson from Contemporary Science Studies. *Sociological Theory* 18, no. 2: 289–307.

Bridgman, Jon, and Leslie J. Worley. 2009. Genocide of the Hereros. In *Century of Genocde: Critical Essays and Eyewitness Accounts*, ed. S. Totten and W.S. Parsons, 17–53. New York: Routledge.

Browning, Christopher. 1992. *Ordinary Men: Reserve Police Battalion 101 and the Final Solution in Poland*. New York: Harper Collins.

Burkitt, Ian. 1996. Civilization and Ambivalence. *British Journal of Sociology* 47, no. 1: 135–50.

– 2006. Dealing with the Ambivalence of Civilization: Elias and the "Cultural Ontology" of Relational Humanism. Paper presented at the conference Elias in the 21st Century, University of Leicester, Leicester, United Kingdom, 10–12 April.

Burl, Aubrey. 2002. *God's Heretics: The Albigensian Crusade*. Gloucestershire, UK: Sutton.

Butler, Judith. 1990. *Gender Trouble: Feminism and the Subversion of Identity*. New York: Routledge.

Calder, James Erskine. 1972. *Some Account of the Wars, Extirpation, Habits etc. of the Native Tribes of Tasmania*. Hobart: Fullers Bookshop.

Callon, Michel. 1988. Some Elements of a Sociology of Translation: Domestication of the Scallops and the Fishermen of St. Brieuc Bay. In *Power, Action, and Belief*, ed. J. Law, 196–223. London: Routledge.

Cannadine, David. 2001. *Ornamentalism: How the British Saw Their Empire*. New York: Oxford University Press.

Carpenter, R. Charli. 2004. Beyond "Gendercide": Operationalizing Gender in Comparative Genocide Studies. In *Gendercide and Genocide*, ed. A. Jones, 230–56. Nashville, TN: Vanderbilt University Press.

CBC News Online Staff. 2004. Turkey Condemns Canada's Armenian Genocide Vote. 24 April. http://www.cbc.ca/canada/story/2004/04/22/armenia040422.html (accessed 9 July 2004).

Chalk, Frank Robert. 1994. Redefining Genocide. In *Genocide: Conceptual and Historical Dimensions*, ed. G.J. Andreopoulos, 47–63. Philadelphia: University of Pennsylvania Press.

– 2000. Panel-discussion paper read at the conference Genocide and Collective Memory, National Gallery of Canada, Ottawa, 26 November.

– and Kurt Jonassohn. 1990. *The History and Sociology of Genocide: Analyses and Case Studies*. New Haven, CT: Yale University Press.

Charny, Israel W. 1982. *How Can We Commit the Unthinkable? Genocide, the Human Cancer*. Boulder, CO: Westview.

– 1994. Toward a Generic Definition of Genocide. In *Genocide: Conceptual and Historical Dimensions*, ed. G.J. Andreopoulos, 64–94. Philadelphia: University of Pennsylvania Press.

– ed. 1984. *Toward the Understanding and Prevention of Genocide: Proceedings of the International Conference on the Holocaust and Genocide*. Boulder, CO: Westview.

Chomsky, Noam, and Michel Foucault. 1997. Human Nature: Justice versus Power. In *Foucault and His Interlocutors*, ed. A.I. Davidson, 107–45. Chicago: University of Chicago Press.

– and Edward S. Herman. 1979. *The Political Economy of Human Rights*. Vol. 1, *The Washington Connection and Third World Fascism*. Montreal: Black Rose.

Churchill, Ward. 1998. *A Little Matter of Genocide: Holocaust and Denial in the Americas, 1492 to the Present*. San Francisco, CA: City Lights.

– 2002. *Meet the New Boss, Same as the Old Boss: Globalization, Genocide and Resistance*. Ottawa: Minto Centre, Carleton University.

Cilliers, Paul. 2005. Complexity, Deconstruction and Relativism. *Theory, Culture and Society* 22, no. 5: 255–67.

Clark, Julia. 1986. *The Aboriginal Peoples of Tasmania*. Hobart, Australia: Tasmanian Museum and Art Gallery.

Comisión para el Esclarecimiento Histórico (CEH). 1999. *Guatemala: Memory of Silence: Report of the Commission for Historical*

Clarification, Conclusions and Recommendations. English ed. Guatemala City: CEH.

Comte, Auguste. 1998. Cours de Philosophie Positive. In *August Comte and Positivism: The Essential Writings*, ed. G. Lenzer, 69–306. New Brunswick, NJ: Transaction.

Conquest, Robert. 1990. No Grain of Pity. In *The History and Sociology of Genocide: Analyses and Case Studies*, ed. F.R. Chalk and K. Jonassohn, 291–300. New Haven, CT: Yale University Press.

Cooley, Charles Horton. 2004. The Looking-Glass Self. In *Social Theory: The Multicultural and Classic Readings*, ed. C. Lemert, 185. Boulder, CO: Westview.

Cooper, John. 2008. *Raphael Lemkin and the Struggle for the Genocide Convention*. New York: Palgrave MacMillan.

Corntassel, Jeff, and Cindy Holder. 2008. Who's Sorry Now? Government Apologies, Truth Commissions, and Indigenous Self-Determination in Australia, Canada, Guatemala, and Peru. *Human Rights Review* 9: 465–89.

Courtois, Stéphane. 1999. Introduction: The Crimes of Communism. In *The Black Book of Communism*, ed. M. Kramer, 1–32. Princeton, NJ: Harvard University Press.

Cove, John J. 1995. *What the Bones Say: Tasmanian Aborigines, Science and Domination*. Ottawa: Carleton University Press.

Cregan, Kate. 2007. Early Modern Anatomy and the Queen's Body Natural: The Sovereign Subject. *Body and Society* 13, no. 2: 47–66.

Culler, Jonathan. 1982. *On Deconstruction: Theory and Criticism after Structuralism*. Ithaca, NY: Cornell University Press.

Curthoys, Ann. 2005. Raphaël Lemkin's "Tasmania": An Introduction. *Patterns of Prejudice* 39, no. 2: 2005.

Dadrian, Vahakn N. 1996. *German Responsibility in the Armenian Genocide: A Review of the Historical Evidence of German Complicity*. Watertown, MA: Blue Crane.

– 1997. *The History of the Armenian Genocide: Ethnic Conflict from the Balkans to Anatolia to the Caucasus*. 3rd ed. Providence: Berghahn.

– 2001. The Comparative Aspects of the Armenian and Jewish Cases of Genocide: A Sociohistorical Perspective. In *Is the Holocaust Unique? Perspectives on Comparative Genocide*, ed. A.S. Rosenbaum, 113–68. Boulder, CO: Westview.

Dallaire, Roméo A., and Brent Beardsley. 2003. *Shake Hands with the Devil: The failure of Humanity in Rwanda*. Toronto: Vintage Canada.

Danner, Mark. 1997. The Horrors of a Camp Called Omarska and the Serb Strategy. http://www.pbs.org/wgbh/pages/frontline/shows/karadzic/atrocities/omarska.html (accessed 30 March 2003).

Davis, Mike. 2001. *Late Victorian Holocausts: El Niño Famines and the Making of the Third World*. London: Verso.

Davis, Robert, and Mark Zannis. 1973. *The Genocide Machine in Canada: The Pacification of the North*. Montreal: Black Rose.

Dawidowicz, Lucy S. 1981. *The Holocaust and the Historians*. Cambridge, MA: Harvard University Press.

de Swaan, Abram. 2001. Dyscivilization, Mass Extermination and the State. *Theory, Culture and Society* 18, nos 2–3: 265–76.

Dépelteau, François. 2008. Relational Thinking: A Critique of Co-Deterministic Theories of Structure and Agency. *Sociological Theory* 26, no. 1: 51–73.

Derrida, Jacques. 1976. *Of Grammatology*. Trans. G.C. Spivak. Baltimore, MD: Johns Hopkins University Press.

– 1982. Différance. In *Margins of Philosophy*, 1–28. Chicago: University of Chicago Press.

Des Forges, Alison Liebhafsky. 1999. *"Leave None to Tell the Story": Genocide in Rwanda*. New York: Human Rights Watch.

Doyle, Mark. 2006 . Rwanda's Mystery That Won't Go Away. 29 November. http://news.bbc.co.uk/2/hi/africa/6196226.stm (accessed 10 June 2010).

Drechsler, Horst. 1990. The Herero Uprising. In *The History and Sociology of Genocide: Analyses and Case Studies*, ed. F.R. Chalk and B.R. Johnston, 97–117. New Haven, CT: Yale University Press.

Drèze, Jean. 1995. Famine Prevention in India. In *The Political Economy of Hunger: Selected Essays*, ed. J. Drèze, A. Sen, and A. Hussain, 69–178. Oxford: Clarendon.

Durkheim, Emile. 1979. *Suicide*. Trans. J.A. Spaulding and G. Simpson. New York: Free Press.

– 1982. The Rules of Sociological Method. In *Durkheim: The Rules of Sociological Method and Selected Texts on Sociology and Its Method*, ed. S. Lukes, 29–163. Trans. W.D. Halls. New York: Free Press.

– 1984. *The Division of Labour in Society*. Trans. W.D. Halls. New York: Free Press.

– 1992. *Professional Ethics and Civic Morals*. 2nd ed. Trans. C. Brookfield. London: Routledge.

– 1995. *The Elementary Forms of Religious Life*. Trans. K.E. Fields. New York: Free Press.

– 2002. *Moral Education*. Trans. E.K. Wilson and H. Schnurer. Mineola, NY: Dover.

Dussault, René, Georges Erasmus, Paul I.A.H. Chartrand, J. Peter Meekison, Viola Rosbinson, Mary Sillett, and Bertha Wilson. 1996. *Royal Commission Report on Aboriginal Peoples*. http://www.ainc-inac. gc.ca/ap/rrc-eng.asp (accessed 15 June 2010).

Ebihara, May, and Judy Ledgerwood. 2002. Aftermaths of Genocide: Cambodian Villagers. In *Annihilating Difference: The Anthropology of Genocide*, ed. A.L. Hinton, 272–91. Berkeley: University of California Press.

Edwards, David. 2000. Half a Million Children under Five are Dead in Iraq – Who Is Responsible? An Interview with Denis Halliday – Former Assistant Secretary-General of the United Nations. May. http://www. medialens.org/articles/the_articles/articles_2001/iraqdh.htm (accessed 28 September 2010).

El-Kaïm-Sartre, Arlette, and Jean-Paul Sartre. 1968. *On Genocide*. Boston: Beacon Press.

Elder, Bruce. 1988. *Blood on the Wattle: Massacres and Maltreatment of Australian Aborigines since 1788*. Frenchs Forest, NSW, Australia: Child and Associates.

Elder, Tanya. 2005. What You See before Your Eyes: Documenting Raphael Lemkin's Life by Exploring His Archival Papers, 1900–1959. *Journal of Genocide Research* 7, no. 4: 469–99.

Elias, Norbert. 1978. *What Is Sociology?* Trans. S. Mennell and G. Morrissey. New York: Columbia University Press.

– 1987. *Involvement and Detachment*. Oxford: Basil Blackwell.

– 1991. *The Symbol Theory*. London: Sage.

– 1996. *The Germans*. Trans. E. Dunning and S. Mennell. Ed. M. Schröter. New York: Columbia University Press.

– 1998. Violence and Civilization: The State Monopoly of Physical Violence and Its Infringement. In *Civil Society and the State: New European Perspectives*, ed. J. Keane, 177–98. London: Verso.

– 2000. *The Civilizing Process: The History of Manners and State Formation and Civilization*. Trans. E. Jephcott. Rev. ed. Oxford: Blackwell.

– 2001. *The Society of Individuals*. New York: Continuum.

Elshtain, Jean Bethke. 1990–91. Sovereign God, Sovereign State, Sovereign Self. *Notre Dame Law Review* 66, no. 5: 1355–78.

Eltringham, Nigel. 2006. "Invaders who have stolen the country": The Hamitic Hypothesis, Race and the Rwandan Genocide. *Social Identities* 12, no. 4: 425–46.

Emirbayer, Mustafa. 1996. Useful Durkheim. *Sociological Theory* 14, no. 2: 109–30.

– 1997. Manifesto for a Relational Sociology. *American Journal of Sociology* 103, no. 2: 281–317.

Engels, Friedrich. 1972. *The Origin of the Family, Private Property, and the State, in Light of the Researches of Lewis H. Morgan.* New York: International Publishers.

– 1988a. The Materialist Conception of History. In *Marxism: Essential Writings*, ed. D. McLellan, 69–71. Oxford: Oxford University Press.

– 1988b. Revolution: Peaceful or Violent? In *Marxism: Essential Writings*, ed. D. McLellan, 71–5. Oxford: Oxford University Press.

Engler, Yves. 2009. *The Black Book of Canadian Foreign Policy.* Vancouver: RED Publishing.

– and Anthony Fenton. 2005. *Canada in Haiti: Waging War on the Poor Majority.* Vancouver: RED Publishing.

Ertürk, Yakin. 1990. Trends in the Development of Sociology in Turkey. *Journal of the Human Sciences* 9, no. 2, 37–55.

Esparza, Marcia. 2005. Post-war Guatemala: Long-term Effects of Psychological and Ideological Militarization of the K'iche Mayans. *Journal of Genocide Research* 7, no. 3: 2005.

Evans, Richard J. 1989. *In Hitler's Shadow: West German Historians and the Attempt to Escape from the Nazi Past.* New York: Pantheon.

Fabri, Antonella. 2003. Genocide or Assimilation: Discourses of Women's Bodies, Heath, and Nation in Guatemala. In *The Politics of Selfhood: Bodies and Identities in Global Capitalism*, ed. R.H. Brown, 42–63. Minneapolis: University of Minnesota Press.

Fackenheim, Emil L. 1977. The Holocaust and the State of Israel: Their Relation. In *Auschwitz: Beginning of a New Era? Reflections on the Holocaust*, ed. E. Fleischner, 205–16. New York: Ktav.

– 1978. *The Jewish Return into History: Reflections in the Age of Auschwitz and a New Jerusalem.* New York: Schocken.

Fanon, Frantz. 1963. *The Wretched of the Earth.* New York: Grove.

– 2008. *Black Skin, White Masks.* Trans. R. Philcox. New York: Grove.

Fausto-Sterling, Anne. 1993. The Five Sexes. *The Sciences*, 20–1.

Fein, Helen. 1979. *Accounting for Genocide: National Responses and Jewish Victimization during the Holocaust.* New York: Free Press.

– 1984. Scenarios of Genocide: Models of Genocide and Critical Responses. In *Toward the Understanding and Prevention of Genocide: Proceedings of the International Conference on the Holocaust and Genocide*, ed. I.W. Charny, 3–31. Boulder, CO: Westview.

– 1993. *Genocide: A Sociological Perspective*. London: Sage.

– ed. 1992. *Genocide Watch*. New Haven: Yale University Press.

Fenton, Anthony. 2005. *"Legalized Imperialism": "Responsibility to Protect" and the Dubious Case of Haiti*. http://briarpatchmagazine. com/2005/12/03/legalized-imperialism-responsibility-to-protect-and-the-dubious-case-of-haiti (accessed 14 December 2010).

Ferroggiaro, William, ed. 2001. *The U.S. and the Genocide in Rwanda 1994: Evidence of Inaction*. Washington, DC: National Security Archive.

Figueroa Ibarra, Carlos. 2006. The Culture of Terror and Cold War in Guatemala. *Journal of Genocide Research* 8, no. 2: 191–208.

Finkelstein, Norman. 2000. *The Holocaust Industry: Reflections on the Exploitation of Jewish Suffering*. London: Verso.

Firestone, Shulamith. 1970. *The Dialectic of Sex: The Case for Feminist Revolution*. New York: Morrow.

Fischer, Edward F., and R. McKenna Brown, eds. 1996. *Maya Cultural Activism in Guatemala*. Austin: University of Texas Press.

Fletcher, Jonathan. 1997. *Violence and Civilization: An Introduction to the Work of Norbert Elias*. Cambridge: Polity.

Fontaine, Theodore. 2010. *Broken Circle: The Dark Legacy of Indian Residential Schools*. Victoria: Heritage House.

Foucault, Michel. 1980. Two Lectures. In *Power/Knowledge: Selected Interviews and Other Writings, 1972–1977*, ed. C. Gordon, 78–108. New York: Pantheon.

– 1984. Nietzsche, Genealogy, History. In *The Foucault Reader*, ed. P. Rabinow, 76–102. New York: Pantheon Books.

– 1988. The Political Technology of Individuals. In *Technologies of the Self: A Seminar with Michel Foucault*, ed. L.H. Martin, H. Gutman, and P.H. Hutton, 145–62. Amherst: University of Massachusetts Press.

– 1990. *The History of Sexuality*. Vol. 1, *An Introduction*. Trans. R. Hurley. New York: Vintage.

– 1995. *Discipline and Punish: The Birth of the Prison*. Trans. A. Sheridan. 2nd ed. New York: Vintage.

– 1998. Structuralism and Post-structuralism. In *Aesthetics, Method, and Epistemology: Essential Works of Foucault, 1954–1984*, vol. 2., ed. J.D. Faubion, 431–58. New York: New Press.

– 2003. *Society Must Be Defended: Lectures at the Collège de France, 1975–1976*. Trans. D. Macey. Ed. A.I. Davidson. New York: Picador.

Freely, Maureen. 2007. Why They Killed Hrant Dink. *Index on Censorship* 36, no. 2: 15–29.

Freud, Sigmund. 2002. *Civilization and Its Discontents*. Trans. D. McLintock. London: Penguin.

Fuentes, Annette, and Barbara Ehrenreich. 1983. *Women in the Global Factory*. Ed. H. Sklar and G. Jacobs. INC Pamphlet No. 2. Boston: South End.

Galeano, Eduardo. 1985. *Memory of Fire: I. Genesis*. New York: Pantheon.

– 1997. *Open Veins of Latin America: Five Centuries of the Pillage of a Continent*. 25th anniversary ed. New York: Monthly Review Press.

Gallie, W.B. 1956. Essentially Contested Concepts. *Proceedings of the Aristotelian Society* 56: 167–98.

Garfinkel, Harold. 1967. Passing and the Managed Achievement of Sex Status in an Intersexed Person: Part 1. In *Studies in Ethnomethodology*, 116–85. Cambridge, UK: Polity.

Gasanabo, Jean-Damascène. 2006. The Rwandan *Akazi* (Forced Labour) System, History, and Humiliation. *Social Alternatives* 25, no. 1: 50–5.

Genocide Watch. 2010a. Directors and Advisors. http://www.genocide-watch.org/aboutus/directorsandadvisors.html (accessed 25 June 2010).

– 2010b. International Campaign to End Genocide. http://www.genocide-watch.org/campaigntoendgenocide/about.html (accessed 25 June 2010).

Gill, Lesley. 2004. *The School of the Americas: Military Training and Political Violence in the Americas*. Durham, NC: Duke University Press.

Given, James B. 1997. *Inquisition and Medieval Society*. Ithaca, NY: Cornell University Press.

Gleijeses, Piero. 1992. *Shattered Hope: The Guatemalan Revolution and the United States, 1944–1954*. Princeton, NJ: Princeton University Press.

Goffman, Erving. 1959. *The Presentation of Self in Everyday Life*. Garden City, NY: Anchor.

– 1961. *Asylums: Essays on the Social Situation of Mental Patients and Other Inmates*. Garden City, NY: Anchor.

Goodman, Lisl Marburg, and Lee Ann Hoff. 1990. *Omnicide: The Nuclear Dilemma*. New York: Praeger.

Gourevitch, Philip. 1998. *We Wish to Inform You That Tomorrow We Will Be Killed with Our Families: Stories from Rwanda*. New York: Farrar Straus and Giroux.

Gramsci, Antonio. 1971. *Selections from the Prison Notebooks*. Trans. Q. Hoare and G.N. Smith. New York: International Publishers.

Grandin, Greg. 2000. *The Blood of Guatemala: A History of Race and Nation*. Ed. W.D. Mignolo, I. Silverblatt, and S. Saldívar-Hull. Durham, NC: Duke University Press.

– 2004. *The Last Colonial Massacre: Latin America in the Cold War.* Chicago: University of Chicago Press.

– 2009. Politics by Other Means: Guatemala's Quiet Genocide. In *Quiet Genocide: Guatemala, 1981–1983*, ed. E. Higonnet, 1–16. New Brunswick, NJ: Transaction.

Grant, Agnes. 1996. *No End of Grief: Indian Residential Schools in Canada.* Winnipeg: Pemmican.

Griffin, John Howard. 1977. *Black Like Me.* 2nd ed. Boston: Houghton Mifflin.

Gunaratana, Bhante Henepola. 2002. *Mindfulness in Plain English.* Updated and expanded ed. Somerville, MA: Wisdom.

Hairapetian, Armen. 1984. "Race Problems" and the Armenian Genocide: The State Department File. *Armenian Review* 37, no. 1, 41–145.

Hall, Stuart. 1997. *Representation: Cultural Representations and Signifying Practice.* London: Sage and Open University.

Hamburg, David A. 2008. *Preventing Genocide: Practical Steps toward Early Detection and Effective Action.* Boulder, CO: Paradigm.

Hancock, Ian. 2001. Responses to the Porrajmos: The Romani Holocaust. In *Is the Holocaust Unique? Perspectives on Comparative Genocide*, ed. A.S. Rosenbaum, 69–96. Boulder, CO: Westview.

Handy, Jim. 1984. *Gift of the Devil: A History of Guatemala.* Toronto: Between the Lines.

Hannum, Hurst, and David Hawk. 1986. *The Case against the Standing Committee of the Communist Party of Kampuchea.* New York: Cambodia Documentation Commission.

Harding, Sandra. 1992. Rethinking Standpoint Epistemology: What Is "Strong Objectivity?" *Centennial Review* 36, no. 3: 437–70.

Harff, Barbara, and Ted R. Gurr. 1988. Toward Empirical Theory of Genocides and Politicides: Identification and Measurement of Cases since 1945. *International Studies Quarterly* 37, no. 3: 359–71.

Hatzfeld, Jean. 2005. *Machete Season: The Killers in Rwanda Speak.* Trans. L. Coverdale. New York: Farrar Straus and Giroux.

Herman, Judith Lewis. 2001. *Trauma and Recovery: From Domestic Abuse to Political Terror.* London: Pandora.

Heyd, Uriel. 1950. *Foundations of Turkish Nationalism.* London: Luzac.

Hilberg, Raul. 1980. The Anatomy of the Holocaust. In *The Holocaust: Ideology, Bureaucracy, and Genocide*, ed. H. Friedlander and S. Milton, 85–102. Millwood, NY: Kraus International.

Hinton, Alexander Laban. 2002. The Dark Side of Modernity: Toward an Anthropology of Genocide. In *Annihilating Difference: The*

Anthropology of Genocide, ed. A.L. Hinton, 1–42. Berkeley: University of California Press.

– 2005. *Why Did They Kill? Cambodia in the Shadow of Genocide.* Berkeley: University of California Press.

Horowitz, Irving Louis. 2002. *Taking Lives: Genocide and State Power.* 5th rev. ed. New Brunswick, NJ: Transaction.

Hovannisian, Richard G. 1990. The Historical Dimension of the Armenian Question, 1878–1923. In *The History and Sociology of Genocide: Analyses and Case Studies,* ed. F.R. Chalk and K. Jonassohn, 250–66. New Haven, CT: Yale University Press.

Human Rights and Equal Opportunity Commission. 1997. *Bringing Them Home: Report of the National Inquiry into the Separation of Aboriginal and Torres Strait Island Children from Their Families.* Sydney: Commonwealth of Australia.

Human Rights Watch Arms Project. 1994. *Arming Rwanda: The Arms Trade and Human Rights Abuses in the Rwandan War.* Human Rights Watch.

Huntington, Samuel P. 1996. *The Clash of Civilizations and the Remaking of World Order.* New York: Simon and Schuster.

Huttenbach, Henry. 1988. Locating the Holocaust on the Genocide Spectrum. *Holocaust and Genocide Studies* 3, no. 3: 289–304.

– 2001. From the Editor: In Search of Genocide – (Re)focusing on the Existential. *Journal of Genocide Research* 3, no. 1: 7–9.

International Commission on Intervention and State Sovereignty (ICISS). 2001. *The Responsibility to Protect: Report of the International Commission on Intervention and State Sovereignty.* Ed. Ministry of Foreign Affairs. Ottawa: International Development Research Centre.

Jeffremovas, Villia. 2002. *Brickyards to Graveyards: From Production to Genocide in Rwanda.* Albany: State University of New York Press.

Johnston, Anna. 2009. George Augustus Robinson, the "Great Conciliator": Colonial Celebrity and Its Postcolonial Aftermath. *Postcolonial Studies* 12, no. 2: 153–72.

Jonassohn, Kurt, and Karin Solveig Björnson. 1998. *Genocide and Gross Human Rights Violations: In Comparative Perspective.* New Brunswick, NJ: Transaction.

Jones, Adam. 2002. Gender and Genocide in Rwanda. *Journal of Genocide Research* 4, no. 1: 65–94.

– 2004a. Afghanistan and Beyond. In *Genocide, War Crimes and the West: History and Complicity,* ed. A. Jones, 383–403. London: Zed.

– 2004b. Gendercide and Genocide. In *Gendercide and Genocide,* ed. A. Jones, 1–38. Nashville, TN: Vanderbilt University Press.

- 2006a. *Genocide: A Comprehensive Introduction*. London: Routledge.
- 2006b. Straight as a Rule: Heteronormativity, Gendercide, and the Noncombatant Male. *Men and Masculinities* 8, no. 4: 451–69.
- ed. 2004c. *Genocide, War Crimes and the West: History and Complicity*. London: Zed.

Kahveci, Erol. 1995. Durkheim's Sociology in Turkey. *Durkheimian Studies/Etudes durkheimiennes* 1: 51–7.

Katz, Steven T. 1983. *Post-Holocaust Dialogues: Critical Studies in Modern Jewish Thought*. New York: New York University Press.
- 1988. Quantity and Interpretation: Issues in the Comparative Analysis of the Holocaust. In *Remembering for the Future: Jews and Christians during and after the Holocaust*, ed. Y. Bauer, 200–16. Oxford: Pergamon.
- 1991. The Pequot War Reconsidered. *New England Quarterly* 64, no. 2: 206–24.
- 1992. *Historicism, the Holocaust, and Zionism: Critical Studies in Modern Jewish Thought and History*. New York: New York University Press.
- 1994. *The Holocaust in Historical Context*. Vol. 1. New York: Oxford University Press.
- 2001. The Uniqueness of the Holocaust: The Historical Dimension. In *Is the Holocaust Unique? Perspectives on Comparative Genocide*, ed. A.S. Rosenbaum, 49–68. Boulder, CO: Westview.

Keefer, Edward C., ed. 2001. *Foreign Relations of the United States, 1964–1968*. Vol. 26, *Indonesia; Malaysia-Singapore; Philippines*. Ed. D.S. Patterson. Washington, DC: United States Government Printing Office.

Kessler, Suzanne J. 1990. The Medical Construction of Gender: Case Management of Intersexed Infants. *Signs* 16, no. 1: 5.

Kiernan, Ben. 2007. *Blood and Soil: A World History of Genocide and Extermination*. New Haven, CT: Yale University Press.

Kinealy, Christine. 2002. *The Great Irish Famine: Impact, Ideology and Rebellion*. Ed. J. Black. New York: Palgrave.

Knockwood, Isabelle. 2001. *Out of the Depths: The Experiences of Mi'kmaw Children at the Indian Residential School at Schubenacadie, Nova Scotia*. 2nd ed. Lockeport, NS: Roseway.

Koonz, Claudia. 2003. *The Nazi Conscience*. Cambridge, MA: Belknap.

Kuper, Leo. 1981. *Genocide: Its Political Use in the Twentieth Century*. New Haven, CT: Yale University Press.

Lacouture, Jean. 1978. *Survivre le peuple cambodgien*. Paris: Le Seuil.

LaFeber, Walter. 1993. *Inevitable Revolutions: The United States in Central America*. 2nd ed. New York: W.W. Norton.

Lambert, Malcolm. 1998. *The Cathars*. Oxford: Blackwell.

Lansing, Carol. 1998. *Power and Purity: Cathar Heresy in Medieval Italy*. New York: Oxford University Press.

Latour, Bruno. 1988. *The Pasteurization of France*. Trans. A. Sheridan and J. Law. Cambridge, MA: Harvard University Press.

– 1993. *We Have Never Been Modern*. Trans. C. Potter. Cambridge, MA: Harvard University Press.

– 2005. *Reassembling the Social Sciences: An Introduction to Actor-Network Theory*. Oxford: Oxford University Press.

Lawrence, Bonita. 2004. *"Real" Indians and Others: Mixed-Blood Urban Native Peoples and Indigenous Nationhood*. Vancouver: University of British Columbia Press.

Lebor, Adam. 2006. *Complicity with Evil: The United Nations in the Age of Modern Genocide*. New Haven, CT: Yale University Press.

Legters, Lyman H. 1984. The Soviet Gulag: Is It Genocidal? In *Toward the Understanding and Prevention of Genocide: Proceedings of the International Conference on the Holocaust and Genocide*, ed. I.W. Charny, 60–6. Boulder, CO, and London: Westview.

Leiby, Michele L. 2009. Wartime Sexual Violence in Guatemala and Peru. *International Studies Quarterly* 53: 445–68.

Leledakis, Kanakis. 2000. Derrida, Deconstruction and Social Theory. *European Journal of Social Theory* 3, no. 2: 175–93.

Lemarchand, René. 1994. *Burundi: Ethnocide as Discourse and Practice*. Cambridge, UK: Woodrow Wilson Center Press and Cambridge University Press.

– 1998. Genocide in the Great Lakes: Which Genocide? Whose Genocide? *African Studies Review* 41, no. 1: 3–16.

– 2009. The 1994 Rwandan Genocide. In *Century of Genocide: Critical Essays and Eyewitness Accounts*, ed. S. Totten and W.S. Parsons, 483–504. New York: Routledge.

Lemkin, Raphaël. 1944. *Axis Rule in Occupied Europe: Laws of Occupation, Analysis of Government, Proposals for Redress*. Washington, DC: Division of International Law, Carnegie Endowment for International Peace.

– 1947. Genocide as a Crime under International Law. *American Journal of International Law* 41: 145–51.

Levene, Mark. 2005a. *Genocide in the Age of the Nation-State*. Vol. 1, *The Meaning of Genocide*. London: I.B. Tauris.

– 2005b. *Genocide in the Age of the Nation-State*. Vol. 2, *The Rise of the West and the Coming of Genocide*. London: I.B. Tauris.

Lewy, Günter. 2005. *The Armenian Massacres in Ottoman Turkey: A Disputed Genocide*. Salt Lake City: University of Utah Press.

– 2007. Can There Be Genocide without the Intent to Commit Genocide? *Journal of Genocide Research* 9, no. 4: 661–74.

Lindqvist, Sven. 1996. *"Exterminate All the Brutes": One Man's Oddyssey into the Heart of Darkness and the Origins of European Genocide*. New York: New Press.

Lippman, M. 1984. The Drafting of the 1948 Convention on the Prevention and Punishment of the Crime of Genocide. *Boston University International Law Journal* 3: 1–65.

Lipstadt, Deborah E. 1993. *Denying the Holocaust: The Growing Assault on Truth and Memory*. New York: Free Press.

Loucky, James. 2001. The Tz'utujil Maya of Guatemala. In *Endangered Peoples of Latin America: Struggles to Survive and Thrive*, ed. S.C. Stonich, 153–69. Westport, CT: Greenwood.

– and Robert Carlsen. 1991. Massacre in Santiago Atitlan: A Turning Point in the Maya Struggle? *Cultural Survival* 15, no. 3: 65–70.

Luis, J.R., D.J. Rowold, M. Regueiro, B. Caeiro, C. Cinnioglu, C. Roseman, A. Underhill, L.L. Cavalli-Sforza, and R.J. Herrera. 2004. The Levant versus the Horn of Africa: Evidence for Bidirectional Corridors of Human Migrations. *American Journal of Human Genetics* 74, no. 3: 532–44.

Lukes, Steven. 1982. Introduction. In The Rules of Sociological Method, by E. Durkheim, in *Durkheim: The Rules of Sociological Method and Selected Texts on Sociology and Its Method*, ed. S. Lukes, 1–27. New York: Free Press.

Lutz, John Sutton. 2008. *Makúk: A New History of Aboriginal-White Relations*. Vancouver: University of British Columbia Press.

Luxemburg, Rosa. 2003. *The Accumulation of Capital*. London: Routledge.

Lyons, Robert, and Scott Straus. 2006. *Intimate Enemy: Images and Voices of the Rwandan Genocide*. New York: Zone.

Lyotard, Jean-François. 1984. *The Postmodern Condition: A Report on Knowledge*. Trans. G. Bennington and B. Massumi. Minneapolis: University of Minnesota Press.

Mace, James E. 2009. Soviet Man-Made Famine in Ukraine. In *Century of Genocide: Critical Essays and Eyewitness Accounts*, ed. S. Totten and W.S. Parsons, 95–126. New York: Routledge.

MacIntyre, Stuart, and Anna Clark. 2003. *The History Wars*. Melbourne: Melbourne University Press.

MacKinnon, Catharine A. 1989. *Toward a Feminist Theory of the State*. Cambridge, MA: Harvard University Press.

Madley, Benjamin. 2004. Patterns of Frontier Genocide, 1803–1910: The Aboriginal Tasmanians, the Yuki of California, and the Herero of Namibia. *Journal of Genocide Research* 6, no. 2: 167–92.

Mamdani, Mahmood. 2001. *When Victims Become Killers: Colonialism, Nativism, and the Genocide in Rwanda*. Princeton, NJ: Princeton University Press.

Mann, Michael. 2005. *The Dark Side of Democracy: Explaining Ethnic Cleansing*. Cambridge, UK: Cambridge University Press.

Manne, Robert, ed. 2003. *Whitewash: On Keith Windschuttle's Fabrication of Aboriginal History*. Melbourne: Black.

Manz, Beatriz. 2008. The Continuum of Violence in Post-war Guatemala. *Social Analysis* 52, no. 2: 151–64.

Marchak, Patricia. 2003. *Reigns of Terror*. Montreal and Kingston: McGill-Queen's University Press.

– 2008. *No Easy Fix: Global Responses to Internal Wars and Crimes against Humanity*. Montreal and Kingston: McGill-Queen's University Press.

Markus, Andrew. 1982–83. The Aboriginal Tasmanians. Book review. *Australian Historical Studies* 20: 467–9.

Marrus, Michael Robert. 1987. *The Holocaust in History*. 1st ed. Tauber Institute for the Study of European Jewry Series No. 7. Toronto: Lester and Orpen Dennys.

Martinez Salazar, Egla. 2008. State Terror and Violence as a Process of Lifelong Teaching-Learning: The Case of Guatemala. *International Journal of Lifelong Education* 27, no. 2: 201–16.

Marx, Karl. 1971. "Preface" to *A Contribution to the Critique of Political Economy*. In *Karl Marx: Early Texts*, ed. D. McLellan, 327–31. Oxford: Basil Blackwell.

– 1979. The 18th Brumaire of Louis Bonaparte. In *Karl Marx, Frederick Engels: Collected Works*, vol. 11, *Marx and Engels: 1851–53*, 99–197. Moscow: Progress.

– 1990. *Capital: A Critique of Political Economy*. Vol. 1. Trans. B. Fowkes. Toronto: Penguin.

– 2000a. Alienated Labour. In *Karl Marx: Selected Writings*, ed. D. McLellan, 85–96. Oxford: Oxford University Press.

– 2000b. Theses on Feuerbach. In *Karl Marx: Selected Writings*, ed. D. McLellan, 171–4. Oxford: Oxford University Press.

– 2000c. Wage-Labour and Capital. In *Karl Marx: Selected Writings*, ed.
   D. McLellan, 273–93. Oxford: Oxford University Press.
– and Frederick Engels. 1976. The German Ideology. In *Karl Marx,
   Frederick Engels: Collected Works*, vol. 5, *Marx and Engels: 1845–47*,
   19–539. Moscow: Progress.
– and Friedrich Engels. 1988a. The Communist Manifesto. In *Marxism:
   Essential Writings*, ed. D. McLellan, 20–49. Oxford: Oxford University
   Press.
– and Friedrich Engels. 1988b. The German Ideology. In *Marxism: Essential Writings*, ed. D. McLellan, 3–19. Oxford: Oxford University Press.
Maybury-Lewis, David. 2002. Genocide against Indigenous Peoples. In
   Annihilating Difference: The Anthropology of Genocide, ed. A.L.
   Hinton, 43–53. Berkeley: University of California Press.
McCreery, David. 1990. State Power, Indigenous Communities, and Land
   in Nineteenth Century Guatemala, 1820–1920. In *Guatemalan Indians
   and the State: 1540 to 1988*, ed. C.A. Smith, 96–115. Austin: University
   of Texas Press.
McCullum, Hugh. 1995. *The Angels Have Left Us: The Rwanda Tragedy
   and the Churches*. Geneva: World Council of Churches.
McDonnell, Michael A., and A. Dirk Moses. 2005. Raphael Lemkin as
   Historian of Genocide in the Americas. *Journal of Genocide Research* 7,
   no. 4: 501–29.
McMillen, Liz. 1994. The Uniqueness of the Holocaust. *Chronicle of
   Higher Education* 40, no. 42: A13.
McVeigh, Robbie. 2008. "The Balance of Cruelty": Ireland, Britain and
   the Logic of Genocide. *Journal of Genocide Research* 10, no. 4: 541–61.
– and Bill Rolston. 2009. Civilising the Irish. *Race and Class* 51, no. 2:
   2–28.
Melson, Robert. 1992. *Revolution and Genocide: On the Origins of the
   Armenian Genocide and the Holocaust*. Chicago: University of Chicago
   Press.
Melvern, Linda. 2000. *A People Betrayed: The Role of the West in
   Rwanda's Genocide*. London: Zed.
– 2004. *Conspiracy to Murder: The Rwandan Genocide*. London: Verso.
Memmi, Albert. 1965. *The Colonizer and the Colonized*. Trans. H.
   Greenfeld. New York: Orion.
Mennell, Stephen. 1989. *Norbert Elias: Civilization and the Human Self-
   Image*. Oxford: Basil Blackwell.
– 1992. *Norbert Elias: An Introduction*. Dublin: University College
   Dublin Press.

– and Eric Dunning. 1996. Preface. In N. Elias, *The Germans*, vii–xvi. New York: Columbia University Press.

Milgram, Stanley. 1974. *Obedience to Authority: An Experimental View*. London: Tavistock.

Mironko, Charles K. 2006. Ibitero: Means and Motive in the Rwandan Genocide. In *Genocide in Cambodia and Rwanda: New Perspectives*, ed. S.E. Cook, 169–89. New Brunswick, NJ: Transaction.

Mirowski, Philip. 1989. *More Heat Than Light: Economics as Social Physics, Physics as Nature's Economics*. Ed. C.D. Goodwin. Cambridge, UK: Cambridge University Press.

Molina Mejía, Raúl. 1999. The Struggle against Impunity in Guatemala. *Social Justice* 26, no. 4: 55–83.

Monbiot, George. 2001. Backyard Terrorism. *Guardian*, 30 October.

Moore, R.I. 1990. *The Formation of a Persecuting Society: Power and Deviance in Western Europe, 950–1250*. Oxford: Blackwell.

Morris, James. 1972. The Final Solution, Down Under. *Horizon* 14, no. 1: 60–71.

Moses, A. Dirk. 2000. An Antipodean Genocide? The Origins of the Genocidal Moment in the Colonization of Australia. *Journal of Genocide Research* 2, no. 1: 89–106.

– 2002. Conceptual Blockages and Definitional Dilemmas in the "Racial Century": Genocides of Indigenous Peoples and the Holocaust. *Patterns of Prejudice* 36, no. 4: 7–36.

– 2004. The Holocaust and Genocide. In *The Historiography of the Holocaust*, ed. D. Stone, 533–55. London: Palgrave.

Mullin, James. 1999. *The Great Irish Famine*. 2nd ed. Moorestown, NJ: Irish Famine Curriculum Committee and Education Fund.

Mundy, John Hine. 2006. *Studies in the Ecclesiastical and Social History of Toulouse in the Age of the Cathars*. Ed. B. Bolton, A.J. Duggan, and M. Goodich. Burlington, VT: Ashgate.

Mégret, Frédéric. 2009. Beyond the "Salvation" Paradigm: Responsibility to Protect (Others) vs the Power of Protecting Oneself. *Security Dialogue* 40, no. 6: 575–95.

Neu, Dean, and Richard Therrien. 2003. *Accounting for Genocide: Canada's Bureaucratic Assault on Aboriginal People*. Halifax: Fernwood.

Nicholls, Tracey. 2009. Solidarity and Paternalism: The Dangerous Ambiguity of the Responsibility to Protect Doctrine. Paper presented at the Midwest Political Science Association 67th Annual National Conference, Chicago.

Ó Gráda, Cormac. 2006. *Ireland's Great Famine: Interdisciplinary Perspectives*. Dublin: University College Dublin Press.

O'Shea, Stephen. 2000. *The Perfect Heresy: The Revolutionary Life and Death of the Medieval Cathars*. Vancouver: Douglas and McIntyre.

Ollman, Bertell. 1976. *Alienation: Marx's Conception of Man in Capitalist Society*. 2nd ed. Cambridge, UK: Cambridge University Press.

Oxford English Dictionary. 2010. *OED Online*. Oxford: Oxford University Press. http://www.dictionary.oed.com.

Palmer, Alision. 2000. *Colonial Genocide*. Adelaide: Crawford House.

Parsons, Talcott. 1951. *The Social System*. New York: Free Press.

– 1966. *Societies: Evolutionary and Comparative Perspectives*. Englewood Cliffs, NJ: Prentice-Hall.

Paul, Daniel N. 2006. *We Were Not the Savages: Collision between European and Native American Civilizations*. 3rd ed. Halifax: Fernwood.

Pietgen, Heinz-Otto, Hartmut Jürgens, and Dietmar Saupe. 1992. *Chaos and Fractals: New Frontiers of Science*. New York: Springer-Verlag.

Plomley, Norman James Brian. 1992. *The Aboriginal/Settler Clash in Van Diemen's Land, 1803–1831*. Hobart: University of Tasmania.

Porpora, Douglas V. 1990. *How Holocausts Happen: The United States in Central America*. Philadelphia: Temple University Press.

Porter, Jack N. 1982. Introduction. In *Genocide and Human Rights: A Global Anthology*, ed. J.N. Porter, 2–33. Washington, DC: University Press of America.

Powell, Christopher. 1999. Crisis of Co-optation: Human Rights, Social Movements and Global Politics. *Alternate Routes* 15: 5–34.

– 2007. What Do Genocides Kill? A Relational Conception of Genocide. *Journal of Genocide Research* 9, no. 4: 527–47.

– 2009. The Wound at the Heart of the World. In *Evoking Genocide: Scholars and Activists Describe the Works That Shaped Their Lives*, ed. A. Jones, 11–17. Toronto: Key.

– 2011. Genocidal Moralities: A Critique. In *New Directions in Genocide Research*, ed. A. Jones. London: Routledge.

Power, Samantha. 2002. *A Problem from Hell: America and the Age of Genocide*. New York: Basic Books.

Prunier, Gérard. 1995. *The Rwanda Crisis: History of a Genocide*. New York: Columbia University Press.

– 2009. *Africa's World War*. Oxford: Oxford University Press.

Recovery of Historical Memory Project (REMHI). 1999. *Guatemala, Never Again! The Official Report of the Human Rights Office, Archdiocese of Guatemala*. Maryknoll, NY: Orbis.

Reisman, W. Michael, and Charles H. Norchi. 1988. Genocide and the Soviet Occupation of Afghanistan. *ISG Newsletter* 1, no. 1: 4–6.

Rennie, David. 2005. Turkey's EU Plans Threatened by Genocide Dispute with the French. http://www.telegraph.co.uk/news/worldnews/1531079/Turkeys-EU-plans-threatened-by-genocide-dispute-with-the-French.html (accessed 22 May 2010).

Republic of Turkey. 1982. *The Armenian Issue in Nine Questions and Answers*. Ankara: Republic of Turkey.

– 1998. Armenian Claims and Historical Facts. Ankara: Ministry of Foreign Affairs Centre for Strategic Research.

Resnick, Stephen, and Richard Wolff. 1995. Lessons from the USSR. In *Wither Marxism? Global Crisis in International Perspective*, ed. B. Magnus and S. Cullenberg, 207–34. New York: Routledge.

Reynolds, Henry. 1995. *Fate of a Free People: A Radical Re-examination of the Tasmanian Wars*. Melbourne: Penguin.

– 2001. *An Indelible Stain? The Question of Genocide in Australia's History*. Victoria, Australia: Penguin.

Rittner, Carol, John K. Roth, and Wendy Whitworth, eds. 2004. *Genocide in Rwanda: Complicity of the Churches?* St Paul, MN: Paragon House.

Robertson, Roland. 2006. Civilization. *Theory, Culture and Society* 23, nos 2–3: 421–36.

Robinson, Eric, and Henry Bird Quinney. 1985. *The Infested Blanket: Canada's Constitution – Genocide of Indian Nations*. Winnipeg: Queenston House.

Robson, Leslie Loyd. 1983. *A History of Tasmania*. Melbourne and New York: Oxford University Press.

Rodney, Walter. 1981. *How Europe Underdeveloped Africa*. Rev. ed. Washington, DC: Howard University Press.

Roseau River Anishnabe First Nation Government. 1997. *Genocide in Canada*. Roseau River Anishnabe First Nation.

Rostica, Julieta Carla. 2007. The Mayan Organizations of Guatemala and Engaging in an Intercultural Dialogue. *Politica y Cultura* 27: 75–97.

Roth, H. Ling. 1899. *The Aborigines of Tasmania*. 2nd ed. Halifax: F. King and Sons.

Rowley, Charles Dunford. 1970. *The Destruction of Aboriginal Society*. Canberra: Australian National University Press.

Rubenstein, Richard L. 1983. *The Age of Triage: Fear and Hope in an Overcrowded World*. Boston: Beacon.

– 1987. Afterword: Genocide and Civilization. In *Genocide and the Modern Age: Etiology and Case Studies of Mass Death*, ed. I.

Wallimann and M.N. Dobkowski, 283–98. Syracuse, NY: Syracuse University Press.

– 2001. Religion and the Uniqueness of the Holocaust. In *Is the Holocaust Unique? Perspectives on Comparative Genocide*, ed. A.S. Rosenbaum, 33–40. Boulder, CO: Westview.

Rubin, Gayle. 1997. The Traffic in Women: Notes on the "Political Economy" of Sex. In *The Second Wave: A Reader in Feminist Theory*, ed. L. Nicholson, 27–62. New York: Routledge.

Rubin, Miri, ed. 2009a. *Medieval Christianity in Practice*. Ed. D.S. Lopez Jr. Princeton, NJ: Princeton University Press.

Rubin, Olivier. 2009b. The Entitlement Approach: A Case for Framework Development Rather than Demolition: A Comment on "Entitlement Failure and Deprivation: A Critique of Sen's Famine Philosophy." *Journal of Development Studies* 45, no. 4: 621–40.

Rummel, R.J. 1994. *Death by Government*. New Brunswick, NJ: Transaction.

Ruthven, Malise. 1978. *Torture: The Grand Conspiracy*. London: Weidenfeld and Nicolson.

Ryan, Lyndall. 1996. *The Aboriginal Tasmanians*. 2nd ed. St Leonards, NSW, Australia: Allen and Unwin.

– 2008. Massacre in the Black War in Tasmania, 1823–34: A Case Study of the Meander River Region, June 1827. *Journal of Genocide Research* 10, no. 4: 479–99.

Said, Edward. 1978. *Orientalism*. New York: Vintage.

Saint-Simon, Henri. 1975. Memoir on the Science of Man. In *Henri Saint-Simon: Selected Writings on Science, Industry and Social Organization*, ed. K. Taylor, 111–23. New York: Holmes and Meier.

Sané, Pierre. 2000. Foreword. In *Report 2000*, ed. Amnesty International, 5–9. London: Amnesty International Publications.

Scanlan, Stephen J. 2009. New Direction and Discovery on the Hunger Front: Toward a Sociology of Food Security/Insecurity. *Humanity and Society* 33, no. 4: 292–316.

Schaller, Dominik J. 2005. Raphael Lemkin's View of European Colonial Rule in Africa: Between Condemnation and Admiration. *Journal of Genocide Research* 7, no. 4: 531–8.

Sellström, Tor, and Lennart Wohlgemuth. 1996. *The International Response to Conflict and Genocide: Lessons from the Rwanda Experience, Study 1: Historical Perspective: Some Explanatory Factors*. Ed. D. Millwood. Copenhagen: Steering Committee of the Joint Evaluation of Emergency Assistance to Rwanda.

Sen, Amartya. 1981. *Poverty and Famines*. Oxford: Oxford University Press.

Sewell, William H. 1992. A Theory of Structure: Duality, Agency, and Transformation. *American Journal of Sociology* 98, no. 1: 1–29.

Shahar, Shulamith. 2009. Cathars and Baptism. In *Medieval Christianity in Practice*, ed. M. Rubin, 14–20. Princeton, NJ: Princeton University Press.

Shaw, Martin. 2007. *What Is Genocide?* Cambridge, UK: Polity.

Shewell, Hugh. 2004. *"Enough to Keep Them Alive": Indian Welfare in Canada, 1973–1965*. Toronto: University of Toronto Press.

Shipley, Thorne. 1995. *Intersensory Origin of Mind: A Revisit to Emergent Evolution*. New York: Routledge.

Simpson, Christopher. 1993. *The Splendid Blond Beast: Money, Law and Genocide in the Twentieth Century*. New York: Grove.

Smith, David Norman. 1995. Ziya Gokälp and Emile Durkheim: Sociology as an Apology for Chauvinism? *Durkheimian Studies/Etudes durkheimiennes* 1: 45–50.

Smith, Dorothy. 1990. *The Conceptual Practices of Power: A Feminist Sociology of Knowledge*. Toronto: University of Toronto Press.

– ed. 2006. *Institutional Ethnography as Practice*. Lanham: Rowman and Littlefield.

Smith, Roger. 1987. Human Destructiveness and Politics: The Twentieth Century as an Age of Genocide. In *Genocide and the Modern Age: Etiology and Case Studies of Mass Death*, ed. I. Wallimann and M.N. Dobkowski, 21–40. New York: Greenwood.

Sousa, Ashley Riley. 2004. "They will be hunted down like wild beasts and destroyed!" A Comparative Study of Genocide in California and Tasmania. *Journal of Genocide Research* 6, no. 2: 193–209.

Stammers, Neil. 1999. Social Movements and the Social Construction of Human Rights. *Human Rights Quarterly* 21, no. 4: 980–1008.

Stannard, David E. 1992. *American Holocaust: The Conquest of the New World*. Oxford: Oxford University Press.

Star, Susan Leigh. 1991. Power, Technologies, and the Phenomenology of Conventions: On Being Allergic to Onions. In *A Sociology of Monsters: Essays on Power, Technology and Domination*, ed. J. Law, 20–36. London: Routledge.

Stewart, Julie. 2008. A Measure of Justice: The Rabinal Human Rights Movement in Post-War Guatemala. *Qualitative Sociology* 31: 231–50.

Straus, Scott. 2004. How Many Perpetrators Were There in the Rwandan Genocide? An Estimate. *Journal of Genocide Research* 6, no. 1: 85–98.

444

References

- 2006. *The Order of Genocide: Race, Power, and War in Rwanda.* Ithaca, NY: Cornell University Press.

Sumption, Jonathan. 1978. *The Albigensian Crusade.* London: Faber and Faber.

Tal, Uriel. 1979. On the Study of the Holocaust and Genocide. *Yad Vashem Studies* 13: 7–52.

Tatz, Colin. 2003. *With Intent to Destroy: Reflecting on Genocide.* London: Verso.

Temelkuran, Ece. 2008. Flag and Headscarf. *New Left Review* 51: 81–6.

Thompson, John L., and Gail A. Quets. 1987. *Redefining the Moral Order: Towards a Normative Theory of Genocide.* New York: Columbia University Press.

- and Gail A. Quets. 1990. Genocide and Social Conflict: A Partial Theory and Comparison. *Research in Social Movements, Conflicts and Change* 12: 245–66.

Tilly, Charles. 1985. War Making and State Making as Organized Crime. In *Bringing the State Back In*, ed. P.B. Evans, D. Rueschemeyer, and T. Skocpol, 169–85. Cambridge, UK: Cambridge University Press.

Titley, E.B. 1986. *A Narrow Vision: Duncan Campbell Scott and the Administration of Indian Affairs in Canada.* Vancouver: University of British Columbia Press.

Tomuschat, Christian. 1999. Failure or Success? An Account of the Work of the Commission for Historical Clarification of Guatemala. *Die Friedens-Warte* 74, no. 4: 433–55.

Totten, Samuel. 2009. The Plight and Fate of Females during and Following the 1994 Rwandan Genocide. In *The Plight and Fate of Women During and Following Genocide*, ed. S. Totten, 107–35. New Brunswick, NJ: Transaction.

- and William S. Parsons. 2009. Introduction. In *Century of Genocide: Critical Essays and Eyewitness Accounts*, ed. S. Totten and W.S. Parsons, 1–13. New York: Routledge.

Travers, Robert. 1968. *Tasmanians: The Story of a Doomed Race.* Melbourne: Cassell.

Tuhiwai Smith, Linda. 1999. *Decolonizing Methodologies: Research and Indigenous Peoples.* London: Zed.

Turnbull, Clive. 1966. *Black War: The Extermination of the Tasmanian Aborigines.* Melbourne: Lansdowne.

Turner, Bryan S. 1992. Preface to the Second Edition. In E. Durkheim, *Professional Ethics and Civic Morals*, 2nd ed., xiii-xlii. London: Routledge.

Turner, Stephen P., and Dirk Käsler, eds. 1992. *Sociology Responds to Fascism*. London: Routledge.

UNICEF. 1999. Iraq Surveys Show "Humanitarian Emergency." 12 August. http://www.unicef.org/newsline/99pr29.htm (accessed 27 February 2008).

United Nations. 2008. *Office of the Special Advisor on the Prevention of Genocide*. http://www.un.org/preventgenocide/adviser (accessed 12 December 2010).

Uvin, Peter. 1998. *Aiding Violence: The Development Enterprise in Rwanda*. West Hartford, CT: Kumarian.

Valentino, Benjamin A. 2004. *Final Solutions: Mass Killing and Genocide in the 20th Century*. Ithaca, NY: Cornell University Press.

van Krieken, Robert. 1998. *Norbert Elias*. London: Routledge.

– 1999. The Barbarism of Civilization: Cultural Genocide and the "Stolen Generations." *British Journal of Sociology* 50, no. 2: 297–315.

Vansinia, Jan. 2004. *Antecedents to Modern Rwanda: The Nyiginya Kingdom*. Madison: University of Wisconsin Press.

Vartanian, Nicole E. 2000. In a Perfect World: Durkheim's Imperfect Conception of Power and the Legitimation of Nationalism and Genocide in Turkey. Paper presented to the American Sociological Association, Chicago.

von Sponeck, Hans. 2006. Failure in Iraq and the Urgency of UN Reforms. Paper presented at the conference Global Violence, Global Justice, University of Manitoba, Winnipeg, 24–26 February.

Wakefield, Walter L. 1974. *Heresy, Crusade and Inquisition in Southern France, 1100–1250*. Berkeley: University of California Press.

Wallerstein, Immanuel. 1983. *Historical Capitalism*. London: Verso.

Warren, Mary Anne. 1985. *Gendercide: The Implications of Sex Selection*. Totowa, NH: Rowman and Allanheld.

Weber, Max. 1978. *Economy and Society*. Vol. 1. Berkeley: University of California Press.

Weitz, Eric D., ed. 2003. *A Century of Genocide: Utopias of Race and Nation*. Princeton, NJ: Princeton University Press.

Wellman, Barry. 1988. Structural Analysis: From Method and Metaphor to Theory and Substance. In *Social Structures: A Network Approach*, ed. B. Wellman and S.D. Berkowitz, 19–61. Greenwich, CT: JAI Press.

Weston, Burns H. 2006. Human Rights: Concept and Content. In *Human Rights in the World Community: Issues and Action*, 3rd ed., ed. B.H. Weston and R.P. Claude, 17–25. Philadelphia: University of Pennsylvania Press.

Weyler, Rex. 1992. First Nations. In *Blood of the Land: The Government and Corporate War against First Nations*, 255–310. Philadelphia: New Society.

Winch, Peter. 1990. *The Idea of a Social Science and Its Relation to Philosophy*. 2nd ed. London: Routledge.

Windschuttle, Keith. 2002. *The Fabrication of Aboriginal History*. Vol. 1, *Van Diemen's Land, 1803–1847*. Sydney: Macleay.

Wittgenstein, Ludwig. 2001. *Philosophical Investigations: The German Text with a Revised English Translation*. 3rd ed. Trans. G.E.M. Anscombe. Oxford: Blackwell

Wittig, Monique. 1992. *The Straight Mind and Other Essays*. Boston: Beacon.

Wollstonecraft, Mary. 1997. A Vindication of the Rights of Woman. In *The Vindications: The Rights of Men, The Rights of Woman*, ed. D.L. Macdonald and K. Scherf, 99–343. Peterborough, ON: Broadview Literary Texts.

Wright, Ronald. 1992. *Stolen Continents*. Boston: Houghton Mifflin.

– 2004. *A Short History of Progress*. Toronto: House of Anansi.

Young, Iris Marion. 2005. *On Female Body Experience: Throwing Like a Girl and Other Essays*. Oxford: Oxford University Press.

Žižek, Slavoj. 2008. *Violence: Six Sideways Reflections*. New York: Picador.

Index

Ireland, 230–1; of Jews, 4, 30,
61, 63, 69, 70, 74, 76, 81, 87–90,
101–6, 154, 193, 269–70; of
Mayans, 183–200; as moral, 26–
37; productivity of, 82, 117, 135,
158, 267; as rational, 101–9; in
Soviet Union generally, 115, 181;
successful and unsuccessful, 13,
36, 55, 57, 158, 247, 261, 267;
of Tasmanians, 204–26, 239,
243, 302; of Tutsis, 4, 275–300;
in Ukraine, 4, 14, 230, 239
Genocide Watch, 97–9
Gökalp, Ziya, 36–7, 267, 271–5
Gramsci, Antonio, 99
Guatemala, 63, 81, 111, 183–200,
247, 304; aftermath and outcomes of genocide, 197–200;
cold genocide in, 186–93; culpability for atrocities, 194; foreign
intervention in, 191–3; hot genocide, 193–6; indigenous civilizing
process, 184–5; mortality from
civil war and genocide, 183–4.
See also anticommunism;
Mayans

habitus 12, 132, 142, 144, 146,
147, 149–55; defined, 132
Halliday, Denis, 100
Hancock, Ian, 89
heteronormativity, 10, 101, 121–4
Hinton, Alex, 68n6, 83, 86n2,
128n1
Hitler, Adolf, 28, 37, 103, 139n9,
268–9
Holocaust. *See* genocide
Holodomir. *See* genocide, in Ukraine
Horowitz, Irving Louis, 115–17,
315–16

humanism, 7, 30, 137n7, 139 187,
266
Huntington, Samuel, 128, 159
Hutu Power, 279, 283, 285–7,
292–6
Hutu-Tutsi differentiation, 279–82,
294
Hutus. *See* Hutu-Tutsi
differentiation

identity-difference, 12, 53–4, 55,
82, 84, 114, 115, 117, 120, 121,
124, 127, 156, 160, 182, 193,
223, 226, 245, 268, 277, 300,
303, 308
ideology, 92–3, 119–20, 165, 193,
196, 285–7, 294, 317
I-identity. *See* we-identity
imagined communities, 73, 79, 248
immanence, 27, 43, 55, 70, 99
imperialism. *See* colonialism
impunity, 12, 56, 99, 113, 116–17,
155–62, 173, 184, 188–9, 191,
197–8, 199–200, 201, 204, 206–
10, 225–6, 238, 244–5, 253, 258,
266, 298–300, 308–10
Impuzamugambi, 286
India, 99, 227–45; British civilization in, 233–4; famine of 1876–
79, 235–9; famine of
1896–1902, 239–42; genocidal
mortality in, 227
Indian residential schools, 5, 15,
213
Informe Proyecto Interdiocesano de
Recuperación de la Memoria
Histórica (Recovery of Historical
Memory Project, REMHI), 197
Inquisition, 173–9, 183
intentionalism, 63–4, 88

social action, 25, 27, 31, 33, 38, 39,
79, 138, 142, 143, 226, 227,
230, 243, 248. *See also* sociology
social facts, 33, 38, 39, 41, 78, 79,
80, 227. *See also* sociology
social relations, 8, 9, 11–12, 14,
18, 19, 39, 42–56, 79, 92–3, 96,
101, 102, 105, 110, 111, 113,
121, 127, 129, 139–40, 149,
168, 172, 182, 207, 229, 243,
302, 305, 307–10; material, 54–
6, 93, 114, 130, 133. *See also*
class relations; figurations; force
relations; gender; power; racialization; relationality; sociology
social structure. *See* figuration
socialism, 108, 111, 113
sociological theory gap, 85–127
sociology: complicity in genocide,
271–5; critical, 42–57, 86, 101,
115, 121, 127, 307; objectivist, 25,
32–8, 40, 42, 45, 51–2, 59, 65–6,
79–80; radical, 18–19, 45, 54, 56,
117, 121, 130, 301, 306–7; relational, 14, 25, 38–41, 42–57, 59,
80, 82, 120, 126–7, 130, 143, 223,
307; subjectivist, 25–32, 40, 42,
59, 61, 63–4, 66, 79–80, 222
sovereignty, 4, 27, 51, 79n8, 93,
105, 107, 116–17, 127, 132–3,
154, 208, 225, 229, 245, 247–8,
269, 303, 310; Guatemalan, 190,
193, 199; in Languedoc, 172,
177, 182; Ottoman, 251–3, 264–
5, 270; Rwandan, 296, 298
Sponeck, Hans von, 100
standpoint, 44–7, 56, 137
Stannard, David, 4, 89n8, 229
state formation, 19, 75, 135, 144,
147–55, 303; in Guatemala,

185–7; in Languedoc, 170–4; in
Rwanda, 277–83, 299; in
Ottoman Empire, 251
subjectivity, 14, 25–32, 33n5, 49–
51, 56, 92, 106–7, 143, 151,
199–200, 226, 247, 249, 270,
294, 300, 308; isomorphic with
sovereignty, 265. *See also*
figurations
symbolic violence, 133, 152–5, 188,
248, 255, 266, 300. *See also*
shame

Tasmania, 204–26, 238, 239, 243,
203; mortality from genocide,
201. *See also* Aboriginal
Tasmanians
torture, 31n4, 32, 63, 94, 165–6,
176, 184, 192, 194–5, 209, 237,
289, 291, 304, 318
total war, 101, 113, 135
Toulouse, Counts of, 171–4, 302
transgender, 122
tribunals: International Criminal
Tribunal for Rwanda (ICTR),
196, 275, 299; International War
Crimes Tribunal (Russell
Tribunal), 73–4, 112; in postwar
Ottoman Empire, 261
troubadors, 170, 172–3
Truganini, 211, 216, 218–19, 221
Turkey. *See* Ottoman Empire
Tutsis. *See* Hutu-Tutsi
differentiation

Ubico, Jorge, 189
Union of Soviet Socialist Republics
(Soviet Union), 14, 54, 61n3, 71,
97, 108, 114n19, 115, 135n5,
181, 190, 192, 199, 230